"Guns up!" Chief barked.

Shawn felt exhilarated each time he heard that call. Emotions he never knew he had swelled up from deep inside until the fear was swept away and all that remained was a rush of adrenaline and a bizarre thrill with each life or death situation. He gave no thought to screaming but somewhere as if from far away he heard himself, " 'YeeeHaiii!' " as he burst through the door. . . .

Also by Johnnie Clark
Published by Ballantine Books:

GUNS UP!

SEMPER FIDELIS

Johnnie Clark

BALLANTINE BOOKS • NEW YORK

Library of Congress Catalog Card Number: 88-91966

ISBN 0-345-33529-5

Manufactured in the United States of America

First Edition: September 1988

Dedication

My thanks and love to Pam Strickler, Ernie Tremblay, Cathy Brubaker, Elsa Houtz, Jesus Quintana, Tony Bowman and P. F. Clark.

I dedicate this book to the memory of Linda Hendry and to the memory of my dad. So young, so brave, and so faithful.

In Him who is Semper Fidelis.

Prologue

The big tent quivered as the prop wash of a low-flying medevac chopper blew red dust through the screen window flaps. A giant black Marine with a blood-soaked bandage wrapped around his left biceps sat up in his cot and followed the sound of the passing chopper with his eyes.

"Another meat wagon from Hue City," he said, checking his bandage.

At the far end of the long tent full of wounded Marines, a young, freckle-faced corpsman pulled back the door flap and poked his head inside. "Listen up!" he yelled. He lifted a clipboard up close to his face so he could read from it in the dim morning light.

Eighteen-year-old PFC Shawn McClellan exchanged a quizzical glance with his A-Gunner, Eric Lukevec, who sat up in his cot and shrugged.

"Anybody in here from One-five?" the freckle-faced corpsman yelled.

"Yo! Here!" Shawn waved from the far end of the tent.

"That is Alpha Company First Battalion Fifth Marines!" the corpsman yelled.

"Yeah! Second Platoon," Shawn said.

"You know a Corporal Dustin Soper Wells, Second Platoon, grunt?"

Shawn McClellan turned to his buddy Lukevec. "Is that Dusty?"

Luke's mouth tightened. He nodded solemnly, then looked toward the corpsman. "Yes. We know him," Luke said.

"You two able to walk?"

"Yeah," Shawn said.

"Affirmative. Meet me in that big green Quonset hut in

1

two minutes," he said, pointing with his thumb. "Says Graves and Registration on a sign out front." The corpsman closed the tent flap.

Shawn and Luke pulled on their mud-caked jungle boots and plodded toward the Quonset hut. The corpsman met them out front. The morning sun wrapped itself in dark gray monsoon clouds.

The two Marines followed the corpsman up a plywood ramp through gray double swinging doors and into a cold, white room lit with fluorescent bulbs. It smelled like soap and chemicals. In the center of the room sat a long, shiny stainless-steel table, mounted with water faucets. A drain at one end emptied into a pipe that led down to another drain in the cement floor. The floor drain was splashed red with fresh blood.

The corpsman pointed to a cot against one wall. "You guys sit over there till I find him." He disappeared through a red swinging door.

Shawn hobbled over to the cot and sat down. Lukevec remained standing.

Two laughing corpsmen carried in a stretcher with a poncho-wrapped body on it. They dumped the body onto the stainless-steel table like butchers throwing down a slab of beef. One of the corpsmen pulled the poncho away and threw it into a galvanized garbage can.

"So what did old Jim tell this mama-san?" the other corpsman asked with a grin. He was tall and had a skinny face.

The first corpsman pulled on a pair of plastic gloves, grabbed a large pair of black scissors, and started cutting away the dead Marine's filthy jungle utilities. He grinned and shook his sandy hair. "He said he got it at China Beach!" He gave a loud, guttural laugh.

"Hey, this jarhead's missing a hand," Skinny-face said.

The sandy-haired corpsman shrugged. "Check the poncho."

"Yeah, here it is," Skinny-face said, pulling the clothes away from the body. There was a baseball-size hole in the dead Marine's side. The blood was dried. A piece of rib stuck out through the hole. The corpsman pulled a yellowed human hand out of the galvanized garbage can. It was severed at the wrist. A green plastic body bag lay in

2

a corner of the room near Luke. Skinny-face unzipped the bag, tossed the hand in, and pulled the zipper back up.

Shawn got up, walked over to the bag and unzipped it enough to look in. He grimaced. "God, Luke, it's half-filled with pieces of guys."

"What do you do with all of these parts?" Lukevec asked.

"A chopper drops 'em into the South China Sea," the sandy-haired corpsman said.

"What?" Shawn asked. "You're kidding."

The corpsman shrugged, then poured a yellow solution over the dead Marine and started scrubbing the naked body with a brush until the liquid lathered like soap.

The red door opened again and the freckle-faced corpsman motioned to Shawn and Luke. They followed him into a cold, cavernous room filled with what looked like huge filing cabinets. The corpsman led them over to one that was pulled halfway out. He unzipped the top of the green body bag inside. Dusty's handsome face appeared.

"Didn't he have dog tags?" Shawn asked.

"Yeah, he had tags, but we've had too many foul-ups with you clowns. Some of these jarheads are wearing each other's tags or two different tags or no tags. The real jokers are the Marines with John Doe tags. They get 'em made up in Bangkok on R&R. Crazy Marines. Where do they find you guys, anyhow?"

CHAPTER ONE

South Charleston, West Virginia
May 1959

Shawn's mother squeezed his hand as she sobbed harder, and
Eddie was sniffing beside him. Shawn wanted to cry too. He
wanted to show everybody how much he loved his dad, but he
couldn't. He stared at the green mountains below, spread out all
the way to the Kanawha Valley. Spring Hill Mountain was the
highest and prettiest of them all. Shawn figured that was the
reason his father had picked it.

> "On a hill far away,
> Stood an old rugged cross
> The answer to all suffering and pain"

Mr. Whitley's clear, strong voice echoed off of the surrounding hills and seemed to trail off into the gullies and valleys below. It was a song that his father had loved, but Shawn never
had. It was just too sad. He hoped that Jesus understood.

A small frog hopped toward the edge of the green felt carpet
that surrounded the bronze coffin. The little frog stopped at a
dark, narrow gap between one of the wood planks and the green
felt. He was going into the grave. Shawn grimaced. Suddenly a
white-gloved hand scooped up the little frog. Shawn looked up.
Uncle Bob winked and walked quietly over. He put his free hand
around the little boy's shoulder and led him away from the ceremony.

Uncle Bob had always been Shawn's hero. This was the first
time Shawn had seen Bob in his Marine Corps dress blue uniform, and Shawn thought he looked neater than anything. He
wished that his dad could see Bobby. When they were far enough
away, Bob squatted down. He opened his hand and the frog
jumped to freedom.

"Shawnie, I know it's hard for a ten-year-old to understand, but your daddy is happy with Jesus right now. He isn't in that box over there.''

Shawn fixed a glassy stare on the escaping frog.

"Do you hear me, Shawn?"

"I know he's with Jesus, but Jesus didn't like Daddy."

Uncle Bob's bright blue eyes opened wider. "Why do you say that, Shawnie?"

"Daddy had a crummy life. He cried because we were poor and he couldn't help." Shawn's bottom lip began to quiver. He bit down hard to keep from crying.

Bob cleared his throat as he hugged Shawn to him. Shawn could feel Uncle Bob trying to swallow back tears. "Jesus loved your dad, Shawn. Remember, after the car wreck, your dad depended on the Lord. Even blind and crippled, he had remarkable faith."

"Why did God still make everything so bad? I'm the only kid in school that lives in a round house."

"Who are you feeling sorry for, Shawn? Your mom and dad or yourself? Marines live in Quonset huts. If it's good enough for Marines, it's good enough for you, isn't it?"

Shawn didn't answer. He bit angrily at his bottom lip and fought back the flood of tears he felt swelling up inside him.

"Shawnie, I know it's been tough. I don't have all the answers, but I never once saw your dad lose his faith just because things got hard. He was one of God's Marines, Shawn, and that's what you have to be."

Shawn turned away from Bob. He could feel the tears running down his face. He remembered seeing tears streaming from underneath his father's dark glasses. Faith. He wondered if faith and tears went together. He wasn't sure he liked either one. Shawn glanced back at the graveside ceremony. He saw Eddie brush a strand of white-blond hair off his forehead, then wipe a tear on the sleeve of his navy-blue suit. Shawn wiped at his own face and sniffed and wished that he had a suit of his own. He wished that he had his dad too.

The climb up the scenic West Virginia mountain to the tree house felt steeper than usual. Shawn could see Eddie's blond head poking through the triangle-shaped window of the little square house. The tree was perfect for overlooking the golf course. Even Sammy Snead played there, and in the winter Eddie and Shawn could see all the way to the Kanawha River. They probably don't even have mountains in Florida, Shawn thought as he started the climb up the friendly familiar oak.

This was it. This was good-bye to the old tree. To their perfect tree house. To Eddie. Shawn pulled himself up to the last limb and pushed through the brown rug that was their door. Eddie's eyes were red. Shawn knew he'd been crying but was determined not to mention it.

"Did you bring the paper and pen?" Eddie asked.

"Yep. Did you bring your Bible?" Shawn asked.

"Yep." Eddie laid the book on the wood box that was their table. Shawn sat on one side of the wood box and Eddie, legs crossed, sat on the other. Eddie pulled a book of matches out of his pocket. "I'll light the candle," he said.

"The candle?" Shawn said, his frosty green eyes showing his surprise.

"No use saving it now." Eddie's voice cracked as he forced a chuckle. Shawn shrugged, then gave a sad nod of agreement.

"I brought my Davy Crockett knife." Shawn laid the small brown pocketknife on the box, then laid down the paper and pen.

"I wish your mom wouldn't do this." Eddie sounded mad.

"She says she just can't live here anymore," Shawn said defensively. "It's been awful hard on Mom, Ed. She's been taking care of me and Dad all these years and you know how we ain't got no money."

"But why Florida? It's so far. We'll never see each other again!"

"She says she just wants to be where it's sunny all the time. But she swore on the Bible that you and me would spend summers together one way or another and she talked to your mom and dad and they said you could come visit every summer."

"I don't trust 'em. You know how they say stuff like that to keep you from crying and then they don't do it."

"She swore on the Bible, Eddie!"

"Well, I ain't lettin' 'em forget!"

"No way!"

"Why St. Petersburg?"

"No reason. We just played pin-the-tail-on-Florida and the pin stuck there on our map."

Eddie nodded solemnly and looked down like he was about to cry.

"You ready?" Shawn asked.

"Yep. I told my mom that we were joining the Marines together when we grow up and get out of high school."

"What'd she say?" Shawn asked as he picked up the Bible.

"She said 'why?' So I told her we wanted to be the best like your uncle Bob and she said that we would grow out of it by the time we reached high school."

"Moms always say stuff like that."

"Yeah."

"Want me to read the pact?" Shawn asked.

"Yep."

Shawn handed Eddie the Bible and picked up the paper and pen. "Okay, put your hand on the Bible. 'We, Shawn McClellan and Eddie Price, do swear here on this Bible that we will always be best friends and see each other every summer and write letters some and then we will join the Marines together in 1967 unless one of us flunks a year. We swear in blood which we will put at the bottom of this paper.' "

Shawn looked up. Eddie nodded, his round face as serious as it was the day he beat up Chuckie Decker. He held out his finger, closed one eye, and bit on his bottom lip. Shawn opened the knife. The blade didn't shine anymore but it wasn't too bad, he thought. He gritted his teeth, aimed, and poked Eddie's finger. A tiny bubble of blood came out. Eddie grimaced with his eyes closed and shook his head as if in pain but made no noise. He pushed the pinprick's worth of blood onto the paper. Shawn handed Eddie the knife, closed his eyes, and held out his finger.

"Ouch!"

"Well, you got tough skin!" Eddie said. "There. Blood."

Shawn pressed his bloody finger to the paper right beside Eddie's blood spot. They shook hands and hugged and the hurt deep in Shawn's stomach was even worse than his finger.

CHAPTER TWO

St. Petersburg, Florida
November 1966

"Help! Ref! He's got my gonads! Help!"

The tan-faced official blew hard on his whistle and pulled on the back of a green-and-white St. Petersburg jersey. "Come on 84! Get off that pile!"

A second official, screaming with his whistle, ran to the piled-up football players. "Get off! Now!"

"Help!"

"Time out, St. Petersburg!" the tan-faced referee shouted as he yanked another player off.

The Clearwater and St. Pete players untangled themselves and ambled back to their respective sides. A pimple-faced Clearwater linebacker, doubled over, clutching at his groin and gritting his teeth, screamed at the referee. "One of those guys grabbed me by the gonads!" His face was flushed like an old alcoholic's.

"Don't be so emotional, pusshead!" Eric Lukevec, a big St. Pete tackle retorted.

The tan-faced referee pointed at Lukevec. "One more word from you and that'll be fifteen yards for unsportsmanlike conduct."

"I'm sorry, Mr. Referee," Luke said innocently.

The referee walked over to Lukevec, grabbed the front of his jersey, and led him back to the rest of the St. Pete players. "Captain McClellan."

"Yes, sir?" Shawn McClellan answered as he grabbed a towel from the water boy.

"Number seventy-two here, Mr. Lukevec, has one more chance before I toss him out of this game. Is that clear?"

"But I'm innocent, ref," Luke said, raising his bushy black eyebrows.

"Mr. Lukevec, I officiated at the St. Pete–Dixie Hollins High game."

8

"Yes, sir."

"I'm the same official who took that forearm pad away from you, Mr. Lukevec, the pad you had saturated with itching powder and sneezing powder. The pad you used to disrupt the entire Northeast High defensive line."

"Nice to see you again, sir," Luke said.

"If this was any other game, I'd have already thrown you out, mister! Captain McClellan, you'd better keep this man in line."

"Yes, sir."

The referee walked away, shaking his head. Shawn McClellan looked accusingly at Luke. Luke grinned.

"That pusshead linebacker has taken cheap shots at you all night, Shawn, and I've become very perturbed," Lukevec said.

"Oh, go get a drink."

Shawn McClellan threw his helmet on the ground and sat on it. The salt of his sweat stung his bright green eyes. He wiped the grit from his boyish face and tossed the towel back to a frowning Sid Boughton, the team's water boy.

Sid laid the towel over a wire rack of empty red-and-white Coca-Cola cups then shook his fist at the eleven tired, discouraged players. "Come on, you guys! We only got seven minutes left! Two scores! We can do it! This is the state championship! We're still in it!"

"Aw, shut up, Boughton!" Joe Elbon snapped. "We don't need a pissant water boy to tell us what the score is!"

Eric Lukevec threw a towel at the red-haired Sid. "We know the score, Sidney," the big tackle said slowly, carefully enunciating each syllable as if the process were a painful one.

Chuck Caldwell, resting on one knee, crushed a Coke cup and threw it at Sid. "We oughta know the score, we're the ones getting our butts kicked in front of nine thousand people." Caldwell stood up. "Go back to the bench where it's safe, Sidney."

The water boy looked hurt and angry. Shawn McClellan walked over to him and gave him a consoling slap on the back, then turned to face the disgruntled team. "That's enough! Sid's part of this team too. The Lord didn't make everybody big, Lukevec, or fast, Chuck."

The dark, handsome boy, named Joe Elbon, nodded and forced a grin. Elbon played end. "Yeah, this is really cute," he said. "We're playing like a bunch of little girls and trying to blame Sid for it."

9

"This is the most frustrating night of my life," Jay Mancuso, the big, dark-haired left tackle, muttered aloud.

"Your life! It was I who cost us that TD in the first quarter," Luke growled in self-consciously perfect English. He spit his mouth guard into the dirt between his size-thirteen spikes.

The middle-aged referee stepped into the ragged semicircle of dirty white-and-green uniforms. He pulled a small white card from the breast pocket of his black-and-white-striped shirt and made a check on it with his pencil. "Captain McClellan," the referee said, forcing an official tone.

"Yes, sir?" Shawn said.

"Your team has two more time-outs. Is that understood?"

"Yes, sir."

The referee checked his pocket watch. "Get your water boy off the field. We resume play in twenty seconds. Good luck." He turned and jogged over to another referee.

Shawn gave Sid Boughton another slap on the back. "Thanks for trying to help, Sid." He turned and faced the team. "Huddle up! Let's score!"

The St. Pete players began howling and shouting and butting helmets.

"Huddle up!" Joe yelled.

"Quiet down!" Lukevec bellowed.

The team settled down and huddled into an oval. Shawn, with his helmet off, knelt on one knee in the center. His wavy brown hair was matted in sweat-drenched ringlets. No one spoke, but all the players removed their helmets as if on a silent command. Shawn bowed his head. The team did the same.

"Father, God, forgive us for our ungrateful attitudes. Thanks for blessing us with this chance to play in the state championship game. Please help us to play at the very peak of our God-given abilities. In Jesus' name, we pray. Amen."

Shawn looked up as the players pulled their helmets back on and snapped their chin straps. Luke's eyes got that glazed-over look. His right eye was brown and his left eye was black, and the black left eye seemed to stare off in its own direction when the big tackle was psyched. Shawn could see that Luke was ready.

"Coach Rudge wants a flat and down pass. . . ." Shawn began.

"No!" Luke pleaded. "Run over the right tackle. I am prepared to knock this guy's jock all the way to Clearwater!"

"I don't know, Luke, we're running out of time. Maybe we better let the Irishman start slinging that sucker," Joe mumbled through his mouth guard.

"Luke's got the eye revved up. Let's go with it," Shawn said. "This better work, Luke, or Coach is gonna have my butt."

"It will appear as if there'd been a great train wreck on the right side of the line," Luke promised soberly.

"Okay, let's try a thirty-six trap. Ready, Chuck? We need a breakaway, buddy."

"Watch my dust."

"On two. Got it? Go!" Shawn shouted. The team slapped their hands in unison as they broke the huddle and hurried to the line of scrimmage. The Green Devil band struck up "St. Pete Will Shine Tonight" from the end-zone bleachers as Shawn paused behind the center. He fought an urge to glance at the St. Petersburg cheerleaders dancing on the asphalt track. Nancy Diez was there—tan and sexy and probably near to tears with concern by now.

The huge, pimple-faced Clearwater linebacker moved up on the line to the left of center. A blitz, Shawn thought. They're playing for a pass. This trap play is going for pay dirt. Shawn put his hands under the center.

"Down!" Shawn shouted and looked right. The St. Pete line dropped like a well-oiled machine to a three-point stance. Joe Elbon glanced at Shawn from the lonesome end position.

"Set!" Shawn barked as he looked left.

"Hut-one!"

"Hut-two!"

The ball slapped into Shawn's hands. Helmets collided with a loud pop as both teams grunted and groaned and fought. Shawn turned to his right and slapped the football into Chuck's gut an instant before someone hit him from the blindside like a truck running over a speed bump. Lukevec's trap block cleaned out a defensive tackle and a second linebacker who got caught in the collision. Someone screamed in agony. Shawn pulled his face mask out of the dirt in time to see Chuck's last juke around a stunned defensive back. The stadium roared as Chuck cleared the goal line, but even the rejoicing fans could not drown out the agonizing scream coming from a pile of players to Shawn's left.

"Didn't you see that?" a St. Pete player shouted at the referee.

Shawn pushed to his feet. The pusshead linebacker pointed at Jay Mancuso, writhing in pain on the ground and clutching his ankle. "Better get a stretcher," he said with a forced chuckle.

Lukevec got to his feet and ran at "Pusshead." He shoved him hard in the chest as the referee reached the scene, blowing his whistle.

"Break it up or you're out of this game, boy!"

"He jumped on Jay's ankle with both knees after the play was over!" Luke shouted at the referee.

"Captain McClellan!"

"Yes, sir."

"You better get this man back in a huddle or he's out of here!"

"My ankle's broken!" Jay screamed.

"Injury time-out!" the ref shouted, and blew his whistle again.

The St. Pete team stood like an angry gang ready for a fight as two paramedics carried Jay to an ambulance parked at the far end of the field.

"All right, let's get your point-after team ready to go, St. Pete!" the referee shouted as he checked his watch and prepared to blow his whistle.

"Huddle up!" Shawn barked.

The players grumbled into an angry huddle around their quarterback.

"We cannot allow that pusshead to get away with this, McClellan," Luke said slowly.

"With that TD we're losing by five points, right?" Shawn asked.

No one answered.

"This extra point doesn't matter," Shawn said. "We have to have another TD to win. If that linebacker was to break free to block the kick it still wouldn't matter, would it, Lukevec?"

"It would be just terrible to see that happen, Shawn."

"Extra point on one! Break!" The team slapped hands and ran to the line of scrimmage with a hint of newfound zeal.

Chuck dropped to one knee to receive the snap from center. Shawn took an extra step back away from the holder and lined up his kick.

"Lukevec! What are you doing at guard?" Coach Rudge bellowed from the sideline.

Shawn pretended not to notice.

"Down!" Chuck shouted.

"Set!" Chuck put his hands out to give the center a target.

"Hut-one!"

The ball sailed straight from between the center's legs and into Chuck's waiting hands just as they had practiced a thousand times. Lukevec jumped aside as the ball was snapped. The pimple-faced linebacker burst through the line untouched. Five feet from the ball he leaped into the air in a flattened out all-or-nothing dive to block the kick, his hands stretching for the extra inch of distance that would make the difference between glory and a belly flop on the turf.

Shawn skipped forward with his eyes on the flying linebacker instead of the ball, now being placed for the kick. Shawn planted his left foot and his right leg swung into the kick like a man going for a fifty-yard field goal. At the last possible instant, Chuck moved the ball. Shawn's kicking foot followed through, going high into the air until the steel cleats of his right shoe sank deep into the groin of the flying linebacker. The nine thousand voices in old Stewart Field seemed to groan in unison as "Pusshead" folded like a matchbook cover. He thudded to the ground on his helmet and knees, with his butt up in the air, and he stayed that way until the stretcher came. Chuck tried to run the ball in for the extra point, but no one seemed to notice that he didn't make it. Luke, Joe, Chuck, and Shawn stood together applauding politely as Pusshead was carried off of the field. He remained curled up in a fetal position all the way to the Clearwater locker room.

"Huh," Luke muttered: "I have never seen a person's eyes open that wide before."

The extra-point team jogged to the sideline. Coach Rudge shook his head and tried to look disgusted. He waved Shawn toward him as he removed his headset.

"Who called that play, McClellan?"

"I did, Coach."

The big round man paused, and for an instant Shawn thought he caught the beginnings of a smile around his eyes. Coach Pagacs cleared his throat and looked away.

"Well"—Coach Rudge shrugged as he put his headset back on—"you're probably gonna be hearin' from that guy's girl-friend."

"Yes, sir," Shawn said. He turned back toward the bench.

"Shawnie!" A girl shouted from the track in front of the

13

stands. It was Nancy Diez. She waved and blew Shawn a kiss. One look at the dark Cajun girl usually gave Shawn weak knees. She had the best body in school and a face that had already won her the Miss Suncoast beauty pageant.

Shawn gave a quick wave then turned toward the field again for the kickoff. He knew it was probably the first time in their seven-month romance that he didn't turn into human Jell-O when she smiled. He looked at the scoreboard underneath the giant Coca-Cola sign behind the St. Pete end zone: ST. PETERSBURG 13, CLEARWATER 18. 4TH QUARTER. TIME REMAINING: 4 MINUTES, 22 SECONDS.

Someone pounded Shawn on the back. He turned to face Joe Elbon. Joe had the happiest face he'd worn all night.

"I could kiss ya if you were prettier!"

"Forget it. The girls might have voted you most attractive, but I think—"

Someone bear-hugged Shawn from behind, picked him up off of the ground, and howled.

"That was the absolute finest kick you have made in three years!" Luke said as he dropped Shawn back to the ground.

Shawn turned. Luke's mouth was open and he looked as if he was laughing, but no sound came out. It occurred to Shawn that Lukevec's silent laugh matched his unique sense of humor rather well. A normal laugh just would not fit Eric Lukevec, Shawn had decided back in the seventh grade when he had first moved to Florida and met Luke.

"You did that pusshead a favor, you know," Luke managed to say.

"Oh, yeah," Joe howled, "a great favor if he plans on being a priest."

"I was speaking about his complexion, Joe. I'm quite sure that every zit on his face popped when his testicles reached his throat."

Joe, still laughing, pointed at Shawn. "Oh, no. Saint McClellan looks worried."

"You think he's seriously hurt?" Shawn asked.

"Get that frown off of your face, McClellan," Luke scoffed.

"That jerk's okay. Don't start feeling guilty, McClellan," Joe said.

"I don't feel guilty, Elbon. I just don't want him seriously hurt; he deserves a good bruise, that's all."

"McClellan!" Coach Rudge called.

14

Shawn jogged over to him with his helmet pushed back. "Yeah, Coach?"

"After the kickoff I want you back in there at safety."

"Brett's doing a good job, Coach."

"Look, McClellan, I was trying to keep you from going both ways, but we need to make something happen out there on defense. We got four minutes to pull this game out."

"Don't take Brett out, Coach. He's playing a good game."

"Look, Shawn, this last four minutes is gonna mean a lot to you guys for the rest of your lives. You'll never forget this night, be it good or bad."

Shawn looked around, then leaned closer to Coach Rudge. "Brett's mom and dad are divorced and he hasn't seen his dad in two years, Coach. His dad drove all the way from Ohio to see him play tonight."

Coach Rudge pinched the bridge of his nose and frowned as if he had a headache. "Go take a seat on the wood, McClellan."

"Everybody stand up for the kickoff!" Coach Pagacs yelled from a few feet away.

Shawn turned to face the field as Fred Adam booted the ball end over end to the Clearwater five-yard line. A short black Clearwater halfback caught the kickoff and twisted away from the St. Pete tacklers like a water bug. He was finally knocked out of bounds at the Clearwater thirty-seven. Shawn breathed a sigh of relief as he headed back to the bench. He sat down beside Joe Elbon and whistled.

"Man, that was close, Joe."

"Why aren't you out there?"

"Brett's doing the job."

"Bull pucky, Shawn! He's too slow, man! If they run by him at safety, it's all over!"

Shawn nodded toward the stands behind them. "Is your dad up there?"

"Yeah. I guess so. He better be."

"So is Brett's."

"Really?" Joe's eyebrows lifted.

"Yeah. All the way from Cleveland."

Joe shook his head. "That turtle's gonna cost us the state. I should have known."

"Where's your faith, man? Besides, Brett earned it. That guy hasn't missed a practice in three years."

Joe turned his face to the field. "You ever wish your dad could see you play, Shawn?"

Shawn leaned forward with elbows on his knees and looked down at his spikes. "Yeah," he said quietly.

He stared at the Stewart Field grass and thought about the green hills of West Virginia and his faith and his dad. *Faith*. He could still hear the bells of old St. Paul's Methodist Church the day he told Dad that he hated that word.

"What would make you say a thing like that, Shawnie?"

"That sermon, Dad! 'Faith can move mountains.' It ain't true."

"Every word in the Bible is true, son."

Shawn looked up at his father's dark glasses and held his arm tighter.

"Then how come nothing happened when I prayed for your eyes to work again?"

Mr. McClellan paused and swallowed and released Shawn's hand. "It has to be the Lord's will, Shawnie." He lifted the dark glasses from his sightless eyes, wiped at a tear, and cleared his throat. "I love you, son."

An explosion of screams and cheers pulled Shawn out of West Virginia and back to the game as Joe leaped off of the bench with his fist in the air. Shawn stood up to see what the commotion was all about.

"Offense!" Coach Rudge bellowed.

"McClellan!" Coach Pagacs shouted.

"Joe, what happened?" Shawn asked as he pulled on his helmet.

"Fumble! We got a fumble!"

"All right!"

"McClellan!"

"Here, Coach!" Shawn ran over to the coach as Joe ran onto the field.

"Listen up, now!" Coach Pagacs put an arm around Shawn's shoulder and looked him right in the eye with his forehead against the front of Shawn's helmet. Shawn could feel his heart pounding. He felt suddenly nervous.

"Calm down!" Coach said firmly as he covered the ear holes on Shawn's helmet with both of his palms to shut out the stadium noise.

"Listen to me. Take a deep breath. Slow."

Shawn inhaled and breathed out slowly through his nose.

"Calm?"

"Yes, sir."

"We got no time-outs. We need a TD. We got a minute and twenty seconds left. Plenty of time. Stay cool. Don't get sacked. Throw it away first. We got sixty yards to go. Go on quick counts. Use the two-minute drill sequence of plays. Got it?"

"Yes, sir."

"Let's win the state championship." Coach Pagacs slapped Shawn on the rear end and shoved him toward the field.

The team was already bent over in a huddle when Shawn pushed into the center. He dropped to one knee. He glanced around the sweaty faces, every one beaming with excitement.

"The two-minute drill. Everybody got it?"

No one spoke.

"On quick count. Ready, break!"

The team slapped hands and ran up to the line of scrimmage. The referee's arm lifted into the air. He blew his whistle and lowered his arm as he pushed the button on his stopwatch.

"Down!"

"Set!" The ball slapped against Shawn's hands. He dropped back three steps and threw a hard spiral at the right sideline ten yards downfield. Joe ran the ten-yard out the same way that he had for the last two seasons. The defensive back was playing off him. Joe caught the ball but the pass was low and he had to drop to his knees to catch it. He couldn't get out of bounds to stop the clock. Shawn slapped himself in the helmet. He had thrown the pass a thousand times and now he was choking. The clock read fifty-eight seconds and counting.

"Line up! Get on the ball!" Shawn screamed.

He paused under the center as Joe Elbon moved into position. "Down!"

The team dropped to the three-point stance.

"Set!"

Shawn took the snap and dropped back three steps. He pumped toward Joe then turned and threw the same out pass to Nick Perry on the left side of the field. Nick caught the ball and ran another ten yards up the sideline before getting knocked out of bounds, stopping the clock. Shawn turned back to check the time. Thirty-eight seconds. He ran over to the sideline. The team hurried into a huddle around the center.

Coach Rudge and Coach Pagacs stood together, studying a clipboard. Coach Rudge grabbed the front of Shawn's jersey as

17

he listened to a final word from the press box through his headset.

"Three-deep zone," Coach Rudge said as he pressed the earphone against his ear to hear better. He nodded and pulled the headset off. He turned to Shawn. "I think they're gonna give us a couple more of those ten-yard outs."

"Coach, I got an idea."

"All right, what is it? Hurry!"

"Let me run a quarterback draw. They know we're gonna pass, they're dropping way back and the linebackers are going out wide or blitzing."

"If you get tackled we can't stop the clock!"

"I know. I can get twenty yards, maybe all the way to the ten-yard line. We line up fast and in a tackle-eligible play I fake throwing the ball out of bounds to stop the clock and flip the pass to Luke."

Coach Rudge looked at Coach Pagacs. Coach Pagacs looked at Shawn.

"Luke only catches that thing one out of three times in practice."

"I know," Shawn agreed, "but if he drops it, it stops the clock, and if he doesn't we win the state."

Coach Rudge pulled hard on Shawn's jersey, forcing him closer. His big rugged face burned with intensity. "Go with it." He shoved Shawn away.

Shawn turned and ran as fast as he could back to the huddle. This was it. He was scared. He looked up at the dark sky. He desperately wanted to call a time-out so he could say a prayer.

When Luke heard his part in the plan, his mouth fell open and his mouth guard dropped to the ground. Every sweaty face in the huddle turned toward him. He, in turn, stared at Shawn.

Shawn grinned and winked. "I think it'll work," he said.

The whistle blew.

"Ready, break!"

They ran up to the ball. Shawn glanced left, then right, to make sure the team was in position.

"Down."

"Set."

The center snapped the ball. Shawn dropped back as if to pass. The St. Pete guards and center pushed the onrushing defense to the outside, creating a hole in the middle of the line. Shawn tucked the ball away and ran. The defense was caught off guard. Shawn was all the way to the thirteen-yard line before the defensive backfield converged on him. He hit the ground hard with the weight of two tacklers on top of him. The Clearwater players were in no hurry to get off. He shoved one Clearwater player to the side, rolled away from the second, and scrambled to his feet, screaming, "Line up!"

He looked at the scoreboard. Sixteen seconds.

The team lined up.

"Down!" Shawn shouted the team into a three-point stance. "Set!"

The center snapped the ball. Shawn dropped back two steps and faked a throw toward Joe then turned and tossed the softest pass he could throw to an all-alone Lukevec. Luke stumbled backward across the goal line with his arms out and palms up, like a man begging for mercy. The ball dropped into his arms. Luke cradled it like a new father holding his baby for the first time. He fell back, bringing his knees up, and rolled into the end zone in a fetal position, wrapped protectively around the pigskin.

The final gun sounded, but no one heard it. The St. Pete crowd, led by screaming, tumbling cheerleaders, stormed the field. A moment later Shawn felt himself being pulled away from the backslapping mania. Nancy Diez was tugging him to mid field, fifteen yards beyond the celebrating mob of students, parents, fans, and players. As Nancy twirled around, her long black hair fell down over one shoulder. Shawn pulled his helmet off and dropped it. Nancy stood on her toes and, putting her arms around Shawn's sweaty neck, pulled him into a sweet, long kiss.

It was all too perfect. He wished that this moment of joy could go on forever. He thanked God for loving him so much.

Suddenly the low bellow of a tuba and the blast of trombones startled Nancy into releasing her hug from around Shawn's neck. She gave a half-startled scream and began laughing at the sight of six St. Pete High band members who had encircled them. She wiped away tears of joy and kissed Shawn again.

"I love you, Shawn McClellan!" Nancy shouted over the horns.

"I love you, Nancy Diez! This is the happiest night of my life!"

"Shawnie! Shawnie!" a familiar voice shouted from behind Shawn.

Shawn spun away from Nancy as his mother, Opal McClellan,

19

squeezed between two band members and rushed into his arms with tears in her eyes.

"Well, don't cry, Mom! We won!"

"Oh, God, Shawnie! I am so proud of you." Opal pulled away to look her handsome son in the eyes. Big tears rolled down her careworn, pretty face.

"I love you too, Mom," Shawn said, kissing away a tear on his mother's cheek.

"Oh, Shawnie, how I wish Dad could be here tonight."

"I know, Mom, I know."

Even the odor of the Greyhound bus, exhaust fumes and all, smelled good to Shawn. There was a whoosh of air brakes, the opening of the bus door, then Eddie bounded down the steps. His blond hair looked whiter than ever and his neck seemed twice as big as last summer. His baggy black-and-red South Charleston High School football jersey couldn't hide the muscles underneath.

"God! He's turned into a monster!" Chuck muttered as Shawn ran at Eddie. Eddie picked up Shawn's one-hundred-and-sixty-five-pound body as if it were a toothpick.

"Let me down, you horse!" Shawn shouted with a laugh.

"Man!" Eddie dropped Shawn to his feet. "I can't believe how hot it is here!" He wiped his forehead then lunged at Shawn again. He lifted him off the ground with another hug. "Gosh, it's good to see ya, little buddy!"

"Same here, Ed, but I'd like to keep my rib cage," Shawn gasped. Eddie dropped Shawn to the ground again and pounded him on the back. "Eddie, you remember Chuck?"

"Heck, yeah." Eddie held out his hand. "Good to see ya again, Chuck."

"Welcome back, Ed." Chuck shook Eddie's hand.

"You look bigger than ever this year!" Shawn said, stepping back to look Eddie over. "What are you benchin' now?"

Eddie looked embarrassed. His pale face blushed. "Not that much." He shrugged and looked around. "On a real good day, if I'm lucky, sometimes over four."

"Four what?" Shawn pressed.

"I don't know." Eddie grinned. "Sometimes four-fifty."

"Four hundred and fifty pounds?" Chuck exclaimed.

Eddie shrugged. "Sometimes."

Shawn laughed and tugged Eddie toward the street. "We got

20

Chuck's old Packard parked out here and we got a party to make. Let's beat feet.''

"Where's the party?'' Eddie asked.

Chuck laughed. "Wait till you hear this one. Lukevec works at the Charles Ford Funeral Home and he's got an apartment upstairs that he stays in on weekends to watch over the place. It's perfect.''

CHAPTER THREE

The Party

The setting Florida sun glistened off the four white pillars of the Charles Ford Funeral Home. It looked like an old Southern mansion. Two huge oaks guarded the front. Eight-foot hedges lined the wide circular driveway leading from the red brick of Mc-Queen Avenue.

Lukevec had gotten the job by making old Charlie Ford himself laugh until he cried. Luke came to Charlie's other Southern mansion, the one he lived in, and told him that if he'd give him the job at his funeral home Luke would never ask out his daughter.

People can do things like that when they look like Luke, Shawn once thought. Luke was a big kid, over six feet tall and two hundred pounds. His big face seemed to come out at you with wild bushy, dark eyebrows. Right in the very front of his hairline he had this double cowlick. His hair was straight as nails and just about as stiff.

Luke's left eye was black and his right eye was brown. When he was in one of his funny moods, he'd let the double cowlick grow long and cut the rest short like a flattop. The cowlicks shot out in two directions like antennae coming out of the front of his head.

Eddie chuckled from the backseat as Chuck pulled the banana-yellow Packard up the long circular drive.

"Does Luke still talk like a robot just learning English?"

"Well, Edward, it would appear to be a safe conjecture concerning Luke's continued effort at proper enunciation," Shawn mimicked, flashing his eyebrows up and down, imitating Luke's impression of Groucho Marx.

Eddie laughed. Chuck turned off the engine and the three got out of the car.

"Where's the apartment?" Eddie asked as he slammed the door.

"Over here, Ed." Chuck waved and walked around the corner of a large garage. On the side an outdoor stairway, covered by a green canvas canopy, led up to a black wooden door. "It's up here." Chuck ran up the stairs. He opened the door. A flash of yellow light beamed down the steps.

A stereo needle scratched out static from an old record as Shawn and Eddie reached the top of the stairs. A blaring rendition of "The Marine Hymn" exploded through the open door.

"Gung ho!" Lukevec greeted Eddie at the door with a can of Budweiser.

"Thanks, Luke!"

"It is good to see you again, Edward." Luke glanced toward the kitchen. "Where is Shawn's beer?"

"Comin' up." Jay pushed Luke aside and pulled Eddie into the apartment with one hand as he handed Shawn a long-neck bottle of Budweiser with the other.

"Where are the women?" Chuck shouted from a small kitchen just to the left of the front door.

"Rachel is already here," Luke shouted. "She's in the head! That's Marine talk." Luke winked at Shawn.

"Where did you find that album?" Shawn asked.

"Junk store."

"I've been hearing some wild tales about you, Luke," Eddie said.

"They often try to demean my character, Edward, and they lie. Well, what do you think of my pad?"

Eddie looked around the living room with an approving nod. Old marble-top end tables with little animal-claw feet flanked a rattan couch with orange cushions. The wood floor was gritty with tracked-in Florida sand. The walls were painted purple with two large posters of the Beatles tacked up over the couch. An old tan-colored recliner sat in one corner, occupied by a guy wearing a brown suit. He had a fedora pulled down over his eyes and a full mug of beer between his legs. He looked dead to the world.

"It's super, Luke!" Eddie held up his beer as if to toast.

"Old Charlie Ford told me I could paint it, so I did."

"I think it's the only orange kitchen in existence," Shawn said. "Who's that?" He pointed to the sleeping character in the brown suit.

"That is my uncle Ralph from Kalamazoo," Luke said. "He

wanted to see what our parties were like, but he drank too much and passed out before anyone arrived."

Luke gave Eddie's shoulder a pat. "Eddie, you look huge!"

"He's benching four-fifty," Shawn said.

"Four-fifty!" Jay exclaimed from behind Shawn. He shook his head in disbelief. He tugged down on his yellow surfer shirt and sucked in his flabby gut.

"You're as big as I am, Jay," Eddie said, his face tinted red with embarrassment.

Chuck stepped into the conversation, grinning contentedly through a face full of freckles. "Yes, but Jay is known to the ladies as Mister Mush."

"And boy, do they love it!" Jay said with a wink.

Luke smirked.

"At least Yvonne Boughton loves it. Is she coming to the party?" Luke asked.

Jay pushed back his straight black hair. "Yeah, she'll be here."

"I was hoping that you would have a few young ladies here to gawk at, Luke, old buddy," Eddie said.

"We have a few on the way. You have not yet had the pleasure of meeting Miss Fancy Nancy, I take it?"

"Shawn's new chick?"

"Yes. A vision that brings out your innermost cravings." Luke flashed his Groucho Marx impression.

Shawn hit Luke with a light elbow. "Keep your eyes on your own girl, you maniac."

Luke gave his closed-mouth grin and flashed his brows again. "A toast!" he shouted, and held up his Budweiser can.

"A toast!" Chuck echoed.

"To two of America's newest jarheads!"

"I'll toast to that," Shawn said with a glance at Eddie.

Eddie's big shoulders drooped. He looked at the floor with his lips tight.

"Okay," Shawn said, "that does it. You've been distant ever since you got here. Something is bugging you."

Eddie looked uncomfortable.

"Out with it," Shawn prodded.

"Well, I got a full scholarship to Virginia Tech to play middle linebacker."

Shawn's heart sank into his stomach. Eddie stared straight into Shawn's eyes. Neither spoke.

24

"What?" Luke shouted.

"That's great!" Chuck echoed. Shawn put an arm around Eddie's neck and the others began slapping him on the back.

Shawn forced a smile. "You big bear, that's super! I'm really proud of you! So why didn't you tell me?"

"Well, I haven't accepted." Eddie paused. "And I'm not taking it unless you change your mind about the Marines."

"Don't be silly, Ed. I'll kick your big butt if you don't take it."

Shawn felt that old familiar lump in his throat. Something had reached into his stomach and squeezed. He felt suddenly alone, sad, as if this was his final good-bye to Eddie. His best friend. His blood brother. He took a quick swig of beer and held out his bottle for a toast.

"To the best middle linebacker in college football." The guys pushed out their beers in a salute. Eddie looked at Shawn as the last stanza of the scratchy album echoed through the apartment:

"If the Army or the Navy ever look on Heaven's scenes,
They will find the streets are guarded by United States
    Marines."

"You're still going," Eddie said.

"Don't sound so ominous."

"Shawn, don't do it. Go on to college. I've saved up some money. I can help out till you get a job. You can go to Tech with me and maybe even get a tryout with the team."

"Let's enjoy the party, Ed, and don't worry about me. I'm going to be okay."

"Hey." A girl with curly blond hair appeared beside Eddie. "Is that guy ever going to wake up?" She pointed at Uncle Ralph, still sleeping in the recliner with his beer between his knees.

"Hi, Rachel." Shawn tipped his beer in hello. "This is my buddy from West Virginia, Eddie Price."

Eddie smiled. "Hi, Rachel. I think you're right." He nodded toward Uncle Ralph in the corner. "I think old Ralph is out for the night."

"I hear women!" Luke howled, and opened the door. A tall, thin blonde wearing brown slacks and a white letter sweater with a big green S stepped in. Jay's whistle drowned out the first chords of "Mustang Sally" by the Young Rascals. The tall blonde danced up to Jay and gave him a kiss on the lips.

"Who's that?" Eddie asked.

"Yvonne Boughton," Shawn said.

"Where's Joe and Sandy?" Shawn asked.

"Right here lookin' for a beer." Joe stepped through the open door carrying a bag of groceries with a yellow bag of potato chips sticking out of the top.

"Where's Sandy?" Shawn asked.

"Here I am." A cute red-haired girl with a perky smile and turned-up nose bounced through the open doorway.

"Hi, Sandy," Shawn said.

"Look what I have for you." Sandy pointed a thumb at the door as a beautiful, dark-haired girl stepped in. It was Nancy Diez.

"So this is Fancy Nancy." Eddie said with a quiet whistle.

Joe moved close to Eddie and cupped his hand around his mouth. "And you should see her in a bikini, man."

"Watch it, buster," Sandy Hendry warned as she drove an elbow into Joe's rib cage.

"Ohhh," Joe moaned. "Hi, babe, didn't see ya there."

"I know." Sandy smiled innocently.

"Hi, Eddie! Remember me?" Sandy asked.

"I sure do, Sandy." Eddie leaned over and kissed Sandy on the cheek.

"So you and Shawn are really going through with it?" Sandy asked him.

"Well, I . . ."

"No," Shawn said. "Eddie got a scholarship to play football. He'd be a fool to join up now. I'm still going, though."

"Did I hear that right?" Nancy said as she twirled Shawn around to face her.

"Yeah. He got a scholarship. Isn't that great? Here, you haven't met him yet."

But before Shawn could introduce the two, Nancy took his hand and led him toward the back bedroom. "I need to talk to you alone," she said. She closed the door behind them to shut out the loud music and turned to face Shawn.

"What's up, Nan?"

"Did you say you're still going through with this?"

"The Marines?"

"Yes. It just doesn't make sense, Shawn! If Eddie's not joining up, why do you have to go through with it? To prove how tough you are?''

"Is that why you think I'm joining?'' Shawn felt the crease between his eyes deepen into an angry frown.

"Why else do people do things like this?''

"We're at war, Nancy.''

"You don't even have a draft card yet, Shawn! And you may not get drafted at all. You can go to school until it's over. Weston Miles went to Canada!''

"Why don't I just put on a dress and learn to prance? That way I could stay right here and avoid my duty.''

"Shawn! I just don't want anything to happen to you. It isn't our war! Let them fight their own war!''

"You heard what the president said. If we let Vietnam fall, it's gonna be like dominoes. Cambodia and Thailand are gonna be dead ducks.''

"I don't believe that, Shawn. And I don't care. I need you to stay with me. We can go to Florida State together. We could have the best time of our lives!'' Big tears filled Nancy's green eyes.

"Are you going to wait for me, Nancy?''

She hugged Shawn tight and sobbed out her answer, "Yes.''

Someone pounded on the bedroom door. "Hey come on, you guys. We got a party out here!'' Chuck shouted.

"You okay now?'' Shawn asked.

Nancy wiped her eyes on Shawn's shirt sleeve and nodded.

"Let's get back out there and have some fun.'' Shawn kissed her, then opened the door and took her over to meet Eddie.

"Hey! Hey! You! You! Get offa my cloud!'' Joe sang out loud in a less-than-melodious voice as he lowered the needle on the turntable.

"Rolling Stones!'' Joe slapped Sandy on the bottom. The music blared.

"I don't believe that guy hasn't moved yet!'' Sandy pointed to Uncle Ralph in the corner, where he sat with his brown fedora still covering his eyes and his feet crossed comfortably on the recliner's footrest. Sandy danced over to the recliner and removed the mug of beer from between his legs. She set the beer on the end table, grinned mischievously, and jumped into Ralph's lap.

As she slung an arm around his neck, the fedora flipped off of his balding head, revealing a deathly pale gray face, closed eyes, and sunken cheeks. His skin was cold and bloodless. Sandy let out a piercing scream that froze the noisy party into silence. She screamed until her voice finally cracked and she clutched at her throat as if she'd injured it. Chuck held his ears. Sandy shot out of the stiff lap of the corpse. She stood trembling for a moment, staring at the dead man's gray features, then clenched her fists, stomped her feet, and wailed hysterically.

She and the rest of the girls ran into the kitchen, hugging and crying. Then in one voice, like the shout of a lynch mob, they screamed, "LUKEVEC!"

The slamming of the bathroom door signaled Luke's escape. Joe Elbon burst into a belly-splitting laugh that brought tears down his face from the slits that were his eyes.

Luke's black, porcupine hair poked out of the bathroom door first, followed by his brown eye. It disappeared only a fraction of a second before an unwashed frying pan, hurled with terrifying accuracy, ripped a piece of molding from the door jamb. Less accurate throws of a glass mug—filled with beer—a handful of knives, forks, spoons, and various kitchen utensils smashed against Lukevec's bathroom bunker, but Luke didn't surrender. Sandy unleashed a parting curse, concerning Lukevec's lack of family history, as she stormed from the apartment with the rest of the girls in her wake.

The party was over. Shawn hated to see Nancy leave, but the sacrifice seemed almost worth it, he thought. This was Luke's finest hour.

After more than a little complaining, Luke and Joe carried "Uncle Ralph" back downstairs to his coffin in viewing room A.

When they returned, Joe held out his hands and nodded proudly as if acknowledging applause. Eddie began to applaud vigorously. Then Chuck followed suit. Eddie stood and pretended to take off a hat.

"Bravo! Bravo!" Shawn shouted with a straight face.

Luke and Joe held hands and bowed like actors taking an encore. "I was only the dumb labor," Joe said. "This was the master's plan." Joe bowed and presented Luke with a wave of his hand.

Luke pushed both palms out and acknowledged the applause with slow nods in all directions until he had made a three-hundred-and-sixty degree turn.

"Thank you. Thank you. Now that the entertainment portion of the evening is over, let us eat!" Luke shouted.

Chuck rushed into the tiny kitchen and yanked open the refrigerator door. "Where?" he asked.

"Bottom shelf behind the two six-packs," Luke said.

"Steaks! Far out, Luke!"

"Steaks?" Shawn repeated with an accusing glare at Luke.

Luke shrugged. "They found their way into my possession."

The grill was full of glowing red embers when the guys reached the backyard patio. A round white metal table surrounded by lawn chairs sat on a small square slab of cement, well lit by four large floodlights. Charcoal smoke filled the warm night air.

Joe nudged Shawn. "Luke's outdone himself. Baked potatoes already cooking. The old man would sure like to be here for this."

"Pull up a chair, men," Luke said as Chuck laid the steaks on the grill.

"All right, who's the chef?" Jay asked.

"I'll cook," Eddie volunteered. "These babies are prime."

"Luke, you didn't really steal those steaks, did you?" Shawn asked.

Luke didn't answer. He gave Eddie a wave of approval. "Go for it, Edward."

Shawn turned an accusing stare at Luke. "Luke, you didn't, did you?"

"How in the world are you ever going to make it in the Marine Corps, McClellan?" Jay asked with a snicker.

"What do you mean by that?"

"Those boys don't wear halos," Joe said.

"They drink and fight and chase naked women," Jay explained. "And then they fight again."

Chuck nodded. "Jay's right, Shawn's too decent."

"I heard they don't allow you in the Marines if you're a virgin who prays."

"Okay, you clowns," Shawn growled.

Jay stood up and checked the steaks, then turned to Luke. "Remember when McClellan talked us into putting a roof on that old lady's house for Christmas?"

"Wait a minute," Shawn said. "We all voted to do that."

"Not exactly a restful holiday season," Luke moaned.

Eddie pointed a spatula at Shawn. "He always used to do

29

things like that when we were kids. One summer he got the whole gang to mow this old crippled lady's yard. We took turns all summer."

Chuck shook his head, suddenly somber. "I just can't see you going to war, Saint McClellan."

Jay laughed, "Yeah, a Bible in one hand and an M14 in the other."

"That's enough you guys," Shawn said.

"What do we get as a going-away present for a guy like this?" Joe said abruptly.

"You don't have to get me anything."

"Joe is correct, Shawn," Luke said. "Exactly what do you really want—besides Nancy Diez?"

"Better get him a bullet-proof vest," Chuck said wryly.

Eddie glared at Chuck. "Don't talk like that, man."

"I tell you what you can give me," Shawn said. "You guys go to church with me and Eddie tomorrow."

"Go sit on it, McClellan," Luke scoffed. "I won't miss you *that* much."

"Are you kiddin'?" Chuck put in. "The church would collapse if Lukevec walked in."

Sunday morning was hot, with no breeze coming through the bedroom windows. It always seemed to feel hotter on Sunday than on any other day of the week. Shawn figured it had to do with wearing a tie.

"I don't know how you guys can live here without air conditioning," Eddie spoke into the bedroom mirror as he pulled on his Windsor. "Shawn," he said, his voice lowered, "if I'm going to take the scholarship"—he paused to watch Shawn's reaction—"I have to leave tomorrow. They want me on campus for physicals and all kinds of garbage next week."

"What time?" Shawn asked.

"Nine A.M."

"Let's call and make reservations."

"Yeah."

"Me and Chuck will drop you off at the bus station the same time I go to sign up."

"Yeah." Eddie sounded uneasy.

"Hey, Ed, you're doing the right thing."

Eddie turned around to face Shawn. He looked serious. "It might be, Shawn, but if anything happens to you . . ."

"That's not for us to worry about. You know that."

Eddie looked at Shawn with a knowing smile. He shook his head and messed up Shawn's hair. "Yeah, but I need my best friend around to remind me."

"You ready, boys? We don't want to miss the bus," Opal McClellan called from the living room.

"We're ready, Mom."

The doorbell rang as Shawn and Eddie walked into the living room. When she opened the door, the surprise on Opal's face matched the surprise in her voice.

"Luke? Hi, fellas." She opened the screen door slowly. "My, don't you boys look nice today!"

"Mrs. McClellan," Luke said seriously, "I think you are the prettiest mom in St. Petersburg."

"Sorry, Luke," Opal said. "The pancakes are all gone."

Joe slapped Luke on the back of the head. "Boy, does she have your number."

Opal turned. "Shawn, it's for you."

The ride to church was hot and cramped but Shawn loved every minute of it. He kept saying silent prayers, thanking God for giving him great friends. And Sunday felt good all day.

Monday came. Saying good-bye to Eddie hurt. Shawn hated getting all teary-eyed, and Eddie kept clearing his throat when they hugged. His eyes were red and wet too. Neither one spoke. Eddie released Shawn from his bear hug, turned, and climbed into the bus.

Shawn's eyes were still red when he stepped into the cold air of the recruiting office. The burly gunnery sergeant stood up from behind his desk as the guys walked in. His khaki shirt and dress-blue trousers were tailored perfectly. Shawn wondered what the colorful ribbons were for but didn't ask.

"Good morning, men." The sergeant's voice sounded even lower than the first time he had talked to him, Shawn thought. "I've just been getting your paperwork ready."

He spread out three sheets of legal-size paper and held out a pen for Shawn. Shawn stepped forward. His stomach felt queasy as he took the pen and he prayed that he was doing the right thing. He leaned over to sign the first paper but someone already had.

"No. Not that one," the sergeant said. "That's Private El-

31

bon's. Yours is the center one. Private Lukevec's is the last one. You'll be glad you joined on the buddy system, men."

Shawn straightened up and turned a stunned look at Joe. "Joe? Are you sure, man?"

"Yeah, I'm sure," Joe said.

"Does Sandy know?"

"She doesn't care."

Shawn turned and signed his name, then looked up at Luke. "Luke, with your grades, you should go to college."

"They would only give me a partial scholarship. If I join for two years, I can get the GI bill to pay my tuition and besides . . ." Luke stopped. He looked around, then shrugged.

"And besides what?" Shawn asked.

"And besides, it is the right thing to do."

"Luke's right," Joe said. He snatched up the pen and signed his name. "We all know right from wrong." Joe handed the pen to Luke.

Luke quickly scribbled his name. "Besides, McClellan," he said, "you have no sense of direction. You would be lost without us."

They laughed. They laughed on the bus that took them to Jacksonville. They laughed about the miserable physical exam. They laughed with pride after being sworn into the armed forces. They managed a couple of sleepy laughs on the all-night bus ride to Parris Island, South Carolina. At Parris Island, the laughing stopped. And so did childhood.

CHAPTER FOUR

Vietnam
January 1968

Flying to war aboard a big orange Braniff Airlines plane with mini-skirted stewardesses wasn't exactly like storming the beaches at Iwo Jima, but when the planeload of baby-faced recruits touched down in Da Nang, Shawn felt more excitement and fear than he had ever felt before. Joe and Luke didn't speak. They didn't have to. Shawn knew they felt the same way.

The blistering sun stung Shawn's eyes as he reached the first step of the drab gray departing ramp. No one knew quite how to act. Scuttlebutt had it that one planeload of Marines had gotten hit on the runway, so everybody was somewhere between ready to duck and ready to march. A barrel-chested sergeant solved the problem by screaming, "Move it! Move it! Move it!" After Parris Island, machine-gun school at Camp Lejeune, and jungle-warfare school at Camp Pendleton, those words made the Marines feel right at home.

They stood in formation beside the plane until everyone had disembarked. The sky was hot, blue, and cloudless. A sleek Phantom jet whined to a stop nearby. Thundering artillery echoed across the airstrip.

Joe whistled quietly. "This is the real potato, gentlemen."

A skinny-looking helicopter floated down one hundred meters to the right of the formation. Its camouflaged body bristled with rockets and machine guns. The roar of another Phantom streaking down a runway grabbed everyone's attention as it sprang off the ground and climbed sharply over the steep green mountains surrounding Da Nang. Joe's right, Shawn thought, this is the real thing. It was scary, but for now the excitement of the adventure outweighed the fear.

The formation double-timed to a processing area at the edge of the airstrip then was quickly marched to an old two-story wood barracks called the Hotel Hilton for the night. Joe got orders for the Ninth Marine Regiment. Shawn and Luke were attached to the Fifth Marine Regiment.

No one slept much that night. Shawn stared at the bunk above him, listening to outgoing artillery and praying occasionally. Each time sleep felt close another salvo of artillery opened fire from somewhere nearby. It sounded like thunder rolling out of the surrounding mountains.

"That's those big 155s, man," a young voice said from a bunk to Shawn's left.

Another Marine whistled from the dark on Shawn's right. "So those are 155s. Man, they sound like they could split the whole earth apart."

"Thank God it's goin' out instead of comin' in," a third voice mumbled.

"They're comin' in at Khe Sanh, I heard, by the hundreds."

Before the sun was up, all Marines attached to units up north, which included the Fifth and Ninth regiments, were herded onto a big snub-nosed cargo plane for a quick flight to a hot dust bowl called Phu Bai. The plane was hot and crowded with sweaty Marines and smelled like somebody had puked. The only place to sit was the floor, and it was covered with metal conveyor rollers that were only slightly more comfortable than broken glass. Somebody had called the plane a flying boxcar. The name fit.

Phu Bai reeked with the stink of burning crappers. Even though they burned the crap in the toilets only every week or so, the stench of burning gasoline, oil, and human excrement hung over the base like a cloud.

By the end of the first sweaty day, the new replacements had been marched through a big tent and issued the tools of the trade. M16 rifle. Ammunition. Two M26 grenades. Web gear. Poncho. Pack. Flak jacket. Helmet. K-bar knife. Bandoliers. Cartridge belt. Canteens. Mess kit. C-rations. Halezone tablets to purify the water. Malaria pills. Salt tablets. Bug juice. Cleaning gear.

Jungle utilities with huge baggy pockets replaced starched stateside fatigues. Jungle boots with canvas uppers and a metal plate in the sole replaced the all-leather stateside boots.

"There's a steel plate in the sole of the boot to protect you from pungi pits," a stocky supply sergeant said with an evil grin, "but it don't stop them from going through your foot."

34

Most of the gear had been used before. Some of it had blood-stains. Some had bullet holes. One Marine refused to take a helmet with a bullet crease. He said it was bad luck. The supply sergeant grinned and tossed him another helmet.

By the second day in Phu Bai, Joe had been quartered in a tent for the Ninth Marines. Shawn and Luke were put in another, with a cardboard sign above the front flap that said A 1/5. Alpha Company, First Battalion, Fifth Marine Regiment.

Most of the men came down with dysentery. Lukevec didn't, but he seemed to think it was his duty to keep a running count on how many trips they each made to the head. If you weren't already sick, just going to the crappers and piss tubes would make you that way. The urinals were artillery casings rammed into the dirt. The crappers were usually wood toilet seats on top of fifty-five-gallon drums put into the ground. The daily temperature was well above one hundred degrees. The men worked hard at staying upwind of the head area.

On the third day the new Marines were marched to a primitive firing range. It seemed like a good idea, as most of them had trained with the M14 rifle from boot camp on. No one knew much about the M16, but the scuttlebutt was all bad. It jammed, it was inaccurate, and it wouldn't knock Charlie down if he was drugged up. The Marines called it the Matty Mattel toy.

The weapon did have a positive side: It was light, and that mattered in the jungle heat. You could carry twice the ammunition that you could with the heavy M14. And the M16 was made for jungle fighting, face-to-face, as it had virtually no recoil. Still, Shawn left the firing range with doubts about the weapon.

Next, the Fifth Marine replacements were marched to a tent filled with rows of benches. Shawn could feel Luke fidgeting nervously beside him. In front of them were rows of white-sidewalled heads. Everyone was sitting at attention on the hardwood benches. Chapel tent on Sunday, Shawn thought. Suddenly a tight-lipped, scowling colonel walked briskly up the center aisle carrying a pointer stick.

"Attention!" someone shouted, and the room jumped to attention. The colonel stepped up on a small wooden platform in front of a black chalkboard. On the top of the chalkboard he printed "Rules of This War."

"At ease! Sit!" His words seemed forced, as if they didn't want to come through his lips. He looked all Marine. He slapped the black chalkboard behind him with the pointer and shouted *"Chieu hoi!"* Then he turned and wrote it on the board as if he were in a hurry.

"When an enemy soldier shouts this, he is surrendering and joining the South Vietnamese Army. He will not be shot! This is a program designed to give the North Vietnamese Army soldiers a chance to change sides. Thousands are doing so. You will honor this. You will not shoot any person not in uniform until he opens fire upon you or others. After someone not in uniform opens fire upon you, you are free to kill that person and you *will* kill that person. . . ."

As the colonel continued bellowing out instructions, the white-sidewalled heads in front of Luke and Shawn began turning to face the Marine on either side. A huge question mark was etched across each young face.

The colonel listed rules about firing near villages or water buffalo. Finally he shouted, "And those are the rules of this war! Until you are told differently, until *we* are told differently, they stand."

Luke rubbed the back of his neck and leaned close to Shawn. "Somebody is out of their mind," he whispered.

"Now hear this!" The colonel slapped the pointer against the chalkboard. "The Fifth Marine Regiment is the most decorated regiment in the corps. Guadalcanal! Peleliu! Ngesebus! Okinawa! Korea! Chosin Reservoir! And more! We now have the highest kill ratio in Vietnam and we intend to keep it! Attention!"

The men jumped to their feet as the colonel marched out of the tent. Shawn felt every kind of emotion he could remember feeling.

"Dismissed!" someone shouted when the colonel was gone. Fear and excitement mixed with doubt as Shawn filed out of the tent with the others into the bright sun.

"Stupid!" Luke growled angrily. "It's no wonder we haven't won yet! The most incredibly stupid thing that I have ever heard of! Let the enemy shoot first?"

"Wonder what Joe just heard." Shawn mumbled.

"Knowing the corps, they probably received a different set of rules for the Ninth Marines. What time are we supposed to meet him?"

"As soon as the indoctrination's over, at the Animal Pit."

"Yeah, a slop-shute complete with sandbags," Shawn said. He forced a laugh, but his thoughts were serious.

"Luke—" he began.

"Yes?" Luke said, staring at a squadron of Army helicopter gunships coming toward the Phu Bai airstrip.

"We're going into combat, man. I mean this ain't no John Wayne movie. I got goose bumps."

They walked to the main dirt road on base that separated the Marine area from the Army.

"It is scary, isn't it?" Luke mumbled. "I sure wish Joe had gotten orders for the Fifth."

"Yeah. Me too."

They turned right on the main dirt street. Fifty yards later they turned left down a walkway lined with rocks painted white. The Animal Pit looked more like a large bunker than a bar. It was made of plywood and sandbags. The only window, visible from the front, looked like a gun slit. An Army MP stood guard in front, beside a row of assorted weapons that were leaning against the sandbag wall.

"Leave your weapons here, Marines." His voice was a low rumble and he looked lean and weathered. His uniform was clean, but his face had that haunted look, as if he had "been there." They handed the MP their rifles and opened the plywood door. It was dark inside and much cooler. Joe raised a hand from the far end of the nearly empty bar. A soldier slapped the side of a loud pinball machine over in one corner as Shawn and Luke sat on stools next to Joe.

Artillery opened up from the north side of the base. Shawn flinched as his bar stool vibrated. His bright green eyes widened. The brown-and-blue Schlitz Beer sign behind the bar sent out enough light to see, but not enough to see clearly. Three black-and-white eight-by-ten photos were pinned to the wall under the sign: President Johnson shaking hands with McNamara, Army generals shaking hands with unit commanders.

The stool vibrated again with the distant sound of thunder, only this thunder came out of long barrels and struck with more than lightning. Glass rattled. Shawn flinched again. A beer-bellied Army sergeant chuckled from behind the bar. He slid a mug of beer past Shawn to Joe.

"Don't get in a habit of flinching, boot, that's outgoing. If you learn to flinch at outgoing, you're gonna jerk at incoming, and by the time your tour's over you'll be one of those vets that

37

go around shaking all the time. How long you been in-country?'' the bartender asked.

"What? In what country?" Shawn asked.

"In-country means Vietnam. How long?" He slid two mugs of beer toward Shawn and Luke, then laid his big forearms on the bar in front of Luke.

"Three days," Shawn said.

"No, Shawn," Luke said. "We have been in Phu Bai for three days but we spent the first night in Da Nang, at the Hotel Hilton."

"The big wood barracks near the airstrip?" the Army sergeant asked.

"Yes," Luke said.

The bartender laughed. "So you just got twelve months to go."

"Thirteen," Joe corrected.

"Oh, yeah, you're Marines." The bartender stood up straight and grabbed a white towel from a shelf behind him. "I don't envy you. When they finally get off their rear ends in Washington and let us invade and end this bull"—he began wiping the bar top hard—"it's probably gonna be you guys that are sent across the Z first. And we've given 'em enough time to booby-trap every tree from here to Hanoi. We'll still turn 'em into rice balls in six weeks, though."

"Got any advice?" Shawn asked.

"Who ya with?" the bartender asked, leaning on the bar again.

"We're in the Fifth Marines, and Joe, on the end there, got orders for the Ninth Marines."

"Ninth?" The bartender's eyebrows lifted. Joe's lifted too.

"Yeah, the Ninth Marine Regiment," Joe said. "Know anything?"

He began wiping the bar top again. "Not much. Just bar talk. We get a lot of Marines cuz you guys don't have your own bar."

"That figures," Luke muttered.

"Well, that's what ya get for bein' Spartans," the bartender said with a mocking grin. "Well, I think it was the Ninth that held Con Thien, up on the Z." He looked at Joe and shook his head ominously. "It was some bad stuff. Hand-to-hand. Held it and kicked some butt, but they took heavy casualties. I hear they call One-Nine the Ghost Battalion, they lost so many guys."

Joe looked at Shawn with an oh-brother look. "That's who I'm with. One-Nine."

"I heard some more for ya then." The bartender's tone told them it wasn't good news. Shawn felt his heart begin beating faster. He glanced at Joe, then back to the round-faced bartender. "It's just scuttlebutt and don't mean nothin'." He paused and looked at Shawn's empty mug. "You need another?"

"Yeah."

The sergeant grabbed the empty mug and turned to pull a tap. "Well, now I heard a couple of Marines in here the other day sayin' that the Ninth was going up to Khe Sanh." Joe's handsome face showed no concern. He took the last swig of beer and slid his empty mug past Shawn to Luke.

"I heard a guy say something about Khe Sanh. You ever heard of it, Joe?" Shawn asked.

"No."

"Well, it's right up on the Z," the fat sergeant said. "I've been hearin' the gooks got T34s up there."

"What's that?" Joe asked.

"Russian tanks."

"Tanks?" Luke said.

"Really?" Shawn asked.

"That's the word."

"Tanks," Joe mumbled, "Good grief."

A sudden burst of harsh sunlight followed by columns of dust shot through the front door. "Hey!" the silhouette of a Marine in battle gear took shape. He was holding the door open with one hand and had a rifle in the other. "Anybody in here from the Ninth Marines?" he shouted.

Joe sat up straight. His face looked strained in the harsh new light. For a moment he didn't speak, then he gave a wave. "Yeah, I am!" he yelled.

"Saddle up! We're movin' out!" the silhouette shouted. The door slammed the bar into darkness. Joe blinked while his eyes readjusted to the dim light. He jumped from the stool and stood rigid, looking at Shawn and Luke. His lips were closed tight. He took two deep breaths through his nose and for an instant looked like he might hyperventilate.

"Well . . ." He held out his hand. "Guess this is it."

Shawn jumped off his stool and gave Joe a quick hug and slap on the back. "I'll pray for you, Joe."

Luke stepped forward and gave Joe a hug too. Nothing more was said.

The walk back to the Fifth Marine area wasn't really a sad one for Shawn. He already missed Joe, but there was so much to think about. Outgoing artillery sent shock waves across Phu Bai and goose bumps up his spine. He kept looking at his jungle boots and then at his web gear and then finally at the M16 in his hand. He was in a war.

Phu Bai was a dust bowl one minute and a mud hole the next. The Army had constructed their half of the base with permanent-looking little buildings made of plywood, tin roofs, and screens to let in air and keep out the biggest mosquitoes Shawn had ever seen. The buildings were surrounded with sandbags. The Marine Corps area was filled with tents that had turned from green to beige in the harsh sun and under layers of dust kicked up by passing tanks and trucks.

A line of big deuce-and-a-half trucks pulled out of the front gate five hundred yards ahead. They turned left, north toward the DMZ. Luke nodded at the trucks as they churned up clouds of dust.

"There goes Joe."

"Probably," Shawn said.

"I think something is wrong between him and Sandy," Luke said. "And he mumbled something that meant he didn't want to talk about it."

"Sometimes I wish I could be more like Joe. You know, the strong, silent type."

"I don't think it's healthy," Luke said thoughtfully. "He keeps too much inside. He'll probably die from ulcers."

Shawn laughed. "I hope we all die from ulcers." He looked down at the hot ground and mumbled a silent prayer for Joe.

Luke moaned. "Are you praying again?" He sounded exhausted.

"Yeah."

Luke shook his head, pulled back the tent flap, and walked in. "I wish that you would curtail that habit. It makes me nervous. I wonder when the Fifth Marines are coming to Phu Bai."

"Who knows?" Shawn said, following Luke into the tent.

"I don't think One-five will be comin' to Phu Bai anytime soon," a husky, curly-haired Marine with a prominent nose said from a cot on the right. He sat up, then stood and extended a hand. "Adelman. Lance Corporal. Call me Burt."

40

"Lukevec," Luke said, shaking Adelman's hand. "This is McClellan."

"Burt." Shawn leaned forward to shake the husky Marine's hand. He looked friendly, Shawn thought. He had that kind of "nice guy" face. "How ya doin'?"

"You guys boots?" Burt asked.

"Yes," Luke said.

Shawn looked down at Burt's jungle boots. "Yours look new too," he said with a grin.

"No," Burt said. He glanced down at his boots. "They cut my salty boots all up when they brought me into First Med."

"You got wounded?" Shawn asked.

"Yeah, almost four months ago now." Burt sat back down on his cot and picked his pack up off the ground.

"Where have you been?" Luke asked.

"Japan. Okinawa. I can't believe I'm actually going back into the bush. I keep pinching myself but I won't wake up." He laid his pack beside him.

"Looks like we got the tent to ourselves," Shawn said. "Mind if we store our gear beside you? I've got a million questions."

"Better ask 'em ASAP," Burt said. "I'm saddlin' up."

Luke and Shawn sat down on the cot next to Burt as he checked the contents of his pack.

"Where are you going?" Luke asked.

"Weapons Platoon, One-Five."

"What company?" Luke asked.

"Alpha Company."

"We're in Alpha Company," Shawn said.

"Second Platoon," Luke said.

"How come Second Platoon only got a couple of new guys?" Shawn asked.

"Just depends on who's taken the most casualties lately. What's your MOS?" Burt asked.

"0331," Shawn said.

"Guns up, bros." Burt signaled a thumbs-up. "Me too. But I don't know what platoon they'll send me to. Machine gunners are all under Weapons Platoon and you get assigned to a grunt platoon from there. You get moved around sometimes, but they try to keep you with the same platoon as much as possible."

"Maybe we're going with you," Shawn said.

"I doubt if you guys are going to battalion first, since they brought you here to Phu Bai. You'll probably go straight to the Second Platoon, wherever they are. Battalion HQ is at Phu Loc, south of here.''

"That's our rear area?" Shawn asked.

Burt chuckled. "Yeah, but it ain't rear enough for me. We used to call it Little Con Thien because it got shelled as much as Con Thien, but only with mortars and rockets.''

"Sounds wonderful,'' Shawn said.

"It ain't Disneyland, but it's better than being in the bush.''

"Is it as bad as they say for machine gunners?'' Luke asked. "In gun school they told us that machine gunners lasted an average of seven seconds in a firefight.''

Burt looked up from closing his pack. His friendly face suddenly looked pensive. "If Charlie shows his butt in the daylight, he gets it kicked, bad. So he tries to only fight at night. The M60 is the most visible target. Those tracer rounds are like a neon sigh, bro.''

"Is there an Adelman in here?'' a high-pitched voice shouted through the tent flap. A young corporal poked his head into the tent.

"Yeah, here,'' Burt said.

"Saddle up. You got a chopper goin' to Phu Loc. Now!'' The corporal disappeared.

"That's my cab.'' Burt stood up, strapped on his cartridge belt, and put on his flak jacket and helmet. "Frankly, boots, I'd rather be in Philadelphia.'' Burt grabbed his rifle, looked down at Luke, and smiled. He turned and walked out of the tent.

Shawn and Luke sat quietly for a minute, then decided to write home.

It rained all night. Shawn stared at the blackness above, listening to the rain pounding against the canvas and feeling cozy and scared but excited. Too excited to sleep.

Luke snored.

The first dim blue shafts of morning light coming through holes in the tent flap told Shawn he had been awake all night. The rain stopped. Suddenly the tent flap jerked open. The boyish corporal peeked in and shouted.

"Saddle up! You got a chopper waitin' at the pad! Ten minutes!''

Shawn and Luke sat up. The corporal's round face disappeared. Shawn's heart began pounding so hard that he could feel his chest moving. His fingers felt like sticks. He couldn't tie up his boot laces. He gave up and stuffed the laces into the tops of his boots. Luke stood up, raised his arms over his head, and inhaled and blew out several times.

"You nervous?" Shawn asked.

"Who, me? Of course not. Going to war is just your average nine-to-five humdrum experience."

Shawn forced a chuckle. "Yeah, just a walk around the block."

Luke took a deep breath and picked up his cartridge belt. "Rough neighborhood, Shawn."

Ten minutes later the round-faced corporal slammed on the squeaking brakes of a jeep. He turned to Luke and Shawn and pointed at a group of Marines loading boxes of C-rations into the back of a CH-46 helicopter.

"That's your ride!" he shouted over the noisy departure of a nearby Huey helicopter gunship. "Semper fi!" He held out his fist with a thumbs up.

A few nervous minutes later they were airborne for their first helicopter ride ever. Shawn peered out of the porthole window between himself and Luke. The fiery copper sun seemed to gain altitude along with the chopper. His stomach rose the way it did on a good roller coaster. The first cool wind he'd felt since reaching Nam blew through an open hatch where a young door gunner sat, one leg dangling in the breeze. Fifteen minutes later the sun was bright and hot. Two mountains loomed larger and larger as the CH-46 descended between them into a hazy valley.

Yellow smoke spiraled up from a square field of tall grass. The wind moved the grass like waves of water. The square field looked as if it had been cut out of a dense jungle on all sides. The door gunner glanced at Shawn and Luke through his dark flight glasses.

"Get ready! The LZ is that big field of elephant grass," he shouted over the noise of the engine.

The chopper circled the valley, banking sharply against the steep face of each mountain, then dropping low and swooping down. The dark figures of Marines in prone positions around the swirling yellow smoke marked a perimeter for the landing. Suddenly the back ramp dropped as the CH-46 bounced lightly, then settled.

"Grab a couple of boxes of C-rats!" the door gunner shouted.

He looked toward mountains on his right then back at Shawn and Luke. "Just thrown 'em out the back, fast!"

Luke laid his rifle down, picked up a box of rations, and heaved it out the back, narrowly missing two dirty Marines carrying a limp body by the four corners of a bloodstained camouflage poncho liner.

"Gang way!" a big reddish-skinned Marine who Shawn thought must be an Indian yelled as he struggled to hold the boot end of the poncho. A square-jawed black Marine holding the other end backed up the ramp, turned to look for a spot on which to lay the dead Marine, then moved over to where Luke's rifle lay.

"Move your weapon, man!" the black Marine yelled, with a hint of a Caribbean accent. Shawn stared at the body in the poncho as Luke grabbed up his M16. The dead Marine's face was muddy. His long, straight nose was smeared with dried blood. Two huge flies landed on his nose.

"Hey! Here's his helmet!" someone yelled.

An Oriental Marine tossed a helmet into the chopper. Shawn caught the flying helmet. It had a thick black rubber band around the camouflage helmet cover. A white plastic bottle of insect repellent was stuck in the band. "Guns up!" was printed in black across the canvas helmet cover. Shawn felt numb, almost dazed by the whole scene. The door gunner threw a green tarp over the dead Marine, then grabbed the helmet from Shawn and laid it on the dead man's chest.

Two loud cracks sounded over the prop wash of the helicopter rotors. The big red-skinned Marine began throwing off boxes of C-rats as quickly as he could. The door gunner ran for his machine gun. The engine revved. The chopper began to lift.

Shawn looked at Luke. Luke was rigid, his eyes wide open. The black Marine with the Caribbean accent grabbed Lukevec's arm and yanked him toward the ramp as the rear of the chopper swung to the left. The door gunner opened fire. Shawn couldn't breathe. He was sure that his heart had stopped.

"Move it, Marine!" the big Indian roared as he grabbed Shawn's arm and pulled him toward the ramp.

Luke jumped out behind the black Marine. With a loud groan Shawn flew out of the back of the chopper, aided by a shove from the red-skinned man. The jump was only a few feet off the ground, but the weight of the gear made the impact feel like the receiving end of a gang tackle. Shawn's seventy-pound pack hit him in the back of his head and the front of his flak jacket shoved a bandolier of M16 clips into his throat. His knee smashed into the butt of his rifle. Gunfire echoed from a mountainside to Shawn's rear. He looked up and into the sweaty face of the black Marine.

"Name's Cager, man," the Marine said. He glanced toward the escaping helicopter. "Can ya chord, boot?"

"What?"

"Can ya hold a chord? Tunes, man?" he asked. He pronounced man like "mon." His teeth were huge and ivory white.

"Sing?"

Another series of sharp cracks rang out from the mountainside. A bullet smacked through the head-level saw grass. Shawn flinched, then shivered slightly. A chill ran up his spine.

"Yeah, man, can ya hold a note?"

"Can't sing a lick," Shawn said. He rubbed his throat and looked at his hand. It was bloody. The edge of an M16 magazine had cut him when he jumped from the chopper.

Cager frowned at Shawn. "Shoulda known they'd send a honky boot who can't jive. You better get Doc to throw some medicine on that cut. It'll be puttin' out pus by tonight, man."

"Cager." The big red-skinned Marine's voice was low and strong. He stood casually behind Shawn. He didn't seem the least bit worried about getting shot.

"Yo," Cager said as he stood up.

"Take those two boxes of C-rats over to Murph's squad, over on that half of the perimeter," he said, pointing.

"Okay, Chief," Cager said, picking up a couple of boxes.

"Why do you call him Chief?" Shawn asked Cager. "Is he Navy?"

"Navy?" Cager laughed out loud. "No, man, he's Chocktaw. Indian."

"Move it, Marine!" the Chief shouted.

Cager leaned close to Shawn and whispered, "And he's bad, man!" Cager laughed again. The Chief didn't. Cager started off through the high saw grass and in a moment he disappeared as if the grass had swallowed him.

"Get up, boots!" Chief grabbed a box of C-rations with both hands and shot it toward Lukevec like a basketball pass. Luke barely rolled out of the way in time. "You carry that!"

He looked toward Shawn. Shawn prepared to jump. "You get the other one. Move it!" With that the big Indian was already

45

deep into the saw grass. Shawn and Luke jumped to their feet, grabbed the C-rations, and hurried after him. Luke slapped at his face like he had been stung. He stopped and turned to face Shawn. There was a thin line of fresh blood from his left temple to his jaw.

"Hey, watch this grass, Shawn; it cuts like a razor!" Luke turned back to the trail of bent grass that the Chief had made.

Twenty feet later Luke broke into a ten-by-ten-foot clearing where the grass was stomped down. A chubby little Marine with glasses sat on one knee tinkering with a PRC-25 radio. Another Marine hovered over his shoulder; his clean-cut collegiate face and the .45-caliber pistol on his hip smacked of officer. The chubby-cheeked guy pushed his glasses back on his very small nose and smiled contentedly as static came from the radio. He looked over his shoulder as if awaiting praise.

"Got it, Lieutenant," Chubby Cheeks said. "She'll work now."

College Face slapped him on the back. "Good job, Chip. We'd be in a GI can without you."

A thin guy with a boyish face and a crop of blond hair sticking straight up on the crown of his head pointed at Shawn and Luke. "Like, boots, man." The thin blonde spoke with a totally deadpan face. Shawn did a double take. The blond guy looked familiar.

"Replacements, Chief?" the lieutenant asked.

"Yes, sir," the Indian mumbled.

Luke stood straight and started to salute.

"No!" the lieutenant snapped. "No salutes in the bush, Marine."

"Sorry, sir," Luke said.

"What's your MOS?"

"0331, sir," Luke answered quickly.

The lieutenant's eyes softened. Shawn's stomach tightened at what he read as compassion. The face of the dead Marine on the chopper flashed across his mind. For just an instant he thought about Burt Adelman and the seven-second statistic.

The chubby radioman pushed his glasses back on his tiny nose like a professor. "I'm Chip Houston."

Luke and Shawn nodded. "I'm Eric Lukevec and this is Shawn McClellan."

"You're both gunners?" the familiar-looking blonde asked, his face never changing.

"Yeah," Shawn said.

Chip the radioman pulled a wad of bubble gum out of his mouth and stuck it on the end of his radio antenna. "Both gunners," he said with eyes open wide. "Kayto's gonna be glad to see you, boots."

"I'm Doc, the corpsman," the blond guy said. Shawn gave a slight wave of hello and wondered how the Doc could speak without his face moving. "My name's Dennis Abernathy."

That's *it*! Shawn thought in astonishment. Dennis. He looks exactly like Dennis the Menace, only bigger.

"I'm Lieutenant Townsend and this is Sergeant Ghosthorse." Shawn turned from Dennis to Lieutenant Townsend. The big Indian stood beside the lieutenant. "We don't have time to talk to you right now but pay attention to what I say."

"Yes, sir," Luke said.

"Sit down."

Sounds easy, Shawn wanted to say, but didn't. The seventy pounds of gear made it difficult to lower himself without falling backward. The lieutenant knelt on one knee. "When you hear 'Guns up!' I want that M60 to the point of contact and firing, and I mean now! Got it?"

"Yes, sir!" they both replied sharply.

"You will clean and oil the gun every time we stop long enough, and you better never go more than a day without cleaning the gas chamber. Who fired highest with the gun?"

"I fired expert, sir," Shawn said.

Lieutenant Townsend looked at Luke. "Okay with you if he's the gunner?"

"Yes, sir."

"That makes you the A-gunner. What's your name?"

"Lukevec, sir."

"Lukevec, you'll carry four or five hundred rounds, always. If he goes down you're the gunner! Got it?"

"Yes, sir."

"Sir, do you mean I get the gun right now?"

Lieutenant Townsend exchanged glances with Chip and the Indian sergeant, then looked back to Shawn. "Yeah. We depend on the gun, Marine. Marines are going to die if you don't come through. You will always be in the center of the column; that way if we make contact at the point or the rear or even on the flanks you guys can get there quick. Are you fast?"

47

Shawn shrugged. "Well, I was a quarterback. But this big klutz was a guard."

"What?" the Chief snapped. "You mean you guys know each other?"

"Since the seventh grade," Luke said.

The lieutenant looked stunned. He exchanged a worried look with the Indian. "Real bright, HQ," Lieutenant Townsend muttered.

The big Indian shook his head. His stony expression didn't change. Luke looked at Shawn and rolled his eyes in a circle, then did his Groucho Marx eyebrow routine. Shawn didn't feel like laughing.

"What's wrong, Lieutenant?" Shawn asked.

"It's an old combat rule, PFC," the lieutenant said. "You never send brothers or best friends into combat together. If one of you doesn't make it, then the other one might not react like a Marine and that could cost someone else his life. That better not happen!"

"Yes, sir," Shawn heard himself answer, but even his own voice was starting to sound unfamiliar.

"Chief," Townsend said.

"Yes, sir?"

"Tell Kayto to stay with the gun team for a couple of days. Then he can go back with Cager."

"We could put a short-timer with 'em for a while, sir."

"Who do you suggest?"

The big Indian pushed his Coke-bottle glasses back up his long nose and lifted his eyebrows. "Dusty. He'd probably teach 'em the most. But, he won't like being next to the gun. Not with a month left."

The lieutenant's mouth tightened and he seemed to go into deep thought for a moment. He pinched the bridge of his nose and closed his eyes as if he had a headache. "You're right," he said. "Take these guys over to the gun and go tell Dusty."

A single shot suddenly echoed across the valley. Shawn and Luke dropped to one knee. No one else moved. Luke peered up from under his helmet. Doc and Chip the radioman looked at Luke with no expression. No surprise. No laugh. Almost bored.

"Okay," Chief growled. "Follow me."

He pushed into the ten-foot-high elephant grass. Shawn hustled to his feet and trotted after him with Luke close behind.

48

Twenty yards ahead the Chief broke through to another flattened square in the tall grass.

Shawn paused and looked back at Luke. "You hear that?"

Luke frowned. "Yeah. Music?"

"They sound pretty good."

Shawn shoved through the razor-sharp grass to the opening. The Oriental Marine sat next to an M60 machine gun, tapping on his helmet with his open hands like a bongo drummer. The black Marine named Cager relaxed comfortably on his back, his head on his pack and his feet on his helmet. Their humming sounded like two musicians jamming; they did it well.

"Kayto." The Chief's commanding voice stopped the music cold.

"Yeah, Chief?" the Oriental said.

"These boots are gunners. . . ."

"Allll riiight, bro!" Kayto jumped to his feet, smiling. "She's all yours, brothers!"

"Chief," Cager said as he got to his feet. "Hey, man, lieutenant's not going to leave two boots alone is he?" Cager sounded concerned. Shawn decided that he liked this Jamaican-sounding Marine.

"Dusty's breakin' 'em in."

Kayto whistled. "How did he take to that news?"

"He don't know yet," Chief said. "I want you to go tell him to—"

"No, way!" Kayto held up his hands like a man surrendering.

"Go tell him to come over here and to bring his gear."

"Okay, but you tell him—okay, Chief?"

"Move it, Marine."

"Which one of you is the gunner?" Kayto asked.

"Me," Shawn said.

"Give me your rifle and bandoliers. Loose clips too."

Shawn peeled off the M16 bandoliers. Kayto grabbed the rifle and threw the bandoliers over one shoulder. He turned and disappeared into the huge grass.

"Better sit down, boots." Cager said. "You learn to save all the energy you got cuz when we start the hump, man, you're going to need it. Take it from a lance corporal who knows."

"Where are you from, Cager?" Shawn asked.

"Baton Rouge, man."

"Baton Rouge?"

"Yes, man," he said. "Cajun, you know?"

Luke dropped his pack and seemed to study Cager for a moment.

"Excuse me, Lance Corporal Cager," Luke said, "but your accent is not a Southern accent, and saying 'mon' in place of 'man' would lead me to speculate that you're from an island in the Caribbean."

Cager smiled. His bright white teeth were a beacon against his dark brown skin. He looked at Shawn, still smiling. "Does he always speak so slowly, man?" he asked.

"Always," Shawn said.

"I was born in Baton Rouge, raised in Jamaica, and graduated from Grambling."

"How about you, Sergeant Ghosthorse?" Shawn asked.

"Are we supposed to call you Chief?" Luke asked.

"Don't matter," the Chief said. His hard black eyes looked huge through the thick glasses.

"What happened to that guy you put on the chopper?" Luke asked.

"Gunner," the Chief mumbled, and turned away as if he didn't want to talk.

"We laid an ambush last night, man. Earl caught one right in the heart." Cager said.

The Chief spun around with an angry stare at Cager, "Fired too long," he growled. "At least a hundred rounds." The big Indian turned back to Shawn. "Twenty-round burst, boot. You fire longer, they zero in on the gun, you're dead. Got it?"

"Yes, sir. I mean, got it, Chief." Shawn's throat felt dry. The continual sweat dripping down his face suddenly felt thicker.

"Gosh, I want to ask questions but I don't even know what to ask." Shawn spoke out loud, but he was talking to himself.

Luke held up one finger. "I have one; how can I avoid smelling like you guys?"

Shawn's mouth fell open. He looked at the big Indian, expecting the worst. Cager laughed out loud. The Chief's lips may have straightened, but calling it a smile would have been pushing it.

"Just wait, boot man," Cager said. "A couple of months in the bush and you won't even be able to smell the difference between clean and filth because everything stinks in the Nam, man. This is the armpit of the world."

"You mothers!" An angry bellow came from somewhere in the ocean of tall grass.

Cager whistled and shook his head at the sergeant.

"Dusty isn't happy, Chief," Luke said.

The Indian looked at the two boots. "You do everything he says. You pick his brain. Quick. You better not do something stupid and get Dusty killed. He's a short-timer. Good Marine."

"He's a salt, man," Cager said with a nod. "He's only got twenty-six days left and he's on the freedom bird back to the world."

The sound of someone slashing angrily through the tall grass preceded the emergence of a rugged, angry, Marine of medium build and height. His dark, handsome features reminded Shawn of Joe Elbon. His face was crusty with the two-day stubble of what could easily become a heavy beard. He had a mustache, as nearly everyone did. His once-black boots looked like well-worn white moccasins that had molded to the shape of his feet. His jungle utilities were sunbaked beige instead of green. He was a mountain man out of another era, and though all of these Marines seemed hard and old, none did as much as this guy. Shawn stared like a little kid seeing his first policeman. He yearned to look like this hard-core Marine. A salt.

Dusty threw his odd-looking pack down beside the machine gun, then angrily threw his rifle against the pack. "You guys are tryin' to kill me! That bloody boot lieutenant doesn't want me to get home!"

"They're both boots, Dusty," the Chief said sternly. "We want 'em to have the best chance they can."

Dusty's fiery dark eyes seemed to soften for a moment, then he turned and spit angrily. "Yeah, yeah," he muttered through clenched teeth, then turned back to the Chief. "But you don't put short-timers beside the gun and you know it, Chief! You've been here four frickin' tours! How many times have you seen it done?" Dusty's face flushed red.

"It's done, Marine," the Chief said.

Luke glanced down. He seemed almost embarrassed at causing so much trouble. Shawn fidgeted nervously with a grenade that hung on the pocket of his jungle jacket. He felt like an intruder.

"Get your hand off that, boot!" Dusty barked. "Look at this!" He stepped forward and pulled the grenade off Shawn's shirt. "Look!" He held the grenade out to the Chief. "They haven't even bent the pins on their frags! You guys are gonna get me killed with twenty-six days left!"

51

"All right," the Chief said calmly, "I'll pull you away from the gun. Two days." The Indian's long, serious face turned hard and looked even more red than normal. "You teach 'em everything they need. Fast. We depend on the gun. We're gonna depend on it after you're home free."

"Affirmative." Dusty held up two fingers. "Two days." He took off his helmet. A calendar in twelve squares was printed all the way around his helmet cover. The days were X'ed off from January 1967 to January 1968. The thirteenth month was on the top of his helmet with a big red circle around February 20. Dusty pointed to it.

"I know, I know," the big Indian said. He turned and disappeared into the grass, then poked his head back into the clearing. "Cager, get over to your position. We're movin' out in ten." With that he was gone and so was Cager.

Shawn and Luke still hadn't sat down. Shawn felt awkward, like an uninvited guest. Luke moved over to the machine gun. He pushed his helmet back and moved his bushy eyebrows up and down until he got a smile out of Shawn. Then he sat and turned to Dusty.

"I'll say this much for you gentlemen: you certainly know how to make a fellow Marine feel welcome."

Dusty smiled. The tension had been broken. He laid his helmet down, then used it for a pillow as he stretched out on his back and crossed his feet. "Where you guys from?"

"We're from St. Petersburg, Florida." Shawn said, sitting down beside Luke.

"Both of you?" Dusty asked.

"Yes. I am Eric Lukevec and this is Shawn McClellan."

"Did you know each other before you joined the corps?"

"Yes," Luke said. "We've been best friends since the seventh grade."

"We joined together," Shawn said. He was glad that Luke seemed to show pride in the longevity of their friendship. Sort of out of character for ol' Luke, he thought.

Dusty groaned. "Just my luck. The corps usually won't let that happen."

"Yes," Luke yawned and stretched. "We know."

Shawn leaned back on his pack. "Dusty, I'm ready for all the advice you can give me."

"Yes. Me too," Luke said.

"Yeah. Well, first thing you better do if you haven't already

52

is swallow a malaria pill and a salt tab. If you miss the malaria pill you'll get it and it'll stay with ya long after this war is over. If you don't take your salt tab you'll pass out from heat exhaustion, guar-rone-teed!" He laughed. "That's the way Dook talks. You ever heard Cajuns talk, from Louisiana?"

"Yeah, I have." Shawn said. "My girl's Cajun."

"Your girl? That sounds official," Luke said. He looked at Shawn and raised and lowered his bushy black eyebrows.

"Dook's a good ol' boy," Dusty said. "You'll meet him. He don't trust no plastic rifle and he ain't carryin' one. He's a riot. Good Marine too. Poor guy ain't got no mail from 'the world' since he came in-country except for some dog food."

"Dog food?" Luke repeated.

"Yeah. We got a bunch of care packages at Christmas time, you know, school kids and churches and stuff. They send you Kool-Aid and real food and newspapers."

"That's good," Shawn said.

"Yeah, but the one guy who really needed mail the most, Dook, got dog food and some letter saying 'Dog food for murderers' or some crap like that."

"Probably from another hero living in Canada," Shawn scoffed.

"Dook put a full magazine of M14 rounds into that package. Lieutenant didn't say a word either."

"Where are you from, Dusty?" Luke asked.

"Wisconsin. Madison." He lifted his head from the helmet, looked over at the boots, and leaned back again. "Better put your dog tags in the laces of your boots and blacken 'em up so they don't catch shine from the moon. If you get blown to bits, the boots always hold together and then they can identify you."

Luke dropped his chin and raised his eyes.

"Shawn," Luke mumbled, "I am really ready to go home now. This is a very stupid place for me to be."

"Gosh, we can't leave yet, we just got here. Rude, rude, rude."

"Keep that sense of humor, boots; you're gonna need it."

"Is the gun really that bad?" Shawn asked. "You guys act like we're doomed."

"You'll be all right. Just be smart and stay alert and you'll take names. It's a tough job. Nobody in Alpha has spent his whole tour on the gun and gone home untouched since I've been here."

53

"Take names?" Shawn asked.

"Yeah. Kick butt and take names. That's when we wipe out a whole unit. Like the 308th NVA Regiment. The Fifth Marines took their name. They had to go back north and start all over cuz we killed three-fourths of 'em."

Dusty looked at the blank faces of the boot gunners and shrugged. "Look, don't freak out, a couple of gunners got KIA'ed, the rest just got nicked and sent home. Just keep your eyes open. If you ever see three sticks about the same length laying on a trail side by side like Roman numerals, that's a gook mark for a booby trap."

"How could anybody spot that in a jungle full of sticks?" Shawn's heart quickened with his question.

"There it is, boot. Another one is when you see something extremely large and something extremely small right beside it, like a huge boulder and a small rock about the same shape. You see that, you sky-out-of-there, bro."

Shawn started to speak but there was nothing to say. He was scared.

"Saddle up!" someone yelled from the tall grass.

"Saddle up!"

"Saddle up!"

The shout echoed from position to position around the perimeter. Dusty frowned as he got to his feet. He grabbed his pack and put it on. His pack wasn't Marine Corps issue. It was bigger and made of a softer canvas. It looked more comfortable than the small stiff pack Shawn had.

"You'll grow to hate those two words," Dusty grumbled. "Maybe as much as you'll hate the other two words: 'Guns up.' "

Shawn started a silent prayer as he joined the column of men that stretched across the elephant-grass valley and up a steep, heavily wooded mountain. The column looked to be about seventeen men long. The brush was green and thick and full of thorns and strange plants that all looked antihuman. The blazing sun made the stagnant jungle air feel like the inside of an oven. The cool shade of the canopy of tall trees was a welcome relief.

No one spoke. Shawn wondered if they weren't supposed to or if maybe the men were just conserving energy. He wondered how anyone could see the enemy in country like this. The top of his shoulder and neck hurt from the weight of the M60. There wasn't any practical way to carry the thing other than laying the twenty-four-pound gun on your shoulder while holding on to one of its two legs. Shawn pulled up the collar of his jungle jacket to shield his neck against the points of the four crisscrossing one-hundred-round belts of machine-gun ammo.

"You gotta face the bullet points out, boot."

Shawn looked back to see who was speaking and nearly lost his balance on the steep mountainside. It was Dusty. He had passed Luke in the column and was close behind.

"You better tie up your trousers around your boot tops next time we stop too," he said.

"Why?" Shawn asked. He grabbed hold of a small tree and pulled himself forward.

"Leeches," Dusty said. Big ones. They'll suck you dry. And don't ever pull 'em off either. You gotta burn 'em off or the head stays in you. Then you'll get infected sure as crap. Now, what are you gonna do when you hear somebody scream 'Guns up'?"

Shawn hesitated. He wasn't sure what to say. Suddenly Dusty poked Shawn in the rear end, hard, with the butt of his rifle.

"You better not be that slow gettin' that gun to the point of contact, boot!" Dusty growled.

Shawn spun around and glared down at Dusty.

Dusty paused in his climb. "Look, boot, you hesitate with the gun and a lot of these guys won't go home, understand?"

"Yeah, I understand." Shawn pushed his anger aside and turned back to the climb. Dusty was right. His mind had to focus.

Excitement, fear, and anxiety scrambled his thoughts but not his senses. Every shade of green was clear and separate from the rest. The rustle of leaves underfoot sounded frighteningly loud. The whole world had to know they were coming up the mountain. Boot paranoia, he thought.

He didn't like this "boot" stuff; the difference between himself and the others was painfully obvious. The men in the platoon were all about the same age as he, but they looked hard. Most of them were thin and even the eighteen- and nineteen-year-olds had that haunted look of men twice that age. Shawn knew why. These guys had faced death. Some of them had killed. It showed in their hollow stares.

At the top of the mountain a single rifle crack echoed from the front of the column. No one seemed to pay any attention to it. Shawn could feel his body pumping with adrenaline. He wanted to be ready. Every clump of bushes looked like perfect cover. Someone could pop up and kill him before he could begin to move the heavy machine gun from his shoulder.

The ache of panic chewed at his stomach. He felt himself shiver. He had to pray. Lord Jesus, please be with me, calm me with Your spirit. My God, don't let me fail the men around me. Father, don't let me fail.

Three mountains and four hours later, Shawn's shoulder felt like raw hamburger, but the fear was gone. Other than the few words from Dusty, he had heard no one speak. At the top of the fourth mountain, under the shade of huge trees and a network of vines that formed almost a solid canopy of dark green, they came upon a trail.

It felt good to walk easy, but Shawn could sense the change in the men ahead by the way they moved—more cautiously, with their rifles at the ready. They followed the trail along the top of the mountain for about one hundred meters. Ten yards ahead the Marine in front of Shawn suddenly dropped to one knee. He turned and held up a hand for Shawn to stop. The Marine had freckles and a pug nose. "Billy the Kid" was printed across the front of his camouflage helmet cover just above the black band that held his white plastic bottle of bug juice and a dirty brown rabbit's foot.

Billy the Kid got to his feet, turned, and motioned Shawn forward. Shawn turned to Dusty and waved him forward. The column moved on cautiously for twenty yards, then stopped again. The big Indian moved swiftly and quietly along the column, whispering an order to each man as he passed. He dropped to one knee beside Shawn and looked toward the front of the column.

"You stay put," he said. "I'll show you where to set up the gun." He stood and moved toward Dusty and then to Luke behind him. A moment later Dusty and Luke came forward and knelt beside Shawn on the trail. Dusty looked worried.

"What's up, Dusty?" Shawn asked.

"I don't know. I don't like it. Chief said we're setting up a perimeter in an old gook position."

Luke scooted closer. "What's wrong with that?" he whispered.

"Ghosthorse didn't like it, and if the Chief doesn't like it, somebody better listen to him."

"Is the Indian that good?" Shawn whispered.

"Listen to what he says and you might make it home."

The Chief rushed past the gun team with a wave of his hand to follow. "Guns up!" he said.

Shawn was up and hustling forward before he had time to think. They moved past the kneeling Marines along the trail until they reached a small, relatively flat area, thirty yards square, on top of the mountain. It was pockmarked with foxholes. Each hole was square and about three feet deep. The dried-up dirt around them looked dark and fresh. The top of the mountain was fairly clear of brush and was shaded by towering mahoganies. The trail led across the mountaintop and down the other side.

The Chief stopped where the trail began its descent and pointed to a spot beside the trail. "Put the gun here and cover the trail coming up."

Dusty signaled a thumbs-up. He dropped his pack and sat down a few feet to the right of the trail.

The Chief hustled back toward the rest of the column.

Shawn set the M60 down on the bipod legs, pointing it down the trail. He sat down beside it and watched Luke fumble for his canteen like a dying man in the desert. His clothes were soaking with sweat.

Dusty pointed at the M60. "Link up two belts when we stop and always carry a fifty-round strip belt in the gun when we're humpin'. The weight of a full hundred-round belt can jam the gun or get tangled up on stuff when you're runnin'."

"What are we doing up here, anyway?" Luke asked. He gave a nervous look at the narrow, winding path leading down hill.

"Just humpin'," Dusty said. "We'll hump all day and sometimes all night looking for Charlie. You better shove down some food, we won't stop again for a while."

Dusty opened his pack and pulled out a can of C-ration eggs. He pulled a rusty little P-38 can opener out of the band of his helmet and started working the can. "Right now we can't make a fire up here, but when we can, you'll need a stove." He pulled an old C-ration can out of a side pocket on his big floppy pack. It had holes cut all around the bottom. It was charred black.

"This is a stove. You put some C-4 in here and light it to cook your food."

"It won't blow up?" Luke asked, his bushy eyebrows raised to their limit.

"No. You need an electric charge to blow it."

"How come your pack is different?" Shawn asked.

57

Luke frowned. "It looks like it holds about twice as much as this thing." He yanked a pack strap off one shoulder.

"It's an NVA pack," Dusty said. He picked it up and opened the big flap. He stuck his finger through a small hole. "Got it at Hai Van Pass. My first confirmed." He dropped the pack beside him.

He did not sound sad, but he wasn't bragging either. Shawn didn't know if he liked this guy or not.

"We'll set up an ambush tonight. Do you have a watch, Lukevec?"

"No."

"You?" He nodded at Shawn.

"No," Shawn said.

"Try to get one."

"Where?" Shawn asked.

"Off a dead gook or dead Marine or wherever. Wear it facedown. If it shows up at night, you'll get us killed. If you fall asleep on watch, somebody might cut your throat—might be Charlie, might be the Chief."

"What's with this Chief character, anyway?" Luke said sullenly.

"His father was one of the Chocktaw Indians that ran the radios on Guadalcanal. The Japs never broke their code through the whole war, and all it was, was Indian Marines speaking Chocktaw."

"Yeah," Shawn said, "I've read about those guys."

"He's all Marine. This is the Chief's fourth tour in Nam and all four as a grunt."

"And he never gets hit?" Shawn asked.

"Seven hearts, boot," Dusty said through a mouthful of eggs and a white plastic C-ration spoon.

"Purple Hearts?" Luke asked in a tone of disbelief.

Dusty stiffened. He cocked an ear and his eyes widened. A muffled thump off in the distance sent a shiver through Shawn. Another thump followed and then another. Dusty jerked back around toward the platoon moving into a perimeter around the mountaintop.

"Incoming!" Dusty shouted. The call reverberated around the perimeter as Marines dove for cover. Shawn and Luke scrambled around behind the M60, flattened out, and stared down the eerie jungle trail.

An instant later the first mortar round exploded somewhere

behind them. Dusty rolled to his right, taking cover beside the trunk of a huge tree. He buried his face in the dirt and covered his helmet with both hands. The second explosion sent rocks and shrapnel smacking through the leaves and brush with terrifying velocity. The ground vibrated as another mortar round tore into the earth somewhere behind the gun team.

Shawn wanted to turn, to see what he couldn't believe. Another ripping explosion jarred the earth. It was closer. He stuck his face in the dirt and tried to bring his whole body under his helmet. Luke, his eyes bulging with fear, jabbed Shawn in the ribs. His face was taut and white. He raised his rifle from the dirt and took aim. Shawn followed Luke's frightened stare down the winding trail to where it disappeared like a snake crawling into the trees below.

"I saw something move!" Luke said. He turned to Dusty. "I saw something move!"

Dusty pulled his face out of the dirt and pushed away from the tree trunk. His dark eyes glanced up as if pleading. "God!" he growled. "I don't believe this! Twenty-six days, God!" He rolled closer to Luke, rose up, and stared down the trail. "You sure?"

"I think so! About fifty yards down." Luke pointed. "That yellowish-looking bush on the left of the trail."

"Don't fire that gun, boot!" Dusty ordered. "Neither of ya! We don't let 'em know where the gun is till we have to." He nudged Luke. "You're the A-gunner. Start linking up the ammo and keep it out of the dirt or the sucker's gonna jam."

Dusty raised up to look left over Luke and Shawn. He lowered his head. "Okay, we got Billy the Kid ten meters back, on our left flank. Don't freak out and blow away a Marine. Billy!" he shouted to his left without raising his head.

Freckle-faced Billy peeked up out of a foxhole twenty yards on the other side of the trail. "Yeah!"

"Gooks down the trail!" Dusty shouted.

"Right!" Billy said with a nod of his helmet. He laid his rifle over the edge of his foxhole.

Dusty looked back and to his right. "Who's on my right flank?" he shouted. A loud birdlike whistle came from the right flank.

Shawn looked back. He couldn't see anyone.

"What was that whistle?" Luke rolled on his side and pointed his rifle to the right. Dusty grabbed the barrel of the M16 and shoved it toward the trail again.

"That's Birdman!" Dusty growled. He closed his eyes and shook his head. "Friggin' boots."

"Birdman?" Luke said, inhaling and then blowing out hard. "Sorry." He aimed back down the trail at the yellowish bush again.

"Birdman, we got gooks on the—" Dusty's words were swallowed by a mortar explosion in the center of the perimeter. Two more quickly followed. A large rock hit the tree trunk to Dusty's right with a solid thud. "They got our position already plotted! I don't believe this!" He lay on his stomach and shouted into the ground.

Luke rolled onto his side and unlinked one of the belts of ammo that crisscrossed his chest. He flipped the ammo belt off his shoulder and tried to link it to the belt already in the gun, but his fingers wouldn't work. Luke blew out again, then squeezed the belts together. Another series of mortar blasts sent shrapnel whistling in all directions. Someone screamed from behind them, but no one looked away from the trail.

Something moved below. Shawn held his breath. Suddenly three little men with green pith helmets darted across the trail near the yellow bush. Shawn felt himself stiffen. He started to squeeze the trigger. Too late.

"Gooks!" Shawn said. "I see 'em—three of 'em jumped across the trail!"

"Hold your fire!" Dusty raised his head to look down the trail. "Small burst! Remember! Small burst!"

Four single shots rang out from Shawn's right. He glanced that way. Billy the Kid fired a fifth shot, then ducked down. Somewhere behind them the perimeter opened fire. Dusty nudged Luke and pulled two grenades off his cartridge belt.

"Get some frags ready," Dusty said. Beads of sweat bubbled up all over his face. He bent the carter pins straight on both grenades and rolled back to the tree trunk on his right. He aimed down the sloping mountain twenty meters right of the trail.

Shawn glanced right to see what Dusty was aiming at. The brush wasn't thick, but the big trees gave the enemy good cover. A mortar round cracked like lightning into the top of a tall tree to their right. The top half of the tree broke clean away. It crashed through the limbs below and hit with the weight of a small building.

"Jesus!" Billy shouted from his hole. "Sounds like they got eighty-twos!"

Two more enemy soldiers dove across the trail from right to left. Luke pointed. Shawn squeezed the trigger. Orange tracers skipped off the ground and into the trees beyond. The gun recoiled with a steady rhythm of deadly power. A surge of adrenaline pushed more excitement through Shawn than he had ever known.

He moved the tracers into the yellow bush, then raked the brush to the right of the trail. Lukevec dropped his rifle and held the long belt of ammo out of the dirt with both hands.

"Cease fire!" Dusty's shout pulled Shawn's finger from the trigger.

"That's a hundred rounds, Shawn!" Luke snapped. He ripped another belt of ammo off his shoulder and linked it up.

"Don't waste ammo!" an angry voice bellowed into Shawn's ear. He turned left. Intense black eyes peered through thick glasses. Shawn flinched at the look on the Chief's face. It was as though the Indian had materialized from the gunpowder air.

"We're pinned down," the Chief said. "Might be here awhile. Conserve ammunition!"

Shawn nodded. He couldn't speak. The Indian pushed away and was gone.

"Man," Luke said. He blew out again. "That guy is scary!"

Shawn stared downtrail. He glanced at his hands. They were shaking. He clenched his fists to keep them still.

"God!" Luke stared at a grenade in his hand. "I have to remember to bend the pins!"

Suddenly Dusty opened fire with four single shots, then stopped. He laid the rifle down, grabbed a grenade from beside him, pulled the pin with his left hand, and held the spoon in with his right. He rose up slightly beside the tree stump to see down the sloping mountain.

A briar bush blocked Shawn's view of Dusty's target. He rose up to look over the bush, then realized what he was doing. He wanted to smack himself for such a stupid move.

Dusty lobbed the grenade, giving it more of a toss than a full throw.

They're close, Shawn thought. He cringed and waited for the explosion. One. Two. Three. The grenade explosion was muffled by the louder blast of an incoming mortar round.

Luke pulled the pin on a grenade and tossed it down the trail.

It bounced twice, then rolled off to the left of the trail. Shawn and Luke buried their faces and pulled their helmets down just as it exploded.

Something hard glanced off Shawn's helmet. Another mortar round hit behind him. He shook from a sudden chill. This wasn't the movies. It didn't seem possible. He didn't feel very brave. Clear your mind. Stay calm. Clear your mind. He bit his lower lip.

"My Father who art in heaven . . ." Shawn spoke quietly, his eyes opened as far as they could. He thought of his dad and his mom and Eddie. The power is in the Word, his dad had always said. Power over fear. But he couldn't remember the Lord's Prayer.

Twenty meters past the yellow bush the branch of a small tree moved. Shawn stiffened. A large black-and-yellow bird sprang from the limb and flew to a higher perch. He sighed and realized that he had been holding his breath. He wondered why the bird didn't fly to another tree. Another mountain. Another country.

Stay calm, he thought, think of Dad. He tried to remember his dad's face, but he could only remember the dark glasses. He could still hear the quiet strength in Dad's voice though. Especially when he had talked about the Bible and the power that was in the Word. "In the beginning was the Word, and Word was with God, and the Word was God. And the Word became flesh and lived amongst us. We have seen his glory, the glory of the only begotten Son . . ."

"Jesus Christ!" Billy the Kid screamed and fired. "Dusty! The woods are crawlin' with gooks over here! Guns up!"

He fired single-shot until his clip was empty, then he ducked down.

Shawn pushed to his knees, grabbed the ammo out of Luke's hands, and threw the long belt over his shoulder. He picked up the gun and ran toward Billy's position. The short run felt like it took forever. The weight of his gear pulled back on his speed until he felt like he was running underwater.

"Comin' in!" Shawn screamed, and dove for the hole. The butt of the M60 knocked Billy's helmet off as Shawn crashed in on top of him. An instant later Lukevec crushed both of them under his two-hundred-fifty-odd pounds of man and equipment.

Luke was still exposed. Shawn squirmed and struggled to get lower for Luke, but there wasn't room in the hole. Luke rolled off Shawn's shoulders and scrambled for the cover of a fallen tree to the left of the foxhole. The woods below exploded with small-arms fire. Bullets sang through the branches and brush and ricocheted with frightening whistles, thudding into the earth all around.

"Get the gun working!" Billy shouted at Shawn. His freckled face was a mask of sweat, dirt, and terror.

Shawn threw the gun over the edge of the hole. Muzzle flashes spit from everywhere. Green tracers streaked overhead and across the perimeter from an enemy machine gun forty meters down the wooded slope. He couldn't see the enemy gunner, but his green tracers shot from a clump of bushes just beside a huge tree.

Shawn shoved the butt of the gun against his shoulder and squeezed off a short burst. Orange tracers zipped just above the enemy position and into the thick woods behind. He squeezed again. Pieces of the bush exploded away.

Billy peeked up to fire as bullets thudded into the earth all around the hole. Chunks of dirt erupted from the hard ground.

Billy jerked backward. Shawn ducked down instinctively. Billy slumped back and his helmet fell off. His left eye was gone, replaced by a clean, dark, red hole. Shawn stared hypnotically as the first trickle of blood dribbled down Billy's ashen face. A vile, bitter taste filled Shawn's mouth. He turned away, and vomit shot out of his stomach in one violent belch.

"Guns up!"

Shawn looked over the edge of the hole.

"Guns up!" Luke screamed, and opened fire from behind the fallen tree fifteen meters to Shawn's left. Shawn shook his head clear. He aimed at a line of muzzle flashes and opened fire. He raked a steady stream of tracers back and forth until the gun stopped. He squeezed the trigger harder. Nothing. Jammed!

He pulled the M60 down into the hole, laid the butt end on Billy's dead shoulder, and unlatched the feed cover. Then he ripped out a piece of the belt to clear the jam and reloaded. A shrill whistle sucked through the air overhead. A moment later a muffled explosion a hundred meters down the slope pushed a cloud of white smoke up through the trees.

Somewhere behind Shawn, Chip the radioman started yelling, "Fire for effect! Fire for effect!"

Shawn threw the M60 over the edge of the hole, rammed the butt against his shoulder, and fired a twenty-round burst at the muzzle flash coming out of the brush below. The artillery rounds whistled by overhead, grew silent, then hit. The earth shook. The sloping mountain to Shawn's front blew apart as if a series of volcanoes had erupted. Giant trees splintered into pieces. White light and orange fire flashed through the green forest below. Big shards of shrapnel ripped through the trees, breaking off limbs with loud cracks. Shawn watched in awe. He felt overwhelmed. He knew it was all real, but it didn't feel that way. Wounded men groaned. Some screamed.

The artillery barrage ceased. A strange silence fell upon the perimeter. Shawn felt sticky, as if his body had oozed out some clammy form of fear. He peeked over the edge of the hole. No movement. The air was thick with the smell of sulfurous gunpowder. His muscles ached. His neck was stiff. He wondered how long the firefight had lasted. The sun had moved across the darkening sky. At least two hours must have passed, maybe more. He felt as though he'd been flexing every muscle in his body for hours, and yet it seemed like the entire battle had only taken a few seconds. He thought about Luke. He made a quick search for the big Polack. Luke lay flat on his stomach, fifteen meters to Shawn's left, behind the fallen tree.

"Luke!" Shawn called, and tensed, ready to move toward Lukevec. Luke turned his big oval face toward Shawn and signaled thumbs-up. Shawn sighed and relaxed then looked to his right at the lifeless, childlike face of Billy the Kid.

There was no pain on Billy's face. He could have been sleeping. Tears clouded Shawn's vision, and he bowed his head. "Father God," he whispered, "please let Billy be with you." He cried. Everything was so confused.

"Never cry, Marine," Sergeant Ghosthorse said. Shawn looked up. The Chief lay on his stomach looking into the foxhole at Billy. He turned his icy black eyes to Shawn. "You can't shoot if you can't see. You understand?"

Shawn wiped his face with his sleeve and nodded yes.

"The gooks pulled back," he said. "Get Foley's poncho, put him in it, carry him over to the CP."

"Foley?" Shawn said.

"Yeah. Billy Foley was his name."

"Where's the CP?" Shawn swiped at an embarrassing tear.

"The command post is always in the center of the perimeter. It's where the lieutenant, the corpsman, and the radioman set up. Get your A-gunner to help you. And, boot, don't ever jump in a gook foxhole. Dig your own fighting hole. Foley should've known better. They booby-trap old holes.''

The Indian jumped to his feet and hustled toward another position on the perimeter. Shawn looked at Billy, then chewed at the inside of his mouth to keep from crying.

Twenty minutes later the platoon moved back down the trail until they came to a clearing big enough for a chopper to land. Billy Foley was loaded in first, then two guys with shrapnel wounds. Someone shouted "Saddle up!" and the hump started again.

The column turned off of the trail and headed due west. Two hours later it circled back toward the trail. The hot sun slowly dipped behind a gray mountain. An eerie twilight settled over the thick forest. It was difficult to see the man ahead of you. Finally the column stopped. Kayto turned back to Dusty and whispered something. Dusty turned back to Shawn.

"We're setting up an ambush on the trail. Pass it back."
Shawn swallowed hard and passed the word to Luke.

A few minutes later Lieutenant Townsend shoved Shawn toward a thorny bush on the right side of the trail. Shawn couldn't tell where the rest of the men were. To Shawn's left Lukevec leaned back against his pack. Dusty did the same on his right. A heavy fatigue overcame Shawn. He couldn't tell if it was physical or mental. He felt overloaded by extremes of emotion he had never known before. Excitement and terror and sadness and fatigue. No one back in St. Pete would believe any of this, he thought.

Luke leaned over and whispered into Shawn's ear so low that he could barely hear. "I was so scared, I almost wee-weed."

Shawn snickered under his breath. The giggle felt good. "I wouldn't know if I did or not, but something about me don't smell Kosher," he whispered. A quarter moon appeared from behind a cloud, casting an eerie blue light over the dark jungle.

He turned to Dusty. Dusty looked strangely comfortable resting against his pack. Shawn had a million questions and just as many doubts. He had to talk about it. He gave a tug on Dusty's sleeve.

"Dusty."

Dusty sat up. "Yeah?" he whispered.

"Today was unbelievable."

"You guys saw some heavy stuff for boots. Stay cool. You'll be dying of boredom most of the time."

65

Dusty took Shawn's hand and shoved a watch into it that had no wristband. "You got first watch, two hours, then Luke, then me. Got it?"

"Yeah."

"Let the fluorescent face of the watch show and we might be dead." With that Dusty fell back and seemed to go right to sleep.

The night dragged on one endless minute at a time. Huge bloodsucking mosquitoes attacked in swarms, but no one dared slap one. Every bush and tree began to look like an enemy soldier, crouching, standing, crawling. Shawn gripped the M60 tighter with each new shadow. He squeezed all feeling from his hands. He decided to pray to stay calm. He prayed and prayed until the first shafts of sunlight stretched across the horizon and he knew that he had not slept. Dusty sat up, yawned, and stretched. He looked at Shawn and shook his head.

"You stood watch all night?"

"Couldn't sleep," Shawn said.

"Neither could I," Luke groaned, and rubbed the back of his neck. "These mosquitoes must use a landing strip."

Dusty rustled through his pack making no effort to be quiet. He pulled out his C-ration can stove and a chunk of C-4 plastic explosive. It looked harmless, like white clay, but this chunk of clay could take down a bridge. He pulled out a brown packet of instant coffee, poured some water into another empty can, lit the C-4, and waited for the water to get hot.

"Saddle up!" someone said, and the hump began again. For the next four days the platoon moved, set up ambushes at night, and moved again. Conversations were short and tired. There was no contact with Charlie, only constant walking through the steaming jungle.

On the fifth day the platoon set up a perimeter atop a rocky knoll. It was infested with giant red ants, like the kind they showed in Tarzan movies.

Lieutenant Townsend and the Chief stood up in the center of the perimeter. The lieutenant pointed toward the gun team, then he turned toward Chip the radioman and mumbled something that brought Chip to his feet. Chip pulled the antenna of his PRC-25 all the way out and started chattering away. Chip was always talking in short bursts, as if he were on the radio. He also collected rumors greedily and kept the platoon informed about all the latest scuttlebutt.

Dusty stood up with his helmet in hand as the Chief approached. He pointed at the calendar on his helmet. "Two days with the gun, Dusty," Dusty said in a mocking imitation. "Two days."

"All right, all right," the hawk-faced Indian said as he stopped beside Shawn and Luke. He looked down at Shawn. "McClellan, I'm putting you and Lukevec with Kayto and Cager for a while."

"Okay by me, Chief," Shawn said. "Okay with you, Luke? As if your opinion matters."

Luke stuck a dirty white plastic spoon into a can of "beans and rocks" commonly known in the real world as beans and potatoes. He looked up at the Chief and frowned.

"Darn." Luke tilted his head and ran his hand through his porcupine hair. "I've already made plans, Chief. I'm not really a Marine, you know, and the moment my congressman finds out where I am he is going to be considerably upset."

Luke tilted his head to the left and tried to look sincere. The Indian sergeant did not laugh. Or smile.

"Where are we anyway?" Shawn asked.

"Thua Thien Province," Dusty said. "Part of Operation Checkers, according to Chipper."

"*That* explains everything," Luke said.

"Well, we're supposed to be blocking one approach to Hue City, but who knows?" Dusty sounded tired.

"Hey, Chief," the Doc called as he walked toward the group. His straight blond hair stuck straight up on the crown of his head. He looked more like Dennis the Menace each time Shawn saw him.

"How can the Doc's hair stick up like that after wearin' a helmet twenty-four hours a day?" Shawn wondered aloud. No one answered.

"You better let me work on that foot," the corpsman said. His lips moved when he talked but it was amazing how stiff and expressionless the rest of his face remained.

"I'll wait, Doc," the Chief said.

The young corpsman's bottom lip came out just enough to make him look sad. He looked at the ground. "Well, all right," he mumbled. He turned with hands thrust deep into his pockets and walked slowly back to the CP.

67

"Why didn't you let him work on your foot, Chief?" Luke asked.

The Chief looked suspiciously over his shoulder as if to make sure no one else would hear him. "Doc's a good corpsman," he said, then shook his head. "But he likes cutting too much. Tearing off dead skin. Works it over with a wire brush." Chief grimaced and shook his head. "Hurts."

"Choppers!" Lieutenant Townsend shouted. "Saddle up!"

"What's up, Chip?" Dusty yelled.

"Little Con Thien!" Chipper shouted from the CP. "Last chance to get your tickets!"

"Little Con Thien?" Luke echoed.

"Phu Loc," Chief said in his usual monotone.

"Is that good news or bad?" Shawn asked.

"Neither," Chief grumbled.

"Is that close to Phu Bai?" Luke quizzed.

The Chief started walking toward the CP, then looked back at Luke. "No. Farther south. Home base for One-Five." He turned away again.

"Chief," Shawn called, "why do they call it Little Con Thien? Isn't Con Thien up near the DMZ?" The Chief gave a wave and headed toward the CP. The big Indian obviously liked conversations kept to a minimum.

Shawn looked at Dusty. "Dust?"

"Con Thien gets shelled all the time." Dusty stretched and yawned and looked around for any loose gear.

"Phu Loc is at the foot of some mountains about a quarter mile west of Highway One, sort of facing the South China Sea. Gets mortared all the time from the mountains."

"That's what this guy told us back at Phu Bai," Shawn said.

"Why"—Luke flashed his eyebrows and tilted his head in one of his better Groucho Marx impressions—"here goes: I repeat, why is the base in such a vulnerable position?"

Dusty shrugged and did his own Groucho imitation: "Why don't we invade the North and finish these little slimeballs off?"

As chopper rides went, the flight to Phu Loc combat base was a long one. One quick stop at the big base called Phu Bai and then south for about twenty minutes. Shawn pressed his face against the round portholes of the troop helicopter like a kid on his first Greyhound bus ride.

From the air Vietnam was deceptively beautiful. To the east

of Highway One was the South China Sea with turquoise water more clear and beautiful than anything Florida could offer. Inland from the sea the land was like a desert of white sand dunes sprinkled with patches of thick brush and bamboo. The terrain rose steadily into a patchwork quilt of perfect squares, rice paddy fields that were of every imaginable shade of green. Then came lush forest with mahogany and oak trees rising two hundred feet into the air. Steep green mountains rose out of the jungle forest into shrouds of gray, misty clouds.

The helicopter flew into a storm of dark, rolling clouds. Rain smashed against the window, distorting Shawn's view. His stomach lifted as the chopper dropped. It circled down toward a large muddy square the size of three football fields, sitting at the base of an endless range of green mountains. A small road branched west off Highway One for about a quarter mile, through a small village of grass-roofed hootches and came to a dead end at the base. The big muddy square was separated into five sections of large tents and surrounded by concertina wire with sandbag bunkers at the corners. From the air, Phu Loc looked like the kind of camp that Shawn and Eddie used to build for their toy soldiers. Sometimes this adventure still felt unbelievable to Shawn.

"Stand by!" the copilot shouted from the front of the chopper.

"Prepare to disembark!" Lieutenant Townsend yelled from beside the door gunner as he put on his helmet. The door gunner cleared his weapon toward the mountains with a five-shot burst. He turned to the lieutenant and shouted over the noisy rotors.

"We took some fire comin' in yesterday!" He pointed to a large mountain rising from the southeast corner of the base. "From that mountain over there."

"That's probably where we're going tomorrow," Lieutenant Townsend shouted over the prop wash.

"Outstanding! Take some names!" the door gunner said as he gave a quick thumbs-up.

The chopper suddenly dropped, banked left, and then leveled out over a big square corrugated-steel landing pad on the northwest corner of the base. The back ramp of the chopper dropped. The men ran down it into the driving rain. A short march to the Alpha Company tents to drop off gear was followed by another march to the mess tent for lukewarm food. Luke looked as pale as Shawn felt. As they left the tent, Shawn paused and put his hand on his stomach.

"Do you feel sort of . . ."

"Sick?" Luke groaned. "Near barfing? In need of a good wholesome vomit? On the verge of—"

"All right, already! Sorry I asked."

"Do you remember which tent is ours?" Luke asked. He ran his hand across his wet face and flipped water onto Shawn. "There are no less than twenty tents, Shawn. Got a guess as to which tent?"

"There were two big concrete-block bunkers right behind our tent. Chief said they were old French bunkers."

"I didn't see them," Luke said.

"They're underground, but the tops are visible."

"Now I see them." Luke pointed between two tents at two long rectangular slabs of cement.

"Yeah, that's them. This is our tent." Shawn jogged over to the tent, splashing mud and water with each step. He pulled back the flap and jumped in out of the rain.

Two rows of fifteen cots each were empty except for five Marines crowded around a deck of cards. Luke rushed in out of the rain and stomped the mud off his boots. A thick-necked, stocky Marine with "Cornhuskers" printed across the back of his flak jacket turned away from the card game to face Shawn.

"Today's Sunday!" he shouted, and he turned back to the card game. He looked like a linebacker—short, wide, and powerful. Shawn looked over his shoulder at Luke, who shrugged.

"Them's boots," a heavyset black Marine mumbled with a glance toward Shawn and Luke. He looked back at his hand of cards as if too tired to say more. Cornhusker turned around again.

"Today's Sunday, boots. If you wanna go to chapel, go on over." He turned back to the game. He nodded at a thin-faced Marine with short, dirty-blond hair. "You playin', Birdman, or pickin' your nose?"

"He got his mind on Bonnie Kay," the black Marine said.

"This ain't playin' cards; cards is what I played in Vegas." The thin-faced Marine grinned. His teeth were yellow and jagged and his cheekbones were so high that he almost looked Oriental. He whistled a mocking little tune as he threw down a card.

Shawn removed his helmet and stomped mud from his boots. "Did you guys already go?" he asked.

The big, sleepy-eyed black Marine peeked over his cards and stared at Shawn. "Say what?"

"To chapel," Shawn said. "You guys already go?"

The cardplayers lowered their hands and turned curious stares toward Shawn as if all five heads were attached to one neck.

Luke moaned. "What an embarrassment you can be," he mumbled quietly so that only Shawn heard.

The high-cheekboned Marine named Birdman whistled and laughed, then nudged the black Marine. "It's your play, Murph." He whistled again.

The cardplayers turned their eyes back to the game.

"Here, Birdman." Murph slapped a card down. He smiled a mouth-load of white teeth. Birdman frowned.

The tent flap whipped open behind Luke. A loud crack of lightning hit near by. Luke jumped. Cager pulled the dripping hood of his poncho back.

"You'll know the sound of incomin' soon enough, man." He laughed. The flap of the tent flipped open again. Kayto stepped in and shook like a dog trying to dry himself. He pulled back his poncho hood, then removed his soft-cover hat.

"Hard rain." Kayto stomped mud from his boots.

"Shoot." Birdman whistled. "You ain't seen rain yet."

Kayto shook his head and pointed a thumb at Birdman. "He kills me."

"You guys wanna go to chapel with us?" Shawn asked Cager.

Luke raised his bushy eyebrows. "Us? You got a mouse in your pocket?"

"We might not get another chance for a while, Luke."

"Good. Then you can't hound me for a while."

"I'll not be joining you 'ither, man," Cager said.

"Ah, come on, Cage," Shawn asked.

Cager pulled off his poncho, shook some water off it, and laid it across the end of a cot. Kayto threw his poncho next to Cager's. They sat down. Still no answer. Cager looked at Shawn as if searching for the best way to explain.

"My parents were Baptist missionaries. They made me go to church and Sunday school all of my life, man. Am I keeping you from being on time?"

"No, we're in no hurry." Shawn sat on a cot facing Cager.

"It's no big deal, man; I was forced to attend church and I promised myself that when I was old enough to make my own decisions, I would never go again."

71

"That is a very logical reaction," Luke said.

"That was the decision of a little boy and it would have faded away were it not for our move back to America. In Grambling, I found that learning was the most exciting thing in the world." Cager's dark eyes opened wide. "My professors opened up my mind, man. I admired them greatly. I became an assistant to Professor Franklin Soper. He was the head of the Humanities Department, a brilliant man."

Luke sat down beside Shawn. "Did you finish up all four years?"

"Yes. Ah, the women, man." Cager got a faraway look in his eyes. "How they loved my accent." He grinned contentedly.

Kayto laughed.

"Birdman!" Cornhusker shouted angrily from the card game. "If I catch you cheatin' I'm gonna squeeze you like a pimple, scumbag."

"Just tell Gooy he's been droolin' over Bonnie Kay." Murphy said with an evil grin.

Birdman said nothing. He gathered up the cards and began shuffling and whistling "The Yellow Rose of Texas."

"Go on, Cage," Shawn said.

"Well, I wanted very much to emulate these men that I admired. They taught us that the Bible was no more than just another creation story. All races of people have their own creation story. The Koran is a Bible too. The Japanese believed that a giant spear came from heaven and hit the sea, and that became the islands of Japan and that the—" He paused. "Let me think. There was a giant involved and the hair or lice or something on his body became the people—"

"And you think that kind of nonsense is the same as the Bible?" Shawn couldn't hide his contempt. "You should talk to this chaplain and see what he says."

Luke moaned. "Oh, no," he muttered as his shoulders sagged forward.

"Put it in your 'diddybag,' Lukevec," Shawn said.

Cager looked back to Kayto. Kayto was stretched out comfortably, hands clasped behind his head for a pillow and feet crossed as he stared silently at the roof of the tent.

"Got anything to say?" Cager asked.

"Think they sing gospel music in the chapel?" Kayto asked with his eyes fixed on the ceiling of the tent.

Cager laughed. "Yes, man, they will today, I hope." He

slapped Luke on the back. "Come, man, it will be good for our minds to talk and argue and sing."

Luke didn't answer. He drooped as if receiving bad news and closed his eyes.

It was still daylight as they sloshed through the mud and rain, but the black clouds made it feel like night. The garbled pitch of bad voices singing an unfamiliar hymn greeted the four men as Shawn pulled back the tent flap of the chapel. Eight rows of benches made from planks supported by empty wooden grenade crates were less than half full with soaking-wet Marines. A tall, willowy Navy chaplain looked terribly uncomfortable standing behind a stack of C-ration cases that served as his pulpit. He seemed nervous, Shawn thought. The four found an empty bench at the rear of the tent. The tent window flaps on both sides and behind the chaplain were open to let in light, but more rain than light poured in.

"Welcome, men," the chaplain said, and smiled. "We have some Gideons over there on that table if you need one." He pointed to a grenade box in the back corner of the tent. No one picked up one of the small Bibles.

"I'm Chaplain John Elliott. We are—" He paused and looked down at the open Bible in his hands. "—in the book of II Chronicles, chapter sixteen, verse nine."

He looked up. "We have an incredible promise here."

He looked back at his Bible and read, "For the eyes of the Lord move to and fro throughout the earth, that He may strongly support those whose heart is completely his."

He looked up with a contagious smile. "It's really encouraging to think that the God who created the universe can actually see each one of us as individuals, important to Him. So important that He wants to come to our aid, if only we have a righteous attitude toward Him. . . ."

The rain stopped and shafts of hot sun streaked through the window flaps as the sermon ended. The chaplain wasn't exactly a dynamic speaker, Shawn thought, but he was a good teacher and seemed to know his facts.

When the Marines began filing out, Shawn nudged Cager. "We gonna talk to him?"

"Sure, man."

They stood together and walked to the front of the tent. Luke and Kayto remained seated.

"Can I help you, men?"

73

"Yes, sir," Shawn said quickly, then hesitated, unsure of how to explain this whole idea. "My friend, here, Lance Corporal Cager—"

"How do you do, sir?" Cager said, extending his hand. The chaplain shook it.

"Well, he has some arguments against the Bible, and I don't agree with some of what he says and some of what he's been told by his college teachers and—"

"That's good to hear, men," Chaplain Elliott said enthusiastically.

"Well . . ." Cager paused and rubbed his chin. "I doubt that you will think it all good, Chaplain. I believe that the Bible is just another creation story and that it is filled with hardly believable fairy tales."

Shawn felt himself wince at Cager's words. He felt bad for the soft-spoken Chaplain and suddenly wished that he had not suggested this talk. But Chaplain Elliott's dark brown eyes were sparkling. He grinned like a cat eyeing a canary.

"That's wonderful, men," he said, and pointed excitedly at the front benches. "Here, let's sit and talk about it."

The timid chaplain's whole manner seemed to change right before their eyes.

Shawn looked at Cager as they sat down. Cager looked wary. He glared at the chaplain for a moment as if he wanted to leave.

Chaplain Elliott slid another bench up and sat down facing Cager and Shawn. The chaplain rubbed his hands together, then gave a single clap. His sudden enthusiasm straightened Shawn's spine with anticipation. "Please, Lance Corporal—Cager, is it?" he asked. "Feel free."

"Well, sir . . ." Cager began.

"Call me John. I'm a captain in Marine Corps rank but in the Lord's house, I'm just John."

"Okay, John. Why is Christianity any different or any better than a dozen other religions? People around the world have their own creation stories, their own Bibles or their own Koran—their own way of believing this or that."

"Well, where do we begin? We could go into the facts of the resurrection, like Christ appearing before over five hundred people after the resurrection and ascending into heaven. There is even more historical evidence of the resurrection in other writings of the time, some by Jewish historians who weren't even Christians. We could touch on the wealth of scientific facts in

74

the scriptures that modern man is just now discovering to be true. Or, we could talk about the hundred-percent accuracy of fulfilled Bible prophesy . . . or whatever you like. Pick a topic."

"I like this," Shawn said. "Go on, Cager, pick a topic."

Shawn looked back at Luke. Luke shrugged and pretended to be bored. He opened his mouth to speak then sat up, rigid. Someone far away screamed.

"Incoming!"

"Incoming!"

"Incoming!"

The warning was drowned out by a series of sharp explosions. A piece of shrapnel ripped through the top of the chapel tent. No one spoke. Everyone in the tent jumped to his feet and ran out. Chaplain Elliott pointed at a circle of sandbags fifteen meters to the left of the tent. The five dashed for the sandbag cover. Shawn dove over the three-foot wall of sandbags just ahead of Luke and the others.

"Sure wish we'd have finished this bunker!" Chaplain Elliott shouted as another mortar round exploded near the Phu Loc perimeter, fifty meters away.

Marines around the area started screaming for someone to get down. Shawn peeked up over the wall of sandbags. Forty meters away, just inside the perimeter wire, a shirtless Sea Bee sat atop a noisy bulldozer working away, oblivious to any danger. Before anyone could get his attention the mortar attack was over.

Shawn nudged Luke and pointed at the Sea Bee. "Can you believe that clown? He's still working. He'll probably never know that he worked right through a mortar attack."

"Where is the head?" Luke asked, "I have to go. You think it *is* over?"

"Sure," Kayto said. "They're out of rounds."

"Where is the head?" Luke stood up and climbed over the bunker wall.

"Ain't much of a head, Luke," Kayto said. "A crapper seat on top of two fifty-five-gallon drums."

Cager pointed back in the direction of the Alpha Company tents. "It's about fifty meters past our tent, over near the wire, man."

"You'll smell it when you're close," Kayto said.

Luke took off at a full gallop.

The chaplain stood up. "I'll have to be on my way too, men." He hurdled over the half-built bunker. "I have a meeting in a

75

few minutes." He checked his wristwatch. "I'd like to talk again, Marines, anytime you want. That's what I'm here for."

"Thank you, Chaplain," Shawn said uncertainly.

The chaplain shook their hands, nodded, and turned away.

Ten minutes later Shawn, Cager, and Kayto were falling asleep on their cots. The hollow thump of a mortar round leaving the tube echoed from the nearby mountains. It seemed to be coming out of a dream.

"Incoming!"

Five quick explosions brought Shawn to his feet. He looked around for Luke, but Luke's cot was empty. The ground shook. The big tent quivered. Shawn ran for the tent flap.

"Luke!" he called as he ran out of the tent.

"Bunkers over there!" Sergeant Ghosthorse barked as he stopped Shawn's dash with a stiff arm to the chest. He pointed to the old French bunkers behind the tent. "Bunkers over there! Move it, Marine!"

"Luke's missin', Chief!"

Marines scurried past, heading for cover.

Ghosthorse looked around and shouted, "Anybody seen Lukevec?"

"I saw him over on the crapper, readin' a magazine!" Dusty said as he ran past the tent.

Sergeant Ghosthorse shoved Shawn toward the bunkers. "Get in those bunkers. I'll find him."

Shawn turned to run for the bunker.

"Hey, boot!" Cager called. Shawn stopped and looked back. "You forgetting something, man." Cager tossed the M60 toward Shawn. Shawn grabbed it. He wanted to explain about Luke but didn't.

The old French bunker had a foot of rank-smelling water in it. Gun slits brought in enough light to see the slimy green walls inside. Three marines stood hunched over in the far corner of the rectangular concrete bunker watching a battle to the death between a giant brown spider and a strange bug with pincers like a crab. A fourth Marine, leaning against the bunker wall, looked sound asleep. The mortars stopped. Shawn climbed up the four steps of the bunker. A foul odor filled the air.

"Oh no, man," a voice behind him groaned. Shawn looked back at a thin, young Marine whose shoulders twitched like he had a nervous disorder.

"What's wrong?" Shawn asked.

76

"They—they—they hit the crapper, man," he stuttered. "You the new gunner?"

"Yeah, Shawn McClellan."

"I'm Jake. They call me Shakey."

"The crapper?" Shawn's handsome face tightened. He closed his eyes tight, covered his forehead with his hand, and prayed, "Dear Jesus, please take care of Luke, and let him be okay, Lord." Shawn opened his eyes. The skinny Marine named Jake was staring at him like he was an officer or something worse.

"What's wrong, McClellan?" Jake asked.

"My A-gunner, Lukevec, went to the head right before the mortars hit."

"We better check it out, bro." Jake turned back to the bunker. "Saddle up, Sleepy!" he shouted at the sleeping Marine leaning against the bunker wall. The sleeping Marine didn't move.

"Who's that?" Shawn asked.

"My partner, Sleepy. He tries to ignore the war. Come on." Jake gave Shawn a tug as he headed back to the tent. They jogged back. Jake looked inside the tent and turned back to Shawn. "It's empty. Come on."

They ran past the tent area. The rancid odor grew stronger. Up ahead Sergeant Ghosthorse stood with a short, black Marine beside a bunker. The black Marine pointed at the smoldering remains of a fifty-five-gallon drum that was lying in the open twenty meters inside the wire.

"Chief!" Shawn called. "Did you find Luke?"

"No, but this guy saw him."

The black Marine shrugged. "I guess it was him. He was just sittin' on the drum reading a magazine when the first rounds started comin' in. That's when I beat-feet into the bunker. Heard a hit on the drum and looked out. Wasn't nothin' but drum and paper and crap left out there."

Shawn started toward the smoldering drum.

"I already looked," the Chief said. "No body out there. He's around here somewhere, don't worry. Did you check back at the tent?"

"We checked it but no one was there, Chief," Jake said.

"Better check again."

Shawn could feel every beat of his heart. The fear made it hard to breathe. He prayed silently as they walked back; it seemed to ease his fear a little, but not much. He knew it was stupid but up until now he hadn't really considered the chances of Luke getting killed, or Joe either. He had thought about himself dying, and he had sort of accepted that possibility, but never had he thought about something happening to Joe and Luke. He felt scared and he prayed again.

Jake pointed at a group of Marines that were standing in front of the tent. "What—what's the commotion, Chief? That's our tent, ain't it?"

"Yep."

The big Indian started running toward the tent. Shawn and Jake ran close behind.

"That's foul, man!" someone bellowed from inside the tent. A moment later the big sleepy-eyed black Marine stormed out of the tent coughing and cursing.

A lean Marine with a red bandanna around his neck and a wad of chewing tobacco pushing out one side of his mouth ran to meet the Chief. "Dad-gum! You gotta do somethin' 'bout this, Chief! Good Gawd almighty!" He stopped, spat tobacco juice at the muddy ground, and wiped at his droopy mustache.

"What's going on, Goody?" the Chief asked.

"That boot, Chief! Smells worse than a dang Yankee! Worse'n a dang sheep herder!"

Luke's big oval face peeked through the tent flap. His bushy brows lifted high on his forehead. His two-tone eyes shifted back and forth like those of a man expecting to be lynched. Stepping out of the tent to the jeers and whistles of the platoon, he shrugged and tried to look innocent. His big face looked wonderful to Shawn. Some of the men pointed. Others held their noses. All of them started laughing.

"Thanks, Lord," Shawn mumbled. Jake gave Shawn a curious stare. Shawn's eyes got misty; he cleared his throat and tried to act nonchalant. He stopped a few feet from Luke and started laughing along with everyone else, but he could still feel Jake's stare. The laughing grew into a doubled-over howl.

Luke was covered with human waste from his boots to his helmet, and he smelled worse than the inside of a Tijuana commode. Pieces of used toilet paper were stuck to his clothes.

The Sea Bees had rigged up shower drums of water for themselves and the office pogues in the rear to bathe. They were off limits to others, but in Luke's case they made an exception. He tried to clean his utilities, but they still smelled atrocious. When he got back to the tent, his cot was sitting outside. Luke was banished for the night. And it rained.

The next morning the platoon zigzagged through the rolling maze of perimeter concertina wire before the sun was up. Shakey Jake took the point as the platoon started up the first mountain. Shawn chugged down a full canteen of Halazone water before they were halfway up.

Two mountains and two steamy valleys later the men began the climb up a third forest-covered mountain. The safety of the base at Phu Loc was already a fading memory. The woods were thick and dark and seemed to be getting more so with each new climb. The platoon stumbled onto a hard clay trail lined with giant, two-hundred-foot-tall mahoganies and oaks. A canopy of vines stretched through the treetops, blocking out any direct sun but allowing millions of pencil-thin shafts of light to penetrate.

The forest was alive with thousands of chattering birds. It was like stepping onto another planet. The temperature had dropped ten degrees according to the thermometer in Doc's helmet band. The column stopped. Kayto turned his sweaty Oriental face back toward Shawn and held up a hand.

"Take five, pass it back."

Shawn looked back at Luke. "Take five, pass it back."

Luke turned to pass the word to Cager but Cager had already passed the word back. He was sitting on the side of the trail and drinking from a canteen. Shawn pulled the heavy M60 off his aching shoulder. He sat down beside the red clay trail with the machine gun across his lap. His body tingled, near heat exhaustion, and for a moment he felt nauseous.

Kayto lifted his helmet and wiped sweat from his forehead. "Better throw down some water, boot. If you don't, you'll pay."

Shawn nodded. He didn't feel as if he could speak yet. He leaned back against a log, twisted slightly to his right, and unsnapped a canvas canteen pouch from his cartridge belt. His waist was sore from the weight of the five canteens. His .45-caliber pistol had rubbed the skin off his right hipbone. He chugged down half of the canteen before he took a breath. The Halazone tablet gave the warm water a taste that reminded Shawn of the chalky-tasting medicine that his mom used to try to sneak into his Kool-Aid when he was a kid.

Shawn looked at Kayto and exhaled hard. "Man, I used to think Florida was the hottest place on earth."

Kayto grinned. "This ain't earth, boot."

"What's the Doc doing?" Shawn asked. The dead-pan corpsman came toward them. The Doc handed each man something from one of his pouches as he passed.

"Salt tabs," Kayto said. "If you forget to take 'em you'll get heat exhaustion. Ain't no fun, bro."

Shawn set his canteen down on the log that he was leaning back on and waited for the Doc to walk by.

"Here, Kayto." Doc Abernathy held out two big white pills. Kayto took them. Doc moved over to Shawn and held out two more pills. "Here, boot, make sure you—"

Doc's mouth stayed open but no more words came out. His blue eyes bulged. The young corpsman's face turned pale. Shawn followed his frightened stare to the canteen on his right. The green plastic canteen was moving. Shawn froze stiff, watching the canteen slide away on the back of the smooth, dark log.

"God!" Doc shouted, and pointed at the giant snake, now sliding past Shawn's pack. Shawn rolled forward into Doc's shins, knocking him to the ground. They both scrambled to the other side of the trail. An M16 opened fire with five single shots. Shawn got to his feet as Luke put two more rounds into the snake.

"What is it?" Lieutenant Townsend shouted from the front of the column.

"It's a snake!" Kayto screamed as he ran up the trail. "A giant snake!"

The lieutenant and the Chief ran down the trail toward Shawn, Luke, and the corpsman.

"Who opened fire? It better be big, Marine," Lieutenant Townsend barked as he ran to a stop in front of Shawn.

No one said a word. All three openmouthed Marines pointed at the thing. It was still moving.

"Holy mackerel!" Lieutenant Townsend looked as dumbfounded as the others. He moved close enough to kick at the tail end with his boot, then walked back to the front of the column. Two by two the men ambled by to take a look at the giant reptile. No one could believe it, except Birdman. He and Goody, the long-necked Texan, strolled by to look before the column moved out. Goody shot a squirt of tobacco juice at the ground and twirled one end of his droopy mustache.

"Good Gawd! I ain't seen no snake that big, even in Texas."

"Oh, sure," Birdman said. He sent out a low hissing whistle

between jagged yellow teeth. "One time I saw a snake over in the Hai Van Pass area that makes this sucker look like an undernourished fishin' worm."

Goody spit again and scrunched up his face like he had just tasted something bitter. "Birdman, there ya go again makin' more noise than a cow pissin' on a flat rock and less sense than milkin' a bull!"

The hump continued. Ambushes at night, patrols all day. Contact with the enemy never came. A week later the platoon walked back into Phu Loc. Somebody in the rear had heard about the giant snake. A team of engineers had gone out and measured it. They said it was over twenty-six inches around. No one ever knew how long it was. Another animal had eaten away part of it before the engineers got there.

The platoon got one hot meal that made most of the guys sick before they climbed aboard trucks for a ride south on Highway One to the bridges at Hai Van Pass. The sun was barely up when the trucks pulled out of Phu Loc. It was still early morning when the Second Platoon reached the first small wooden bridge on the winding road leading through Hai Van Pass. Four salty-looking Marines were leaning over the guardrail, drinking coffee out of C-ration cans as the two trucks passed.

"Skate duty again!" Birdman shouted, then whistled at the Marines on the bridge.

Shawn peeked over the tailgate as they crossed the bridge. A familiar face stared back through the clouds of hot beige dust kicked up by the trucks.

"Hey, boot!" Burt Adelman waved.

Shawn waved and elbowed Luke. "Hey, Luke. It's that gunner we met at Phu Bai."

Luke gave a sleepy nod and closed his eyes. A couple of miles later the trucks stopped and Lieutenant Townsend shouted the platoon out. The hump began. As usual, no one seemed to know why or where the platoon was going. Hai Van Pass was steep, rugged mountain terrain. The climb was hot and long enough to make Shawn's legs ache for a rest. Two hours later he wasn't sure he could continue. His brain felt like it was boiling inside the heavy steel helmet. Finally the word came back down column to take fifteen. Shawn collapsed to the rocky ground and remembered how cruel the DIs on Parris Island had been to the weaklings and "fat bodies." Now he knew one reason why.

By late afternoon the platoon had reached the top of Hill 1614, the highest peak in the Hai Van Pass. The column wove down the back of the pass to a misty valley that looked almost prehistoric. The jungle floor there was shrouded in a damp, blue ground fog.

A sudden chill rushed in a wave of goose bumps over Shawn as the temperature dropped dramatically.

Visibility was practically zero when Kayto turned and whispered, "We're settin' up a perimeter."

Night brought more fog. Shawn's clothes were soaking wet from his own sweat. The chill turned into a shivering cold. He pulled his collar up and shrank into his flak jacket like a turtle trying to hide his face from the huge, whining mosquitoes. The whole country seemed like one insane contradiction after another. He had been nearly fainting from heat exhaustion two hours earlier, and now he was trying to warm his body with his own breath. Shawn tried to think of something funny to get his attention off the cold. Nothing came to mind.

Something strong grabbed tight around his helmet and jerked his head back. His muscles flexed for a panicked response, but it was too late. The cold steel blade of a K-bar touched his throat and Shawn knew that he was about to die.

"You got fire watch, Marine?" the Chief whispered in a guttural, menacing voice into Shawn's ear as the blade pressed harder against his throat.

Shawn heard leaves rustle beside him as Luke sat up straight.

"It's my watch, Chief," Luke whispered. "I didn't hear you."

The Chief pulled his knife away and released Shawn. "Pull your E-tools off your packs," he whispered.

Shawn swallowed and tried to breathe again. "Why?" he asked.

"If we see Charlie here, it's hand-to-hand." Sergeant Ghosthorse turned and crawled into the fog.

Shawn leaned close to Luke. His heart thumped with fear and anger. If he'd known that Luke was asleep, he'd have punched him right in the mouth. "If you ever let somebody sneak up on me like that again I'm wrapping this M60 right around your fat head!"

"I'm sorry, man. The Chief is too quiet. . . ."

82

"I don't wanna hear it, man. The gooks are quiet too! Just don't let it happen again."

For a few minutes Shawn and Luke sat rigid, stunned and frightened, staring into the cold black fog. Finally Shawn laid his small shovel beside him and tried to sleep. He thought of home and Nancy until fatigue overwhelmed him.

"Shawn. Shawn." Luke tugged Shawn out of Nancy's warm embrace. Shawn pulled his collar down from his face and opened one eye. "It's your watch," Luke whispered.

Shawn sat up slowly and waved away a dive-bombing mosquito.

Luke leaned close. "Do you have any idea just how big these mosquitoes are?" he whispered in Shawn's ear.

Shawn rubbed his sleepy eyes. A rustle in the brush to their right took Shawn's breath away. Luke stiffened and aimed his rifle at the noise.

"My God!" A panicked voice came out of the dark fog. A branch broke. The sound of someone struggling became clear. "Smitty! It bit me! Snake! Get him!"

A stomping, hacking sound cut through the fog like a knife. Silence.

"Cager? Kayto?" Shawn whispered.

"Corpsman up. Pass the word."

The nervous night felt as though it would never end, and though the warm grasp of daylight never actually reached down into this strange gray valley, it felt immeasurably better than the black night.

Dook, the quiet Cajun who refused to carry a plastic rifle and would only carry an M14, had been bitten by a snake. The location of the bite changed each time a new person told the story. Birdman said that Dook got it "where the sun don't shine," but nobody ever took Birdman's word for anything. Smitty, the chunky blooper man, killed the six-foot brown snake with his entrenching tool. Doc said it was not poisonous so Dook was not medevacked. Dook "guar-rone-teed" the Doc's death if he died from the snakebite. Everyone was too tired to question his logic.

The hump through the bush continued at the same murderous pace. They climbed up and down mountains and through valleys of razor-sharp elephant grass. The strain of constant walking and the stress of trying to stay alert had a bizarre effect on the mind, Shawn noticed. One hour of one day seemed to last an eternity. Thirteen months was unfathomable. Shawn now understood how these nineteen-year-old Marines could look so old.

On the third day they walked into a thick jungle with a natural corridor that led through a valley and into a wooded paradise with fields of soft grass and wildflowers in a rainbow of colors. The air smelled fresh, like after a rainstorm. The Chief said it was called the Garden of Eden by the old salts. The name fit.

Beyond the Garden of Eden was more harsh jungle. They ran into a paved, one-lane road that seemed to spring from nowhere and lead to nowhere. It was pockmarked with bomb hits. Elephant grass grew tall out of every crack and crater. The road wound deeper and deeper into the thick jungle. Still no contact with the enemy. Someone said they had only been out a week this time. It felt like a month. The platoon turned back.

The diesel engines of two big deuce-and-a-half trucks were already rumbling as they neared a small combat base at Hai Van. Rumors about Khe Sanh had been mumbled through the tired, dirty column before the first man climbed aboard a truck. Words like "cease-fire" and "Tet" and "New Year's" seemed to be on everyone's lips. The trucks rolled across the bridges of Hai Van Pass, heading back to Phu Loc. Shawn and Luke were in the lead truck. A gaunt young Marine waved the truck to a stop on the last bridge.

"You got a corpsman on board?" His voice cracked with strain.

"Yo!" Doc Abernathy jumped over Birdman and Goody. He leaped over the tailgate of the truck with his medical pouch and ran forward.

"Quick, Doc! Our gunner tripped my booby trap! I told him to stay put!"

"Where?"

"Over here!" another Marine shouted from the bush to the left of the dirt road.

A few minutes passed before the Doc came back to the truck. He shrugged and said something to Lieutenant Townsend. The lieutenant shook his head and got back into the cab of the truck as the Doc climbed into the back.

"How bad, Doc?" Birdman asked.

"Anybody here know Burt Adelman? Third Platoon gunner."

84

"I know him, Doc. Darn nice feller." Goody moved his large wad of tobacco from one side of his mouth to the other.

"He's dead. He went out to take a crap in those rocks up there." Doc pointed at a wooded rise on the left of the road. "Tripped his buddy's frag. Looked like he knew it and tried to run but got his boot caught between two big boulders."

Doc's long Dennis the Menace face seemed to get longer. "Found him hanging upside down, like, he was still quiverin' away, but he was a goner."

Chip radioed for a medevac. The trucks pulled away. The gaunt young Marine hung over the wood railing of the one-lane bridge and threw up. He fell to his knees with his head in his hands as the trucks rounded a curve and Shawn could no longer see him. The image lasted all the way to Phu Loc.

They stayed in Phu Loc for as long as it took to climb out of the trucks, walk through the base, and hump back into the mountains. During the second night outside of Phu Loc, the sky over the base exploded with streaking tracers and lightninglike flashes from explosions of all sizes. Second Platoon was too far away to help. Orders were to stay put until daybreak. Chipper picked up radio transmissions from all over. It sounded like every base camp around was getting hit. Word whispered around the perimeter: one hundred percent alert. No one would have slept anyway.

The next day started with a five-mile forced march back to Phu Loc. The camp was a mess. Troop tents had been blown up, and garbage was strewn everywhere. A gunny sergeant had been killed and the base commander seriously wounded, but scuttlebutt said casualties were light.

Two days of rebuilding bunkers spawned a new rumor. Second Battalion, Fifth Marines were fighting house to house in Hue City. Alpha was either going there or to another meat grinder called Khe Sanh.

"They're calling it the Tet Offensive," Chipper said with a shrug as the long convoy of trucks carrying Alpha Company started down Highway One.

Shawn didn't care what colorful name they gave it; judging by the panic on the faces of the thousands of refugees streaming south on both sides of the dirt road called Highway One and the constant helicopter traffic above, this was big. Ghosthorse ran a whetstone back and forth on his K-bar knife. Goody wrote a letter.

Dusty took off his helmet and stared at the calendar of days X'd off. He spit some of Highway One out of his mouth and put his helmet back on. He twisted at one end of a dirty green towel wrapped around his neck and chewed at the inside of his mouth.

An hour later Shawn wasn't sure if he was scared or excited. It was like in the old war movies—rolling toward a crucial battle in the back of big trucks. He stood to see the front of the convoy. It could be Rome or Paris, he thought.

Cager stood up beside him. "We'll know now, man," he said with his rolling Jamaican accent.

"Know what?"

"That is Phu Bai." He pointed at the big base to the left of the road. The crowded village of Phu Bai, just in front of the base, looked busier than usual. "If the lead truck pulls left into Phu Bai, we might skate longer, man."

"How far is Hue City?"

"Nine miles, man, just nine miles." Cager nodded toward Dusty and shook his head. Dusty sat staring at a photograph wrapped in a plastic bag.

"Who's the photo of?" Shawn asked Cager.

"A four-year-old daughter, man."

"Gosh, I didn't think he was that old."

"Yeah, man, Dusty's twenty-two, I think." Cager said.

The brake lights of the lead truck flashed red through the cloud of dust kicking up behind it. Huge black rain clouds rolled in from the western mountains covering the base. The lead truck turned left. Cager sighed aloud and sat down.

CHAPTER FIVE

Bad Rope in Phu Bai

"All right, Sergeant," Lieutenant Townsend shouted over the noisy diesel engine of the big deuce-and-a-half truck, "get 'em out of that truck and form up in front of the tent!"

"Aye-aye, sir." Chief waved a salute from the back of the truck, then unlatched the tailgate and let it drop.

"Move out, Marines!" He jumped down and pointed to a spot in front of the Second Platoon tent. Shawn jumped out quickly. No one else moved fast.

"Make sure those weapons are on safety! Clear your chambers! Pull out the magazines! Check the pins on your frags! Hurry up! Form up!"

The platoon formed into three lines.

"Move it, platoon!"

"Platoon?" Luke said, looking around as if searching for something. "This is the platoon? I thought this was a squad."

Grins spread across the seventeen dirty, unshaven faces of the men. Forty-four men made an official platoon. But then, this was not an official war.

"Listen up!" Lieutenant Townsend shouted away the tired laughter. He turned to Chip the radioman, said something too low to hear, then looked back at the men. "Chipper says he picked up a transmission for medevacs. Some recons stepped in it, so don't go far and don't get drunk at the slop-shute. Matter of fact you better get over to the chow hall and get a hot meal while you can." The lieutenant turned to the Chief. "Top sergeant is going out with us next time, Chief. Thought you'd want to know."

The stone-faced Indian nodded.

"Dismiss the men."

"Aye-aye, sir." Chief saluted sharply. Lieutenant Townsend replied. The Chief turned to the men. "Dissss-missed!"

The men scrambled into the tent, stripping off their helmets and packs as they hustled for the nearest empty cot. A new energy bubbled out of the dirty, fatigued faces as they rushed to rid themselves of the heavy gear.

Shawn picked up the machine gun and threw it over his shoulder. "Where did all that energy come from?"

"Are we late for something?" Luke asked. They entered the tent. Kayto sat horseback style on the first cot, pounding out a jivy beat on his helmet between his legs with two grenades. Cager, with one boot resting on Kayto's cot, was singing "The Midnight Hour" while he pulled off bandoliers, one at a time.

"Hey, boot," a hairy-faced Marine with a Southern twang called out from the back of the tent.

"He must mean you." Luke shoved Shawn from behind.

Shawn pointed to two empty cots on the right. "How 'bout there, Luke?"

"I prefer a view, but okay." Luke tossed his helmet onto the nearest cot. Shawn laid the M60 on the other cot and began dropping his gear.

"Hey, gunner." The hairy guy motioned to Shawn.

"Tell him to get off his butt and come over here," Luke growled.

"Probably should."

"You going to write Nancy?"

"Yeah, probably."

"Tell her that I love her bod. Let us go feed. I am starving for hot food."

"You were born starving," Shawn said, and walked over to the hairy-faced Marine. "How ya doin'? My name's McClellan." He put out his hand.

The Marine ran a quick wipe across his walruslike mustache and grabbed Shawn's hand with a firm grip. "Dook." His lips seemed to stick out when he said his name. He shook Shawn's hand once and motioned to an empty cot next to him. "Have a seat, bro."

Shawn plopped down. A small cloud of dust shot up from the cot.

"Where ya from, Marine?" Dook asked with a deep Southern drawl.

"West Virginia, originally, but I've lived in Florida since I was eleven. How 'bout you?"

"Loo-zee-anna. Glad to hear you're a Southern boy. The gunner is mighty important."

88

"How's that snakebite, Dook? I heard you wrestling around that night up at Hai Van Pass. Scared me to death too."

Dook looked at the back of his right hand. "Got me on the hand; it's fine now. No thanks to that goofy corpsman. He's from California, ya know." Dook held out his hand. "Glad to know you."

"Nice meeting you, Dook." Shawn extended his hand. Dook gave it one firm shake. Shawn stood up to walk back to his cot.

"Hey, gunner."

Shawn looked back.

Dook lifted his chin and twirled one end of his walrus mustache. "How'd LSU do in football?"

"I think they were seven and three," Shawn said.

Dook nodded and lay back on his cot.

"Hey, Dook," Shawn called back.

Dook lifted his head.

"My girlfriend is a Cajun. From Gonzales."

Dook sat up straight. He smiled, but Shawn sensed a hint of sadness in his dark brown eyes. "Jambalaya capital of the world," Dook said. "Black hair?"

"Yep. Boy, is she good-lookin' too." Shawn could almost see Nancy's long black hair against the olive skin of her face.

"Does she write ya?"

"I hope so. I haven't been here long enough to know yet."

"If she does, could you—" He paused and looked around the busy tent. He motioned Shawn to come closer. Shawn did. "Would ya, if it's no trouble, now, maybe ask her how things are back home?"

The burly Marine looked tough enough to chew nails, but suddenly Shawn felt sorry for him.

"I'll make sure she does, Dook."

Shawn smiled but felt empty inside. He remembered Dusty's story about the dog-food package. The press back home had been spitting on their own troops for a while, but Shawn hadn't paid much attention to it. He wondered if the liberal press could make people care so little about their own fighting men. He shook his head and decided that he was blowing one sad story out of proportion.

Luke led the way to the chow hall. The hot meal made Shawn queasy. His stomach wasn't used to real food now. Luke insisted on a beer chaser at the "Animal Pit." The bar was a little more alive this time. Most of the tables were filled. There was standing room at the bar. Rugged-looking soldiers leaned over their beers and laughed, not in a really happy way, but the kind of laughter that comes from nervous fatigue.

Shawn and Luke leaned on the bar with beers in hand. A young Marine with a blackened face, dressed in camouflage utilities, pretended to fire a rifle as he described a kill to four other Marines. Some men spoke in whispers. Some were loud. Shawn listened. The same names and phrases kept echoing through the barroom chatter.

"Tet Offensive."

"Division size."

"Khe Sanh."

"Hundreds of confirmed."

"KIAs."

"Hue City."

"The Fifth Marine Regiment."

"Boo-coo gooks, man, it was hand-to-hand, bro."

"I wonder how ol' Joe is doing?" Luke said, staring at the naked lady on the clanging pinball machine in the far corner.

"I've been praying for him," Shawn said.

"Do you always have to throw that crap in?" Luke's bushy eyebrows came together in a frown.

"I pray for you too, Luke," Shawn said, grinning. "Why don't we ask somebody in here about the Ninth Marines?"

"What do you want to know?" A short husky Marine turned on his bar stool to face Shawn. He had a sergeant's chevron on his soft-cover hat.

"We got a buddy with the Ninth Marines," Shawn said.

"He's in a meat grinder, bro." The sergeant's eyes were serious. "They got sent up to Khe Sanh to help the 26th."

"What's going on at Khe Sanh?"

"You ain't heard?" Shawn and Luke leaned closer. "Khe Sanh is surrounded by forty thousand gooks."

Shawn felt the air go out of him. He looked at Luke. Luke's eyes opened wide.

"Really," Luke said in a tone that rang with doubt.

"Yeah, really." The sergeant turned back to the bar. Luke looked at the wood floor covered with red dirt from a war's worth of jungle boots. He looked up as the Chief walked through the door with his hand on the black handle of his K-bar knife.

"Chief." Luke motioned him over. "Buy you a beer."

The Indian walked over and put an elbow on the bar between

Luke and Shawn. "Beer!" he barked once toward the bartender, and looked at Luke. "You guys written home yet?" He pushed his thick-lensed glasses against the bridge of his long nose.

"No," Luke said.

"Do it tonight. That's an order."

The Chief's order aggravated the grumble of Shawn's nervous stomach.

"Sure, Chief," Luke said. He dug into the big cargo pocket of his jungle utilities and pulled out the funny-colored money he had been issued the first day.

"How much MPC you got?" the Chief asked.

"This? My Monopoly money?" Luke held out a purple-colored bill with a strange-looking lady on it.

"Don't carry much on you. Can't spend it in the bush. If Charlie gets a chance to search your body, he uses your MPC."

Shawn leaned around Luke. "The scuttlebutt sounds bad, Chief."

Chief turned to take a mug from the bartender. Luke tossed out some Monopoly money. Chief drank the mug down in one long gulp and slid it back at the bartender.

"Beer."

Luke looked at Shawn and whistled. "Thirsty Indian," he said, and tossed some more money on the bar.

"You got any plastic bags?" the stone-faced Indian mumbled.

"No," Luke said.

"Get some. Put your letter-writing gear in it and wallet and crap paper. The rains are coming."

"The monsoon?" Shawn asked.

"It rains all day and all night," the Chief said. "Rains hard. Rains soft. Gives you bad headaches from pounding off your helmet. Nothing stays dry. Keep the gun covered with oil, always. Weapons will rust in ten to twenty hours. They jam, you're a KIA."

Chief's face and eyes never seemed to change. It was hard to tell if he was sad or mad or just always serious, but whatever else he was, he was the way Shawn had always thought an Indian would be.

The Chief sniffed. "Don't put on too much bug juice. Wind blows, Charlie smells it, you die." He turned to take another mug of beer from the bartender. He drank it down in one long gulp again.

He slid the empty mug toward the fat bartender. "Beer."

91

Luke dug for more money.

Chief looked at Shawn. "You hear 'Guns up,' you beat feet, Marine." He looked at Luke. "Don't run after him until he has a ten-yard start. He gets hit, you pick up the gun." His black eyes grew more intense. "You leave him. Doc takes care of the wounded, you take care of the gun. Got it?"

"Right, Chief," Luke said.

The Indian took another mug of beer and downed it again in one long gulp. He slid the mug away, pushed away from the bar, and walked out the door. Shawn and Luke exchanged nervous glances. The big 155 artillery pieces opened up from the north end of the base and Shawn's bar stool vibrated with each salvo.

"This Tet thing must be big, Luke."

"Sometimes this feels like a strange dream, you know?"

Shawn nodded slowly. "Yeah, like it isn't really happening." He ran his finger along his upper lip. A few hairs, but no mustache. He wanted one. He wanted to look like the hard-core Marines around him instead of some baby-faced kid.

The bar door opened again. The daylight was fading fast. It felt so safe in Phu Bai, nothing like the fear in the bush. Chipper came through the door with helmet, flak jacket, pack, and radio already on. Luke looked toward the ceiling with eyes closed, dreading the words.

"Alpha One-Five! Second Platoon! Saddle up! ASAP! We got choppers waiting!"

Shawn pressed his face against the round window of the twin-rotored helicopter. A dim green light lit the inside of the CH-46. Everything below was pitch black. How could they possibly know where to land?

Lieutenant Townsend stood up and held on to the ceiling of the chopper. He walked over to Sergeant Ghosthorse and looked down at a long rope piled up beside him. He turned and shouted toward the cockpit, "How far?"

The copilot leaned back toward Lieutenant Townsend, held up five fingers, and shouted, "Five minutes! Get your men lined up before we kill the light!"

The lieutenant gave him a thumbs-up, then turned to face the platoon. Seven men sat against one wall facing eight on the other side of the chopper. "We have to drop down by rope!" he yelled over the popping rotors. "There's no LZ!"

Shawn couldn't believe his ears. He looked at the heavy black machine gun in his lap and wondered how he could manage it. There was no shoulder sling on the gun.

"Let me carry it down," Luke shouted into Shawn's left ear. He reached for the gun.

"No, Luke." Shawn pushed his hand away from the M60. "It's my problem, I'm the gunner."

"I'm bigger and stronger than you, stupid. Now give me the gun."

"You're also a big klutz."

"One!" Lieutenant Townsend tapped the helmet of the man nearest the door gunner's open hatch. "Two!" He moved to the next Marine.

The Chief was next in line. Chief got to his feet and yanked Dusty up with him. He pulled Dusty to the other side of the chopper, put Dusty between Luke and Shawn, then squeezed in between Shawn and Smitty, the fat blooper man. The M79 looked like a sawed-off shotgun. It was only twenty-eight inches long and weighed six pounds, loaded. It made a funny *bloop* sound when fired—hence the name blooper gun. Smitty was too big to carry the little M79 grenade launcher. He was the one who should be humping the M60, Shawn thought.

"Twelve . . . thirteen . . . fourteen . . . fifteen . . . ready!"

"LZ ahead!" the pilot shouted from the front. "Lights out!" The eerie green light turned to black. The chopper slowed, then hovered just above the tips of tall trees swaying in the wind. Shawn shoved his nose against the window. The beam of a small flashlight flicked on and off in the blackness below.

"One!" someone shouted in the darkness, and Shawn's heart pounded. He grabbed the gun and stood it on the butt end between his legs. "Two! Three!" Shawn felt Luke grip his left arm. "Four!" His mind raced from home to Nam and back to home and Nancy. Pray. Pray. He shook his head to clear his thinking, then looked at the dark floor of the vibrating helicopter.

"Dear Father, please protect us and keep us from getting hurt; in Jesus' name I pray."

"Twelve!"

"Smitty, you're next!" Chief shouted, and nudged the short, round Marine. Smitty moved to the open hatch, got to his knees, and slowly put one foot out of the open hatch as he gripped the rope with all of his strength. The Chief stepped to the hatch. He paused as if he were waiting for something. A faint scream came from below.

"The rope broke!" someone yelled.

"Get outta here!"

A moment later the chopper banked sharply and strained for altitude. The Chief stumbled back to the bench beside Shawn. No one spoke. A few minutes later the dim green light came back on. A barely discernible smile cracked at the edges of the Chief's mouth.

"What happened, Chief?" Shawn asked.

"Smitty's fat."

"Is that why you moved over here?" Shawn asked with a smile that was turning into a laugh.

"Bad rope. Smitty's fat." He turned away.

Dusty leaned back and closed his eyes. Shawn laughed. Then Luke laughed until he doubled over. Huge tears ran down his face. The door gunner looked at the four grunts as if they were crazy.

"I love this guy!" Luke said, wiping laugh tears from his eyes. He leaned out to see past Shawn. "Chief! Can I buy you another beer?" The Indian's expressionless stare remained fixed straight ahead, but he nodded yes.

The ride back to Phu Bai was quiet. A million questions ran through Shawn's mind, but the biggest was: What would the platoon do without a gun? The Chief didn't seem worried about it. If he wasn't worried it was probably okay, Shawn thought. Dusty look relieved. The chopper settled onto a landing pad of corrugated-steel planking two hundred meters from the Alpha Company tent area. Luke, Dusty, and Shawn followed the Chief to the tent. He walked fast. When he reached the tent, he looked back.

"Hurry up! Drop your gear."

"I'm gonna sack out, Chief." Dusty plopped down on the nearest cot.

"Get a letter off to that baby girl," Chief said gruffly.

"Yeah. Good idea, Chief."

Shawn and Luke dropped everything onto their cots and followed the Indian back to the Animal Pit. The bar was filled with soldiers. Most of them wore the Screaming Eagle patch of the 101st Airborne. They looked clean. Their fatigues weren't beige from the hot sun and their boots didn't look like moccasins from months in the bush. The Chief found a table with three chairs in a dark corner.

Luke headed for the bar. "I'll get the beer."

"What are we supposed to do, Chief?" Shawn asked. He pulled out a chair and sat facing the Indian. The Chief looked around the noisy room full of soldiers, then back at Shawn.

"We'll get another chopper tomorrow. Something big is up." The Chief's words came out in a slow ominous tone.

"Why?"

"The 101st wasn't here yesterday. Khe Sanh's getting pounded."

"My buddy, Joe, is there."

"Ain't no place to be."

Luke set three cans of Budweiser on the round table. He pulled out a chair, grabbed a beer, and held it up for a toast. "To old rope."

Shawn touched cans with Luke. The Chief didn't bother. He slugged back the can of Budweiser.

"Chief says something big is coming down, Luke." The excitement in Shawn's voice brought a frown from his friend.

"Wonderful, Shawn. I am glad that you have found the bright side to this news."

"I can't help it! This is exciting; I mean I'm scared, but sometimes I'm just really hyped up. It's like seeing a movie, only I'm in it."

Luke stared at Shawn for a moment in silence. "You are sick, Shawn; seek help."

The Indian put his empty can down and peered at Luke through one eye. "Beer?"

Luke signaled a thumbs-up. "Yes, I'll have another." The Chief walked toward the bar. Luke blew out a low whistle. "Man, that guy is bad."

"There it is, bro. If somebody had told me there were guys like that in the corps, I wouldn't have believed it."

Luke leaned back with a laugh. "Can you see us bringing the Chief to one of the parties back in St. Pete?"

"He'd be a perfect blind date for Benita George." Shawn chuckled and leaned his chair back on two legs. He looked up at the granite jaw of the big Indian standing over him and swallowed the rest of his laugh like it was unchewed meat. He smiled.

The big Indian set five cans of beer on the table. He pushed two cans toward Luke and Shawn, then pulled the other three to himself.

"So, Chief," Luke said hesitantly, "where does your family live?"

"Reservation. Oklahoma."

"Wow!" Shawn surprised himself by saying it out loud. "I never met anyone who lived on a reservation."

"I'm splitting you two up as soon as we get another gunner." The Chief's words pierced the jovial mood like an arrow.

"What?" Luke asked, sitting straight up in his chair. "Why?"

"It's best."

"Ghosthorse." A low commanding voice turned all three heads. A tanned older man with clear blue eyes and a large gray handlebar mustache walked up to the table. The Chief jumped to his feet and nearly stood at attention.

"Sir, it's good to see you." The Indian walked around the table and stood in front of the other man. They looked straight into each other's eyes, then the Chief put one hand on the older man's shoulder, and the old Marine did the same.

Shawn squirmed in his chair. He felt out of place. The Chief turned back to Shawn and Luke.

"Boots, this is Sergeant Major O'Connel."

"How do you do, sir." Luke pushed his chair aside, stood up and put out his hand. "PFC Lukevec, sir."

Shawn stood up. "PFC McClellan, sir."

Sergeant Major O'Connel shook Luke's hand, then Shawn's. The Chief pulled over an empty chair from another table.

The sergeant major sat down. He took off his soft-cover and laid it on the table, then pulled out a four-cigarette pack of C-ration Lucky Strikes. He struck a match and cupped it with his hands, instinctively hiding the light. He blew a large smoke ring into the air and started laughing, low at first, then louder and harder until everyone in the bar was looking at him.

The Chief finally smiled, a real smile, not a straight-mouth grin. Luke and Shawn exchanged grins and shrugs. Finally the sergeant major leaned forward with his elbows on the table and stopped laughing. He shook his head as if in disbelief and laughed again. He cleared his throat and put on a serious scowl.

"I was over at the com shack," the sergeant major began, then paused and blew another smoke ring. "Heard about a rope breaking and sort of figured I'd find you here." He shook his head again. A grin sent small lines of age across his face and around his eyes.

"Bad rope," the Chief said with a straight face.

The sergeant major turned to Luke and Shawn. "His daddy and me were on the 'canal.' " His bright blue eyes sparkled. He took another puff off his Lucky Strike and seemed to look past the bar to another time and another place. "That big horse carried me through a swamp under fire." He looked back at the Chief. "How is he?"

"Last I heard, he was in the hospital on the reservation. Liver."

"Why won't he stop drinking?" O'Connel pounded the table with a closed fist.

"Can I buy you a beer, Sergeant Major?" Luke asked.

"What's your name, again?"

"Lukevec, sir."

He looked at Shawn. "And you're Irish?"

"Yes, sir."

"Don't call me sir, Marines. I'm no butter-bar officer, by God."

"You are above an officer, sir," Luke said. "That's what they taught us in boot camp."

The sergeant major sat up straight. He looked pleased. He laughed and pounded Luke on the back. "I'll have that beer, PFC."

Luke stood up, searching through his big cargo pocket.

"No." The sergeant major pulled a small wad of MPC out of his starched shirt pocket. "Here." He handed it to Luke. "At eleven cents an hour, you can't be buying too much beer, PFC."

"Thank you, Sergeant Major." Luke took the money.

"A round for everybody," the sergeant major said. He turned a serious face to the Chief. "Okay, Chief. No more of this bad-rope crap."

"Aye-aye, sir."

"Don't give me that. We need Marines like you in the bush, not in some brig! Now, if you want an R&R just tell me! You got about four of 'em coming."

"I will, Sergeant Major."

"Something big is coming, Chief."

"I know."

"What do you think is up, Sergeant Major?" Shawn asked, sliding his chair closer to the table.

"You seen all of those choppers comin' and goin'?"

Shawn nodded yes.

"All medevacs out of Hue City. First Med is overflowing with casualties. I hear it's house to house."

Shawn could feel his heart speeding up. His skin tingled from a rush of adrenaline.

"You going out with us on the OP?" Chief asked.

"I think so, if I get the 'Bird's' okay."

The wood planks of the bar's floor vibrated through the boots that stood on them. An instant later the thunder of distant explosions sent a hush through the noisy bar as if the air in the room had been sucked away. A series of cracking explosions rattled glasses hanging behind the bar. Suddenly, with no sign of panic, the room began to empty.

"Get to your bunkers!" someone shouted from the plywood door. Shawn got to his feet as Luke came back with four beers. Shawn looked at the Chief, then at the sergeant major. They didn't move. The sergeant major reached for his beer. Luke stood rigid. He looked ready to run or sit, whatever the order might be.

"Envelop and secure that beer, Marines," the sergeant major growled.

They both sat, staring at the strange lack of concern on the faces of the two "salts." Shawn envied their confidence. He wondered if either of them ever prayed. Deep in his heart he doubted that they did. Another series of explosions sounded closer.

"What is happening, Sergeant Major?" Luke asked.

"Nothin', PFC," he mumbled. "Just some mortars."

Chief pulled off his thick glasses and cleaned one lens on his jacket. "That first one was a 122, Sergeant Major."

"Was it?"

The Chief nodded. "Yep."

And so it went. Talk of old wars. Talk of the new war. The mortar and rocket attack continued for an hour, the "salts" barely noticing while the "boots" squirmed in their hard wooden chairs like men sitting on nails. They finally drank their fill of beer. It ended with the same old question. "When will they let us invade and win?" No one knew.

For the rest of the night Shawn lay on his cot, staring wide-eyed into the darkness. He tried to say his prayers, but his mind wandered from Guadalcanal to the Chosen Reservoir. If he could just be half the Marine these men were, he thought. Even Luke was impressed, and Luke was never impressed. The backfiring sounds of helicopter medevacs coming and going continued through the night. The tent quivered as they whipped by low overhead. Hue City.

"Saddle up, Marines!" The Indian's shout brought on the morning.

"What about chow?" Luke yelled.

"No time for chow! Chopper waiting!"

Excitement pushed its way through the sleepiness as they jogged toward the landing pad. The morning sky was gray. A light drizzle began.

They passed a group of boot Marines standing in the chow line. Shawn could feel their stares. He felt a bit "salty" himself, and he liked it. He felt meaner too. But then how could a man not feel mean with four hundred rounds of machine-gun ammo crisscrossing his chest like a Mexican bandit? An M60 over his shoulder, grenades hanging here and there, a .45-caliber pistol and a K-bar for good measure. All I need is a mustache. He almost smiled at the thought.

The airstrip buzzed with activity. A wounded Huey gunship floated down with black smoke billowing from the main rotors.

"This way!" the Chief shouted as he ran past a sandbag bunker and turned right toward a larger bunker. A Hispanic Marine sat on top of the large bunker with a headset over his ears. He pointed the Chief toward an old Korean-era chopper that looked like a big bug. Under the cockpit were painted two funny black-and-white eyes, just under one eye, a big purple heart. The Marines ducked under rotors as they climbed in. Shawn tapped Sergeant Ghosthorse on his helmet.

"Chief!" He shouted over the prop wash of the helicopter. "Are we going to Hue?"

"No."

Shawn sighed with relief; then, for some reason he did not fully understand, he felt disappointed.

Twenty minutes later the shaky old helicopter descended toward a flat brown rice paddy surrounded by a tree line on three sides. The platoon formed a circle around a rising funnel of green smoke. The tires of the old chopper sank into muck long enough for the three riders to jump out. The lieutenant shouted those hated words even before the old war bird had lifted off.

"Saddle up!"

No one mentioned the bad rope. No questions were asked. By noon the sun was sucking water and salt out of the platoon faster than it could be replaced. An hour later a driving monsoon rain hit the Marines with a stinging force, hard enough to raise small welts. The rain fell all night and all day. It rained until each man's skin looked yellow and wrinkled. There seemed to be no purpose to the continuous hump other than to set up the endless ambush. No enemy was to be seen, only the leeches to be burned off in the morning after they filled with your blood and weighed enough to be felt hanging from blue skin.

The second day began with the clang of one of the old metal canteens bouncing off a steel rifle. Dook wiped his walrus mustache and spit angrily at the dented canteen. A Marine with a sheepish expression and dark bags under each eye struck a match and scooted up beside Dook.

"Now keep it out of the Yankee rain, Blaine, or I guar-rone-tee . . ."

The sheepish-looking Marine sucked in his cheeks and touched the match to Dook's throat. A long, bloated leech dropped to the mud. A trickle of blood ran down Dook's throat. He pulled out his rusty K-bar and grinned as he stabbed the black, slimy leech over and over. Shawn watched and couldn't help wondering what strange little diseases he'd be taking home with him—if he went home.

"PFC McClellan."

Shawn looked to his left. The lieutenant was coming his way. The round healthy face of the college-grad lieutenant would have looked more at home above a letter sweater.

"Yes, sir."

Lieutenant Townsend stopped beside Shawn and knelt down on one knee. Rain cascaded off his helmet and splashed into Shawn's eyes. "Sorry about that." He removed his helmet, revealing a short crew cut with the customary white sidewalls. "I never had the chance to tell you and Lukevec how well you did that first day. That was a hard way to break into the bush and you both reacted like Marines."

Luke sat up straight, pride and surprise pushing his mouth slightly open. "Thank you, Lieutenant."

"Thank you, sir," Shawn said. He felt his chest expand.

"Remember to keep your gun oiled. The rains are coming."

"Yes, sir," Shawn said.

"We do keep it oiled, sir." Luke said clearly.

"See that you do, PFC."

"Lieutenant!" Chipper called from the center of the perimeter, which circled a small barren rise just above a dense jungle area.

"Yo!" The lieutenant waved Chip over.

Chipper walked toward the gun team carrying his radio in one hand and a can of "beef and rocks" in the other. He looked less like a Marine than most of the men. Shawn wondered how Chip or Smitty ever got out of boot camp looking so round. He remembered the "fat bodies" couldn't leave Parris Island until they were lean and mean. Chip was chubby and so was Smitty, but they were not soft and sloppy by civilian standards. Maybe they just looked heavier because the rest of the grunts were lean.

Chip dropped the radio beside the lieutenant and handed him the receiver. He pulled out the antenna. A big round wad of pink bubble gum was on the tip. "We got a replacement coming in on a chopper, Lieutenant."

"Alpha One . . . Alpha One . . . Alpha Two . . . Over." Lieutenant Townsend sang a pretty good call, but nothing compared to the rhythm of the Chipper.

"Alpha Two this is Alpha One . . . We got a bird at 0900 at LZ Lima-Foxtrot-Zero-Wun-Thuh-ree-Ate-Fo-wer . . . Copy."

"That's affirmative, Alpha One." The lieutenant handed the receiver back to Chipper and shook his head in disgust.

"Is this the guy, Lieutenant?" Chipper asked through a mouthful of food. Lieutenant Townsend nodded and walked back to the CP. Chip spooned out another bite of food and squatted down between Luke and Shawn.

"Hey, I never got to ask you guys about the world, man." Chip's words came in a quick burst. "Minis, I hear the women are wearing skirts up to here!" He slapped his dirty white plastic spoon against his hip.

"I didn't see too many in St. Pete," Shawn complained. "Did you, Luke?"

"St. Petersburg is always behind. I did spot a couple, though."

"That's right. He nearly fell out of a car window screaming at one," Shawn said.

"I was merely showing my appreciation."

"Chip, what's with this chopper?" Shawn asked.

"Well . . ." Chip paused and looked over his shoulder suspiciously. "Keep it to yourself, but we got a bad egg comin' in."

Luke leaned closer. "What?" He wiped rainwater from his big bushy eyebrows.

"Some clown who keeps getting kicked out of other units. The sir don't like it either. Bad enough without no loony tunes runnin' around."

Chip sat down with a splash. "So, come on. What's happening in the world?"

"The Beatles." Luke shrugged.

"The Young Rascals too," Shawn said.

"What about TV, they ever say anything about us?"

"Yeah," Shawn said.

"Protesters get more press than the guys dying," Luke growled. "The news will search the country until they find a group of drugged-up hippies crying about something, then they build it up like it is the only news they can find."

Shawn pulled a can of meatballs and beans out of his pack and frowned. "One night on the news, they did this ten-second blip on some Army guy winning the medal of honor, and then the whole rest of the news was about Jane Fonda and a bunch of hippies against the war. It was like the guy saving his whole squad and getting killed wasn't worth going into."

"Ain't selling enough papers, bro. That's what it all comes down to. What sells the most papers."

Chip checked the portion of a poncho tied over the PRC-25. "Can't let baby get wet." He gave the radio a pat. "Where's Cager and Kayto?" He looked around.

"Water detail," Shawn said.

"Any good movies out?" Chip asked.

Shawn pointed at Luke. "That Mrs. Robinson movie."

"That was good. And *Bonnie and Clyde* was okay," Luke mused aloud.

"Where you from, Chip?" Shawn asked as he turned to search his pack for his C-ration can stove.

"New Mexico. Right down the road from old Goody's place."

Shawn pulled out his C-ration can stove. "Who's Goody?" he asked. Luke handed Shawn a small chunk of C-4 and hovered over a book of matches that he pulled out of his helmet liner.

"Goody is that good ol' boy, the one from Texas."

"A mustache that hangs down from the edges of his mouth?" Luke asked as he struck the match.

"Chews tobacco all the time?" Shawn asked.

"Yeah, that's him. He always sets in with the Birdman. He's the third-squad leader. Lance corporal. Funny guy too."

"Every time I see that guy—" Shawn paused to hold his helmet over the tiny stove to shield Luke's match from the rain. "—he looks real down."

The small chunk of C-4 turned into a hot blue flame. Chip stared at the flame as he pushed his glasses back on his wet button nose.

"Yeah, well, Billy the Kid was Goody's main man."

Shawn's stomach tightened. He wanted to say how sorry he was but didn't.

"I forgot you were there," Chip said. "The first time's always bad. I better be makin' it back to the CP." He stood up with the PRC-25 radio dangling from one shoulder strap and blew a bubble and popped it.

Shawn stared at the blue flame until Chip was gone. Billy the Kid. He knew his memory of Billy would stick with him until the day he died. His freckled face, the dark hole where his eye should have been, the crawling line of dark red blood, would always remain, like an old photograph.

Luke poked Shawn with his C-ration spoon. "Do not go getting all depressed on me; this place stinks enough, Shawn."

"I wonder if Goody blames me."

"If he blames anyone, it would be me. I am the A-gunner. I should have been beside you feeding the gun, not Billy."

"Maybe he blames both of us."

Luke looked mad. He cranked his P-38 opener around the top of a can of ham and limas. The grunts called it ham and mothers. The lima beans looked like Crisco that had already been used. Luke was quickly becoming popular because he was the only man in the platoon who would eat the stuff.

"Heat yours first," Shawn said. He sat up, pulled out his Bible wrapped in plastic, and hunched over it. Rain still found the small white pages, but he didn't care. He needed it. An empty feeling of blame gnawed at his insides. How did Billy die? They were trying to knock out the gun. Billy died instead. Focus on the Word, he thought. He turned the pages hoping that something would jump out at him, something that would help the gnawing inside.

"Shawn." Luke's big oval face wrinkled slightly with annoyance.

"Yeah."

"I'm curious about something."

"What?"

"Here you sit feeling bad. Worrying about that guy dying beside you."

"I don't know if it's worrying so much but, yeah, I'm thinking about it."

"Well, whatever you choose to call it, Shawn, how is reading from that book really going to make the slightest bit of difference?"

Shawn grinned.

"It makes me feel better. I see what it says about certain problems that I might be having. . . ."

"You're worrying."

"Okay, yeah, I'm worrying."

"And that makes you stop worrying?" Luke asked sarcastically. "It explains why Billy the Kid got blown away instead of you, the gunner, the one they were aiming at?"

Instead of answering, Shawn opened to the Gospel of John. "Here's what Jesus said, Luke: 'I am telling you the truth: when you were young, you used to get ready and go anywhere you wanted to; but when you are old, you will stretch out your hands and someone else will tie you up and take you where you don't want to go.'

"He was saying Peter would also die on a cross. Then Peter turned and saw John and said: 'Lord, what about this man?' And Jesus answered him: 'If I want him to live until I come, what is that to you? Follow me!' "

Luke shrugged. "So."

"He's telling Peter, and me, that it's basically none of our bloody business what he does with someone else; we're just to follow Jesus."

"Is Peter supposed to have really died that way?"

"He grew to be an old man and was crucified, but he asked to be crucified upside down because he said that he was unworthy to die like the Lord."

The popping of helicopter rotors turned Luke's head. A shout came from the center of the perimeter.

"Guns up!"

Shawn sprang to his feet, grabbed the M60 and three belts of

104

ammo, and ran toward the CP. The Chief stood beside the lieutenant. Luke propped his can of food against a rock, grabbed his rifle and three belts of ammo, and chased after Shawn.

"Where, Chief?" Shawn shouted as he neared the CP.

"Goody saw movement in the brush on that small hill over there!" Chief pointed to a bump on the landscape two hundred meters to the south. Shawn ran past the lieutenant, Chip, Doc, and the Chief. He ran over the crown of their small hill and down the slight slope until he came to Birdman and Goody. They were flat on their stomachs, pointing straight ahead. Shawn hit the ground and aimed at the invisible target.

"Can ya see 'em?" Goody's Texas twang was crisp and clear as a cowbell. His droopy mustache matched his cowboy voice perfectly.

"No. I don't see anything," Shawn said.

"What do we got?" Luke slid in beside Shawn. He linked up a belt to the fifty-round strip belt and held the ammo out of the mud with both hands.

"I don't know yet." Shawn searched the green hill with his gun sight. Nothing. The popping of the chopper rotors grew louder.

Goody pulled his chin off the stock of the M16 and spit a shot of tobacco juice straight ahead. "If they're gonna shoot, they'll wait'll she lands." He nudged Birdman to his right. "Ain't that right, Birdman?"

"I 'magine so, Goody."

The old Korean-era H34-D circled once and dropped like a big ugly grasshopper. Its three tires sank into the mud just beside the CP. An instant later Russian AK-47 rifles cracked from the small hill. Shawn fired. His tracers sputtered into the green hill. Goody and Birdman opened up single-shot, quickly emptying a clip of eighteen rounds apiece and jamming in another clip with barely a loss of rhythm.

Someone cursed the Marine Corps. Shawn glanced back at the chopper. A tall, lanky Marine jumped out of the old chopper as it bounced once and labored into the air. White muzzle flashes spat from the green brush along the ridge of the enemy hill. Shawn lay on the trigger for what felt forever. Orange tracers from the M60 raked across the enemy ridge line.

Then it was over. Shawn tingled from the vibration of the gun. He searched the hill again through his gun sight. Nothing moved.

Only stillness in the steady drizzle. He looked at Luke. Luke smiled.

"Good shooting. I think you knocked out two of those muzzle flashes."

Goody spit a shot of dark brown juice toward the enemy hill and came up on an elbow to look over Luke's prone body. His jaw bulged to one side with his chew.

"Weren't bad, boot." He winked at Shawn. Shawn felt like he did well. And Goody didn't seem to blame him for Billy the Kid's death. Shawn thanked God for that.

"Now what about it, Goody?" Birdman sat up on the other side of the Texan. He leaned on his rifle butt in the mud. "You givin' me your sister's address or not?" Birdman sounded mad.

"There ain't no dad-blamed way I'd let my baby sister date no Marine!"

"Now how you gonna be, Goody? That's just plain foul!" Birdman whistled, sharp and loud. His high cheekbones looked even bonier when he sulked.

Goody shook his head no. "There ain't no way, dude! No green-machine Marine is gonna amble any closer than Dallas to my little Bonnie Kay; I don't care if it was the duke himself!"

"That's real raw, Goody. Ya save a guy's life and how's he treat you? Real raw, bro."

The rain dripping off Birdman's long, skinny nose, combined with his brooding face, made it look like he was crying.

Goody looked at him, closed his eyes, and shook his head no. "She ain't even seein' no movie with Marines in it!"

Shawn laughed. "What you got against Marines, Goody?"

"We ain't no good! We drink, fight, chase whores. Ain't no way no Girene gets my sister's address. No ex-Marines, no future Marines, no boy whose father were a Marine! Noooo way!"

Birdman looked dejectedly at the ground and shook his head slowly from side to side. "That's raw, bro, real raw."

"What does Bonnie Kay look like, Goody?" Luke asked.

"Noooo!" Goody groaned, turned his head, and spit another shot of juice. "Ain't no Marine even lookin' at a likeness of Bonnie Kay."

"I saw her." Birdman's narrow eyes opened wide then closed to a squint as he strained to describe Bonnie Kay's beauty. "She's like a perfect chick. Long blond hair, perfect face, God! What a body!" His voice rose.

"Me and yooz'r goin' to fightin' real soon, here!" Goody's neck seemed to stretch longer with each word.

"Real raw, Goody," Birdman said sadly as he drooped back into his depressed look.

"Saddle up!" The call echoed around the muddy hill.

The hump was on. The weight of Shawn's gear pushed his shoulders forward like an old man's. It was over a hundred pounds, counting the machine gun. With the rain the gear got heavier until your pack straps would rip the tops of your shoulders right through the flak jacket.

The column struggled along the side of a steep mountain. A dark jungle ravine was below. Kayto stopped ahead of Shawn. He pulled off a one-hundred-round belt of machine-gun ammo, tossed it into the ravine below, and continued on. Shawn was stunned.

"What are you doing?"

Kayto looked over his shoulder. "Too much weight." He sounded unconcerned.

An hour later Kayto did the same thing with his E-tool.

Shawn wondered what would happen if they ever had to dig in. Two hours later he pondered dropping his own E-tool along the trail. He couldn't do it.

The new man's name was Neader. He was ugly, his face was scarred, his skin was furrowed and oily, and his dark eyes looked permanently angry. He had the tattoo of a giant black spider across his back with two of the legs creeping all the way over his shoulders and joining at the base of his throat. He was distant and unfriendly. He wouldn't say where he was from, but the nasal quality of his voice hinted at New Jersey. He'd been given the choice of the Marines or prison, for what crime he wouldn't say. Scuttlebutt said he may have fragged a lieutenant in his last outfit, but no one could prove it.

PFC Neader was put in a fire team with Kayto and Cager, who were taken out of the gun team and sent back to Murph's squad. By Neader's third day with the platoon, Kayto complained his C-ration peaches and poundcake had been stolen. Peaches and poundcake were worth more than gold. Somehow the peaches always tasted cool, even when it was a hundred and twenty degrees. Then it was Cager's Tabasco sauce that he had received with his last care package from the world. Cager had the broad shoulders and back of a strong man. He wasn't tall but he was powerfully built. And he wasn't a fool. He knew he could beat the Tabasco sauce out of Neader, but making an enemy in the bush could be suicide. Kayto and Cager let it drop.

Late in the afternoon of February 10 the platoon circled into a perimeter on the east bank of the Ta Trach River, seven miles west of Phu Bai in Thua Thien Province. The rain eased up and slowed to a steady drizzle. It seemed as if it never actually stopped raining. The downpour just changed velocity. A steep forest-covered mountain looked down on the small clearing where the men rested.

Chip tossed out a green smoke grenade. A sleek Huey gunship circled above. Two passes. No shots. Then a CH-46 troop helicopter swooped out of the gray sky as if from nowhere. Within moments the platoon of mud-soaked men loaded on.

Chip the radioman squeezed in between Luke and Shawn as the chopper got airborne. He chewed fast on his bubble gum like he was nervous. He pushed his glasses back up his small wet nose and looked at Shawn.

"Hue City."

CHAPTER SIX

Hue City

The helicopter began to circle the Phu Bai airstrip. Through the porthole over his shoulder Shawn could see two more CH-46 helicopters, one circling two hundred meters behind the other. He leaned closer to the glass. Two more choppers were now visible against the gray-white sky. His stomach lifted like it always did on a roller coaster just before the plunge. Eyes popped open. Marines clutched their rifles. The helicopter seemed to stop a few feet above the landing pad, then set down with no bounce. The rear ramp dropped. Sergeant Major O'Connel stood at the bottom of the ramp in full battle gear and holding a pump shotgun.

"Move it, Marines!" Sergeant Ghosthorse shouted the tired men out of the helicopter.

"Move it, Marines!" Sergeant Major O'Connel echoed into the chopper. "Form up over here, Lieutenant!" He pointed toward a long column of mud-covered Marines lining the edge of the corrugated-steel landing pad.

The rain felt cold from the wind of the helicopter rotors as Shawn moved toward the end of the column of hardened faces. He tried not to stare, not to look too boot. Some sharpened bayonets while others squeezed oil onto the bolts of rifles from small green plastic bottles. One bearded Marine squatted with his grenade launcher between his legs as he calmly worked a whetstone across the already razor-sharp shovel end of his E-tool.

Shawn fell in line behind Luke. Another chopper load of Marines landed to their right.

A young Marine with a pencil and notepad sat on his helmet looking at Luke. "This looks big, bro. How do you spell it?"

Luke closed his brown eye and rubbed his chin thoughtfully, "Someplace called Way, only they spell it H-U-E, I think."

Fifteen big deuce-and-a-half trucks began cranking up their diesels at the far end of the airstrip.

"Saddle up!"

"Saddle up!"

"Saddle up!"

The word moved down the column. Then one platoon at a time began climbing aboard the trucks. A few minutes later the convoy passed through the barbed-wire gate of Phu Bai, turned left on Highway One through the village of Phu Bai, and headed north toward Hue City. The last refugees from Hue City and the villages around Hue all the way to Quang Tri Province were straggling south. They carried every possession they could, everything from broken bicycles to squealing pigs. It was like a scene out of an old World War II movie, except for the constant helicopter traffic above. Another chopper ripped by just overhead.

"My Gawd, how many does that make?" Goody asked as another chopper ripped by just above the convoy.

Birdman whistled. "Real meat grinder, bro. That's the twenty-third medevac chopper that I've counted."

"All those choppers are medevacs?" Shawn asked as another helicopter whipped by less than a hundred feet above the road.

"I guar-ron-tee they ain't doin' road traffic reports, boot." Dook gave a knowing nod at Shawn.

"This must be the way cattle feel on the way to the slaughter," Luke said.

"First guy that moos gets the butt end of my rifle," Dusty snapped angrily. His dark eyes darted nervously from a chopper above to the worried faces around him. He pulled his flattened leather wallet from inside his helmet liner and unwrapped the protective plastic. He opened his wallet and stared at a color photo of a dark-haired little girl wearing a sky-blue sweater.

Twenty minutes later the trucks pulled off the road just before reaching a steel bridge that crossed a small canal. Sergeant Major O'Connel ran up to the tailgate of the platoon's truck the instant it stopped.

"Hurry up! Move it, Marines! Second Platoon! You're sittin' ducks!" He unhooked the chain and dropped the tailgate with a loud bang.

"Form up over there to the right of that bridge on this side of the canal! Move it! Dig in a perimeter!" He shoved a shell into his pump shotgun as the men jumped off the truck and ran toward the canal bridge. The other platoons spaced out along the canal facing the old city. A tattoo of explosions, big and small, echoed from the north. Shawn felt a surge of adrenaline and goose bumps shoot down his arms.

"We're on the left flank!" the sergeant major shouted as the diesel engines of the trucks strained to speed back toward Phu Bai before nightfall. "Vietnamese Marines are replacing their airborne troops up ahead. That'll be good. Think we can depend on them."

"Chief." Lieutenant Townsend pointed to his left. "Check each foxhole." He turned back to the old man. "Who we working with, Sergeant Major?"

"We got the Third ARVN Regiment fartin' around on the outskirts of the city, Two-Five and B Company of the First Marines have moved up here." He reached under his flak jacket and pulled a crumpled map out of his shirt pocket. He squatted down on one knee. The lieutenant followed him down and lent a hand, holding one edge of the map.

"Here." The sergeant major pointed to a blue line on the map. "The Second Battalion Fifth Marines moved west, here, paralleling the Perfume River and the city. They took the jail, the province HQ, and the hospital. The last organized resistance south of the river ended yesterday."

"Okay, we got Two-Five here."

The sergeant major looked up from the map with a hard stare. "It's been all house to house, Lieutenant. Some brutal stuff; it wasn't this bad at Inchon."

O'Connel glanced up at the platoon of young faces, digging in with ears cocked to hear any scuttlebutt that might blow their way. He looked back at the map. "See the Citadel, here?" The sergeant major pointed.

"Yeah, I got some specs on it. It's surrounded by a moat, outer wall of dirt and stone thirty feet high and twenty feet thick, and it's supposed to be over two miles square."

"It's already been agreed on. The colonel put out the order that we stop there. The ARVNs get to finish it off for the sake of morale."

Lieutenant Townsend gave an evil grin. "If that gives these useless riceballs some fighting spirit, we'll gift wrap that sucker."

"We won't get much heavy airpower, Lieutenant. They don't want to damage the city."

"Tanks?"

"I heard that Two-Five lost a dozen tanks already."

The lieutenant looked toward the platoons of digging Marines then back at the old sergeant. "Are you with us or are you going with the colonel and the CP?"

"I thought I'd tag along with your Marines, if you don't mind."

"Mind?" Lieutenant Townsend smiled and patted the old Marine on the back. "God knows I'm gonna need you."

"Where's that long-necked Texan of yours?" the sergeant major asked.

"Goody!" the lieutenant shouted over the exploding rockets of an attacking Phantom F-4 jet. The jet streaked overhead at treetop level then shot straight up into the gray sky. "Goody!" he shouted again.

"Yessir!" The Texan stuck his shovel in the mud a few feet to Shawn's right. He spit a stream of brown juice at the ground and walked over to the lieutenant.

"Feel like sharing any of that chew with the old corps?" the sergeant major asked with a grin half hidden under his majestic silver handlebar mustache.

"You bet, Sergeant Major." Goody dug deep into his cargo pocket and pulled out a clear plastic bag wrapped with rubber bands, which he tossed to the sergeant major. The sergeant major removed the rubber bands, pulled out a big pinch, and stuck it in one side of his mouth. He grinned contentedly and tossed the bag back to Goody.

"That Goody is a funny character," Shawn said as he shoveled out a spadeful of muck.

"He does make that chew of his look almost palatable," Luke said.

"Did you hear what the sergeant major said?"

Luke looked over at the old Marine and the lieutenant as they studied the plastic-covered map like two guys cramming for a final exam. "Yes, I heard."

The distant popping of M16s was answered by the louder cracks of Russian AK-47s. The familiar chatter of the M60 machine gun opened up in another part of the smoking city of Hue. Shawn looked across the old steel bridge, then up and down the canal.

"Wonder why we didn't go on across that bridge today,"

Shawn said, staring at the tree-lined streets on the other side of the broad canal.

"Take a guess," Luke muttered.

Shawn sniffed and frowned. "This place smells funny, don't you think?" he asked Luke.

Cager stopped digging and sat on the edge of his fighting hole a few feet to Shawn's left. He pushed his helmet back and let the rain hit him in the face.

"It smells," he said with his Jamaican roll, "but it sure ain't funny, man."

"That's dead gook, boot," Kayto said. He grabbed Cager's shovel and started digging.

"They're sweet now, man," Cager quipped.

"That's a big affirmative, boot," Chip the radioman said quietly as he walked up behind Shawn and Luke. "But get back Jack when it gets hot." Chip made a face like he was sick.

"What's the scuttlebutt, Chipper?" Kayto asked.

Chip knelt down on one knee, blew a bubble, then popped it. "It ain't official, but the word is this ARVN unit found a place just on the outskirts of Hue where Charlie executed about three thousand civilians."

"Get back," Cager said slowly.

"Three thousand?" Luke's mouth fell open with his question.

"Wonder if that reaches the papers back home," Kayto scoffed.

"Get out of Dodge, Gyreene," Chip growled, and walked away.

"Cager," Shawn said.

"Yeah."

"What are Arvins?"

"Army of the Republic of Vietnam. A-R-V-N and it spells useless, man."

"There it is, bro," Kayto said, "They ain't worth a pimple on a Marine's butt!"

The night was a confusion of the colors and sounds of war. No one slept. It made the fireworks display back at the old St. Pete Million-Dollar Pier look like two cents. Green tracers from enemy machine guns shot out of orange fires, arching across the black, rain-swept sky as they chased after the deadly helicopter gunships. Rockets from the gunships sparkled like comets toward the city.

The first shafts of the sun warmed the gray horizon. The rain fell heavily as the black clouds of the northeast monsoon struck the barrier of the Hai Van Mountains and curled back on Hue. It was cold. Shawn felt stiff and water logged.

"Saddle up!" The word came out of the dark corner of the circle of foxholes. Shawn could hear his teeth grinding. Maybe it wasn't cold. Maybe it was his nerves. He slapped himself on the face to stop.

"Follow me!" The Indian's silhouette motioned the gun team toward the narrow steel bridge.

"Pass the word! We got Marines crossing the bridge!" a deep voice called from the darkness ahead.

The platoon gathered, crouching, just off the bridge and mumbled with apprehension. Shawn could feel his heart pounding through his flak jacket. He had never felt such anticipation in his life.

Lieutenant Townsend's voice silenced the mumbling platoon. "When I give the word, I want you to run across that bridge as fast as you can run. Is that clear?" No one spoke. "Okay. Form up a perimeter as soon as you get across."

"Aye, aye, sir," Ghosthorse snapped.

A series of explosions echoed from the city. Shawn felt close to hyperventilating. His eyes bulged to see through the darkness.

"Get ready!"

Shawn tensed until his back ached.

"Go!"

The noise of charging boots on the steel bridge sent adrenaline pounding like liquid dynamite through Shawn's body.

They were dead, Shawn knew it. Every gook from here to Hanoi could hear them coming. The run felt like a mile but Shawn knew it was only one hundred meters at the most. Someone stumbled up ahead. The crash of a helmet bouncing, a plastic rifle sliding across the metal bridge, and a groaning curse. He felt dirt! The end of the bridge. Marines stumbled into a perimeter like scared drunks.

The hasty perimeter didn't last long, though. The Second Platoon moved forward as the rest of Alpha Company crossed the bridge and brought up the rear. Small-arms fire sounded closer and louder. The sickening stench of a rotting human drifted by with a light breeze and Shawn swallowed back the urge to vomit. The sun brought depth to the shapes around him. The platoon moved slowly, in a staggered column, down a narrow street of demolished white blockhouses. At the end of the street the column turned right. A square three-story building stood out in the center of what appeared to be a well-kept city park. Large, old oak trees were scattered about a beautiful green lawn that covered an acre of land. Park benches of iron and wood sat shaded under the oaks.

"Wow, man, this looks civilized," a voice whispered from behind.

"Hey, brother, just like downtown," another Marine quipped.

Shawn searched for movement, too scared to comment.

"Doubletime," a voice ahead turned to pass the word. The men began to run.

They ran straight across the rain-soaked lawn, and up a tier of long marble steps to a row of sandbags three feet high. An M60 barrel rested on the top of the sandbags. Two Marines peeked over and motioned the men past. The platoon jumped over the barricade and ran through the debris of what had once been large, double-glass doors. Dried blood smeared the white-tiled floor. Bullet holes had cracked the beige plaster walls all the way down the twenty-foot hall. Heavy fumes of ether burned Shawn's eyes.

"Halt!" Lieutenant Townsend held up a hand. "This is it for now. Sit down and chow down while you can."

The rest of Alpha Company split up by platoons throughout the hospital. The men sat, played cards, and ate. All day and through the night. Somebody said it was the University Hospital. No one cared.

February 12

The morning began with another run that stopped at the edge of the Perfume River, aqua blue and as wide as the Mississippi. The monsoon rains had filled the ancient river to the top of its banks, and the water was choppy with thousands of tiny whitecaps. Two big LCM landing craft sat along the river's edge, their steel mouths open like sea monsters waiting for food. Marines were the food. Alpha Company hurried into the landing craft. The ride was loud with engine noise, cramped with rifles sticking in ribs. Then came the call: "Incoming!"

The men crouched as bullets rang off the hull like out-of-tune church bells.

115

"Hey, man, we get a ribbon for this!" a faceless voice shouted from the rear of the LCM.

"No way, bro, you gotta land under fire!" another Marine yelled.

An artillery fire mission whistled across the river and rumbled like thunder in the city. Two more bullets rang off the hull.

Goody shifted his chew from one cheek to the other and shouted toward the rear of the landing craft, "By Gawd, boot, them bells yer ahearin' sure ain't horseflies mating on the dad-blamed bulkhead!"

The men laughed, but the laughter was tense, forced.

The LCMs finally reached the other side. The Navy pilot pointed the LCM toward a small dock between two white block-houses. The swift current made the landing craft smash into the dock. Incoming fire stopped as the boat wedged between the houses on the third try. The ramp dropped with a thud, and men ran out of the boat with weapons at port arms. Somebody screamed "Gung ho," then everyone started yelling. They ran past the two houses and into a red-brick street.

"Move out!" someone shouted.

The men charged forward, west through Gai Lon, a village of small white blockhouses, already secured.

"How far can we go without seeing Charlie?" Kayto half sang his question from behind Shawn. The column moved within sight of the outer red-brick walls of the ancient Citadel.

"It looks like a castle," Shawn said aloud. He could see the moat.

Luke glanced over his shoulder five yards ahead. "It probably was."

No one would believe this back home, Shawn thought. How do you tell anyone you charged a castle in 1968? The wall stood a good thirty feet high with battlements spaced every hundred meters along the top. Small-arms fire cracked continuously from the other side of the massive walls. The platoon ran forward down a narrow dirt road and stopped at a twenty-foot wide moat around the Citadel. Two Vietnamese floated facedown in the algae-covered moat.

The lieutenant and the sergeant major ran across a small bridge that looked like a drawbridge. They were met on the other side by an ARVN officer carrying an old M1 carbine. The ARVN pointed back down the road. The lieutenant turned and ran back across the bridge with the sergeant major close behind. They stopped in front of Chip, within ear range of the gun team. Townsend grabbed Chip, spun him around, and pulled the field phone to him.

"Alpha One . . . Alpha One . . . Alpha Two. Over."

"Alpha One . . . Captain Ramsey . . . Go on, Robb."

"This ARVN captain doesn't want us in his compound, skipper. Says we'll draw fire."

"Tell that worthless slimeball that these are United States Marines! We ain't looking for a place to hide! We're here to kick some butt and take some names, mister!"

"Aye, aye, skipper." The lieutenant handed the field phone to Chip. He looked ready for a fight.

A surge of pride swallowed up the anxious fear that Shawn was beginning to feel. Lieutenant Townsend ran back across the bridge. He stopped with his chest in the ARVN's face. The ARVN tried to step back but his left spit-shined boot was pinned under Lieutenant Townsend's muddy right jungle boot. The tall lieutenant looked even bigger as he barked down at his dwarfish counterpart. The cowering ARVN pointed back the way the Marines had come. Lieutenant Townsend turned and hustled back to the column.

"Move out! Back this way!" Lieutenant Townsend grabbed Chip's arm and jogged past the column, pulling Chip along with him. "Doubletime!" he shouted.

The men ran at doubletime in column, spaced ten yards apart. Back down the dirt road, then down a narrow brick street with one-story French-style houses. Most of the white stucco houses had garage ports on the side with old vintage 1945 to 1950 automobiles that seemed in remarkably good condition. Some had flat tires or collapsed roofs from the weight of bombed garage ports, but none looked rusty and the big chrome bumpers and grillwork on each one shone like new.

The column turned at the dead end of the street, between two demolished houses and up an embankment. Railroad tracks paralleled the road on the other side. Three dead, green-clad NVA soldiers lay rotting just on the edge of the tracks. Shawn froze for a moment to stare. One was facedown in the mud. The other two were spread-eagled on their backs, their mouths open in a silent scream. Both were bucktoothed and young.

"Move it!" the Chief barked from just ahead. Shawn pulled his stare from the dead enemy and hustled forward.

The column moved quickly along the tracks for a hundred

117

meters, then broke across the tracks. They crossed a rice paddy of foot-deep mud, leeches, and water. On the other side of the paddy a tree line rimmed the northern corner of the once-busy city. Through the thin tree line, rows of small white houses formed a Vietnamese suburbia. Two Huey gunships dove and circled over the little neighborhood. They dropped low like angry bees, stinging with their sizzling rockets then darting away as green enemy machine-gun tracers shot into the gray sky after them.

The platoon moved through the tree line with Lieutenant Townsend walking point. The men rounded the corner of the first house on a narrow brick street and walked in a scattered column down the center. Bomb craters pockmarked the road. It could have been a village in France. Once-lovely archways were now riddled with bullet holes. South Vietnamese soldiers peeked from open windows with curious smiles as the American Marines walked past. Shawn sensed they knew something he didn't. It irritated him; why, he wasn't sure, but their smiles or grins or whatever they were seemed almost sinister. From the balcony of a bullet-riddled two-story house, an ARVN stood up behind an old .30-caliber machine gun and grinned down.

"Jake," the lieutenant called out.

"Yo."

"Take the point."

Someone farther back started humming the theme from the television show "Combat." Cager picked up on it. Then Kayto. Shawn found himself humming along. Most of the platoon started humming. Luke looked over his shoulder at Shawn and shrugged.

"Why not?" He began to hum too.

"I always loved that show," Shawn said.

"Where is Vic Morrow when you need him?" Luke scoffed.

Suddenly, Shawn wanted to pray so bad it hurt. His heart pushed blood to his ears until they felt hot. Will I die here, Lord?

The narrow street took an L turn to the right, then at the end, a left. Shakey Jake, the nervous point man, ran to the corner of a beige house. He peeked around. The Second Platoon ran forward to the side wall of the house and crouched down one behind the other.

"Radio up!"

Chip hustled over to the lieutenant and the old sergeant major. Lieutenant Townsend grabbed the field phone off Chip's PRC-

25 backpack. A few moments later Chip came back down the line repeating the word.

"First, Third, and Weapons Platoon are moving up the streets on our flanks, so don't blow 'em away!"

"Fire in the hole!" Shakey Jake yelled. Jake pulled the pin on a grenade, hunched down, gripping tight to the spoon, and crept around the corner. An instant later he jumped back around the corner, flattened against the wall with a grimace on his face, and covered his ears with both hands. The wall shook with the explosion. Bits of dirt and cement jarred from the roof and walls.

"Guns up!"

Shawn's stomach tightened. He took a deep breath, stood up clutching the M60, and ran forward to the lieutenant. Luke followed. They crouched down beside Lieutenant Townsend, who kneeled behind Jake. The loud cracks of Russian AK-47s opened up somewhere nearby. The lieutenant tapped the wall of the beige house with his thumb.

"I want the gun set up in here. See that house straight across the street?" The lieutenant leaned out away from the wall and pointed.

"Yes, sir," Shawn said.

The house looked abandoned. It had no door and only one round window. Beside it was another small blockhouse about ten feet away. A fifty-five-gallon black drum sat on the corner of the second house, catching rainwater draining off the tile roof.

"I'm sending Dusty's fire team across the street to secure that house with the round window," the lieutenant said. "See it? The house with the fifty-five-gallon drum on the front corner."

Shawn leaned away from the wall to get a better view. "Yes, sir."

"All right. Now the third house down from that one is a two-story job. It's got a little balcony upstairs with a white curtain hanging over a doorway leading onto the balcony."

"West side, facing the street?" Luke asked.

"Yes. Now, Jake said he saw movement behind that curtain, so keep an eye on it."

"Got it, Lieutenant," Shawn said. He looked at Luke. "Ready?"

Luke tapped the magazine of his M16. "I better go first; there might be a Charlie still in there. I doubt that you can quick-draw with that cannon."

"Okay."

Shawn moved against the wall as Luke skirted around the three Marines. The rain stopped and the air turned stuffy and hot. Luke peeked around the corner and looked back at Shawn. His two-tone eyes were filled with fear.

Shawn wiped the stinging sweat from his eyes and pushed off after Luke. They ran past an open window. Luke scurried through the front doorway with Shawn close behind. The room was cloudy with dust from the grenade explosion. There was a two-foot square hole in the wood floor where the grenade had blown. Luke searched the dusty room with his rifle, then moved slowly toward the back room of the two-room house. A broken bamboo chair and a straw mat seemed to be the only furniture left. Luke jumped through the doorway to the back room. He looked back out and signaled thumbs-up. Shawn moved to the window. He folded back the bipod legs of the M60 and laid the barrel on the wooden windowsill. He aimed at a small round window just to the left of the open doorway in the white block-house across the street.

"Ready, Lieutenant!"

A ripping explosion from farther down the street shook the floor beneath Shawn. Luke tore off a belt of ammo and linked it to the fifty-round strip belt that was already in the gun.

"Hold your fire! Smitty's comin' in!" The chunky Marine hustled past the window and dove through the open door. He rolled to his right until he stopped at Luke's feet. "I'll fire through the door." His words came in labored gasps.

Smitty's chubby cheeks were always flushed red but they looked redder than usual. He stayed on his back as he broke the M79 grenade launcher, the blooper gun, in half like a mini-sawed-off shotgun. He pulled a blue-tipped round out of the ammo pouch. The blooper gun fired a forty-millimeter round that was about three inches long and a couple of inches in diameter.

"What are you doing?" Luke asked.

"I stole this one from the Army." Smitty tucked the blue-tipped round back in the pouch on his cartridge belt and gave it a pat. He pulled out another one and loaded it. "This one is HP, that other one's for personnel." He snapped the barrel back, rolled to the edge of the doorway, and aimed at the open door-way across the street. "Man, I sure feel bad for old Dusty," he said, his jaw against the wood stock of his M79.

120

"Yeah," Luke said, his eyes fixed on the house across the street. "He should be back in the rear with twenty days left."

"Can you see anything?" Shawn asked.

"No," Smitty grumbled.

"Open fire! When ready!" the lieutenant's shout from the side of the house caught Shawn by surprise. He sighted in on the round window straight across the street.

Bloop! Smitty fired. A small white explosion shot dust and debris from the open door across the street. Shawn squeezed the trigger. The round window exploded into glass, wood, and hunks of cement.

"Friendlies crossing!" someone shouted.

Dusty ran across the street just to the left of Shawn's stream of tracers, hunching forward, rifle in his left hand and a grenade in his right. He slid in behind a charred telephone pole, looked back, and held up a hand. Shawn stopped firing. Kayto and Cager darted across the street, jumped over a line of rocks that served as a curb, and flattened out in the muddy ten-foot-square front yard.

Dusty took three steps into the tiny yard and threw the grenade through the front door. He dove to the ground. Smoke and fire exploded through the window and open doorway. Kayto and Cager ran through the door firing. An anxious silence came from the house.

Kayto's head peeked back through the doorway like a cautious turtle coming out of his shell. "All clear!" He waved Dusty forward.

Dusty got to his feet and ran for the safety of the house. The automatic clamor of a heavy machine gun boomed from Shawn's right. Dusty dove through the door as pieces of the blockhouse exploded away in chunks.

"That's a .50-cal, man!" Smitty yelled, and rolled away from the door.

"Where is he?" Shawn leaned forward in the window to see down the street.

Smitty rolled back to take a look out of the doorway. "I can't see him."

Luke peeked over the windowsill. "He must be on our side of the street. God." He slumped back down. He looked pale.

"What's wrong?" Smitty looked up from the floor.

"They got Dusty." Luke spoke in a dry monotone voice. He

stared down at the dirty wood floor and sagged forward as if he were under a mountainous weight of despair.

Shawn looked out the window. Dusty was flat on his stomach and motionless just inside the doorway of the house across the street. His muddy jungle boots hung over the threshold. A brackish taste filled Shawn's mouth. He wanted to spit but there wasn't any saliva.

"Corpsman up!" Cager screamed, his voice wavering as if in agony.

Kayto and Cager grabbed Dusty's prone body under the arms and dragged him away from the open door.

"Give me cover!" Doc screamed from the corner of the house, then stepped out far enough to shout through Shawn's window. "Here I go. Guns!"

Shawn sent a stream of tracers into the next three houses along the narrow street. Doc's long, gangly legs had him across in three giant strides. He dove the final five yards, landing just inside the door with his feet hanging out. The big enemy gun opened up again. Its rhythm of fire sounded much slower than the M60 but louder, booming out each heavy round. Again pieces of the small white house tore away in large chunks. Shawn stopped firing and stared across the street. Cager looked around the edge of the splintered door jamb as Doc crawled out of sight. Cager's shining black face glistened with sweat and strain.

"Knock out that fifty, Lieutenant!" We got rounds comin' right through the cement walls, man, like they ain't here!''

"Where is he?" Townsend shouted back.

"He's firing from the east side of the street! Two houses down from you!"

"Guns up!" Lieutenant Townsend shouted from the corner to Shawn's left. "Get across the street and put some fire on that fifty!"

Shawn pulled the gun out of the window and threw a long belt of ammo over his shoulder.

"Ready, Luke? I'll set the gun up between Cager's house and the next one!"

Luke gathered up four hundred rounds that he had piled beside the gun. He threw the four belts over his left shoulder, grabbed his rifle, and stood up. "Fourth and goal from the ten yard line," he said through gritted teeth. His two-tone eyes sparkled under a current of anger.

122

"Yeah. Gung ho, brother," Shawn said quietly, then turned and shouted across the street, "Cager!"

Cager's glistening face peeped out at the bottom of the doorway. "Yeah, man."

"Hold your fire! Here we come! We're going for the drum on the corner of the house next door!"

Cager signaled a thumbs-up and crawled out far enough to get an angle of fire at the enemy gun. Shawn ran through the door. His heart and his breath seemed to stop. The sprint felt agonizingly slow under the burden of his gear. An eternity later he ran between the two battered homes and flattened against the side of the house next to Cager's. He rolled behind the fifty-five-gallon drum that sat at the front corner. Luke slid in at Shawn's feet like he was stealing second base.

Shawn pulled down the bipod legs of the machine gun. He looked around the drum. Nothing. No movement. No incoming fire.

He stretched out prone and took aim at the third house down on the east side of the street. It had a front porch and looked slightly larger than the houses beside it. A ten-meter gap separated each house on the street. Fallen telephone cables were draped through trees singed black by the fire of earlier mortar attacks. Every house had been hit. Some weren't too bad, others were nothing but rubble. Shawn wondered why they hadn't just flattened the whole place.

A burst of fire from the enemy .50-caliber machine gun cut his thoughts short. Luke yanked Shawn behind the corner of the house. The first rounds hit high, splintering away big chunks of cement and slapping with terrifying force against the side of Cager's house.

Shawn rolled on to his side as the fifty stopped firing. "I saw him, Luke! He's in that house with the porch out front! I saw his flash comin' out of the porch!"

"He saw us too, man!"

Shawn rolled out again, just enough to aim around the drum. The enemy machine gun was on about a forty-five-degree angle across the street to Shawn's left. The first drops of more rain beaded up on the oil-coated barrel as he squeezed off a twenty-round burst. Orange tracers disappeared into the darkness under the porch roof. Suddenly the frightening muzzle flash of the .50-caliber machine gun erupted from the inner darkness of the porch. Mud and cement exploded around Shawn and Luke. Dirt

123

stung Shawn's face like hot grease. Shawn fired again, this time gripping the trigger through twenty, then fifty, then a hundred rounds.

The gun jammed into silence. Shawn pulled back the cocking-lever handle. Luke wiped mud from his hands on Shawn's pack, then flipped open the feed cover, ripped out the jammed round, reloaded, and snapped and latched the cover. Shawn pushed the gun around the drum again. He backhanded the water from his eyes, took aim, and fired.

"Comin' over!" Smitty yelled as he broke into a hunched-over sprint from the beige house. He cleared the curb, ran through the muddy front lawn, and dove over the cringing gunners. He landed like a great water balloon. Mud splashed against the sides of both houses. Shawn ceased fire and pulled back behind the corner of the house. M16s opened up from Cager's house. The answer was quick from the .50-caliber. Big pieces of Cager's house exploded away under the power of the heavy gun. The firing stopped.

Smitty crawled forward and peeked around the corner. "Where is it?" he asked, his chubby face flushed red.

Shawn nodded toward the enemy position. "See the house with the porch?"

"Third house down?"

"Yeah."

"He's in the porch."

Shawn leaned back, resting his pack against the wall. He stared straight ahead at the huge bullet holes in the side of Cager's house. A few had blown clean through the concrete block. He looked to his right. A headless dog lay sprawled in a shallow mud puddle.

"Hey." Shawn motioned toward the dead dog. "Is anybody covering our rear?" He looked at Luke, then Smitty. Luke shrugged. Smitty shrugged.

"Good idea," Luke mumbled. He got to his feet and moved to the back corner of the house. When he saw the dead dog, he held his nose, dropped to one knee, peeked around the corner with his M16 at the ready, then pulled back and signaled a thumbs-up.

"I'm gonna put a round in that porch." Smitty said.

The *bloop* of Smitty's grenade launcher echoed between the houses. Shawn leaned out to see the shot. A loud white flash erupted from the porch as the round exploded. An instant later

124

the .50-caliber returned fire. Pieces of cement burst from the corner over Shawn's head. Smitty looked up then jerked back, wild-eyed, his face bleeding under both eyes.

"You okay, Smitty?"

"Yeah, I think so." Smitty wiped his hand across his face and looked at the blood. "I'm okay. Cement cuts."

"McClellan!" the lieutenant shouted through a lull in the firing.

"Over here!" Shawn yelled.

"McClellan!" Chip peeked around the lieutenant. He held his PRC-25 radio field phone. "I got a gunship coming in with rockets! Show him which house . . ."

Another blast of fire from the enemy gun drowned out Chip's voice. Shawn signaled with a thumbs-up then turned to Smitty. "You okay?"

"Yeah, this probably won't even get me a Heart."

"Go trade places with Luke. I need an A-gunner."

Smitty jumped to his feet and ran to the opposite end of the house. A moment later Luke splashed in beside Shawn.

"I gotta point out that fifty for a Huey. Hold the ammo out of the mud."

Luke stretched out on his stomach to Shawn's right. He tossed the long ammo belt over his shoulder so it could lie dry on his back.

"Hey, Chip!" the corpsman shouted from Cager's house. "We need a medevac, ASAP!"

Shawn gritted his teeth. He knew it was for Dusty. He closed his eyes and prayed. Dusty's too short to die, God. Please, Jesus, don't let him die. Let him make it home after coming so far.

The popping sound of a helicopter gunship banking sharply echoed up and down the narrow street. The chopper buzzed low overhead then lifted high, turned, and dove. Shawn squeezed the trigger. His heart pounded as fast as the vibrating gun. Orange tracers painted a golden arrow pointing to the porch of the enemy house. His whole body vibrated to the powerful rhythm of the gun. All he could feel and see and hear was the power of the M60. Four rockets smoked a fiery trail through the gray sky. The helicopter broke away at the last instant, peeling skyward like an old World War II fighter plane. The enemy house shook like a volcano had erupted from inside. Smoke and debris shot into the air. Hunks of concrete crashed into the street with crushing thumps. Smitty leaned around Luke, knelt on one knee,

125

and aimed down his short barrel. *Bloop!* A smallish explosion shot from the burning rubble.

"Rake it over, Shawn!" Smitty yelled.

"Don't waste ammo," Luke said.

"He's history," Shawn answered without looking away from the burning house.

"Always make sure, boot," Smitty snapped angrily. He broke open his M79 and shoved in another round. "I've seen 'em open up when they didn't have any legs left! They get so doped up they don't even know they're dead!"

Smitty closed his fat little shotgun-like weapon and took aim again. *Bloop!* He jerked slightly with the recoil. The round exploded. Shawn looked at Luke as if to ask his opinion. Luke shook his head no.

"Chip!" Doc shouted again. "Call off that medevac."

Shawn was stunned. No need for a medevac. Dusty was dead. He looked at Luke and tried to swallow the lump swelling up in his throat. Luke stared at the smoldering ruins. He picked up his rifle, stood behind the drum, and emptied a twenty-round clip into the enemy house. He knelt down on one knee with a blank stare that Shawn had never before seen on Luke's face.

The Chief slid around the corner of the beige house. He moved like a cat past the front, then jumped against the side wall of the next house, which was white and had a bamboo door. The Chief was directly across the street from the gun team. He pulled a grenade pin, held the spoon tight, stepped around the corner of the second house, and tossed the frag through a window. He flattened out back around the corner as smoke and debris shot through every opening. Goody, Dook, Neader, and Birdman ran around the lieutenant one at a time as the Chief kicked open the bamboo-slat door and starting firing his rifle. He jumped into the house just as a series of shots rang out from the west side of the street. The men scrambled in behind the Chief, bullets ricocheting off the other side of the wall behind them.

"McClellan!" Lieutenant Townsend shouted. "You got Charlie on your side of the street! Two houses down and upstairs!" The lieutenant aimed at the place and fired four shots.

"Guns up!" the Chief shouted from inside the door directly across the street.

Shawn's heart froze. A Phantom jet whisked by overhead. Shawn followed the smoke of its afterburner and for a moment wondered what it was like to be out of the rain, roaring through the silent clouds. Luke jumped to his feet, splashing mud into Shawn's face. Shawn stood up with the M60 on his hip. He looked across the street and bit his lower lip.

"I'm starting to feel like one of those ducks in a shooting arcade," Shawn mumbled.

"Please, do not quack. You ready?"

"If I go down, Luke, you grab up the gun. See ya later, Smitty." Shawn took a deep breath and ran. "Quack, quack!" he yelled.

The loud cracks of the Russian AK-47s sent a shiver down his spine as he lunged for the doorway. The bamboo door opened as he dove the last few feet and landed hard on the dirty wood floor. Luke crashed in a moment later with a groan as he hit the floor beside Shawn.

Shawn rolled over on the gritty floor and looked around the room. Birdman stood leaning against a wall to Shawn's right, picking his long skinny nose. Goody knelt on one knee beside Birdman. He chewed his tobacco faster than usual.

"I want the gun team set up between this house and the blown up one next door where that fifty was." The Indian sergeant sounded mad. "Make sure the gook on that fifty is dead. We need fire on that two-story house across the street. Move it, Marines!"

"They obviously did not stress hospitality on that reservation." Luke's words came so slowly that Shawn thought the Chief would boot him through the door before he finished.

"Hold on, Chief," Dook said as he leaned his M14 rifle against the wall under a window. The window faced the street to the left of the doorway. It had been considerably enlarged by some type of explosion and was now less square than octagonal. Dook pulled an LAAW from around his neck.

"What are you doing?" Sergeant Ghosthorse barked.

"How 'bout I put a LAAW round in that house before the gunner makes a run for it. I guar-ron-tee that'll slow things down on that end." Dook gave the three-foot long cardboard cylinder of the light anti-armor weapon a friendly pat. He pulled up the plastic sight. It was a use-it-once-and-throw-it-away rocket launcher.

"No. Save it. We might need it later."

Neader, the new man with the bad reputation, lit a cigarette in one corner of the empty room then laughed. "Blow 'em up, man!" he yelled.

Chief turned his stone face to Neader. "Why aren't you over there with Cager and Kayto? You're in Dusty's squad."

Neader's angry eyes stared straight into the Chief's. "Nobody told me to go, man."

"Go!" the Chief snapped. The muscles in his neck flexed.

Neader gave his ugly face a nervous scratch. He took a last puff of his cigarette and threw it angrily to the floor. "No sweat, man." He got to his feet. He moved to the door and shouted, "Cager! I'm comin' in!" He darted across the street. Russian AK-47s opened up. Neader dove through the door of Cager's house unscathed. The shooting stopped.

"Guns up!" Chief barked.

Shawn felt exhilarated each time he heard that call. Emotions he never knew he had swelled up from deep inside until the fear was swept away and all that remained was a rush of adrenaline and a bizarre thrill with each life-or-death situation. He gave no thought to screaming, but somewhere as if from far away he heard himself yell, "Yeeehaiii!" as he burst through the door.

He ran to the side of the house next door where the .50-caliber gun had been. The porch was gone, along with most of the roof and the back of the house, though parts of the roof still burned hot through the drizzle. Most of the side wall was still intact. Luke slapped up against the side wall just behind Shawn. Smitty waved from behind the drum, straight across the street.

Shawn peeked around the corner at the two-story house on the other side of the street. It was next door to Smitty's. The front door was barricaded waist-high with sandbags, and there was a small square paneless window on either side. The fifteen-foot-long upstairs balcony was intact. Its wooden railing had been painted red. Opening onto it was a small wood-and-glass door with torn white curtains hanging from the top.

"Smitty!" Shawn called out loud, then cringed with the fear that he'd given away his position.

"Yeah!" Smitty yelled.

"You better chuck a frag into that house!"

"The two-story house? I can't reach it from here!"

"No! Not the two-story house! The one you're up against! If there's a gook in there he's got a clean shot at us!"

Smitty signaled with a thumbs-up. He rolled on his side, pulled a grenade off his cartridge belt, and yanked out the pin. He crawled around the corner and lobbed the grenade into an open window. He scrambled back around the drum as the grenade exploded.

"Smitty!" Cager shouted from the doorway where Dusty had been killed. "Comin' in!"

Kayto followed Cager through the doorway. They sprinted between the first two houses on the west side of the street and dove in behind Smitty and the fifty-five-gallon drum. A moment later Neader followed. All four crawled away from the corner drum far enough to open fire. They fired across the street into the smoldering porch where the enemy fifty had been. Shawn flattened against the side wall and turned a frightened face to Luke.

"Must be gooks on the other side of this wall!"

"Still alive?" Luke asked in disbelief as he pulled a grenade off his belt. He pulled the pin, held the spoon, stepped out, and tossed the frag over the wall. The wall shook with the explosion. Cager kept firing. Then Smitty shot another blooper round.

"Cover our back, Luke! I'll open up on that two-story place."

Luke dropped to one knee with his back to Shawn and rifle ready.

Shawn stepped away and fired a twenty-round burst into the bottom of the two-story house. Suddenly the street crisscrossed with green tracers. Two machine guns opened up from the west side of the street from the bottom windows of the two-story house. Automatic-rifle fire shot from the balcony and the roof. Another enemy machine gun opened up from Shawn's right on the east side of the street. Then, just as quickly as the enemy fire had started, it stopped.

Suddenly a hissing sound, like air escaping from an automobile tire, made Shawn cringe; it grew louder and closer. A rocket followed by a trail of smoke ripped into the corner of Smitty's house three feet above the drum. The street quaked from the blast. Shawn turned with the gun and dove toward Luke's back as shrapnel slapped against the walls of the houses. He pulled his face out of Luke's flak jacket and looked across the street. Blue smoke hovered around a large hole in the corner of the house. A cloud of white smoke spread like a ten-foot-square patch of fog. Shawn straightened his helmet, pulled his M60 off the back of Luke's legs, and peeked around the corner again.

Luke took a deep breath. "Man! What was that?"

"Some kind of rocket," Shawn answered with eyes glued to

the patch of fog. Then he heard the call. Just as he knew he would.

"Corpsman! Up!"

The gangly corpsman ran out of the doorway where Dusty had been hit. He darted through the smoke and dove behind the fifty-five-gallon drum. Shawn stared at the smoke until the rain began to push it into the muddy ground. Finally he could see the boots of one of the men lying on his back. The Doc was leaning over the downed Marine, working frantically, grabbing gauze from his canvas bag and stuffing it into the wounded man's stomach.

"We need a medevac!" Doc shouted.

"Got it comin', Doc!" Chip shouted.

Cager and the corpsman got the wounded Marine to a sitting position, then knelt down, shoved a shoulder under each limp arm, and lifted him to his feet. The man's helmet dropped and Shawn could now see who it was: Smitty. His fat cheeks looked pale. His eyes were closed. Cager and Doc locked hands under Smitty's rear end and lifted his dangling boots off the ground in a chair carry.

Kayto waved at Shawn. "Give 'em cover!" he shouted.

Shawn crawled beyond the corner of the house. He was exposed, but it was the only way to fire down the street. He squeezed off a twenty-round burst into the balcony of the two-story house, then raked a stream of bullets across the bottom windows. From the corner of his eye he could see Cager and Doc start across the street, running at an angle toward the beige house. Luke jumped out from behind the corner, knelt down beside Shawn, and emptied a twenty-round clip into the two-story house. His fire was from the hip and erratic, but maybe it made somebody duck. That was all that mattered. Kayto and Neader opened fire from behind the drum. The Chief's squad opened fire too.

Luke rolled back to the corner. Shawn fired again. He fired until the gun went silent. Out of ammunition. He rolled with the M60 back behind the wall. Something stung his face like hot grease. He yelped. Lieutenant Townsend ran out and met Cager and Doc in midstreet. He grabbed Smitty's feet and the three made it to safety behind the beige house.

"You hit?" Luke grabbed Shawn's face. His eyes were wide with concern.

"No. I burned my face on the barrel of the gun." Shawn

130

winced and pushed Luke's hand away from his blistering right cheek. He opened his eyes wide as a thought suddenly struck him. "Luke! Think that's worth a Purple Heart?"

"God! You make me barf, McClellan."

"Well, it was just a thought. I sure would like to get one. Well, you know what I mean."

"I don't believe we are really having this conversation, Mc-Clellan . . ." Five rapid shots from Neader across the street ended Luke's sentence. The enemy reply was swift. A rocket shot from a position farther down the street landed short, exploding in an old crater in the road.

"Comin' in, Kayto!" Dook yelled as he ran across the brick street in a hunched-over, all-out sprint. White muzzle flashes spit from the windows of the two-story house. The whine of a near-miss ricochet sucked the air by Shawn's left ear. Dook dove over Neader and rolled behind the drum to the side of the house. Shawn watched as Dook broke the tape on the small plastic LAAW tube. Shawn had fired the LAAW at Camp Geiger. It was like a mini-bazooka. Dook kneeled on one knee, pulled up the plastic sight, and moved out from the drum. He pulled the trigger. The back blast of fire darkened the wall of the house behind him. The sixty-six-millimeter rocket made a sucking sound as it sped toward the enemy rocket position. A quick explosion. The wet air reeked of sulfur. Dook scratched his hairy face and signaled a casual thumbs-up at Shawn before moving back behind the drum.

"How much ammo we got?" Shawn asked as he pulled a belt off his shoulders.

Luke fingered the two belts crisscrossing his flak jacket to make sure. "I got two belts left."

Shawn flipped up the feed cover of the M60 and laid in the first bullet of a one-hundred-round belt. He looked at Luke. "Well, I only got two hundred left." He closed the feed cover, leaned his back against the wall, and looked across the street at Kayto, Dook, and Neader huddled against the wall behind the black drum. He looked back at Luke. Luke squatted with his butt against the wall. His big funny face was covered with mud. Shawn felt strange seeing Luke this way. Almost guilty. If it wasn't for me, Luke wouldn't be here, he thought. He leaned his head back hard, hitting his helmet against the wall. Enough of that crap, he told himself; I'll be dead if I don't concentrate on what I'm doing.

One of the old Korean-era helicopters lumbered down behind the tree line separating the houses from the rice paddy field. The two funny eyes painted on the nose seemed to help the old bird find its way. Chip had thrown out a red smoke grenade to mark the spot. Luke nudged Shawn's attention away from the medevac.

"Smitty must be alive." Luke sounded hopeful.

"Yeah," Shawn said. "What are we supposed to do?"

"Got me. It's suicide to go down this street!"

"I'm scared, Luke." Shawn wiped salty sweat and grit from his lips. His face felt numb. His green eyes burned from the strain of trying to see everything.

Luke punched him hard in the shoulder. "Wake up!" Their eyes met.

"Yeah. Yeah."

"Incredible deduction!" Luke said, his bushy eyebrows lifted higher on his forehead than usual. "Go on with it!" he growled.

"With what?"

"You know perfectly well what. Your mumbo-jumbo." Luke looked to his right and then left; his rifle was nervous and ready.

"What mumbo-jumbo?"

Luke tilted his head and looked at Shawn with clear irritation on his big oval face. "Pray." He forced the word between clenched teeth. Shawn's mouth fell open but no words came. Luke's face contorted as if in pain. "Don't give me that stupid look. Hurry up!" Luke motioned with his right hand like he was shooing away a fly. "Do whatever makes you feel steady."

"Okay," Shawn mumbled.

He wasn't sure what had just taken place, but for some reason he felt good about it. He stared toward the street, trying to clear his mind enough to pray, but he was too hyper to think any deeper than a three-word prayer. Jesus, please help. A few moments passed with only the staccato of small-arms fire coming from another part of the city. The clouds grew darker. It started raining harder.

"Well?" Luke said.

Shawn turned back to face him. "Well, what?"

"Well, my hearing is flawless and I have yet to hear a word."

"You don't have to say a prayer out loud." Shawn paused and wondered if he should even try to explain. "God hears our thoughts."

"Of course." A hint of sarcasm came through Luke's tone.

"Of course what?"

"You better scream at the top of your lungs. What would God be doing here, the armpit of the world."

"McClellan!" someone shouted.

"Yeah!" Shawn yelled.

"We got a Huey coming in on that two-story house!" It was Chip the radioman. "Show him where it is when I give the word!"

"Right!" Shawn crawled into the street far enough to get an angle of fire on the two-story house. Neader opened up across the street at a target to Shawn's right. Shawn looked back at Luke, who was covering their rear. "Luke!"

"Yeah!"

"Neader keeps shooting at something just to my right."

Luke nodded.

"Guns! She's comin' in!" Chip shouted.

Shawn squeezed. Orange tracers shot into the first-floor window like a big pointer stick. Shawn raked a steady stream of bullets across the sandbagged door and into the second window on the first floor. A loud *whoosh* shot from the sky. Then another. Like giant sparklers two rockets flashed down to the front of the two-story house. Shawn jerked back behind the wall. Rocks, wood, smoke, and fire filled the street. Cracking AKs opened up on the Huey gunship. The helicopter swooped low over the street then sped away. Two more enemy machine guns from farther down the street sent a hail of green tracers into the gray, rainy sky.

Shawn looked up. The Huey lurched with each hit like a bird trying not to fall. A rocket streaked just beneath the gunship, arching over the trees beyond. Black smoke billowed from the helicopter's rear rotor as she disappeared from sight.

The sandbagged door of the two-story house was gone. A gaping hole that almost formed an archway had been blown out of the front of the house. Two dead NVA soldiers lay half covered by debris four feet in front of the house, near the curb. The bent barrel of an old .30-caliber machine gun lay in the middle of the street. The NVA opened fire. White muzzle flashes spit from the balcony of the two-story house.

Shawn pulled the M60 back, got to his knees, and aimed it like a rifle at the balcony. His tracers hit low. He lifted his aim. The red wood balcony began splintering into pieces until one four-foot section broke away. It tumbled to the ground, landing with a heavy thump on one of the dead NVA soldiers below. Shawn stopped firing. He pulled back. Bullets thudded and ricocheted around him.

"I'm out of ammo, Luke!"

"This is it." Luke handed Shawn two belts of one hundred rounds each.

Shawn grabbed both. He threw one over his shoulder then lifted the feed cover of the machine gun and put in the first round.

"Lay down some fire!" the Chief shouted.

Shawn leaned on one knee and slowly peeked around the corner. He aimed at the balcony and opened fire. Shawn felt the splash of mud and water and knew that the Chief had rolled in beside Luke. He ceased fire and ducked back behind the wall. He looked past Luke to the big Indian, now squatting with his helmet off. His breathing came hard and fast. His thick glasses were smeared with mud and water. He pulled the glasses off and cleaned the lenses with a small, olive-green cloth that he kept inside his helmet liner.

"We're pulling back." His piercing black eyes looked angry. He put his glasses on, tucked the cloth in his helmet liner, and slapped the steel pot on his head.

Luke turned to Shawn. He did his Groucho eyebrows and grinned. "This is an outstanding command decision."

"Shut up, boot," Ghosthorse snapped.

"Sorry, Chief," Luke said.

"Kayto, Neader! Dook!" The Chief leaned forward like a sprinter ready for the shot. "Give me cover, I'm comin' over!"

"I thought you said we're pulling back," Shawn said.

"Gotta get Dusty. We don't leave Marines behind. Lay down some fire."

Shawn turned back to the street. He felt sick about Dusty. He remembered the photo of the little girl in the blue sweater. Neader opened fire. Shawn leaned away from the corner of the wall and squeezed off a burst at the two-story house. The Chief was across the street in six quick strides. He dove in headfirst, flying past Kayto, Neader, and Dook. A moment later the three ran back to Dusty's house. They scrambled through the doorway like madmen. Then Dook darted out of the house with three rifles under his arm. He was across the street before the Chief's voice boomed through the door.

"Guns!"

The Indian came out first. He struggled to hold the weight of the dead Marine by one end of a muddy green poncho. Neader clutched at the other end with both hands. Dusty's boots dangled limp and lifeless from Neader's end of the poncho. Shawn opened fire, spraying bullets up and down the two-story house.

"Cease fire! Shawn! Cease fire!" Luke shouted as he grabbed hold of Shawn's pack and dragged him back behind the wall.

"Guns! Pull back to that next house with Birdman's fire team!" Lieutenant Townsend shouted from the corner of the beige house.

"Right! Birdman! Hold your fire! We're comin' in!"

A loud, sharp whistle that sounded like someone calling a dog was Birdman's answer. Shawn elbowed Luke and took off. He could hear enemy rifles open up. With each furious stride he felt himself wince with the expectation of a bullet screaming through his back. Mud and water spit from the earth with each near miss. Ten feet away from the doorway his right foot slid forward as if he had hit a banana peel. He landed on his left knee and slid into a split. He felt Luke's strong right hand snatch his left triceps with a viselike grip that half yanked, half dragged him through the door. They collapsed in a heap on the rough wood floor. Shawn landed on Luke's stomach with his full weight. The first chuckle came from Luke. Shawn lifted his face from Luke's chest. He stared at the big, funny face for a moment, then exploded into laughter.

Luke began to cackle. Shawn rolled to his right, off Luke and onto his pack, the gun landing beside him. He laughed until his eyes shut. Laughter felt wonderful. He thought he could hear someone talking, but it didn't matter. He needed this laugh like a starving man needs food.

"We ain't safe yet, ya dang boots!" a familiar voice complained.

Shawn squinted an eye open, searching for the Texan with the western mustache. Goody crouched beside the shattered bamboo door, still open and swinging crookedly from one rope hinge at the top.

Goody looked at the laughing gun team and shook his head. "Dang boots," he repeated out of one side of his mouthful of chew, then turned and spit a long stream of brown juice at the wall behind him.

"I saw boots laughing like that once," said Birdman from a squat beneath the bombed-out window to the left of the door.

"Here we go, walkin' behind a horse again," Goody griped.

"Gunners too," Birdman said, paying no heed to Goody's insult. He pulled out a C-ration four-pack of Marlboro cigarettes. "Got a light?" He looked at Goody as he stuck a wet cigarette in the side of his mouth.

Goody took off his helmet and pulled out the liner. Four green matchbooks lay inside the helmet. He tossed Birdman one then put the liner back. "I dang sure ain't seen no boots laughin' in a shoot-out like this." Goody shoved on his helmet hard as if to emphasize his point.

"This ain't that much," Birdman said, cupping his light. He blew out a smoke ring that dissolved quickly in the damp air.

"Birdman, you ain't ever seen nothin' like this in your entire life, boy. If I'm lyin', I'm adyin'!" Goody's voice rose to a near squeal of exasperation.

"Oh, sure." Birdman waved his hand as if waving away Goody's criticism. "Hoi An," he said casually. He cocked his head back and peered over his high cheekbones at Goody.

Goody moved the wad of tobacco from one side of his mouth to the other then turned his head to the wall and spit. He looked back at Birdman. "Boy, you never saw nothin' near this at the Hoi An."

Birdman gave Goody a scoffing wave. "Oh, sure. Now maybe you didn't, but where I was the air was all lead."

"Birdman, you got more bull in you than the en-tire state of Texas." Goody peeked around the edge of the doorway then leaned back against the hanging door. A single bullet shot through the open door and smacked into the back wall of the room.

Shawn crawled to the front wall. He moved to Goody's left and sat with his back against the wall. Luke crawled to the corner on Shawn's left and sat with his rifle between his legs. No one seemed to give the near-miss sniper round a second thought.

"Oh, sure," Birdman began again. "Remember old Burt's gun team?"

Goody nodded. "Yep. Elias—city boy. But I liked him."

"When he was boot, I found him laughing his fool head off right in the middle of the biggest shoot-out you ever saw."

"You ain't seen no bigger shoot-out than this right here in your en-tire military career."

Birdman waved off Goody's words as he pulled his bony chin back and down like a pelican swallowing a fish. "Oh sure. Like that time they tried to put me up for the Silver Star over on the Rock Pile."

"Ain't nobody, never, no how, put your lazy carcass up for no Silver Star. You are so full of—"

"Oh, sure," Birdman said matter-of-factly. He leaned out to make eye contact with Shawn. "I told them where they could put their medal."

A burst of automatic-rifle fire ripped across the front of the house. A solid thud went through the wall and vibrated Shawn's spine. He held his breath and knew that the wall had just saved his life.

Goody turned to Shawn and Luke. He shook his head from side to side and gave one end of his droopy mustache a slow, thoughtful twist, then pointed at Birdman with his thumb. "Silver Star. That boy's got more tales than any cowhand or Girene I ever heard tell of in my en-tire life."

Birdman waved off Goody's criticism. "Oh, sure. Told a full bird where he could put his medal. Common knowledge. I told the Old Man, 'I got no use for your piece of tin.' "

"Could you please elaborate on the fate of Mr. Burt—Elias, was it?" Luke asked.

"Old Burt, he's a sad story," Goody turned his head and squirted tobacco juice at the floor, then started again. "He'd only been here 'bout two months and he already had two Hearts, nothin' bad. Just some little holes from a mortar or somethin'. But one more time and he was goin' back to the world." Goody stuck out his bottom lip and shook his head.

"Three Hearts and you go home?" Shawn asked.

"Yep," Goody nodded.

Shawn turned to Luke. "I never knew that."

"We was in a firefight in this vill and this gook pops up out of a hole with an AK. Old Burt had him dead with the gun, but then this kid runs right by, right between Burt and the Charlie. So Burt don't shoot, then the kid is out of the way and this old mama-san runs by, so he don't shoot again. Then the Charlie sees Burt and Burt starts to fire but another old woman runs right between 'em and Burt holds his fire again but the gook don't. He blew away the mama-san and hit Burt right in the heart."

Shawn looked at the floor. "Man," he said, "I wish somebody would tell America the truth about what's going on over here."

137

"Yeah, don't we all, bro," Birdman muttered.

Russian AK-47s opened fire from down the street. Shawn felt suddenly nervous and vulnerable. "What are we supposed to do, just sit here?"

"We're sittin' tight until the Chief yells," Goody said.

"I wonder what Bonnie Kay is doing right now." Birdman sighed. He smiled contentedly. His dark brown eyes turned into narrow slits when he smiled.

Goody spit. "Boy, now I done told ya, Bonnie Kay ain't to be talked about by no useless Girene!"

"Probably wearing one of them mini-skirts . . ."

"Hush up!" Goody barked.

Birdman stopped. He looked like a puppy that had just been scolded. Shawn grinned at the angry Texan.

"I wanna see a picture of this sister of yours, Goody."

Goody turned his determined stare back to the street. "Low-life grunt Marines," he mumbled.

Birdman laughed. His protruding cheekbones became more prominent when he showed his jagged yellow teeth. He looked Oriental when he smiled. "You need any ammo, boot?" he asked, and grabbed a belt of machine-gun ammo draped over one shoulder.

"I sure do," Shawn said.

"I hate carrying this crap." Birdman pulled the belt of ammo over his head and tossed it past the open door to Goody. Goody handed it to Shawn.

"They all hate to carry it until they have to scream 'Guns up.' They change their mind, right quick," Goody said.

"Goody!" Lieutenant Townsend's voice brought Shawn to his knees with the M60 held tight to his chest.

"Yo! I'm here!" Goody shouted through the doorway.

"Cover fire! We got a fire team crossing!"

"Right!"

Goody rolled past the open door then moved over to the blown-out window beside Birdman. Shawn slid over to the doorway, pushed the M60 barrel and bipod through the door, and aimed at the two-story house. Luke jumped over the prone Shawn and took aim standing over him.

"Why are they sending a fire team back across the street when they just told them to pull back?" Luke asked.

"He always talk so slow?" Birdman asked.

"Always," Shawn said with eyes fixed on the two-story house.

"Now!" Goody shouted.

The four Marines opened fire at the two-story house. Dust and cement spit from the walls with each hit. From the corner of his eye Shawn caught the movement of Marines running toward the house where Dusty had died. A muzzle flashed from the balcony of the two-story house.

Shawn lifted his fire. Tracers ripped up the front of the house to the balcony. A rifle fell between two wood posts of the balcony railing and tumbled to the ground. A green-clad soldier wearing a pith helmet rolled toward the white curtain door leading onto the balcony. Shawn fired. A ten-round burst tore a section of the white curtain away just as the man dove through. Shawn released the trigger. He hammered his fist down on the wood doorstep in frustration, then pulled the M60 back and rolled out of the open door.

Luke looked down at Shawn. "You hit one."

"Yeah, I know," Shawn mumbled to himself as much as answering Luke. His stomach churned and for a moment he felt like puking. He felt strange. He wanted to kill that man, he knew it, and he was angry that he had missed. Confirmed. He wanted a confirmed kill. Shawn stared out of the door at the rain smashing against the brick street and tried to remember why he believed in what he was doing. His stare traveled past the red-brick street and all the way home.

Eddie's big friendly smile was so clear that Shawn grinned at the memory. He could still hear old Ed laughing. "You couldn't even kill a bird when we were kids, now how could you shoot a Vietnamese?"

"I don't know, Ed. I just really believe they're evil."

"Who?"

"Communists!"

"What do you know about communism?"

"I know it's anti-Christ."

"What about 'thou shalt not kill' and 'turn the other cheek'?"

"Self-defense and war don't come under those commandments. Remember, the same people God gave the law to—Israel—he led into war to destroy ungodly nations."

"Well, maybe you and me think that way, and it's easy to sit here and talk about this stuff, but what are you going to do, Shawn, if you really shoot somebody?"

"I don't know. . . ."

Now he knew. Shawn stared at the machine gun. The acrid

smell of gunpowder was strong. Now he knew. He could do it, all right. Pulling the trigger was no problem. Confirmed. But could he justify wanting a confirmed?

"Goody! I'm comin' in!" The lieutenant's shout pulled Shawn back. He leaned right to look through the doorway. Shots rang out from down the street. He could hear boots splashing through mud. A bullet whined as it glanced off the front of the house. The lieutenant ran through the door and ducked down on one knee. He gasped for air for a few seconds before looking at the four Marines. He sat back against the bamboo door and let out one last gasp.

"Okay, here's the situation." He pushed his helmet back on his head. "We're setting up around this end of the street for tonight. I put men out back of this house and the one over there." He pointed with his thumb across the street. "We have to take this street tomorrow or the First Platoon will be flanked on the other street over there."

"How?" Goody asked squarely.

"Just what we've been doing, Marine, only better. We'll move in on one house at a time with cross-street cover. We'll hit it with the M60 and the blooper gun first, then we have to rush it with a fire team, toss frags, go in shooting."

Birdman whistled. "Man, Lieutenant, we're bound to lose some men that way."

Lieutenant Townsend's expression turned hard, like it was a reflex action. His eyes were red with fatigue. The stress of command was stealing the youth from his collegiate face. Dark pouches puffed under his eyes. "We'll get some help from tanks, but—"He paused as if too tired to finish."—but, it's still up to us to secure each house and there's only one way."

"I could give the corps another way . . . sir," Birdman snapped, then looked around nervously as if he knew that he should have kept his mouth shut.

"Let's hear it, Lance Corporal."

"Why don't we just flatten this dump?" Birdman smashed his rifle butt on the floor.

"Hue is the ancient imperial capital of Vietnam. It stinks, but they don't want it destroyed." The lieutenant checked his watch, then looked at Shawn. "How much sixty ammo do we have left?"

"A couple of belts," Shawn said.

Luke slumped to the floor beside Shawn and sighed aloud. "I am really tired. I don't think I could carry four hundred rounds."

"We'll get some tomorrow," Townsend said.

"How bad is Smitty, Lieutenant?" Shawn asked.

"He'll live. I don't know how he got that much shrapnel in his stomach with a flak jacket on. I'm setting the CP up in that first house."

Lieutenant Townsend got to his feet. He took two big breaths then ran through the doorway and back to the beige house. Strangely, no one fired a shot. It seemed to signal a lull for the night to come.

The battle raged sporadically through the night, first one section of the city exploding into a fierce exchange, then suddenly going quiet, only to be followed by another section erupting in gunfire. The air was thick with smoke. Shifts in the wind mixed the stench of rotting bodies with whiffs of the sulfurous smell of gunpowder.

Shawn, nearly gagging, wondered how bad the smell would be without the continuous rain. Streams of deadly tracers sputtered out of the black sky as helicopter gunships worked over targets pinpointed by gunners on the ground. Green tracers from enemy guns shot into the sky like fireworks.

"Shawn," a voice whispered from the window. Shawn turned his eyes from the door. "You awake?" Luke whispered.

"Yeah. Is it my watch?"

"No. Goody is out front under this window. What does all the fireworks remind you of?"

"The Fourth out at Passagrille Beach."

"I knew precisely what you were thinking."

"You too?"

"Yes." Luke sighed. "What I would give right now just to sit and stare at the bikinis walking up and down in front of the old Don Cesar Hotel."

"Yeah. A bikini on Nancy Diez would be fine," Shawn said, trying to visualize the beautiful, olive-skinned Cajun, her shimmering black hair down to her tiny waist and her muscular, tan legs. He loved her. He pushed the thought away and remembered his DI's warning that women won't wait, so don't expect them to.

"I would suggest that you transfer your thoughts," Luke said.

"Right." Shawn leaned back and listened to the rain smacking against the tile roof. He sat still for what felt like a long time. Then he heard movement outside.

"Comin' in," Goody whispered.

"Okay."

Goody crawled through the doorway and nudged Shawn's leg. "Your watch, boot."

"Where should I go?"

"Just set up under the window so you can see down the street."

"Right." Shawn crawled through the door.

"Wait," Luke whispered. "Here." He handed Shawn the barrel end of his M16 wrapped in a poncho. "Give me the gun."

Shawn slid the M60 over to Luke. Shawn knew why. He'd be too slow reacting with the twenty-four-pound machine gun. Shawn crawled through the doorway, then moved left to a spot under the window. He took off his helmet and pulled the poncho over him. The rain was cold on his face and head. He sat with his back resting against the wall and stared down the dark street so hard that his eyes stung.

A flare suddenly popped open somewhere behind Shawn. The blackness burst into shapes and long dark shadows. A white muzzle flash shot from the first floor of the two-story house. Bullets thudded into the mud in front of Shawn. He stiffened, then jerked to life. He rolled and scrambled toward the door, his fingers digging into the water-soaked ground for traction as he sprang forward, landing in the doorway. Luke grabbed him by the seat of his trousers and yanked him inside as bullets flattened with a smacking sound against the house. Marines opened up from every position. Ten minutes later the flares stopped and night engulfed the street like a black velvet blanket. It was quiet again.

The first sliver of daybreak brought with it a frightening sense of urgency. Always before the day felt safe. Now it meant certain death for some. Maybe all. It might be a last chance to write a letter. Shawn groped through his pack and pulled out a plastic pouch. He removed the rubber band and tried to flatten his writing paper on the mud-caked floor.

"Good thought," Luke mumbled, his head resting on one elbow like a kid watching TV on the living-room rug.

"Yeah, if I can see what I'm writing," Shawn said, staring down at the paper. "What do you say when it might be your last letter?"

"You writing Nancy?"

"Yeah, and Mom."

"Make it romantic to Nancy. And patriotic. You know, a little Hemingway, and a little Paul Revere, and tell her that I said that she had the best wheels and the best rump in St. Pete High."

"She had the best helmet too."

"Teresa Sikes had a great helmet."

Shawn raised his eyebrows. "True."

"And Jody Abbot or Kathy Brubaker or Marie Ball were not exactly slouches."

Shawn nodded. "True."

"How about Pam Edmondson? And Bonnie Baker? And what about those four junior-varsity cheerleaders that burned me in effigy? Nice helmets. Fine trunks too."

"You mean Betty Sue Palmer and Lori and Amy and Pammy?"

"Yes. Fine helmets. Big wazzos too."

"True. You know, Luke, you never did tell me what you did to those girls to make them hate you so much."

Luke sighed as if the memory was a pleasant one. "I know. You would never have approved."

"How do you know?" Shawn asked. "I might have loved it."

"No way. Trust me." Luke grinned and glanced at the street. His grin faded. "It's getting lighter outside."

"Yeah."

"Scared?"

"Yeah, but not as scared as I thought I would be. I mean, I'm as scared as I thought I would be but I feel so hyped up that I sort of forget everything else. You know what I mean?"

Luke sat up quickly and grabbed for his rifle. The squishing sound of mud under boots, scurrying closer, snapped Shawn's head toward the open doorway as he groped for the machine gun.

"Friendlies! Comin' in. Hold your fire."

"Come on, Murph," Goody whispered through the blown-out window.

Murph's squad rushed through the open doorway behind the big hulking black corporal. Murph's droopy eyes searched the small room until he found Birdman.

"Birdman?"

"Yo, Murph," Birdman said, then gave a soft whistle as if to prove his identity.

"Goody?"

"Yep."

"Saddle up, bros. This is roll call."

"Gawd-awful Marine Corps!" Goody shot tobacco juice out of the open window. "Ain't even lettin' a man eat breakfast?"

"Don't fret now, Goody," Cornhusker said from behind Murph. "That chow's just gonna make you a fatter target."

"I hear it make's you bleed faster," another voice added.

" 'Tenant says to drop our packs here to lighten up," Murph said.

"Cornhusker," Goody said.

"Yeah, Goody." The stocky Nebraskan dropped his pack.

"If I'm a KIA, don't you let that Birdman go through my saddlebags now. He'll be lookin' fer Bonnie Kay's address and picture and they ain't no Marine gettin' near my sister!"

"What if I get killed too?" Cornhusker asked.

"You got a sister, Cornhusker?" Birdman asked with a hint of excitement in his tone.

"Good God almighty," Murph whined, and shook his head in disbelief. "If my mama could hear this, she'd know the Marine Corps just ruins a man's mind. Saddle up. Move out. Guns?"

"Yeah, Murph," Shawn said. His heart was pounding. He felt out of breath.

"You set the gun up where that gook .50-cal was? Give us cover. Get a line of fire on that two-story house. We're gonna be crossin' the street and hittin' that house with the Chief on the west side. Lieutenant's bringing the rest of the men down this side."

"Man, this sounds screwed up!" a Marine griped from behind the stocky Cornhusker.

"Yeah, what happened to the friggin' tank?" Birdman asked.

"It still might show. They don't know. I think that's what the lieutenant's waitin' on. Go on guns, move out."

"Who's covering our right flank?" Shawn asked.

"I hear something!" Cornhusker said.

"Shhhh." Murph rushed to the blown-out window and stood beside Goody.

No one spoke. Tension roared through Shawn's ears and he

suddenly felt light-headed. The rumble of a giant diesel engine brought a huge grin to Murph's face.

"Your mama, gooks," he muttered quietly.

"Tank." Goody's whisper sounded like a shout.

"This is it, move out, guns!" Murph pushed Shawn and Luke toward the door.

"Ready, Luke?" Shawn clutched the M60 with both hands. He flipped off the safety and pulled back the cocking lever.

"Frankly, I'd rather be in Philadelphia."

Luke led the way through the door and along the front of the house. Then they made a noisy, splashing dash to the next house. Shawn flattened up against its block wall behind Luke. Luke peeked around the corner. The first white shafts of the dawn illumined the low gray clouds of the monsoon and silhouetted the houses across the street. The rumble of the tank sounded closer. Luke looked back at Shawn.

"Ready?"

"Yeah."

The sudden burst of an M60 machine gun echoed from another part of the city, then rifles, the popping of the American M16s mingling with sharper cracks of the Russian AK-47s. The war awakened just a moment too soon for Shawn. It was like a signal had been given and the whole world knew he was coming.

"Here goes nothing," Luke mumbled.

Luke stood in a crouch and moved cautiously around the corner with his rifle ready. Shawn followed, the gun on his hip, ready to move quick, though the truth was that the twenty-four-pound M60 was too heavy to outquick a rifle in a shoot-out. Each step was an effort. He shook his head once to clear the fear and stared at the black outline of the two-story house that was now directly across the street. Acrid smoke still seeped through the rubble that had once been a porch. A four-foot-tall stone wall was all that remained of the front of the house. The roof had also collapsed. The thud of stone falling against stone froze Shawn stiff. Luke dropped to one knee. The wind of an object whistled past Shawn's right ear. Something splattered into the mud behind him. A second later something bounced off the top of the four-foot front wall to Luke's right. A ripping explosion blew Shawn forward, into the back of Luke's hard flak jacket, just as another grenade blew pieces of the four-foot front wall out into the street. His ears screamed in shock and pain. The white explosion stole his vision. He grabbed at the back of his right thigh. His hamstring felt like someone had just ground a lit cigar into it. Luke moaned. Shawn rolled off Luke and fumbled for the M60. An AK-47 opened up full automatic from across the street. His fire was high.

Two more potato mashers splashed as they hit the brick street and rolled to a stop five feet to Shawn's left. He buried his face in the mud and covered his helmet with both hands. One . . . two . . . three . . . four . . . five. Duds. Shawn pulled his face out of the mud and gasped for air. He spit mud out of his mouth as a fifth Chi-Com grenade bounced off the brick street and splattered in the mud ten yards ahead. Shawn tried to crawl under his helmet. One . . . two . . . three . . . dud!

"Come on!" Luke yelled. He turned and crawled past Shawn back the way they had come. Marines opened fire at the two-story house.

Shawn laid the M60 over his shoulder with the butt end resting on his back and low-crawled after Luke. Mud flew from Luke's boots into Shawn's face as he scrambled like a madman after Luke, who disappeared around the corner of the house. Then Shawn released his grip on the bipod leg of the M60, dropped his chin to the muddy ground, breathed, and prayed.

The burning in his hamstring cut his prayer short. I'm hit, he thought, I'm really wounded. He touched the back of his right thigh. Something felt warm and sticky between his fingertips. Blood.

Shawn lifted his chin from the mud to look for Luke. Rain bounced off the ground and splashed into his eyes. He blinked to clear his vision. The sun was higher. The dark had lightened to dim gray. The shadows of Marines, hunched over and moving forward with rifles ready, could be seen clearly now on the other side of the street.

Shawn felt sort of happy. He had a wound. He thought of Nancy. He couldn't wait for her to get the news—would Marines in dress blues bring it? No chance, he thought. Mom will get it. *Oh no*. Mom will have a breakdown or something. Shawn groaned aloud at the thought.

"Shawn," Luke whispered. "You okay?"

"Yeah. I mean, no, I mean, I'm okay but I'm wounded."

"Where at, in the mouth?" Luke snickered.

"I thought we bought the farm, Luke."

Luke's face quivered. He looked hard at Shawn. "We put in a down payment, buddy."

The ground vibrated under tons of steel as the long barrel of a giant green monster rounded the corner of the beige house with grunts walking cautiously on both of its flanks. Shawn watched as it chewed up the brick street. His peripheral vision caught a puff of smoke shooting from the top of the two-story house. A B-40 rocket hissed through the air. The gunner in the open hatch of the turret couldn't duck in time. The rocket exploded. Fire and pieces of orange; glowing shrapnel blasted from the right side of the turret. Lieutenant Townsend scrambled onto the tank, pulled the bleeding man free, and lowered him into the arms of Doc Abernathy and the sergeant major. Most of the tanker's forehead was gone. He was dead.

"Corpsman! Help!" Another crew member shouted as he climbed out of the turret hatch, holding his groin and grimacing in agony.

The big gun rotated toward the two-story house. Two small fires burned on the tank's hull. Suddenly the street shook with the angry roar of the monster and a nearly instantaneous explosion. In the front of the house, a huge, gaping hole replaced the doors and windows on the first floor. An NVA soldier bolted from the rubble and into the street. He fired erratically with an AK-47 as he ran. A hail of M16s riddled him before he got ten yards. He rolled and twitched for a moment, then curled up in a fetal position and stopped moving. The cannon fired again. A *whoosh* of wind and a loud blast filled the street. The balcony on the two-story disappeared. The third shot from the tank brought the front wall crumbling to the ground in a pile of smoke and stone. Someone screamed from the rubble. The cannon fired again. Shawn and Luke ducked back behind their wall as rocks and shrapnel thudded everywhere with back-breaking force. The screaming stopped.

"On line! Fix bayonets!"

The sound of boots running toward them mingled with ghostly echoes from the walls.

"You hit?" The corpsman with the Dennis the Menace face yelled as he came to a stop beside Shawn.

Shawn nodded at the corpsman and looked at Luke. "I think this is our ride, Luke."

Luke forced a tired smile.

The floor of the old H34-D medevac chopper was stained brown with dried blood. Meat wagon, Shawn thought. Shawn, Luke, and a corporal from Two-Five gazed blankly at four poncho-covered bodies as the medevac chopper sped low over Highway One. Shawn's mind was jumbled. Thoughts and memories seemed to mix and skip through his head with no particular pattern. He barely noticed when the chopper settled onto a landing pad at First Med in Phu Bai. Navy corpsmen rushed the wounded Marines to first-aid tents. Their wounds were slight. The corporal from Two-Five had a bullet wound in his calf. He was taken straight into surgery. Shawn had a small horseshoe-shaped hole in the back of his right thigh and a couple of smaller holes in his left calf. Luke had three tiny holes in the back of his neck, all of them minor. He had a slightly bigger piece of shrapnel in the cheek of his rear end. Their wounds were cleaned and dressed. They both got shots to fight infection.

They spent the night in the first-aid tent. Fatigue was overwhelming. Shawn fell into a deep, black, dreamless sleep.

"Reveille, grunts!" a deep-voiced corpsman yelled, ending the best sleep that Shawn could remember having had since landing "in-country."

He sat up in his cot and forced one eye open. The light was dim; the sun wasn't fully up. Every cot in the big tent was taken. Sleepy-eyed Marines sat up and tried to wipe the night from their eyes. Some were still covered with Hue City mud; it looked red like Georgia clay when it dried. Most of the young Marines sat, stiff with blood-soaked bandages or slings; others groped sleepily for crutches stashed under their cots.

"I hate this green machine," Luke whined as he sat up with both eyes still closed.

"You lie, GI," Shawn said sleepily. "You love this. Travel. Adventure. Career opportunities. Attitude check, PFC."

Luke closed his eyes, dropped his chin, and gave Shawn his middle finger. "Here is my attitude, McClellan."

"All right! Listen up!" the corpsman yelled from the front of the tent. "We need help unloading gear and wounded Marines coming out of Hue City. Volunteers up!"

"Yo!" Shawn gave a wave. "We'll help."

"We?"

"Can you two walk?"

"Yeah."

"Follow me to the doc, we'll get you two on the light-duty roster."

"We?"

* * *

Ten days later Shawn and Luke joined up with the Second Platoon again. The battle was over for Alpha Company. There had been more casualties since Shawn and Luke left, but no one that they knew personally. Chip said that the Fifth Marines were taking over bridge duty from Hai Van Pass to Phu Bai. "Skate duty," he said. Shawn felt an ominous chill as they climbed aboard the trucks to leave Hue.

On February 22, 1968, the Marines took their final objective, the southeast wall of the Citadel. By prior agreement, the Marines stayed out of the fight for the Imperial Palace. At dawn on the twenty-fourth, the red, green, and yellow flag of the Republic of South Vietnam went up over the Citadel. Scuttlebutt said that the First Battalion Fifth Marine Regiment was no longer a complete fighting unit. Casualties were high. At one point One-Five Marines took one casualty for every three feet gained. U.S. Marine losses were 142 killed, 857 wounded. U.S. Army losses were 74 killed and 507 wounded. South Vietnamese losses were 384 killed and 1,830 wounded.

Compared with the North Vietnamese Army, U.S. casualties were light. The NVA had committed at least eight battalions, perhaps eleven, to the battle. Command of this division-sized attack had been given to the Sixth NVA Regiment. NVA losses were enormous, over five thousand killed and eighty-nine captured. The communists had assassinated thousands of civilians during their brief occupation of the unfortified city. Some estimates ran as high as five thousand murdered.

CHAPTER SEVEN

Truoi River Bridge
February 23, 1968

The jarring ride down Highway One, away from Hue City, made Shawn feel as if he were awakening from a nightmare, as if it hadn't really happened. Then he glanced around the truck full of sullen stares. This was no dream. He didn't recognize some of the faces. Some were from First Platoon and some from Third Platoon. That's what Hue had done to One-Five. Two platoons could now fit into one truck. Even a boot knew what that meant.

"Gunner." Birdman whistled from the floor of the truck, his feet resting on the tailgate. He looked at Shawn with an upside-down, wide-open gaze. "Didn't you get medevacked?"

"Yeah. They said it wasn't bad enough to stay in bed at First Med, so they put us on light duty."

"Where you been?"

"Luke and me have been helping with the wounded, loading 'em off choppers and stuff."

"You dumb jackass, boot," Neader snarled from a back corner of the truck. "You could be in a clean bed right now in Da Nang or Phu Bai or even Cam Rahn Bay."

Luke held out his hand as if introducing Shawn.

"Not Mr. Volunteer, the All-Green Marine, PFC Shawn McClellan."

"Don't give me grief, Lukevec," Shawn said. "You wanted to help too, and you know it. Besides, what difference does it make, man?"

"Big difference, boot." Neader grinned maliciously. "You could have had a forty-eight-hour Heart and now ya don't, and that's bad luck all over cuz three strikes and you're dead."

"What is he talking about?" Shawn asked. He could feel the anger making the crease between his eyes deeper.

"You boot jerk," Birdman said. "That was the first thing I learned when I got in-country, bro."

"What?"

Corporal Murph pushed his helmet back on his head and gave Shawn a sleepy-looking stare. "It means that if you get hit, bro, and hospitalized for forty-eight hours, twice"—Murph held up two fingers—"Yooz gonna pass go and you will collect a ride on the freedombird back to the world."

"What?" Luke asked.

"Otherwise, my man, you have to get hit three times to go home," Birdman said with a yellow-toothed grin.

"Are you serious?" Luke leaned forward on the truck bench to look down at Birdman's bony face.

"If I'm alyin', I'm adyin'." He held up his hand as if to swear in.

Luke looked back at Shawn. It was hard to tell whether Luke was mad or scared, but Shawn knew that it was somewhere in between the two. Shawn shrugged his shoulders and looked his buddy in his two-tone eyes. "Nobody told me, Luke," he said.

Neader laughed. "Yeah, Lukevec," he taunted, "have that one put on your white cross at Arlington."

Birdman began to whistle the "Marine Corps Hymn."

Luke leaned forward, elbows on knees and his big face buried in his hands. Neader's mocking cackle grated on Shawn's nerves like nails on a chalkboard. For a moment Shawn considered moving close enough to kick Neader in his pitted face.

The drive was slow. The rain had stopped and the sun blazed down on the convoy. Lead trucks had covered the men with a blanket of hot beige dust. The road was jammed with refugees from Hue and the surrounding countryside. The communists had shoved thousands of murdered civilians into mass graves. Some had been buried alive, and others bludgeoned to death to save ammunition. Panic was written on the faces of the mothers scurrying along the roadside, clinging to their children. They carried or dragged all of their belongings, or all that was left of their belongings. Small boys with sticks pushed and whacked the family water buffalo, the most prized of possessions. There seemed to be no end and no beginning to the mass exodus, just carts and bicycles loaded with everything people owned, piled high. It was over one hundred degrees, but many of the refugees wore four or five layers of clothes. Pain was stamped into their faces. The loss. The fear. How could anybody not want to fight against the cause of such suffering? Shawn watched the endless, cowering columns as they covered their faces from the dust kicked up by the big trucks. Finally the squeal of brakes in need of repair signaled a halt by the convoy. Someone shouted the Second Platoon out of the trucks.

"Listen up!" The chattering platoon stilled at the Chief's command.

They stood in two lines of five men along the side of the road. The convoy was headed south across a big steel bridge. It looked like an old train bridge but was strictly for road traffic. The Marines stood in front of a group of small white block buildings with tin roofs surrounded by rolls of concertina wire. ARVN soldiers, huddled in groups around the blockhouses, chattered and snickered and pointed at the Americans. Across the road a huge camouflaged parachute was spread fully open, the corners tied to trees, like a giant tent. It shaded fifteen lean, tan Marines sitting around writing letters and cleaning weapons. Most wore tiger shorts, boots, and no shirts.

"As it stands now . . ." Lieutenant Townsend began, then paused to wave at an ARVN lieutenant standing just to the left of the bridge and beside a large sandbag bunker. He looked back at the platoon.

"Alpha Company will be on bridge duty while we get replacements. Listen up! I ain't saying it twice! One platoon on the bridge, two in the bush. The platoon on the bridge will work with the CAP Marines"—he pointed over his shoulder with his thumb at the Marines under the giant parachute—"and the South Vietnamese Army troops over here in the compound."

He nodded toward the block buildings behind the platoon. "We'll be here a couple of days until Third Platoon shows up to take our place. We should be getting some replacements. The minute these replacements show up, I want you squad leaders to get 'em squared away. Is that clear?"

No one answered.

"Okay, go ahead and stow your gear in this first blockhouse over here. I want a guard posted on the door, to be relieved every hour. You have till"—he turned up his palm to check his watch—"sixteen-hundred hours."

He gave a nod toward the south side of the bridge. "There's a Vietnamese barber in the vill over there. You will have shaves and Marine Corps haircuts by sixteen-hundred hours."

"That sucks," Neader hissed from behind Shawn.

Lieutenant Townsend ignored it. "That ARVN officer says

152

there is also a hootch over there on the starboard side of the road that serves food."

"Far out. Vietnamese McDonald's," Kayto quipped.

"Shut up, Marine," Chief growled.

"You get the runs from that Vietnamese food," Lieutenant Townsend warned. "And it's just too bad. If we move out, you will just crap on the hump. No whores either. Scuttlebutt says the VC got women posing as prostitutes. They say they got razor blades inserted where every Marine wants to be."

The depleted platoon winced and made a chorus of groans.

Birdman whistled. "Whoa, right down the middle."

"Weapons will be locked and loaded, but on safety. Dismissed."

"Neader!" Chief barked. "Kayto. Birdman. You got the first three shifts on the gear so that our ARVN allies don't borrow anything."

"Get back!" Neader snapped.

"Yeah, Chief," Kayto snarled.

"What gives?" Birdman asked. "Boots should get stuck with that garbage, not salts."

"Should have kept your mouth shut in formation. Move it! Neader's got first watch."

"He'll steal more than the ARVNs, Chief," Cager said with a mischievous wink at Ghosthorse.

Neader's pitted face flushed red. "You better tell Sambo, here, I don't forget this trash."

"You want a piece of this Sambo, Neader?" Cager handed Kayto his M16 and stepped toward Neader with clenched fist. Neader brought his rifle up to use the butt end as a weapon. Sergeant Ghosthorse moved between the two with his long arms out. He gripped the front of each man's flak jacket.

"Attention!" Lieutenant Townsend shouted. The sergeant glared at each man then released his grip. "What's going on here, Chief?"

"Nothing, sir."

"Private Neader! This is your last stop, Marine. You screw up here and you go to the brig in Da Nang and then on to Leavenworth. Is that clear, Private?"

"Yeah." Neader glared at Cager.

Lieutenant Townsend stomped forward and put his face an inch away from Neader's. "I don't think I heard you, mister."

"Yes, sir!"

Lieutenant Townsend had the look of a man expecting trouble as he walked away. Shawn didn't envy him his job. These were hard men. Though most had been only boys a few months ago, some of them looked like they would blow your head off without flinching. Neader was one. Shawn said a silent prayer for the lieutenant.

"Come on." Luke tugged Shawn toward the compound.

They stored everything but rifles in the small blockhouse, then headed for the vill. Truoi Village was fairly typical of most of the small villages in Vietnam. The Truoi River was the village's lifeblood. Small grass hootches lined the south side of the river. Each hootch was either built over the entrance to an underground bunker or right beside one. At night the people slept underground, on floors of rotting bamboo and straw mats. A few had dirty rags that were used as blankets. Everyone seemed to cough with a deep sickness from living and sleeping in constant dampness. In the day they worked the rice paddies, standing in leech-infested water and the human excrement used for fertilizer. By the age of twenty-five the village women were already old, haggard-looking, and wrinkled from the torturous sun. The big steel bridge looked out of place in the primitive surroundings, but then nothing really seemed to fit in this strange place. Convoys of the world's most powerful and modern Army rolled up and down Highway One as women squatted along the river beating clothes with rocks. Phantoms screamed overhead while mothers squatted on the doorsteps of grass hootches picking lice out of their children's hair and killing them between their teeth like apes do. The people were quick to smile as Shawn and Luke passed by, almost as if they wanted to show off their blackened or missing teeth. Shawn paused on the side of the dirt road and sniffed.

"You notice how everything smells like fish?"

"Fish is a very Christian way of phrasing it, Shawn," Luke said with a grin.

"Hey, GI, GIs, you number one, you buy Coca-Cola, two buck MPC?" A tiny boy on a large, rusty old Schwinn bicycle wobbled to a stop beside Luke and nearly fell over under the weight of a huge backpack. He had a bundle of clothes strapped to the handlebars. The little black-haired boy smiled and nodded his head as if to help the answer be yes. He stood on the tiptoes of his black rubber sandals just to peer over the bundle strapped

154

to his handlebars. He wore an American Army coat that went all the way down to the shins of his black pajamalike trousers.

"Two bucks!" Luke exclaimed.

"You right, GI. We got special today, buck-fifty." He grinned and made a quick search of the bundle on his handlebars. "Here, GI." He pulled out an eight-ounce bottle of Coke and held it up, beaming with pride.

"We are not GIs," Luke said, stepping closer to inspect the bottle.

"So sorry, GI. You Marines. Marines no like to be called GI. I know. I number-one Coke boy, Phan. For Marines, Coke only one buck MPC."

Shawn laughed as he reached into his cargo pocket. "Here, Phan." He pulled out a small roll of the colorful Monopoly-like money they called Military Payment Certificates and handed the little boy a bill.

"You number one, GI." Phan handed the bottle to Shawn.

"Marine," Shawn corrected.

"So sorry, Marine. You number one."

"A buck for eight ounces of hot Coke," Luke scoffed. "You are number one at something." He gave Shawn a pat on the shoulder.

"You need open?" Phan asked.

"Yeah," Shawn said.

"I rent opener, ten cent." Phan pulled a small rusty bottle opener out of his coat pocket and held it out.

Shawn looked down at the boy, then at Luke. Luke closed his eyes and shook his head. Shawn chuckled as he thumbed through his roll of bills looking for one that said ten cents.

"What do you do with all of this loot, Phan?" He handed the boy a blue-flowered Monopoly-sized bill and took the opener.

The boy snatched the bill like he was afraid Shawn would change his mind. He shoved the money into his coat pocket. "I help old man, old woman."

"Your parents?" Luke asked.

"Parents, dead. Just old man, old woman, I live with them. I help."

Shawn fought back an urge to ruffle the little boy's soup-bowl haircut. "Where do you live?"

"I live small village, close Hue City."

"Hue City?"

"No more. VC come, they kill all people, village chief."

155

"They killed everyone?" Luke asked.

"You work government, they kill. You Christian, they kill. You not help VC, they kill."

"Where are you living now?"

"I find place for old man, old woman."

"You mean you have found a place, or are you looking?" Shawn asked.

"I look. I find," he said confidently. "I build, then get old man, old woman."

"Where is the old man and old woman?" Luke asked.

"Close Hue City. They wait."

Shawn thumbed through his money again. He looked at Luke. "Luke, how much will a haircut cost?"

"How should I know? I came with you, remember?"

"Well, it can't cost more than three bucks." Shawn counted out three dollars of the MPC and put the three back into his pocket. "Here." He held out the rest of the money to Phan. "I want twenty-two Cokes."

Phan's dark eyes grew large. He looked at the money, then at Shawn, and then at the money again.

"Take it." Shawn put the money into his small hand.

Phan looked up at the American in near panic. "I . . . I no . . ."

Shawn held up ten fingers twice, then added two. "Twenty-two."

"I no have," Phan said. He looked at the ground as if he were ashamed.

Shawn patted the boy's head. "No, no. Not right now. You bring to me, here at the bridge when you get them."

Shawn spoke slowly and pointed across the bridge at the compound of blockhouses.

The little boy's eyes squinted. He nodded his head and put the money in his pocket. Shawn popped the cap off of his Coke and handed Phan the opener. Phan looked apprehensive as he pedaled away.

"Shawn." Luke sounded tired. He looked at Shawn with a half smirk, half smile and shook his head slowly from side to side. "I know that we are not from the big city, McClellan, and that your hillbilly youth has something to do with this, but . . ."

"What are you talking about, Lukevec?"

"Of course, you know that he probably suckers no less than two Americans per day with that story."

156

"I don't think so," Shawn said, but inwardly feared that Luke was probably right.

"Is being naive a prerequisite for the biblical version of heaven or is it your own individual quality?"

"Well, actually, the Bible does say that unless a man comes to the Lord with a childlike faith, he won't make the team."

Luke slapped Shawn on the back and laughed. "Then, my good buddy, you are a sure bet for first string." Luke turned and walked away. Shawn followed him into the village, past a group of staring Vietnamese. You couldn't help wondering if any or how many of the villagers were Viet Cong. There was no way to know, of course, not until they shot at you.

Shawn felt for the .45-caliber pistol on his hip. "You know, I feel sort of naked without the M60. I bet I couldn't hit the bridge with this thing."

"Where's our barber shop?" Luke asked.

"I bet that's it." Shawn pointed to a plywood-and-grass hootch with two Marines standing in front.

"Yes, I think you're right. Looks like Goody and Birdman?"

"Yeah." Shawn waved. Goody sent back a lazy thumbs-up.

The barber's hootch was about seventy meters south of the big steel bridge. The bridge was probably another ninety meters long, and the compound was twenty meters beyond the north end of the bridge. Shawn felt a twinge of apprehension over wandering so far away from the compound without the rest of the platoon. He glanced at the trail that ran parallel to the south side of the river. It looked dark and mysterious. That was where most of the people lived, along the river. The tin-roofed hootches along Highway One seemed to be the business district. They walked past a dozen of them to reach Goody.

"Is this the barber, Goody?" Shawn shouted over the passing rumble of the lead truck of another convoy. Goody pulled his dirty red bandanna up over his nose and mouth like a cowboy-bandit as clouds of red dust kicked up by the convoy covered the men.

"Yep," he said through the bandanna. He pulled Luke closer as the two stopped in front of the hootch. "Here's the way it's done, boots." He nodded at Shawn. "He gets his hair cut, you stand right there with your rifle off safety so the papa-san knows it, then you switch and the other guy stands ready."

"What for?" Shawn asked.

157

"The VC used to play barber; they'd cut your throat with a straight razor when they could. It's just playin' it safe."

Shawn lifted his helmet and ran his hand through his wavy brown hair. "You think I really need a cut?"

Luke grinned and pulled on one of Shawn's curls until it was straight. "It is over an inch, Marine," he said formally.

A few minutes later it was their turn. Shawn sat on the wood stool and stared at the leathery face of the old man rubbing the slightly rusted blade of the straight razor against a piece of wood. The hard dirt floor of the hootch was covered with hair and the rotting plywood walls were bare. Luke stood close by with his rifle in both hands. The old man seemed unperturbed by the Americans' precaution. His eyes never once met the Americans' eyes directly as he went about his business. Shawn wished that he could talk to him, just to be friendly. The old man finished cleaning the blade and moved toward Shawn. The sound of boots running brought Shawn's eyes to the open door. Kayto peeked in. He wore his pack and gear.

"Saddle up! Second Platoon, saddle up!"

The suddenness of the march away from the relative comfort of the bridge caught the remains of the Second Platoon cold. The column of tired men grumbled quietly to themselves as they filed on the path along the river. They headed west through Truoi Village. Shawn watched the villagers pretend not to notice the Marines passing. Not one would make direct eye contact with him or even show the slightest interest. The Vietnamese seemed to be always half cowering in fear, and yet, at the same time, they seem completely aware of everything around them. It was an irritating quality that was beginning to grate on Shawn's nerves.

Two hundred meters farther, where the village ended, the river veered away from the trail and to the right. It led to rice fields, now empty of workers as night and the death that came with it approached. While the hot copper sun sank slowly behind the western mountains, the small column of Marines struggled to keep their balance crossing the last, narrow rice paddy dike. The terrain rose slightly then turned into rolling hills strewn with rocks. Beyond that, the land rose steadily, growing more harsh with each step.

After two hours, Shawn found, it was hard to keep his mind on any single thought for more than a few minutes. He stared at

Cager's back for a while, then down at his own boots humping along step after step. They were starting to look a little salty. He thought about his mom and the allotment he was having taken out of his pay. I hope she gets air conditioning for the house, he thought. Please take care of her, Jesus.

Cager dropped down on one knee. He turned and motioned Shawn down with his hand. Shawn dropped and waved Luke down behind him. Visibility was not good. It was the most dangerous time in this dangerous country. That eerie hour when it isn't dark and isn't light, when a man's eyes can't be trusted and sticks look like barrels and rocks turn into helmets and mistakes equal death.

"Guns up!" someone ahead whispered.

Cager looked over his shoulder with one hand cupped around his mouth. "Guns up!"

"Guns up!"

Shawn's heart began pounding like a drum in his ear. His bladder suddenly ached, and he tightened his stomach muscles to keep from urinating. Grasping the M60 with both hands, he ran forward in a crouch. Luke! Shawn glanced back over his shoulder. Luke was up and running. Shawn ran forward up a rocky, narrow path, sidestepping each man every ten meters. The path led to the crown of a small rocky knoll. Shawn could see three men on their stomachs. The gray silhouette of Lieutenant Townsend's hand waved him forward then motioned him to stay low. Shawn's knees strained to bend lower and still run. He dove to the left of the trail. The ground was rock hard. A moment later Luke crashed in beside him with a groan.

Goody spit a quick shot of tobacco juice. "See 'em?" He pointed straight ahead. The path continued over the knoll, sloped down gradually for twenty meters, then up another barren knoll. Beyond that was the black background of thick brush. Shawn squinted to see something, anything, in the dim gray terrain ahead.

"See it, Shawn?" Lieutenant Townsend whispered from Goody's right.

"No."

"To the left of the path on the rise ahead." Goody pointed again.

Shawn squinted. Nothing. Just a lumpy gray outline of the knoll against the black tree line beyond. Shawn's eyes opened wide, straining to bring in more light. There was something round. He could see the dark outline of round objects along the top of the knoll. Helmets. His heart seemed to jump against the inside of his chest.

"I see 'em! Helmets?"

"Yep."

"How . . ." Shawn stopped short with his question. This was no time for a boot quiz on how Goody spotted the ambush, if that's what it was. "Now what?" he asked.

"Chipper up!" the lieutenant whispered back down the column. A moment later the little moon-faced radioman jogged forward and knelt low behind the lieutenant.

"Chip, get Alpha One."

Chip laid his rifle down and reached over his shoulder for the antenna. He gave it two quick tugs to extend it and pulled the field phone around. "Alpha One . . . Alpha One . . . this is Alpha Two . . . over."

"Alpha Two . . . Alpha Two . . . this is Alpha One . . . over."

It seems like we're always too loud, Shawn thought as he searched the darkening knoll ahead for movement. Visibility dropped with each passing moment. Lieutenant Townsend took the phone from Chip and held a small plastic-covered map close to his face.

"We want fire support for coordinates . . . wun . . . thuh-ree . . . seven . . . ate . . . fo-wer . . . over."

"Wun . . . thuh-ree . . . seven . . . ate . . . fo-wer . . . roger. That is affirmative . . . over."

The lieutenant handed the field phone back to Chip. "Chipper, send the sergeant major up here."

Chip shoved his antennae down, grabbed his rifle, and hustled down the path. A few moments later the sounds of boots coming up the rocky path signaled the approach of the old sergeant major. Why the old man wanted to be out there was a wonder to Shawn. He had nothing to prove. He'd been through two wars already. He was a real Marine. The stuff legends are made of. The sergeant major knelt on one knee a few feet below the crown of a small hill and leaned on the stock of his pump shotgun.

"What we got, Rob?"

"Look's like four helmets on the ridge of that next knoll."

"Where's the Chief, Lieutenant?"

"I didn't call him up yet."

"Let's see what he says. What were you going to do?"

160

"I was going to send you and a squad over here on the left flank. We got fire support ready, 105s out of Phu Bai."

"Affirmative."

"Goody," Lieutenant Townsend whispered.

"Yessir."

"Go get the Chief and get back with your squad."

"I'm here, Lieutenant." The big Indian sergeant's soft voice startled the sergeant major. He flinched, then looked over his shoulder with a frown.

"You sucker. Your dad used to do that to me. I threatened to make that friggin' Indian wear a bell."

Ghosthorse showed no expression.

"Chief," Lieutenant Townsend said. "We got four helmets showing on the ridge of the knoll up ahead. I'm sending the sergeant major over to flank 'em on the left while we hit 'em straight on."

"I think it's a trap, Lieutenant." The Chief's tone was calm.

"Could be. I thought of that too."

"Helmets on a ridge line. Sun setting behind 'em. Smells."

"Think they got it plotted for mortars?" the sergeant major asked.

"They might have a couple of men there to open fire and draw us in." The Chief raised himself up to get a better view. He looked to the right. "There's a hill, maybe two hundred meters north. I'd put my tubes there."

Lieutenant Townsend exchanged glances with the sergeant major, then both looked in the direction of the hill. Lieutenant Townsend brushed at a whining mosquito near his eye then rubbed the back of his neck. "Sergeant Major?" he said.

"Sounds okay to me, Lieutenant."

"You feel like taking Murph's squad and laying down some fire on that knoll, Sergeant Major?"

"Affirmative. We'll light 'em up, Rob."

"Time check."

"Eighteen-forty-five."

"Chief."

"Affirmative, sir,"

"Sergeant Major, you lay in that fire at nineteen-thirty hours."

"Aye, aye, Lieutenant."

"Let's move out, Chief."

The night dropped over the land like a blanket. The column closed up until no one was more than a rifle's length away from the man in front of him. An ambush now would kill many. Shawn stumbled forward. He felt the skin rip away from his shin and gritted his teeth to keep from groaning out loud. He wanted to curse but didn't. A thud from behind turned Shawn's head. Luke moaned. Luke had found the tree stump too. The ground was hard with waist-level bush. Pockets of briars with thorns like small nails dotted the landscape. Compared with the dense jungle farther west, this was relatively soft going, but traversing anywhere in Vietnam at night was painfully slow at best. Shawn wondered what they'd do when they got to the hill. It would be sort of nice to know the plan for a change.

The ground began to rise to an incline. The round top of a hill rose up out of the ground ahead.

The crescent moon peeked through a gap in thick dark clouds above. The column stopped, each man quietly dropping to one knee. They stayed there, no one moving a muscle, no one coughing or twitching or swatting at the swarms of bloodsucking mosquitoes. It felt like an hour passed, but Shawn knew it probably wasn't.

"Guns up!" The whispered call came from the darkness ahead.

Shawn turned and whispered to Luke, "Guns up."

Even the two whispered words shot through Shawn like an urgent scream. He pushed himself up and his legs buckled slightly under the weight of his pack. He started forward. Each step was too loud. Brush scraping at his trousers sounded like a small tank moving forward. Part of him desperately wanted to chicken out. He could see the sergeant major, Lieutenant Townsend, and the Chief huddled at the point of the column. Shawn and Luke rushed up beside the huddle and knelt down. The Chief turned to the gun team and motioned them to follow. He stood and whispered back to the lead man in the column.

"First squad up."

Four Marines stood and moved forward behind the gun team. They moved up the hill, circling slightly to the right. Other than a few scattered bushes, the hill was barren. The lieutenant led the rest of the men straight ahead. The incline wasn't steep, and the footing was good. Ten meters from the crown of the rounded hill the palm of the Chief's hand shot back at Shawn like a traffic cop stopping a car. The Indian knelt. Each man did the same.

The Chief checked his watch. "Two minutes," he whispered. "If Charlie's here, he'll be on the back side of this hill to keep us from seeing the flash. They'll have a spotter on top. Pass it back."

Shawn slid back to Luke and whispered the message. Luke moved to the man behind him.

Shawn began to count. Two minutes, a hundred and twenty seconds, no time-outs. Giant mosquitoes whined at his ears. His palms felt sticky and cold. He lost count. That's about a minute, he thought, and started counting again. He licked nervously at the salty-tasting sweat dripping off of his nose. Crazy memories of Nancy and Eddie and Joe and his mom raced through his mind. He thought of Uncle Bob and his dad . . . semper fidelis . . . always faithful. He tried to concentrate on a verse to clear his thoughts and push away the fear:

"Do not fear what you are about to suffer. . . . Be faithful until death, and I will give you the crown of life."

Murph's squad opened fire. Shawn flinched, and he gripped the M60 tighter. Russian AKs exploded in a hail of return fire. Turning, he could see the muzzle flashes clearly. It was like having box seats. A few moments later the AKs ceased. Murph's squad kept firing.

"*O daw?*" a panicked Vietnamese shouted from the darkness.

"*Khong biet! Khong biet!*" Another NVA answered from the top of the hill. He was close. Close enough for the Marines to hear his high-pitched voice crack from strain. The first thump of a mortar round leaving the tube echoed from the dark hill. Shawn could hear the clink of another round against the metal tube. They were close. The frightening thought of hand-to-hand fighting flashed through his mind. He touched the handle of his K-bar knife on his left hip then touched the .45 on his right hip. They were there if he needed them, but neither one made him feel any better. A series of thumps began.

The Chief motioned the men to follow. He led them around the edge of the top of the hill. Light flashed across the dark terrain. Shawn shivered. They moved on around the hill until the enemy mortar crews were in sight. Just below the crown of the hill an area had been dug out and flattened. Four mortar tubes sat in a row about twenty meters away and slightly uphill from the Marines' position. Two pith-helmeted mortarmen manned each tube. They worked feverishly. Each round shot from the tube with a white flash. The sporadic flashes made a strobelight effect. The enemy soldiers seemed to move in jerky motions, like figures in an old film, as they shoved in rounds and closed their ears with both hands.

Someone grabbed Shawn, yanking forward and down. "Gun, here. Fire when I do." The Chief quickly spread the other men down the side of the hill.

Luke flattened out to Shawn's right and linked up two belts of ammo as fast as he could. Shawn took aim at the nearest NVA mortarman. Suddenly someone to Shawn's right opened fire. Shawn pulled the trigger. The first enemy mortarman stiffened, his arms reached up in agony as the phosphorescent end of one M60 tracer round broke off the lead bullet and sizzled into his spine like a tiny hot fire. He fell forward. Shawn raked tracers from left to right across the backs and sides of the enemy mortar crews. The strobelight vanished, but he fired the machine gun until he knew no one could be alive, until the barrel glowed red-hot and he could feel the heat on his face. He released the trigger. There was a dead silence.

Suddenly the rustle of weeds underfoot froze Shawn stiff. A shadow emerged from the darkness in front of him. The wind of a man's frightened feet breezed past Shawn's ear and down the hill into the jungle night behind him. A few seconds later M16s opened up fire from the top of the hill in one final burst then ceased. It was over.

Shawn stared down the dark hill, wide-awake the entire night. The phosphorus tip of the tracer burning into the mortarman's back played over and over in his mind. There was no doubt, even in this strange war of shadows and muzzle flashes; Shawn knew this was a confirmed. His. God saw it, he thought. He saw it before it happened. Should I say I'm sorry, Lord? You know what I feel. Satisfied? Maybe . . . How should I feel, Lord? Dad always said to pray for wisdom and God promises to give it.

He prayed.

Daybreak felt safe. A new beginning, another day alive, every daybreak in the bush felt like a relief. The first gray beams of light were greeted by a shout from the other side of the hill.

"Hot-diggitty-dog! He's mine, bro! Don't nobody claim him!"

Luke opened one eye and groaned, "Who is that maniac?"

Shawn sat up straight. His neck ached and his left hand was puffy and white from some insect bites. He looked toward the mortar tubes. "Sounded like Neader."

"That would figure."

"Luke."

Luke rolled slowly onto his side and rested his head in his hand supported by an elbow. "Yes."

"I've been feeling weird all night."

Luke's bushy eyebrows lifted as his black eye seemed to grow larger than his brown eye. "Could it possibly be that the designated feeling known to you as 'weird' could have originated during an unusual occurrence?" His eyebrows fluttered.

Shawn closed his eyes and growled. He looked back at Luke's big face and couldn't help grinning. "Sometimes, Luke, you can be very difficult to talk to."

"Yes."

The Chief stood and pulled his pack straps over his broad shoulders. "Saddle up. Link up a perimeter with the lieutenant around the top of this hill."

"Why didn't we do that last night?" Shawn asked.

"Too risky," the Indian said gruffly. He started up the slope then looked back. "Move it! Get a body count!"

The sun was hot from the moment the first rays touched skin. The platoon spread into a perimeter around the top of the hill and waited for Murph's squad to link up. Shawn followed the Chief over to the bodies of the dead NVA mortarmen. The body count was lower than expected. None of the salts seemed surprised. Three confirmed. Blood trails down the side of the hill where others had been dragged away by comrades proved the count was higher, but only confirmed counted. The dead men were NVA Regulars. They wore khaki uniforms with green pith helmets and tire-tread sandals called Ho Chi Minhs.

Shawn stared at the dead man by the first mortar. He lay facedown. A large hole in the back of his blood-soaked shirt was burned black around the edges from the phosphorus end of the tracer bullet. The heel of his left foot was shot away, along with half of his black rubber Ho Chi Minh tire sandal. Long columns of giant red ants had already started burrowing into the bloody stub, foraging for food. Shawn swallowed back a mouthful of vomit.

"They all have gun holes. Good shootin'," Chief said. "M16s too."

Shawn pulled his eyes off of the dead man at his feet.

The Chief stood over another body lying against the third mortar tube. "You okay, Marine?" he asked.

Shawn looked around, half expecting to see someone behind him. No one was near. A rush of pride pulled his shoulders back. Marine. Chief usually called him boot. "I'm okay, Chief." He looked down at the dead man. "I guess I know for sure this time," he said quietly.

"Your confirmed."

"Yeah."

"He's an officer." Chief nodded toward the body. "Pistol's yours. Take it."

Shawn looked at the holster on the man's hip and shrugged. "I don't know."

"Go on. That's what all the yelling was about this morning. One of the gooks ran over the top of the hill and into the lieutenant's men. Neader says he got him. Birdman said it was his. He had an SKS."

"What's that?"

"Russian sniper rifle, single shot. You can take it home. Can't take anything automatic."

"Chief." Shawn hesitated and looked at the dead NVA officer. "Chief, do you believe in Christ?" he blurted, half wincing at the expected reaction.

The Indian's face showed no change. He pushed his thick glasses against the bridge of his long straight nose. "You mean God?"

"Yeah, Jesus Christ."

"I thought he was the Son of God."

"He is. They're one and the same."

The Chief shrugged his shoulders. "Don't know, don't give it much thought."

"How many NVA and Viet Cong have you killed? Confirmed."

Ghosthorse shrugged, turned, and walked back up to the perimeter. Shawn looked down at the body again, then at the pistol. He closed his eyes.

"What a joke you are. Blow the dinks away then pray for 'em." Neader's nasal twang identified him before Shawn opened his eyes.

"Stuff it in your diddy bag, Neader. I don't pray for the dead."

Neader snickered as he walked over to the dead NVA officer. "I'm takin' that pistol unless you plan on prayin' me out of it." He shoved the stiff corpse over with his boot, leaned over, and removed the dead man's belt, holster, and pistol. He pulled the long-barreled pistol out of the holster, held it by the barrel, and hammered the dead man hard in the mouth with the butt end. He pulled a broken yellowish tooth out of the dead man's mouth.

"What are you doing?" Shawn demanded.

"Addin' to my necklace, choirboy." He pulled a string necklace of black-and-yellow teeth from under his collar and grinned his ugly grin at Shawn, then took an ace of spades playing card out of his helmet band and shoved it in the dead man's mouth.

The chopping sound of rotors overhead signaled the approach of a supply helicopter. Chip tossed out a green smoke grenade as Shawn walked back to the perimeter. A minute later the old bird bounced down in the center of the perimeter. The enemy mortars were loaded aboard. A new boot replacement stumbled out of the helicopter with a bundle of mail under one arm. The helicopter door gunner tossed out three big boxes of C-rations and the old Korean-era chopper lifted off. No matter how often Shawn watched a helicopter lift off, he always ached to be onboard, flying away from the heat and filth of the torturous jungle.

"If I get ham and mothers again—" Luke stopped his threat short.

Shawn pulled his longing gaze away from the chopper.

"Thought you liked them."

"No more." Luke looked accusingly at Shawn. "Have you been giving your C-ration cigarettes to Dook?"

"Why?"

"I knew it!"

"So what? They're mine to give."

"We could be getting peaches and pound cake for those cancer sticks."

"We got a new man," Shawn said to change the subject.

Luke moaned. "Yes, and he had a grenade hanging off every available thread."

"Don't look now but Chipmunk is bringing him this way." Chip bounced across the top of the hill with the new man close behind. He stopped beside Shawn, blew a bubble, and popped it.

"Hello, gentlemen," Chip said. He thumbed through a handful of mail. He pulled out three letters. "Lukevec. Lukevec. Lukevec." He dropped them on Luke's lap.

"McClellan. McClellan." He tossed two to Shawn. Then he held a pudgy hand out toward the replacement. "Gentlemen, this is PFC Rice."

"A gunner?" Shawn asked.

"No, but he's with you guys for now."

"Name's Rice, C. J. Rice." The stern-faced boot stepped toward Luke with his hand out. Luke shook hands.

"I'm Lukevec, and this is Shawn McClellan."

Shawn waved. C. J. Rice stepped over to Shawn to shake hands. Shawn leaned forward to shake. Rice squeezed Shawn's hand until it hurt.

"I believe men should shake hands, especially Marines." He nodded his head once at the end of each statement as if to confirm it. "That's the way men in the Old West did it." He nodded and brushed his sleeve across his pencil-thin mustache.

Shawn forced a smile. Liking this guy was going to take some effort, he thought.

"Hey, Shawn! A letter from Joe." Luke tore at an envelope.

"Outstanding."

"Better sit down. C. J., is it?" Luke asked.

"Affirmative," he said with a nod. "That's my name. Don't call me anything else."

Luke looked at Chip. "Moving out soon?"

"That's affirmative," Chip said. "We're movin' out in a bit." He turned and walked toward the next position.

"Listen to this." Luke nudged Shawn and read from Joe's letter. "I got an R&R date. April twenty-ninth for Sidney. See if you guys can get the same date so we can party together." Luke looked at Shawn for a reaction.

"Sounds great to me, man."

"Listen to this. 'Khe Sanh was like a nightmare. They overran part of our perimeter one night. It was hand-to-hand. I killed a gook with my E-tool when the sixty jammed. Maybe we can talk about it in Australia. Tell Shawn I got stuck with a Bible-reading Holy Roller for an A-gunner. He's worse than Shawn! Write soon. Joe."

Luke laughed and pounded Shawn on the back. Shawn smiled and forced a chuckle.

"You a Bible thumper?" C. J. asked, his face serious. He lowered a shoulder to slide one pack strap off. A smoke grenade dropped off his cartridge belt. The cylinder-shaped can rolled against a rock by Shawn's boot.

"I wouldn't call myself a Bible thumper, but . . ."

"He is a Bible thumper," Luke said.

"I don't take to bein' preached at," C. J. said with his confirming nod.

"I don't take to bein' blown away by some ignorant boot." Shawn kicked the canister back toward C. J. then elbowed Luke in the shoulder. "And don't call me a Bible thumper, Lukevec."

Luke's bushy brows rose until they almost reached his porcupine hairline. "What in the world? Where did that come from?"

Shawn turned his angry eyes back to C. J. C. J. looked mad. "Bend the pin on that smoke grenade before you kill somebody." Shawn stood up with his letters and walked toward the CP.

Luke jumped up and followed after Shawn. He laid a hand on Shawn's shoulder. "Hey, Shawn. What is it?"

Shawn faced Luke. He felt embarrassed at losing his temper. "Just leave me alone for a minute, okay? I need to be alone for a minute."

Luke looked worried. He shrugged. "Sure." He turned and walked back over to C. J.

Shawn walked over to a large flat rock and sat down. He gazed out at the endless hills and valleys of green and wondered why he was being so emotional. The land looked like a wavy green ocean, deceptively quiet during the day, or at least most of the time. He needed to pray and he knew it; that was the only way he could make his insides peaceful and quiet. Nothing else ever helped. He remembered his dad's dark glasses staring down at him.

"Don't sit around worrying about this or that, Shawnie, just lay your cares upon Jesus. If you're one of his kids, he hears you and he will be with you until the end."

Shawn smiled at the memory. He missed his dad. He bowed his head and prayed for what felt like a long time before walking back over to the gun position. Luke was eating C-rats and C. J. was dabbing oil on his rifle.

"I owe you guys an apology. I'm sorry for acting like such a jerk," Shawn sat beside Luke.

"No sweat, Marine," Luke said as he grabbed a pink envelope out of Shawn's hand.

"Hold it, grunt. I ain't that sorry," Shawn said, grabbing the envelope back.

Luke sniffed like a hound dog on the trail. "Perfume. Woman. Nancy Diez." He groaned.

Shawn began to tear open the letter. He paused and closed his eyes. "Boy, Luke, I can almost see her. Tan muscular legs,

169

perfect face, yellow mini-skirt.'' Shawn sighed, opened his eyes, and looked at Luke. "You ever dream in color?"

"Read, please," Luke nudged impatiently.

"You know, Luke, I think they've been lowering the amount of saltpeter in the C-rats."

"Shut up and read." Luke pinched the bridge of his nose as if he had a headache.

Shawn began to read. " 'Hi Good-Lookin'; how's the cutest boy in the Marine Corps doing? My sorority sisters suggested that I keep you up on what's really heavy and happening.' "

"This is really boring stuff, McClellan," Luke said dejectedly.

"Yeah, I know. They never write what you really wanna hear."

"It is your own fault, McClellan."

"How's that?"

"You are so bloody conservative, she probably wouldn't think of writing you anything too exciting for fear of you going into cardiac arrest."

"Sit on it, Lukevec."

"Now me, if I ever get married, she'll have to be a sweat hog."

"You're probably right, Luke," Shawn said, mimicking Luke's slow monotone.

"I'm serious, Shawn. A beautiful girl will make your life horrible, but a big fat sloppy girl will treat you like a king."

"McClellan!" Chip shouted from the CP. "Get your gun team's C-rats."

Ten minutes later the sergeant major brought Murph's squad up the hill. They barely filled their packs before someone shouted "Saddle up." They were not happy.

The week passed the way all weeks passed in the bush. One, tired miserable minute at a time, each man staring at the man in front of him as the hump labored on endlessly. The platoon never quite reached the mountains and that was fine with everyone. Another week came and went, but it felt as though a month had passed. Still no contact with the elusive enemy. Sometimes it felt as though the platoon had humped into the twilight zone, the passage of time had changed, and twenty-four hours took twenty-four days to pass by.

C. J. Rice was turning out to be a know-it-all boot who didn't want anyone telling him what to do. Shawn liked him less each day. The third week started as always, with a long hump. At noon they set up a perimeter on an unknown hill and chowed down.

Shawn scratched at a trickle of sweat running down his temple as he glanced around the perimeter of weary Marines. He shook his head and forced another bite of ham and mothers then nearly gagged.

"Why do you eat such food, man?" The Caribbean-sounding accent seemed to fit Cager's smile.

"I'm losin' too much weight, Cage." Shawn patted his stomach. "But, God, you're right, this is awful!" He grimaced.

Luke peeked up from tending to his C-ration can of coffee that was starting to bubble over a chunk of blue-burning C-4. "Cager, you're walking as silently as the Warrior."

"You got an English accent?" C. J. asked as he poured a packet of coffee into an empty C-ration can.

"Yes, I would suppose that it sounds a bit English. I'm from Jamaica, originally."

C. J. poured water into the can. "How'd you get in the corps?"

"My family now lives in Baton Rouge." Cager squatted down beside Shawn and pretended to sneak a peek into the can of ham and lima beans. Shawn shoved down another spoonful of con gealed lima beans. Cager watched as Shawn swallowed and nearly gagged. He closed his eyes and shook his head as if a chill had come over him.

"I should rather be thin, man," Cager said with a fake shiver. "My family sent me some hot sauce in my last care package—"

"So it was your package!" Luke pointed an accusing finger at Cager. "Chipper told us that someone got a care package."

Shawn pointed his plastic spoon at Luke and looked at Cager. "He's been lookin' for that package ever since we got mail two weeks ago."

Cager grinned. "It was me, and the hot sauce is my treasure."

"It would take a great deal more than seasoning for this to emulate food," Luke said.

"Yes. This is true, but my mother's homemade hot sauce can do wonders, man." Cager stood up and turned to walk back to his position.

"Thanks, Cage," Shawn said. Cager waved.

171

A few minutes later Kayto strolled up with no shirt on and carrying a pint-size bottle of dark red sauce. "Cager's got a water detail, he sent this over." He handed Shawn the canning jar of sauce and turned to C. J. "Whoever's going on the water detail, meet Cage over on the other side of the hill."

Shawn made a quick check of his five canteens, then tossed three empty ones to the ground beside C. J. "Your turn, Rice."

"Why me?" C. J. asked angrily.

"It's your turn, PFC," Luke said with a mocking tone.

"Look, I don't wanna be a nag, man, but"—Shawn pointed at C. J.'s cartridge belt laying on the ground at his feet—"you really better bend the pins on those frags and smoke bombs."

"When's the water detail leave, Kayto?" C. J. asked.

"In a minute. Go collect everybody's jugs and meet on the other side of the CP."

"Everybody's canteens? Who says?"

Kayto rolled his eyes in frustration. "That's the way it's done, boot." He emphasized the word "boot" with a forced grin.

C. J. tossed his C-ration can of coffee into the dirt. "This sucks."

"C. J." Shawn said quietly. "We bury the cans out here so the gooks don't use 'em."

"Use 'em for what?" he snapped.

"They shove in some C-4 or whatever's handy. . . ." Shawn began.

"A detonator and some wire . . ." Luke added.

"And you got a Marine with no foot," Kayto finished with another grin.

C. J. snatched up his canteens. Luke tossed him two more. C. J. stomped away, grumbling, toward the next position.

Kayto sat down. "Man." He shook his head and groaned.

"Yes, we concur," Luke said with a polite smile.

"Boots like that don't last long," Kayto mused aloud, "How's the fire, man?"

"Fire?" Luke asked. Kayto winked at him and nodded at Shawn.

Shawn finished stirring in a few drops of sauce and took his first bite. He swallowed. The back of his tongue burned hot. He opened his mouth and started blowing. His eyes grew larger. "Wa . . . water."

Kayto snickered through his nose.

"Well, how's the fire, bro?"

Shawn put the can down on the ground and flattened both hands into the dirt as if he were trying to push the ground away.

"Shawn, have you been thinking about Nancy's skivvies again?" Luke said softly, pinching his eyebrows together in a squint of mock concern.

Kayto's eyes and mouth closed; he started laughing through his nose like a dog sniffing for food. He opened one eye, pointed at Shawn's flushed face, and sniffed even faster.

"Waa . . . waa . . . ter!" Shawn moved onto all fours, searching like a blind man among the packs and weapons until he found a canteen. His hands shook as he unscrewed the lid and downed the better part of a canteen of Halazone water. Kayto rocked back and forth, holding his stomach and sniffing out laughter through his nostrils. Tears streamed down Luke's face; he bobbed his head and pointed silently.

Shawn gasped. "What's in that stuff?" He blew out and wiped sweat from his eyes.

"Cajun sauce," Kayto blurted.

"That ain't like any Cajun sauce I've ever had."

" 'Tenant says fer you to get ready 'n saddle up."

Shawn looked behind him. Dook stood over Shawn, his pack and helmet already on and his M14 in hand.

Shawn grabbed the can of C-rations and stood up. "Dook, you're from Loo-zee-anna." Shawn handed him the can. "Take a bite of this."

Dook looked at the can suspiciously. He gave his walrus mustache a wipe with his sleeve then handed his rifle to Shawn. He spooned out a bite and chewed slowly. His big hairy mustache moved in circles with each chew like a cow enjoying a mouthful of grass. He stretched his neck and swallowed.

"Ummmm." Dook closed his eyes. "That there's right next to heaven." He opened his eyes to the stunned stares of his comrades.

"You really like that?" Shawn asked.

"You mean it isn't burning your mouth out?" Kayto asked.

Dook looked at Shawn, his dark eyes almost sad. "I guar-rone-tee that's finer than anything that's touched my mouth in a coon's age. Be askin' too much fer 'nother bite?"

"It's yours, Dook."

Dook looked shocked. He hesitated for a moment then spooned into the ham and mothers as if he feared that Shawn would change his mind.

Luke held up a hand. "Wait, Dook. Any takers? Ten to one this stuff is not hot compared to—"

"Birdman!" Shawn called to the skinny Marine putting on his pack twenty meters away. "Come over here for a minute and give us your opinion on this matter."

Birdman grabbed his rifle and helmet, then hurried over. Obviously the men needed his expertise.

"What can I help you with?" He pulled up on his drooping cartridge belt.

"Birdman," Luke began seriously, "we say this is the spiciest sauce any of us have ever tasted." Luke reached for the can. Dook handed it to him reluctantly. Luke gave it to the stern-faced Birdman.

"Birdman." Dook raised his chin and looked accusingly at the bony face. "Yooz ever had Cajun cookin'?"

Birdman turned his head and waved Dook away with his usual you-got-to-be-kidding scoff. "Mannnn." He looked back at the Walrus. "Are you jivin' me? There ain't a food I ain't had twice."

"I knew that," Luke said matter-of-factly. "That is precisely what I just finished telling these gentlemen." Luke's brows fluttered. Birdman whistled, then spooned out a tiny dab of the now-reddish ham and lima beans.

"What?" Dook pointed at the dirty plastic spoon. "You ain't about to taste no sauce in that puny bite."

Birdman looked insulted. His face took on the look of a man having been challenged. He dug out a heaping spoonful, opened his mouth, and shoved it in. The first change became apparent by way of Birdman's high cheekbones. They turned pink right before the eyes of the four Marines. They studied him as if he were a scientific experiment. His blue eyes opened wide, so wide they seemed about to pop out of his head. Then they got red and misty and tears ran out and over his cheeks. Luke pointed, his mouth open wide and his head bobbing in silent laughter. Kayto bent over, laughing through his nose so hard that he began snorting obnoxiously. Dook just grinned contentedly. Shawn laughed loud and long. Birdman began pounding on his chest with his mouth open and eyes looking startled. Shawn handed him the canteen. He began chugging it down.

"Guns up!"

Shawn grabbed the M60 in one hand and two belts of ammo in the other.

Luke grabbed his rifle. Kayto scooped up three belts of ammo and handed them to Luke. The gunners ran up the slope to the crown of the hill where the CP was. Lieutenant Townsend waved them forward. Doc Abernathy stood up and put on his helmet. The Chief pointed to a cloud of red smoke near the small stream fifty meters away.

"Let's go!" Chief shouted, and started down the other side of the hill in the direction of the smoke. Shawn and Luke ran past the lieutenant and the Doc.

"I'm comin'!" Doc shouted.

The Chief led the way down the hill, through twenty meters of head-level elephant grass that had a trail beaten down by the water detail. At the edge of the field of elephant grass was a wooded area with thick waist-level vegetation. Beyond that was the stream. The wooded area was covered with a red, sulfurous fog. Someone moaned in pain ahead.

"Marines comin' in!" Chief shouted into the smoke.

"Corpsman up!" The shout sounded like Cager. The moan turned into an agonizing scream. Shawn shivered and prepared to fire as they moved into the sulfurous fog.

"Corpsman!" Chief growled. Shawn moved through the thick brush to see what the Chief had stopped to stare down at. Cager had the smoking body of C. J. Rice pinned to the ground C. J.'s face was red and black. His clothes were burned away except for small patches of green cloth stuck to the skin of his legs. Sleepy held C. J.'s boots as he writhed in agony. Two other Marines knelt a few feet away facing the stream with weapons ready.

Chief turned. "Doc, get over here!" He looked back to Cager. "What happened?"

"The pin on a will'-peter got caught on a twig. It went off on his cartridge belt!" Cager's eyes misted over. "We couldn't put it out!"

Doc pushed by Shawn and the Chief. He dropped down and put his ear to C. J.'s smoking chest.

"He'll make it," Doc said, "but we better get an evac, ASAP."

Doc broke out a morphine packet. They made a litter from two rifles and a poncho.

Twenty minutes later the medevac chopper lifted off from the small hill. Doc said C. J.'s chances were good, but he was going to be one ugly Marine from now on. He had been a know-it-all jerk, but he was still a Marine. Shawn felt sorry. Luke had scribbled something on a piece of paper and shoved it in C. J.'s pack before they tossed it into the chopper with him. They watched the surrounding hills looking for muzzle flashes of incoming fire. The chopper was safely away, and then came the inevitable call.

"Saddle up!"

"Hey, Luke," Shawn said as the column trudged off the hill. "What'd you write on that piece of paper that you stuck in C. J.'s pack?"

"Well . . ." Luke hesitated.

Shawn looked over his shoulder. Luke avoided eye contact.

"I merely sent him off with my regards."

"And?" Shawn said.

"And, two small blueprint-type drawings of grenade pins, one bent and one not bent." Luke's bushy black eyebrows fluttered up and down. He did his closemouthed grin.

"That's mean, Luke."

"Yes." Luke sighed aloud. "You better say another prayer for me."

The platoon humped for five hours. They seemed to be heading back toward Truoi Bridge, but Shawn could never tell for sure. He often wondered why he had such a terrible sense of direction. He could never tell north or south or east or west, at least not until the sun dropped, and even then he had to stop and think hard. Eventually they crossed a rice paddy and Shawn was sure they were heading back to Truoi.

The walk through the village was different than before. Shawn felt safer just being around people. The hustling activity on Highway One was a welcome sight. Bicycles, mopeds, trucks, jeeps, and even a giant steel monster tank looked good. The tired, dirty column of Marines crossed the bridge with a new spring to their step. At the barbed-wire entrance to the ARVN compound an ARVN soldier pulled back the roll of concertina wire for the platoon to enter.

"Hey, GI Marine! Me souvenir you Coke!" Shawn searched for the small voice. Phan, the little Coke dealer, sat on the turret of an old rusting French tank next to the compound. He waved at Shawn, then held up an eight-ounce bottle. "Me souvenir you Coke!"

Neader stooped down just inside the wire of the compound and picked up a small rock. He stood up and threw it at Phan.

It broke against the barrel of the old tank. "Who's that gook yellin' at?"

Phan flinched. He looked scared.

Shawn's face flushed warm with anger. "Neader!" he shouted from outside the compound wire. "He's talking to me! Leave him alone."

"Careful," Luke said quietly. "Your crease is showing."

Neader glared through the concertina wire that separated the two. "Yooz better say a bunch of prayers, dude, before you screw with me."

Sleepy and Jake walked past Shawn. "Smash his ugly face, McClellan," Sleepy said.

The line between Shawn's eyes deepened. For a moment he considered fighting.

"Marine, me souvenir you Coke," Phan shouted.

Shawn turned away from the stare-down with Neader. The little boy waved and smiled. His face looked so innocent, his smile so genuine.

"Go see the kid," Luke prodded.

Shawn glanced back at Neader, who grinned with contempt then walked away. The urge to knock his jagged, yellow teeth right out of his ugly face swept over Shawn again but he knew it was wrong. He turned to Luke.

"Here." He handed Luke the M60. "Stow this in the compound for me, would you?"

"Sure." Luke grabbed the gun and laid it over his shoulder. Shawn felt lopsided without the heavy M60. The gun was part of him. It felt odd without that twenty-four pounds of steel lying against the side of his neck. He waved at Phan and walked toward him. The old French tank looked so small compared to the new American monsters. It must have been sitting there for fifteen or twenty years, Shawn thought. He jumped over the small block wall that separated the old tank from the road.

"GI, number one. I wait, you come back, every day." Phan held out an eight-ounce bottle of Coke in each hand.

"Thank you, Phan. That is very honest of you." Shawn reached up for the boy. "Let me help you down."

"Take Coke." Phan handed Shawn two bottles then reached inside the open turret-hatch of the tank and pulled out three more.

"What's it like in there?" Shawn asked.

"Number ten. Boo-coo snake."

"Why do you keep the Cokes in there?"

"Bamboo viper nest. He bite. You KIA. Nobody steal."

"But—" Shawn began, then decided the kid must know what he's doing. "Did you find a place to live for the old people?"

Phan handed down the Cokes. Shawn cradled them.

"I find." He pointed at the village across the bridge. "Number-one bunker." He frowned. "Number-ten house. No wall. Rain in."

"Let's go take a look."

Phan looked happily surprised. He climbed off the turret and jumped from the edge of the tank. Shawn had forgotten how small Phan was. Standing straight with his shoulders back, he only came up to Shawn's belt. Shawn dropped the Cokes off with Luke, who was determined to sleep away all memory of the last couple of weeks, then followed Phan across the bridge. Phan turned left just past the bridge. They followed the well-trodden path east along the river for two hundred meters. It was the same path the platoon had taken through the village, only now Shawn was going east, toward the South China Sea. It was spooky being so far from the bridge all alone. He wondered if it was a mistake, a Marine this far down the trail by himself. He asked Jesus to protect him. That made him feel a little better. To his left an old woman squatted along the riverbank with a small boy sitting between her legs. She fingered the boy's straight black hair then pinched something from his scalp. She put it to her mouth and bit it, then searched for more. Shawn stared as he walked past and, not watching forward, plowed into the back of Phan.

"Sorry, little guy."

"Here." Phan pointed to a grass-roofed hootch on four posts to the right of the trail. "Need wall. Be number-one house."

An old woman squatted by a small fire to the left of the hootch. She looked up from stirring a black kettle, filled with some fishy-smelling substance, hanging by a metal rod over the fire. She smiled and nodded her head up and down. Her mouth was red from chewing on a betel nut. Her teeth were black. Her face looked like old leather and her gray hair, tied on top of her head by a piece of dirty string, was badly in need of washing. She stood and bowed, looking at the ground, then bowed again and again. Shawn bowed back.

"How do you do, ma'am," he said, feeling ignorant for not

speaking her language. She mumbled something to Phan and scurried across the trail, down to the riverbank.

Phan pointed to a spot beside the fire. "You sit. You chop-chop."

"I'll sit, little buddy, but I better skip eating." Shawn sat on the damp ground and looked at the hootch. "So, what are you going to do about the walls?"

Phan shrugged and looked at Shawn with a who-knows face. The old woman scurried back across the trail to the fire carrying two wooden bowls and four chopsticks. She scooped one bowl into the black kettle and handed it to Shawn. Shawn started to speak, to say no thanks but when the mama-san's dark eyes looked suddenly very sad, he smiled.

"I'm honored. Thank you."

Her dark eyes seemed to sparkle as she grinned and handed him two dark-stained, hand-carved chopsticks. Shawn looked into the bowl as he arranged the sticks between his fingers. He felt nervous. It was brown rice mixed with gray bits of fish. Something moved in the rice. Then two or three grains of rice moved as if some tiny creature were burrowing underneath. He'd seen her cooking it. How could something be moving around in it? Maybe he was seeing things. Fatigue, he thought.

"Chop-chop," Phan said, gesturing with his chopsticks. He brought his bowl to his mouth and began scooping in bites with his dark eyes glued expectantly on the green-eyed American.

A lump of air filled Shawn's throat. He looked for more movement in his rice. He looked back at the little boy, his black eyes still staring over the edge of his bowl as he scooped bite after bite. Shawn swallowed the lump, brought the bowl close to his mouth, his fingers struggling to get the two bamboo sticks into position. He closed his eyes and scooped in the first bite. He chewed harder than normal, grinding his teeth between bites, figuring that it would be better to put something dead into his stomach than anything still crawling.

"It's very good." Shawn smiled and lied. "I mean, food is number one."

Phan nodded happily with his mouth stuffed full. The old mama-san smiled her black-toothed smile, spit a stream of red betel nut juice at the ground, turned, and walked into the underground bunker to the left of the hootch.

"Papa-san sick. He sleep," Phan said.

Shawn looked at the hootch then turned back to Phan. "A

few sheets of plywood would just about do the trick on your hootch."

Phan's eyes opened wide. "Yes. American wall." He pointed at Shawn with his chopsticks. "You can get?"

"I'll ask the Chief. I'll try."

Shawn finished up his food and excused himself. He knew that it was improbable, but his stomach told him he had dysentery even before he reached the compound. Highway One was already deserted as Shawn walked across the old bridge. The villagers had begun to fade into their dark holes for the night. It seemed like such a miserable life. Abject poverty in the day and death at night if you dared venture from your spider-ridden hole. Either the Cong kill you, or the ARVN or the Americans do, or you die of some disease from sleeping in constant dampness. Even so, these little people would choose this existence over communism. Shawn knew it was true; he'd seen it with his own eyes and heard it with his own ears. He was doing what was right. It was right, no matter what the media was feeding the people back home.

Luke's big face popped up over a sandbag on the gun bunker at the north end of the bridge. "Where have you been?"

"I had dinner with Phan." Shawn patted his stomach and crossed his eyes.

"That good, huh?"

"Let's just say that this was the first food that ever walked into my mouth. Where's the Doc? I think I better get something for my stomach. I ain't feelin' so hot."

"Good thought. He's in that first house, where we dropped off the weapons. This is our residence for the night, probably for as long as we have bridge duty."

"Oh, okay. You have the gun?"

"Yes, I was just giving her an oil massage."

"Good boy, Luke. I'll be back as soon as I throw up on the Doc."

The compound consisted of two rows of four small blockhouses with tin roofs separated by a narrow dirt street. The Marines were in the first house. The Doc sat with four others scattered lazily around an upside-down helmet with a loose deck of playing cards piled in.

"Hey, Doc," Shawn called from the makeshift wooden door. The young Dennis the Menace look-alike sat up straight on the hard dirt floor.

"Like, you paged, man?"

Chip the radioman pointed a finger at Doc. "Dobie Gillis!" he blurted with his back resting against the PRC-25.

"Wrong. Maynard G. Crebbs."

Shawn put a hand to his stomach and moaned, "Doc, I ate some food . . . and—"

"You need somebody to change your diaper, boot?" Neader's nasal tone came from the far corner of the dimly lit room. Shawn's stomach rumbled. He felt queasy. He wanted to blast back at Neader, but now was not the time.

"You over at the north-end gun bunker?" Doc asked.

"Yeah."

"Meet you over there after this hand."

"Okay." Shawn turned and walked back to the bunker.

By the time the Doc arrived Shawn had lost his cookies twice. He remained bent over at the waist with hands on his knees. The Doc handed him two big white pills that looked like horse vitamins. He gagged them down with half a canteen of water.

Luke leaned over to study Shawn's face. "He has turned a rather nice shade of Marine Corps green," he said with his big face sticking out and not smiling.

"Doc, how long will I feel like this?" Shawn wiped sweat from his forehead.

"A night or so. Those pills should, like, KIA any parasites you swallowed."

"How did you end up here, Doc?" Shawn asked.

"It's a mystery to me, man."

Shawn sat down and slumped against the outside wall of the bunker. "Does everybody in California talk like that?"

"We had a Dobie Gillis fan club on campus. How about Florida?"

"What about Florida?" Shawn asked.

"Do very many people talk like Lukevec?"

"I beg your pardon," Luke said.

"No. He's one of a kind," Shawn said.

"I do not know exactly what you are trying to imply," Luke said, dragging out his syllables even more than usual.

"Like, you feel any better, McClellan?" Doc asked.

"A little."

"You do look less green, Shawn. Now, I should like to have an explanation." Luke said.

181

"Like, man, I know people speak slow down south but you put me to sleep in midsentence."

Luke did not smile.

"Chip told me that you went to Berkeley," Shawn said.

"Only for a semester." Doc kicked at something on the ground near the entrance to the bunker. "Hey, man, you got rats in there."

"You are kidding." Luke sounded serious. "I thought they were small raccoons."

"Isn't it weird how everything like, ugly and like, dangerous and like, creepy and like, crawly is extra big over here?"

"It is. That rat could kill some cats back home," Shawn said.

"Why did you want to be a corpsman?" Luke asked.

Doc took off his soft-cover hat and pressed down on the crop of white hair sticking up on the crown of his head. It immediately sprang back up. "Well, I really didn't decide to be a corpsman. It sort of just happened, ya know, man? I mean, my best friend got killed up at the Rock Pile in sixty-seven. I was low, man, really down. They started protesting the war at school and makin' signs calling Marines baby killers and Jane baby came to spread her communist trash at a rally so she can keep her mug on the front page, and I was down, ya know, really down, man, over Bobby and Bobby wouldn't kill no babies so I get with ol' Jim Kelly, he's a chem major, and make the biggest stink bomb you ever saw."

"You have been around Chip too long," Luke said. "You sound like you're calling in artillery."

"Jane Fonda?" Shawn asked.

"The commie-lovin' . . ."

"So what happened?" Shawn asked.

"They pop me in jail for inciting a riot and my old man is really ticked off cuz he's a doctor, plastic surgeon, big-time liberal, him and my mom. They're so embarrassed, they don't want to look uncool cuz it's uncool in Hollywood to be anything but left-wing twits, ya know what I mean, man?"

"So how'd you end up in the Navy?" Shawn persisted.

"Well we had some hot words and my old man says that at least the protesters had the decency to do things legally, but I knew they were paying people ten bucks to show up and march for the cameras. Anyway, they said I better straighten up or they were cuttin' off the funds so I said, 'Sit on this.' " He held up a fist. "So I joined the Navy."

"You should have just joined the corps. You're in it anyway," Shawn said with a laugh, then held his gurgling stomach.

"I think I wanna wear a white coat someday, so this will give Dr. Abernathy good practice, I figure." He stood up straight. "By the way, any jungle rot to report?"

"Just a scab," Luke said.

"I got something on my foot. Keeps getting sort of pussy," Shawn said.

Doc's face beamed and he tilted his head as if he had just heard good news.

"Far out, man. Like, you can lose your foot to that stuff. Get your boot off."

He dropped to one knee beside Shawn. Shawn took off his boot and sock. Within seconds the young corpsman had his first-aid kit open. He attacked the foot with the glee of a mad scientist who just found a half-built Frankenstein in his basement.

Luke thoroughly enjoyed it and made mention of the fact more than once and even helped point out possible danger areas on Shawn's foot that the Doc otherwise might have missed. The Doc was quick to jump on each danger zone with his lance or his wire brush, which he used in much the same manner as an auto-body man trying to sand away years of rust from a piece of metal. He ended each mini-surgery by applying a burning, red, foul-smelling solution known to the platoon as "Doc Abernathy's elixir." Shawn figured the smell alone would keep the giant rats from biting him and hoped that it might even keep the mosquitoes away.

Night came on quickly. So did the hungry mosquitoes.

The night drifted by slowly, like all nights in the Nam. Shawn wondered if his eyes would be any good after the war. It didn't seem natural to stare so hard into blackness every night. Morning came. Each morning started the same way along Highway One. Engineers, more commonly known as human mine sweepers, would walk cautiously, one nervous step at a time, sweeping back and forth with their metal detectors like men vacuuming the dirt road. In back of them was usually a tank and a squad of Marines for cover. Each day they would find the mines and blow 'em and each night the Cong would put in new ones. Shawn watched the engineers approach. He gave the lead engineer a thumbs-up when they started across the bridge.

"How's it goin'?" Shawn asked.

The engineer paused and wiped sweat from his eyes. "Pretty

good. They let us bomb Haiphong last month," he shouted, and continued across the bridge.

Shawn turned to Luke. Luke pretended to be asleep on top of the bunker; his head was on his pack and he was curled up in a fetal position around the butt end of his rifle. The barrel stuck up like an antenna.

"Luke."

Luke moaned.

"Luke, what'd that guy mean?"

A spitting sound followed by a splash of tobacco hitting the dirt turned Shawn's head.

"Means they ain't got no mines, ner food, ner nothin' else, 'less'n we let 'em." Goody turned and spit again. "We bomb Haiphong Harbor, they got no ammo. We stop, Russians ship in more."

"That's crazy. Even the U.S. can't be that stupid."

Goody shrugged with his hands shoved deep into his baggy pockets. "Chipper says the preacher's comin' in, figured you'd wanna know."

"Why? Am I the only one interested?"

Goody chuckled. "Probably." He walked away.

"Goody."

"Yep." Goody looked back over his shoulder. His jaw pushed out on one side like he had a tennis ball stuffed into it.

"Do you know how I can get hold of some plywood?"

"Yep."

"How?"

"I know how I could," he spit, "but I don't know how you can."

"What's that mean?" Shawn said with his irritation showing.

"I'd just requisition it off the Sea Bees."

"What Sea Bees?"

"The ones that come out 'ere ever' day to help build that hootch over there for the CAP unit."

"You mean steal it?"

Goody shook his head yes and gave Shawn a condescending smile as he walked away. Shawn looked toward the big parachute that shaded the CAP Marines across the road from the ARVN compound, then turned to watch Luke crawl off of the bunker like a bear coming out of hibernation.

Luke leaned his M16 against the bunker and stood up. He stretched and yawned and chuckled. "The old Doc really did an outstanding job on your foot last night. He is one odd human being."

"I bet it's tough having your folks against you like that, especially when you might get blown away without seeing 'em again."

"Screw him. Little rich Daddy's baby."

"Sometimes you can be awful hard on people."

"Well, old buddy, we can't all wear halos." He grinned and fluttered his brows. Luke's sense of humor could be grating, sometimes mean, but one flutter of his thick bushy eyebrows combined with that big silly grin made it difficult to stay mad at him.

By 0900 the chaplain arrived via jeep from Phu Bai. Lieutenant Townsend ordered the platoon to gather by the abandoned French tank for chapel service.

Shawn was glad to see the tall, soft-spoken chaplain again. There was almost an aura around Chaplain Elliott's face as he stood in front of the old French tank praying silently while the men sat on the ground waiting. Shawn had seen that aura before. His dad's face used to have it. Shawn stared at the chaplain but could almost see his dad's dark glasses and hear his calm, assuring voice.

"Sometimes, son," his dad would say, "a man doesn't have to have eyes to see the Holy Spirit in another man's face." Dad's big strong arm hugged him close. "Sometimes the Holy Spirit can glow through the darkness. . . ."

The chaplain had closed his eyes to lead them all in prayer, but suddenly Chip the radioman and Lieutenant Townsend were beside him. Chip had his full gear on. A bad sign.

The chaplain opened his eyes. "What is it, Rob?" he asked the lieutenant.

"We got choppers on the way. Recons 'bout to get overrun up on Hill 600."

The chaplain turned to the rustling men and smiled. "Looks like my prayer was a bit long-winded."

The platoon laughed a nervous laugh with no joy in it.

"Quickly, men, go into battle with the words of our Lord in your hearts and minds." The chaplain opened his Bible and read aloud, "Deuteronomy 7:21, 'You shall not dread them, for the Lord your God is in your midst, a great and awesome God.' "

"Saddle up! Move it, Marines!"

Shawn knew it was a cornball feeling, but he couldn't fight

185

the sensation of excitement. He felt almost noble. Almost ready. And almost scared enough to wet his trousers. The men scrambled for their gear. Shawn jumped to his feet and ran to the chaplain.

"Chaplain!"

"Shawn, it's good to see you!" Chaplain Elliott slapped Shawn on the back.

"It's good to see you too, sir. Look, I wanted to help a small Vietnamese boy and these two old people he's taking care of. They live in the vill"—Shawn pointed in the direction of Phan's hootch—"over there on the east side of the bridge. His name is Phan. They don't have any walls for their hootch. They need four sheets of plywood, depending how big, maybe more. Can you help?"

"Saddle up, McClellan!" Sergeant Ghosthorse barked.

"Comin', Chief."

"I'll do what I can, Shawn," Chaplain Elliott said firmly.

"Thanks."

"Take care, Marine."

"Semper fi, Chaplain." Shawn signaled a thumbs-up and ran for his gear.

CHAPTER EIGHT

"Two Forty-eights"

Two Chinook choppers picked up the platoon, using Highway One for a pad. Shawn stared at Sergeant Ghosthorse as he sharpened the shovel end of his E-tool with a wet rock until it glistened like a razor. He remembered Joe's letter. The thought of hand-to-hand combat flashed through his mind and he shivered.

"You cold?" Luke asked from beside Shawn.

Shawn shook his head no and pulled up the feed cover of the M60 for another check.

Cornhusker laughed. "Twenty-one," he said. He forced a nervous grin at Murph as he slapped down an ace of spades on his thigh.

"Bro," Murph complained, "you is one lucky honky."

"There it is, Murph. I was born in Nebraska."

"Hey, Jake," Murph called toward the rear of the chopper. "Shakey Jake!"

"Yeah, Murph, yeah." Shakey clutched at his rifle standing on butt end between his legs.

"Be cool, bro. You got your Mattel on safety?"

"Yeah, Murph," Shakey answered quickly.

"Give your boy Sleepy, a nudge." Murph looked across the isle of the chopper at Shawn and smiled. "Sleepy makes me nervous when he yawns through firefights."

Shakey Jake leaned to his right to stare close up at Sleepy's face. "Sleepy, Sleepy, Sleepy," Jake repeated, his bug eyes twitching nervously from side to side. Sleepy opened one eye and stared into Jake's twitching pupils. Sleepy's open eye began to move from side to side also.

"Jake!" Sleepy bellowed. "I hate when you do that!" He gritted his teeth and closed his eye.

"Murph says to wake up."

"If I wake up I have to be here, Jake! I hate here!" Sleepy pulled his helmet down over his eyes.

A burst of M60 fire turned Shawn's head toward the door gunner. He released the trigger and watched his orange tracers arc toward the green blanket below, then turned toward the lieutenant squatting just behind him.

"Clearin' the gun! Hot LZ!" he shouted through the wind of the open hatch. He picked up a plastic bottle of oil and squeezed out a stream on the barrel.

Shawn reached inside his flak jacket and felt for the little Bible. He looked at Luke. "You hear that, Luke?"

"Hot landing zone."

"Wonder what old Chuck Caldwell is doin' today?" Shawn grinned.

"He is in class at SPJC trying to look up skirts." Luke looked nervous.

Shawn started laughing, slowly at first, then harder and harder until tears streamed down his face. Everyone but Sleepy gazed suspiciously at Shawn. He elbowed Luke. "Remember," he gasped between loud belly laughs, "when you dressed that stiff up for the party?"

The hint of a grin appeared on Luke's lips.

"And remember," Shawn said, wiping at tears in his eyes, "when Sandy Hendry plopped down in his lap?"

Luke started giggling. The serious faces of the other Marines exchanged questioning glances.

"She lifted off that stiff like a rocket!" Shawn screamed. Luke howled.

Lieutenant Townsend looked at Ghosthorse with one raised eyebrow. The stone-faced Indian nodded once and turned up his thumb.

"Lieutenant!" The copilot leaned out of his seat and shouted from the cockpit back into the chopper.

"Yo!" Lieutenant Townsend yelled.

The copilot pushed back on his dark glasses and pressed against one ear of his olive-green flight helmet as if to receive a transmission more clearly. "It's a hot LZ! Real hot! Tell your men they better be quick cuz it don't sound like we're going to touch ground for long!"

Lieutenant Townsend gave the copilot a thumbs-up signal and turned to the men. "Everyone hear that?" he shouted. "Sleepy!" he bellowed angrily.

Jake elbowed Sleepy hard. Sleepy jumped, pushed back his helmet, and blinked.

"I'm puttin' my boot up the rear end of the last Marine off this bird!" Sergeant Ghosthorse yelled.

Shawn's stomach fluttered as the helicopter began to descend. He leaned toward Luke to get a view out of a porthole as the CH-46 banked sharply. A Huey gunship seemed to pause in the air as orange-and-red fire shot two rockets toward a charred and smoking mountain slope. Near the top the mountain leveled off like some giant had taken a bite out of one side of it. The rest of the mountain rose to a steep peak. A large, permanent, wood-and-wire antenna that looked like an ugly little brother to the Eiffel Tower stuck straight up from the highest point on the peak of the mountain. It was a small base with maybe fifteen bunkers spread out from the leveled-out area all the way around the top of the mountain and ringed with concertina wire ten to fifteen yards thick.

The bottom of the helicopter felt as if it had dropped away. The CH-46 swooped down fast. The rear ramp lowered as the chopper leveled out for a landing. The door gunner opened fire at muzzle flashes on a nearby hill. A loud *crack-crack* made Shawn flinch as a bullet smacked through the wall of the helicopter just above Shakey Jake's head. Shakey lunged forward from the bench to all fours.

"Move out!"

"Jump!"

Sleepy grabbed Jake by the back of his pack and pulled him down the ramp on his butt. The chopper hovered five feet above the ground. Jake rolled off the end of the ramp with a shriek as the rest of the men pushed forward and jumped. Shawn's knees buckled under the eighty pounds of gear. He crashed forward onto the wavering floor of the chopper, scrambled to his feet with a lift from Luke, and sprinted down the open ramp. The jump to the ground wasn't that far, but the weight of his gear made the landing feel like a car wreck.

"Get up!"

"Move it!"

"Move it!"

"Move it, Marines!"

"Get that gun set up over here!" A Marine in a floppy bush hat waved from the top of a sandbag bunker just on the edge of the level part of the hillside.

"Guns up!" Chief shouted at Shawn and pointed at the Marine on the bunker.

Shawn pushed up and ran after Luke. The chopper lifted above their heads as they ran. The smacking sounds of bullets hitting the thin hull of the helicopter rang in Shawn's ears.

"Hold that chopper!" an angry Marine screamed. Then more men screamed somewhere behind Shawn.

"We got wounded!"

It was too late. Shawn knew it. Another twenty seconds and Charlie would have blown the chopper out of the sky. The cracks of Russian AK-47s sounded from every direction.

The thirty-meter sprint felt like a hundred times that. Luke dove into the small opening of a sandbag bunker that faced in toward the perimeter. Shawn stopped short of going inside. The bunker entrance had three bamboo steps going down, walled by four-foot-high sandbags on both sides. The rest was level with the entrance walls, approximately four feet above ground. Shawn peeked up on the roof of the bunker. The Marine in the bush hat was on his stomach, firing single-shot at a target down the slope of the mountain.

"Move over, I'm comin' up with the gun!"

"Come on up and get a tan, bro."

Shawn laid the M60 over the edge of the bunker roof, jumped, and pulled himself up. He flattened out beside the bush hat.

"Welcome to Hill 600." The round-faced Marine smiled. His face was blackened and he wore camouflage utilities. Shawn was immediately envious. He wanted camouflage utilities. Every grunt in the Fifth Marines wanted them.

"Don't fire that sucker yet," Bush Hat cautioned. "Mr. Charles will have our butts tonight if he knows where the guns are."

"How long have you been here?" Shawn asked.

"Shawn!" Luke yelled from inside the bunker.

"Yeah, Luke?"

"I'm comin' up!"

"Stay put, dude!" Bush Hat yelled. "We ain't got a target and we ain't got room!"

"Talked me into it," Luke replied slowly.

"Balman, Tony," Bush Hat said.

"I'm McClellan."

"Guns!" Lieutenant Townsend shouted from the edge of a large oval bunker near the center of the leveled-off portion of the hill.

"Here!"

"Stay there for now! Conserve ammo!"

Shawn signaled with a thumbs-up then turned to look back down the hill. Ten feet beyond the bunker the hill sloped down gradually. Concertina wire, at least fifteen feet thick, ringed the hill at that point. The brush and trees had been cleared another twenty feet beyond the wire. From that point on the jungle was dense all the way to the bottom of the hill. Four smaller hills, covered with forest, surrounded Hill 600. Each one was scarred with artillery hits or charred black from napalm strikes. The shooting stopped except for a single shot here and there around the perimeter.

"We should start getting mortars soon," Tony said, his eyes scanning the hill.

Shawn followed the thick string of wire around the right edge of the hill with his eyes, then turned back to Tony. "It looks pretty secure."

Tony closed one eye and gave Shawn a you-got-to-be-kidding glare. "Secure?" He shook his head. "You grunts kill me. Put some wire around you maniacs and you think you're back in the world."

"You aren't a grunt?" Shawn asked, then wished that he hadn't sounded like such a boot.

"Recon."

"What are you doin' holding a hill?"

"Well, this is the only hill we ever really held, that I know of. It's a relay base. We got a couple of 'prick twenty-fives' here. We relay radio messages from the deep bush."

"Mac!" Shawn turned at the call. Squatting at the entrance of the bunker was Sergeant Ghosthorse. He pointed back at the big round bunker where the lieutenant was. "CP's over there. Stay here. Medevac comin'. Duck some heads."

"Right, Chief."

"Hey, what's the poop?" Tony asked the Chief.

"Bravo company makin' a force march from the south. We hold till they relieve."

"How long will that take, Chief?" Shawn asked.

"They won't get here," Chief said matter-of-factly. He looked left. "Anybody in that trench over there?"

"Yeah," Tony said. "There were two from our team over there."

"Chief"—Shawn squirmed to see past his own boots—"what do you mean, they won't make it?"

"I would like to second that question." Luke quipped from inside the bunker.

"Oldest NVA tactic in the Nam." The Indian sounded disinterested. "Hit an outpost, outpost calls for help, they ambush the relieving column." The Chief stood up and ran toward the trench.

"Oh" was all that Shawn could muster.

Luke poked his head out of the bunker. He peered up onto the roof. "What exactly does that mean for those persons holding the hill?"

No one answered.

"Indian?" Tony asked.

"Yeah," Shawn said.

"We got one too—well, had one. KIA. He was a good Marine. We called him Chief too."

"You did?"

"Yeah, I guess they call every Indian in the corps Chief."

The distant thump of mortar tubes echoed from the far side of the smaller hill directly to Shawn's front. "Incomin'!"

"Incoming!"

"Incoming!"

The call reverberated around the top of Hill 600. Tony scrambled off the roof of the bunker with Shawn close behind. The first round hit the slope of the hill just below the wire and to the left of the bunker. The second round hit the leveled ground. Shrapnel whistled through the hot air. Shawn dove into the bunker behind Tony. The bunker was deep enough to stand up in if you weren't too tall. It was damp and musty. Pornographic pages from magazines were scattered haphazardly on the sandbag walls. Three small windows bordered in by split logs brought in enough light to see two huge, hairy rats in one corner. A black Marine with a boyish face sat on a case of C-rations with his back wedged into another corner of the bunker. He was brushing oil onto the bolt of his rifle with a red toothbrush. He looked up at Tony.

"They waste it yet, bro?"

Tony crouched to look up and out of the entranceway. "Still there."

"Charles must be losin' his touch," the black Marine mumbled as he brushed.

Tony unbuttoned his breast pocket and pulled out a small

Timex wristwatch with no wristband. "Mr. Charles don't KO that tower by the end of the hour . . ."

"Bro, my MPC is ridin' on Charles." The black Marine did a good imitation of Cassius Clay; he pointed at Tony and held his chin high. "The tower hits the canvas by the hour, and dollars of MPC goes to the man that hollers—and that be little ol' me."

"Get your MPC, Freddy," Tony said. He turned to Shawn and nodded at the black Marine. "This is Cassius Charles Caldwell."

"I'm Shawn McClellan. This is Eric Lukevec."

"We met," Cassius said. "Does this dude do downers, man?"

"I enunciate properly," Luke said.

"I knew a guy hooked on downers who talked like that, man. His brain was fried, bro."

"My brain is functionally outstanding," Luke said.

"We got a buddy back home named Caldwell," Shawn said.

"Twenty-five to one says we're no relation," Cassius said.

"Right," Luke said.

Cassius glanced down at Shawn's boots. "How long you dudes been in-country?"

Tony stepped over to the window facing the smaller hill straight ahead. "They gotta be a little salty," he said. "McClellan here thought this place looked secure."

Cassius brushed at the site on the end of his M16. "Grunts."

"This is our fourth lovely month on vacation," Luke said.

"Been catching the sights, have you?" Cassius asked.

"Our tour guide has not missed a thing. The imperial capital of Hue was the highlight of our trip."

"Hey, don't leave out that mad metropolis Truoi Vill," Shawn added.

"Get back, Jack. You guys were at Hue?" Cassius's tone turned serious.

Tony turned away from the window. "Fifth Marines?"

"Alpha One-Five," Shawn said. "Why?"

Cassius looked like he was whistling, but he made no sound.

"We heard that most of One-Five caught green bags home," Tony said.

"Yeah," Shawn said quietly, and looked at Luke. A surge of pride pushed goose bumps up his spine and down his arms.

"A lot of guys did," Luke said.

"Were you gunners in Hue, man?" Cassius asked.

"Yes," Luke said stoically. "And we were out-standing-in-our-field."

"Ah." Cassius waved off Luke. "You're BSin', me, bro."

"No he's not."

"How'd you skate through it?" Tony asked. He glanced out the window. The mortar rounds ceased landing.

"We got hit," Luke said.

"Just slightly," Shawn explained. "A few splinters of shrapnel. Where are you guys from?"

"California," Tony said.

"Cassius?"

"Louisville."

Shawn chuckled. "Makes sense."

"How 'bout you?" Tony asked.

"St. Pete, Florida," Shawn said. "Well, via South Charleston, West Virginia."

"Both from St. Petersburg?" Tony asked.

"Chopper." Cassius pointed through a gun slit, turned, and moved toward the entrance of the bunker.

The popping rotors of the medevac dropped down quickly. Two Huey gunships prepped the surrounding hills with rockets and machine-gun fire. Shawn ran out of the bunker with Luke on his heels. They set the gun up on the roof and took aim at the tree-shrouded hill directly ahead. Cassius and Tony flattened out beside two fighting holes about ten meters to the right of the bunker. Then nothing. One or two single shots cracked from the jungle below. The wounded recon Marines were loaded onto the medevac chopper. It lifted into the air, swung out over a dense narrow valley between Hill 600 and a smaller hill to the east, then climbed safely out of range.

"Gooks must have pulled back," Tony said.

"Yeah. Maybe," Cassius muttered in a way that said he didn't believe it.

The rest of the day labored by slowly with the four Marines exchanging high school football stories mixed with a tale or two about Tijuana. Shawn liked Tony and Cassius. They were honest about most things and easy to talk to. They admitted that neither had had a confirmed kill, though they had been in Nam for nearly six months. That wasn't unusual. Admitting it was. Recon Marines were supposed to find the enemy without making contact. They were highly trained in everything from paratrooping to scuba diving. Shawn stared into the gray jungle dusk beyond the wire and remembered watching the recons do pull-ups off a pole sticking out from the water tower at Camp Geiger, North Carolina. The physical challenge had really excited him; he knew that he was up to it. He was the battalion push-up champion at Parris Island and could run twenty miles in full combat gear faster than anyone there. He would be a recon now if it hadn't been for old Staff Sergeant Gerald McCully, an old hard-core Marine grunt, who had drawn a line in the dirt with the butt end of his M14 while the troops stood at attention near the rifle range.

"Any Marine that wants to join Force Recon, step over this line! Any Marine that just wants to find the enemy, step over this line! Any Marine that joined the corps to fight, stay put!"

Sometimes Shawn wished that he had joined the recons. Tony already had ten scuba missions and a couple of parachute drops. It sounded really exciting.

Cassius stood up fast. "You hear somethin'?"

No one answered.

"Shawn," Luke called from the left-side bunker window. "You see movement?"

Shawn squinted, then rubbed his eyes. An odd glow covered the mountains to his front with a yellowish tint as the last moments of daylight evaporated into darkness. "No, don't see a thing."

"Shut up in there!" An angry whisper from the bunker entrance took Shawn's breath away.

"Chief?" Luke whispered.

"You got claymores out?" Ghosthorse asked.

"Yeah," Tony said.

"When'd you put 'em out?" Chief asked.

"Cassius," Tony whispered.

"Yeah?" Cassius mumbled.

"When did you put out the claymores?"

"Was it light when you set 'em out?" Chief barked impatiently.

"Yeah. Before you guys got here."

"You dumb boot . . ." Chief growled something in Choctaw under his breath.

"What's the matter, man?"

"I want volunteers." The big Indian stepped down into the

195

dark bunker. "You smell that?" There was a long pause of silence before Tony sniffed out loud twice.

"Smoke?" Shawn asked.

"Yeah, sort of sweet," Tony said.

"That's opium." Chief growled. "They're getting ready. By now sappers have probably turned the claymores around. I want two men from each position to crawl through the wire and turn them back around."

"I'll go, Chief." Luke stepped forward.

"No way, Luke," Shawn said. "You're too big. I'll go, Chief."

Cassius stepped toward the entrance. "Haulin' or crawlin' I can't be beat, just step out da way of my happy feet."

"Flip ya for it, Cassius?" Tony said.

"Get that two-headed coin back in your pocket, honky."

"All right." Chief stepped up and out of the bunker then whispered back in. "It's McClellan and the other guy. One of you bring a weapon, the other one don't. Feel around real slow before you pick up the claymore. It might have a frag under it with the pin out and the spoon held in by the legs of the claymore. Move out." He ran toward the next position.

"Man, that dude's spooky," Cassius said.

Shawn pulled his .45-caliber pistol out of the holster on his hip, chambered a round, and flipped it off safety. "You bring your rifle, Cassius, I'll turn 'em around. How many did you put out?"

"Two. The detonator is in a foxhole right next door. Let's just follow the wire."

"How do we get through the concertina?"

"Straight down the slope, directly in front of the bunker, we got the three rolls of wire tied together." He paused and looked toward Tony. "Or is there four rolls?"

"I don't know, four maybe."

"Anyway, it works like a snake." He zigzagged with his hand to show Shawn the pattern.

Doubt squeezed on Shawn's bladder. He was scared and he knew it, but at the same time he felt anxious and ready for the adventure. "I'll just follow you," he said.

"Let's go."

"Shawn," Luke called quietly.

Shawn paused at the entrance. He could feel his heartbeat quickening. "Yeah."

"If you get killed, can I have a dozen or so children with Nancy?"

"You'll think my name was Casper, I'm gonna haunt you so bad." Shawn turned and followed Cassius up the steps, stopped, and whispered back into the bunker. "And every kid's gonna come out lookin' exactly like me."

"Probably come out holding little Bibles," Luke retorted.

Shawn followed Cassius to the fighting holes, ten meters to the right of the bunker. A hazy quarter moon put out just enough light to see the shapes of objects. They crawled along the rocky ground for twenty meters, then followed the detonating wire up to the first roll of four-foot-tall concertina wire surrounding the perimeter. Cassius reached the concertina first. He looked back over his shoulder and pointed left. They crawled left until they were directly below the bunker. Shawn watched nervously as Cassius felt for the tie of rope that held the wire together. The air was wet and thick as if a fog might be settling over the hill. The quarter moon bathed the cleared-out area beyond the wire in a dim blue light that seemed to cast a million shadows all the way to the black tree line twenty meters down the slope. There seemed to be the shadow of a fallen log ten meters to Shawn's right and ten meters down. Adrenaline pushed through his body. A log, it's only a log, he said, trying to calm himself. His heartbeat felt out of control. He looked at Cassius. He was already through the second roll of wire and was snaking left between it and the third. The path through the wire made an S shape. Shawn wiggled through the opening in the first roll.

Cassius jerked slightly then froze stiff. Shawn strained his eyes to see what Cassius was staring at. Rocks and mounds of dirt looked like men, fallen branches looked like rifles and machine guns. Shawn reached for his pistol. Cassius looked back at Shawn and motioned with his hand to go back. They crawled backward. Slowly. One move, then freeze and wait with eyes straining. A rustle of leaves and a branch cracking underfoot from the black tree line below sent a violent shiver up Shawn's neck that made his head shake. Shawn backed through the opening in the first roll of concertina wire. He rolled right and pulled out his pistol from the holster.

A chilly breeze slapped cold against Shawn's perspiring face. The sweet smell of opium was strong now. A shadow moved below, then another, and then the clink of web gear rubbing against something metallic. Cassius backed through the wire.

He didn't bother retying the concertina. He rolled toward Shawn and whispered into his ear.

"Beaucoup gooks. Forget the claymores."

Shawn crawled toward the bunker with Cassius right beside him. Behind them, the rustling sounds of moving men grew louder. Shawn crawled around to the entrance of the bunker and stood to a crouch by the sandbag entrance. Cassius stood up beside Shawn and stared back at the wire. He grabbed Shawn's biceps and squeezed it hard.

"There were three pith helmets right where the claymore was." Cassius released Shawn's arm and wiped sweat from one eye and took another deep breath.

"Come on." Shawn tugged Cassius down into the bunker.

"Claymores okay?" Tony asked.

"Forget the claymores, man! Charlie's everywhere!" Shawn blurted, then struggled to catch his breath.

Tony turned back to the bunker window and pushed his face halfway through.

"Christ, I can't even see the wire," Tony growled.

A clang like two metal pots being smashed together echoed from beyond the wire. Somebody shouted a command in Vietnamese from the black jungle below. Suddenly the darkness was alive with clanging pans and shouts and screams but still no shots.

Shawn grabbed the M60 from Luke. "We better get on deck, Luke!" He darted out of the bunker and up the bamboo steps and slammed face-first into something hard. A flak jacket. Ghosthorse. Shawn jumped back. For an instant he wanted to deck Ghosthorse just for scaring him.

"Chief! You scared the livin' crap out of me! Forget the claymores—"

"Shut up! Don't open fire till they reach the wire."

"Where is the relief column, Chief?" Luke asked from behind Shawn.

"Chip picked up a transmission. They were callin' for medevacs a few miles from here. Better have your E-tool handy. Twenty-round burst, gunner." The big Indian turned and vanished toward the next position.

"Friggin' Injuns," Tony mumbled from inside the bunker. "Ghosthorse. They sure named that one right."

Shawn laid the gun on the bunker roof and climbed up after it. Luke followed.

"I'll set the gun up on the deck, Luke."

"Right behind you."

"Tony. Cassius. You staying in the bunker?"

"No," Cassius whispered. "We'll be in the fighting holes on your right."

A chorus of Vietnamese voices rose over the clamoring noise below.

"Get back, Jack!" Cassius sounded scared. "They gettin' all juiced up."

Tony peeked over the edge of the bunker. He slapped Shawn's boot. "They're getting doped, all right. Charles is out there mainlinin', bros. He ain't even gonna know he's dead till tomorrow."

Shawn looked at Luke. Beads of sweat dripped down Luke's big face, glistening like tiny moon balls as he worked frantically to link up belts of M60 ammunition.

"God, I'm scared stiff, Luke." Shawn lifted his chin from the stock of the M60 and blew out hard.

"Me too. How many frags you got?"

"Four. I think I got four."

"Stupid bunker!" Luke growled

"How many you got? Straighten the pins!"

"Right."

"Did you hear the Chief?" Shawn asked with his eyes straining to see movement.

"Why have a bunker if you can't be in it when the shooting starts?"

"The relief column got hit. They ain't comin'."

"This looks bad, Shawn."

Luke's nervous fingers couldn't squeeze the end of one belt together with another. He jerked his hands away from two belts of ammunition and slapped himself hard in the face. He grabbed up the two ends of the M60 belts again and snapped the belts together then pressed his nose and chin into the sandbag roof.

"God, Shawn."

"We better say a prayer, Luke."

He tried to think of the right words, but all he could think of or hear were the maniacal screams and banging pans.

"God, Shawn," Luke mumbled again as he lifted his face from the sandbag and stared into the wire below. "They can overrun us."

Shawn forced himself to take a deep breath and gave up looking for the right words. Just pray fast, he thought. "Dear Jesus, please protect us, and forgive us for being jerks, Lord. We're sorry for all of our sins. . . ."

A cluster flare shot into the air and burst an eerie red light over the mountain slope and valley below.

"Trip flares," a voice from the darkness whispered. "They hit one of our trip flares."

"I see somethin'!"

"Psst. Psst," Tony called from the darkness to Luke's right. "We got trip flares in the wire, wait till they hit 'em."

"That's too close," Luke whispered to Shawn.

The thump of mortar rounds leaving their tubes echoed through the hills. The wait for that first explosion turned every muscle hard with anxiety, then the earth shook and kept shaking with chaotic fury. Shrapnel whistled through the air, singing off rocks or thudding with deadly force as it found earth, sandbags, or flesh. Someone screamed in agony from the CP bunker. Flashes of white light blinked on and off with each ripping explosion, but still no Marine fired.

Suddenly a red flare shot into the air to Shawn's left, hissing as it climbed then popping open with red light and floating down under a miniature parachute. Three North Vietnamese soldiers were halfway through the concertina wire. Two stood straight, holding the wire for the third to climb through. They were close. Shawn could see the outline of their web gear and the AK-47s slung over their shoulders. Another flare shot up like a tiny rocket and then another to the right of the bunker. An M60 machine gun opened up on the far side of the hill.

"Corpsman up!" A shout came from the center of the perimeter.

"They're in the wire!" someone from Shawn's left shouted, and opened up with an M16.

"Fire!" Luke screamed, and elbowed Shawn as he grabbed for his rifle.

Shawn squeezed off a burst of fire at the three NVA in the wire to his left. The first tracers shot high over their pith helmets and into the dark valley below. Shawn lowered his fire until a steady stream of tracers shot into the stumbling figures. The flare burned out. Only the black night remained. Shawn ceased fire. His night vision was gone. He was blind.

"Gooks in the wire!" someone screamed, and fired, far to Shawn's left.

Another trip flare shot into the air to Shawn's right. Then a ripping explosion tore a gaping hole through the wire as the remains of a human bomb flew through the air like pieces of a broken doll. A green flare shot into the black air from Shawn's right. The mortar barrage stopped. He followed the flare with his eyes for an instant then looked back to the slope in front of him. A chilling scene took his breath away.

"Jesus Christ!" Luke said, his mouth open and gawking in terror.

Luke clutched at Shawn's arm until he drew blood. Straight ahead, a long line of helmeted NVA soldiers emerged from the tree line. Suddenly another ripping explosion tore open the wire where Shawn had fired at the three NVA. He mashed his face into the sandbag and tried to crawl inside his helmet as rocks and dirt and shrapnel and pieces of the dead NVA smashed against the bunker. An enemy officer screamed, exhorting his men forward. The line of NVA walked forward, stumbling like drunks, shouting and firing almost haphazardly. Their aim was pitiful, some even shooting into the ground in front of them as they came up the slope while others shot wildly into the air or far over the tops of the Marine positions.

"Ready! Aim!" Sergeant Ghosthorse's voice rang clear from the right of Shawn's bunker. Shawn turned. There in the dim flickering light of the red flares, the Chief had four M79 blooper men on their knees, aiming at the line of skirmishers. "Fire!" All four fired at once. The explosions staggered the line of enemy soldiers.

"Reload!" Ghosthorse turned toward Shawn; the reflection of the flares and rifle flashes bounced off his thick glasses, making his eyes beam like some science fiction monster. "Get that gun working, Marine!" he screamed.

Shawn flinched, then took aim and fired. Orange tracers sputtered through the air, raking back and forth along the line of oncoming soldiers like a murderous laser. Luke fired his M16 until it clicked. He ripped out a magazine and shoved in another as fast as his hands would work.

"Aim!" Chief shouted again.

"Fire!" A second barrage of M79 rounds ripped into the now-ragged line of NVA. Screams and explosions mixed into one continuous roar.

"Ready!"

"You better throw good!" Luke screamed back toward the

entrance of the bunker. Shawn glanced over his shoulder. Five Marines knelt behind the bunker. A green flare popped high over the wire, bathing the landscape in a mixture of red and fluorescent-green light.

"Pull pins!" Lieutenant Townsend screamed.

"Throw!"

Shawn ducked his face as the Marines cocked their arms to throw. The spoons of two of the grenades bounced off Shawn's back as the frags sailed overhead toward the enemy below. A burst of AK fire ripped into a sandbag to Luke's right. He jerked and grabbed his face.

"You hit?"

"No. Just dirt!"

The grenades exploded amid more screams. The line of skirmishers stopped firing. They began to fall back, some groping for weapons, others dragging dead and wounded comrades back down the hill to the tree line. The Marines ceased fire at almost the same moment. It was perfect fire discipline, Shawn thought. He looked at Luke, still holding his face.

"You okay?"

"Yeah, it just stings."

The drone of a plane above lifted Shawn's head.

"We got Puff ready to work!" Chip yelled from the CP bunker. "Spot 'em! Guns!"

Shawn squeezed off five short bursts toward the tree line beyond the wire and beyond the cleared-out area. A few seconds later a roar came from the sky. Every eye looked up as a giant golden arrow of orange tracers wavered toward the tree line below. Shawn laid on the trigger. He swept his fire back and forth to mark the target. A loud sucking noise shot out of the black trees. From the corner of his eye Shawn caught the white flash. He released the trigger of the M60 and glanced right.

"Incoming!" a startled voice shouted from the center of the perimeter.

Luke dropped his rifle, buried his face in the sandbag roof, and covered his helmet with both arms. Shawn froze. A B-40 rocket spiraled straight toward the bunker like a huge sparkler. Shawn shoved his face into the bunker and bit through his lower lip and waited to die. His ears screamed in pain. He felt himself flying through the air.

* * *

"Knock knock." He felt a sledgehammer smashing the top of his head. "Hey, like, anybody home?"

Shawn opened one eye then winced from a stabbing headache. The flickering green light of a faraway flare illuminated the worried sweaty face of the young corpsman looking down at him.

"Doc?"

"Stay cool, McClellan. You're okay, bro."

"My left knee feels, oh! Crap! Doc! My shoulder hurts. My knee's bleeding! Hey, Doc, I'm hit?"

"Outstanding deduction, Sherlock. Charlie can't put no B-40s over on you, bro." The corpsman slit Shawn's left trouser leg open with a K-bar.

"Luke. Is Luke okay?" Shawn tried to sit up. A sharp pain like a needle going into his ear brought a groan.

Doc pushed against Shawn's chest.

"Sit still. Luke's okay. Peppered his butt good, though." He began wrapping gauze around Shawn's knee.

"I'm right here, Shawn." Luke sounded weak. "Just thinking about those round-eyed nurses in Da Nang."

"Luke! You okay, really?"

"Yes. I think so."

Shawn could feel warm blood running into his left armpit. He felt scared. "How bad are we, Luke?"

"Just some shrapnel," Doc said. "Now shut up and think about the sack time in a real bed under a real roof comin' your way."

"Of course, Shawn—" Luke paused and groaned. "—you realize what this means."

"What?"

"This would have been our second forty-eight-hour Heart, if you had not volunteered us in Phu Bai. We would be going home, Shawn. The world. Mini-skirts. Big American wazzoos. Bikinis. Cheeseburgers."

"All right; enough. You're killing me. I'm sorry. I'm sorry!"

"Oh, that helps me immensely, PFC McClellan."

"How did I get hit on the left?" Shawn asked. "I saw the rocket coming from the right."

"That one sailed right over us," Luke said. "Killed a recon back there. We got hit by the one coming from the other side."

"I never saw one coming from the other side," Shawn said.

"Like, you never do, grunt," Doc said as he shoved a short needle of morphine into Shawn's thigh.

Shawn and Luke rested against the shattered remains of the bunker for the rest of the night. The morphine took away most of the pain and brought on a sense of euphoria. Listening to the moans and whimpers of the dying enemy below while floating on a morphine high made for a grotesque combination. Heavy fog settled over the hilltop like a wet gray blanket.

By daybreak the morphine had worn off and the pain became intense. Being able to see felt warm and safe. Shawn closed his eyes tight. A rush of pain shot through his shoulder.

"Don't bother praying, Shawn," Luke said.

Shawn opened his eyes and looked at the big sad face resting against a wall of sandbags beside him. "What?"

"I know what's wrong now."

Shawn twisted to get a look at his shoulder, but it hurt with movement, so he slumped back against the sandbags.

"Yes, Shawn. You have been praying to the wrong God. Look." Luke held out a small jade Buddha.

"Yeah, right, Lukevec."

"Yes. Goody took it off of a dead gook. Old fat Buddha baby is in charge over here and that explains why every time you pray, I almost get killed. In fact, old fat Buddha is buried not too far from here."

"I suppose he is. China?"

"Yep."

"Sort of funny how the God I pray to conquered death, and all the others are still in the dirt."

Luke squinted then opened his eyes wide as if a light of comprehension glowed across his stoic face for the first time.

"Medevacs!" Ghosthorse shouted from the bunker to Shawn's left.

"Choppers comin'!"

"Body count!"

"Alpha! Pass the word!"

Shawn looked at Luke. "I thought we were dead last night."

"So did I."

"Gunners," Tony called from his foxhole. He struck a match and cupped the flame instinctively from view. He lit a cigarette then took a long drag as if he had been waiting a long time to do so. "You get to Da Nang, look us up at First Recon Battalion."

"Where?" Shawn asked.

"Where in Da Nang?" Luke asked. "Shawn has zero sense

of direction. He would have us heading toward Hanoi.'' Luke slurred his words. He still looked drowsy from the morphine.

"Just diddy-bop over to Freedom Hill and ask somebody. They'll point you.''

Cassius stood up in the hole next to Tony. "Beaucoup cold beer and hot mama-san!'' He stretched and yawned and looked toward the wire. "Get back, Charles.''

Shawn sat up straight and peered around the edge of the bunker. Two NVA bodies hung grotesquely from the concertina wire. They were naked except for shorts. They were covered with sand and dirt and weeds that stuck to their oil-coated bodies. It was a well-known sapper—suicide squad—camouflage technique. A few yards away a lone forearm and bloody hand dangled from the wire.

A loud whistle signaled the approach of Birdman. "Woo, lookin' good.'' He whistled again. "One, two, three, four, over there's one, that's five, get back! Charlie could take roll call in a phone booth today, bro.''

Neader walked past the bunker without a word. He was stripped to the waist. He had a farmer's tan on his arms, but he was pale white from the waist up, revealing a giant black spider tattooed across his back.

"Get back, Jack!'' Cassius yelled from his fighting hole. "Grunt, you got a real beauty humpin' your back.'' He laughed.

Neader glanced over his shoulder and continued toward the wire. "Blow it out your diddy bag, boot!'' He growled through his nose as much as his mouth. He gave Cassius the finger.

"Up yours, Jack,'' Cassius replied.

Neader stopped at the wire where the sappers had opened a three-foot section with satchel charges the night before. He searched the ground for booby traps, then stepped slowly through the blown-out area of the wire. He walked over to the khaki-clad body of an NVA soldier lying facedown. Neader moved around behind the body and kicked the corpse hard in the groin. He slowly rolled the body over with the barrel of his M16. He knelt down by the head, removed its pith helmet, drew back his fist, and punched it hard in the mouth.

"That dude's really sick,'' Cassius said.

Neader rolled the head of the corpse to one side and smacked it in the back until a couple of teeth fell out. He then picked them up, put them in his trouser pocket, and searched the pockets of the dead man. He pulled out some paper bills that looked like MPC, stood up, and counted it as he walked back through the wire to the perimeter. He walked past Shawn, Luke, Tony, and Cassius as if they were not there.

"What is he doin'?" Luke asked.

"He's makin' a necklace," Tony said. "We got a guy that does that." He reached out a hand to Cassius and pulled him up out of his fighting hole.

A mocking whistle preceded the Birdman's customary that-ain't-nothing wave. "That ain't nothin', guns. When I first got in-country, ears was in. Man." He whistled and held his nose as if something stunk.

" 'Twern't that bad," Goody said as he ambled up beside Birdman like a cowboy after a long ride.

"If I'm lyin', I'm adyin'," Birdman complained.

"You only been here three months longer than the gunners! You'd think it was three years the way he goes on!"

"They stunk bad," Birdman persisted. "And three months 'in-country' is the same as three years of normal life."

"After a while ears turn just like cowhide. Just like a little piece of leather on yer cartridge belt," Goody said, marveling. He looked toward the wire. "I think you boys stepped in the spit over here last night."

Goody walked toward the perimeter wire. He nudged the hand that hung from the wire by the severed tendons of a forearm. He looked back at the others and shook his head. "That ol' boy ain't gonna be strumming no guitar."

Birdman whistled. "Hey, put a cigarette between the fingers. We can get Dave Blaine's camera and take a picture and send it to Bonnie Kay!"

Goody started back to the bunker. "I ain't yer fool, boy! You waste your own dad-gum cigarettes."

"Cheapskate."

"And don't let them ugly lips be speakin' of Bonnie Kay."

"Raw. Real raw, Goody."

Goody looked toward the northeast sky. "We better pack 'em on over to the CP, Birdman."

"Medevac?"

Birdman cocked an ear toward the sky. They both came over to Shawn first, laid their weapons against the sandbags, and sized up the task.

"I'll get his feet," Birdman said.

"Yep," Goody mumbled. He leaned over and grabbed Shawn under the arms.

They locked arms to form a chair under Shawn's rear and carried him to the CP bunker. They sat him down gently with his back against the front side of the CP bunker, then turned back to get Luke. It started raining. The slapping of rain against plastic turned Shawn's head right. Four bodies wrapped in ponchos lay five feet away. Flies buzzed around them. They were side by side. Scabbed-over rivulets of blood snaked from under the ponchos like the legs of a spider. The muddy jungle boots of each dead Marine were all that showed. Shawn stared for a moment, watching as water cascaded off the nearest poncho and ran in little streams toward his boots. He belched and swallowed back the bile of his empty stomach. Someone cleared his throat. Shawn looked away from the dead Marines. Dook stood a few feet away with his M14 rifle under one arm, like a quail hunter.

"Hey, Dook."

"Glad you're okay, McClellan. Saw those B-40s headin' for your tracers last night and, well . . ." Dook paused and swiped at his walrus mustache. He looked uncomfortable. "Glad you're okay." He turned and walked away.

"Thanks, Dook." Shawn felt warm inside.

Old Dook never talked much, and it felt special that he chose to use his few spoken words in such a way. Shawn watched the lonely Marine walk away until footsteps coming from the opposite direction caught his attention. It was Lieutenant Townsend and Sergeant Ghosthorse.

Townsend walked up and knelt down on one knee, with the butt of his rifle resting on his boot. He smiled and shook his head. He took off his helmet and scratched his jarhead haircut. Townsend's clean-shaven face always looked out of place to Shawn. Everyone else had a mustache. Even the Chief had a few hairs over his lip. The lieutenant had lifer stamped across his college face, Shawn thought. He was the only Marine Shawn ever saw shaving in the bush.

"Sergeant Ghosthorse tells me you and Luke fought like Marines last night." The lieutenant's blue eyes were all business.

Shawn felt himself sit up straight against the sandbags. "Thank you, sir."

"Here's Lukevec, Lieutenant," Ghosthorse said.

Lieutenant Townsend stood and helped Goody and Birdman lay Luke on his side. "How ya feeling, Luke?"

"I'll be fine, sir," Luke said slowly, "as long as I never sit down for the rest of my life."

The lieutenant chuckled and glanced toward the sound of the rain splashing off the poncho-covered bodies. His smile melted away. He turned back to Shawn. "Chief tells me that this would have been two forty-eights for you men if you hadn't volunteered to help with the wounded coming out of Hue. Doc concurred. Is that true?"

"Yes, I, guess so, sir," Shawn stuttered, and wondered what was coming.

"Lukevec?"

"Sort of, sir."

"We didn't even know about forty-eights at the time, Lieutenant," Shawn said.

"That doesn't matter. I'm putting you both in for a Navy Commendation Medal with Combat V for valor. I'm sorry that you won't be going home with this Heart but I'm also glad we'll be getting you back."

"Thank you, sir," Shawn muttered in quiet surprise.

"Thank you, Lieutenant," Luke echoed.

"Thank the Chief, here. I thought this was your ticket out."

"Lieutenant," Sergeant Ghosthorse said. "Who do you want on the gun?"

"We got a gunner comin' from First Platoon, I hope." He scratched his head and put his helmet back on. "Put Cager and Kayto back on it for now."

"We got medevacs!" Chip the radioman shouted from inside the CP bunker. The call echoed around the perimeter. Chip tossed out a yellow smoke grenade.

The landing took no fire. The dead were loaded first and shoved to the rear of the helicopter, then Shawn and Luke were lifted in. Shawn couldn't fight the feeling that he was somehow abandoning the guys. The old helicopter seemed to struggle to get off the muddy hill. Tired, dirty Marines signaling thumbs-up seemed to shrink away as the medevac gained altitude. Shawn turned to look at a flapping poncho. Wind rushing through the open hatch was blowing it on and off the face of a dead Marine.

Shawn leaned against Luke's shoulder and stared. It was like the dead Marine was playing the peekaboo game that mothers play with babies. Luke turned and found himself face-to-face with Shawn. They stared into each other's eyes. Shawn wanted to speak but there was nothing to say. They both sank back and stared out at the dark rainy sky, for what seemed like a long time.

"Luke," Shawn finally said.

The noise from the prop wash drowned out his voice.

"Luke." He nudged Luke.

"What?"

"Who are those KIAs?"

"Three of them are recons and one is that new boot from Arizona."

Shawn stared out of the open hatch where the door gunner now stood and stretched. The pain in his shoulder seemed to be getting worse. He looked under his shirt at the bloody bandages. The gauze wrap was beginning to cut into his armpit and for the first time in a while he wondered if he might be hurt worse than he thought.

The door gunner adjusted his flight helmet as he knelt down near the open hatch. "You guys are lucky. Phu Bai is filled up," he shouted. "We're taking you two to Da Nang."

Shawn nodded and wondered if that was good or bad. Good, he figured—if anything was really good in Nam. At least Da Nang was a big, relatively safe city.

"That might be nice," Luke said.

"There it is, bro," the gunner yelled over the prop wash. "At Freedom Hill they got a movie theater. You also got round-eyed women, nurses, and Red Cross girls." He held up a finger. "Numba one, GI."

Shawn closed his eyes and tried to picture Nancy. Would she cry when she heard? Pray maybe? I'll send her my Purple Heart, he thought. Medal! He opened his eyes and turned to Luke.

"Luke, we're getting a medal. Isn't that neat? Luke! How can you sleep so easy? Sleep and eat. You'd make a good pet."

He leaned back. He closed his eyes and tried to dream of round-eyed girls.

CHAPTER NINE

Round-eyed Girl

"PFC McClellan?" a soft, sensual voice whispered. A large, rather silly grin spread across Shawn's sleeping, boyish face.

"Talk about an 'eatin' grin,' Marine, you got one." A crude, guttural voice shattered the dream.

Shawn opened one eye. A young American girl with clean, tanned skin and short brown hair smiled down at Shawn with ridiculously white teeth. He opened his other eye then closed one again as if taking aim at the lovely vision.

"Open 'em, Girene. You ain't dreamin'." The guttural voice came from the hospital bed to Shawn's left. He tried to look left. A sharp pain in his shoulder forced out a loud grunt and jerked him flat again.

"Don't try to move, Marine." The pretty girl's face scrunched up as if she felt the pain. She gently touched Shawn's bandaged shoulder. "Is it very bad?" Her big round green eyes seemed so sincere.

"Gosh, you're really pretty," Shawn said.

"Gosh!" The guttural voice barked like a drill instructor then laughed loud and sloppy like a fat man with food in his mouth. Shawn's face felt warm and he knew he was blushing. He wanted to close his eyes to keep from facing the grinning beauty leaning over him.

"Hush up, Carl."

"Sorry, Miss Elsa."

"Thank you very much, PFC." Her soft voice nearly brought an audible sigh from Shawn. "I'm here to help you write a letter home." She paused and looked at a chart in her hands. "Yes."

"Letter?"

"Yes."

"Since you're left-handed you won't be able to write for a while. Married?"

"No," Shawn blurted.

She leaned down and pulled a small, gray wooden stool close to the bed on Shawn's right. She sat down and crossed her tan legs. She picked up a pad and pencil from a gray metal wash-stand between Shawn's bed and the next.

"Who is your next of kin? We should write them first and let them know that you're all right."

"I guess my mom," Shawn said. He leaned forward slightly to sneak a glance at her legs, then tensed with fear that she had seen him. He felt nervous. He reached up to scratch his nose and suddenly remembered that he wasn't left-handed.

"What's the address, PFC?" Her voice matches her soft green eyes perfectly, Shawn thought. He took a deep breath and fought back a sigh. He looked at her long legs again.

"PFC?" She leaned forward slowly and tilted her head side-ways just enough to make eye contact with Shawn, whose eyes had fallen into a trancelike stare at her legs. She has beautiful eyes too, he thought. Green eyes. Soft, sexy eyes. Shawn closed his in embarrassment. His face flushed red and he swallowed a dry lump before opening his own eyes again.

"I'm really sorry, ma'am. I'm not usually so rude, I. . ."
She smiled again and Shawn felt himself melt.

"Don't feel bad. You've just made my day. I'm Elsa Houtz."
"You must get this all of the time."

"True, but"—she winked—"I don't see too many shy Ma-rines coming through here."

"Look, Elsa, I, ah, well, what I'm trying to say is that I don't feel right, lying to you. I'm right-handed." Shawn heard his words but could not believe he was actually telling her.

"Oh, I'm sorry, your friend over in the next ward—well, ac-tually it's the next Quonset hut, but we call them wards—Lu-kevec?"

"Yeah, how is he?"

"Oh, he's fine. But he told me that you were left-handed." She uncrossed her legs and stood up from the stool.

Shawn's heart sank. She was leaving. He would probably never see her again. What a jerk. What a little-kid jerk, he thought. She turned to walk away.

"My name is Shawn, Shawn McClellan," he called after her.
She looked back and winked again. "I'll come and visit." She turned and walked down the aisle and through two swinging gray doors at the far end of the round-roofed Quonset hut.

"You married or somethin', boot?" the deep voice in the next bed asked.

Shawn waited until the swinging doors closed and he could no longer watch the beautiful girl's walk before turning to face the guttural Mr. Carl. He looked just like his voice. Fat, short neck, short-cropped hair on top with Marine Corps white sidewalls, a big broad face with a flat nose like a boxer.

"I'm not a boot, Marine," Shawn said clearly.

"I got more time in the chow line than you got in the corps, boy."

Old Carl was probably speaking the truth, Shawn thought. He looked to be somewhere between thirty-five and forty years old. He reminded Shawn of an older, harder version of Tony Horning, the Cornhusker. Boot or not, there is a limit, Shawn decided.

"Boy!" Shawn exclaimed with a tone of indignation. "You see a boy here, you better call his mama."

Shawn lifted his head from his pillow and stared at the wide face of the old vet and waited for a reaction. He felt rather pleased with his response and wished old Luke could have heard it. Carl gave him a long searching look before he seemed to relax with a half grin.

"I was beginnin' to think they slipped in a Navy squid. Who ya with, Marine?"

"Alpha One-Five."

"Grunt?"

"0331."

"Gunner." He raised an eyebrow. "Shrapnel?"

"Yeah, a B-40 rocket."

Carl pointed down at his foot and lifted a sheet up. He had a cast up to his knee. "Shrapnel broke my ankle. I work in supply here. They hit us with 122s a couple of weeks ago."

"I thought Da Nang was pretty secure."

"Compared to the bush, it's skate city."

Shawn rolled his head right. "This place looks packed."

There were two rows of twenty or thirty beds and each was occupied by a young man with short-cropped hair. Each man seemed to be bandaged in a different place.

"Been this way since Tet started," Carl said. He sounded like he always needed to clear his throat but couldn't.

"Mr. McNamara oughta be dragged in here by his lip just to see these guys," Carl growled.

Shawn looked over at him again. Carl stared at the ceiling. His fists were clenched. His short hairy forearms flexed into rocks.

"Like McNamara, do ya?" Shawn kidded.

"If that jerk-off hadn't stopped us from bombing Haiphong, the war would be over."

"You think they're afraid of China coming into it?"

"That's stupid! The Vietnamese hate the Chinese twice as much as they hate us. Nah, that wouldn't happen. But maybe the pogues in Washington are too stupid to ask an old salt." Carl rolled onto his side to face his young counterpart. "In sixty-seven I had sea duty. I was ranking NCO on the flagship for all operations in Southeast Asia. Admiral Warren Sharp was the head honcho for the Allied Forces in Nam." Carl chuckled. "Little guy didn't come up to my chin." He smiled. "That's one swab jockey I'd hit any beach with."

"How long *have* you been in the corps?"

"Twenty years, come July."

"Wow," Shawn mumbled as he tried to guess at the stocky man's age.

"I served with Admiral Sharp once before."

"Sharp didn't like McNamara?" Shawn asked.

Carl raised up onto an elbow and looked into Shawn's eyes, "I stood guard in the planning room of an aircraft carrier right out there"—he nodded toward the swinging doors—" and listened to the admiral tell the commanding officers what happened when he met with McNamara and Johnson. Sharp gave 'em top-secret reports from British and South Vietnamese agents inside Hanoi that verified the NVA were literally starving in the field. No food, no ammo, nothin'! The bombing of the North was kickin' butt and takin' names, brother. They were ready to crawl to the peace table on our terms. They couldn't even get a ship into Haiphong Harbor. They lost most of their antiaircraft weapons and Sam missiles and they couldn't rebuild 'em as fast as we knocked 'em out."

Carl fell back on his pillow with a look of disgust.

"Then what?"

Shawn tried to sit up. He had to hear this. It didn't have the ring of loose scuttlebutt. This old salt had a clean line of fire.

Carl put his hands behind his head and shrugged his massive shoulders.

"They gave him orders not to bomb beyond a certain parallel.

213

That parallel just happened to eliminate Haiphong Harbor as a target. It got so bad that they wanted to okay every bomb run and McNamara would say, 'You can bomb this oil depot but you can't bomb this refinery.' "

"That's crazy!"

"Insane. Old Sharpie told him to put it where the sun don't shine."

"Then what?"

"They relieved him of command. A bloody sad day for the American fighting man."

"What's goin' on? Why would they do that?" Shawn searched the rugged Marine's face for some hint that he was lying. He wanted this to be a lie.

"I got a feelin' we're never going to know, grunt. You can't let civilians run the military after they're already in combat. Pretty soon you're gonna have to ask Washington before you open up with that sixty."

Carl looked at the ceiling with his hands behind his head.

Shawn lay back on the pillow. He wished that Carl had never opened his mouth. What reason was there? What possible reason could there be for not invading, for not bombing, for not letting us win?

He closed his eyes. For the first time he noticed the softness of the pillow and the clean sheet under him. A mattress. The pillow cover smelled freshly laundered and memories of helping Mom get the clothes off of the line before a summer shower hit went through his mind.

"Well, where is she, Mc . . . Clellan?" That slow effort to enunciate every syllable could only be one person. Shawn opened an eye. Luke grinned, then moved his big bushy eyebrows up and down. Shawn smiled and laughed at the sight of his big friend standing on crutches beside the bed. He wore the same blue pajamas that everyone wore.

"Shawn . . ." Luke dragged out the name almost sleepily. "Tell me her exact location, Shawn."

"She left, Luke."

"That was a very short letter, Shawn," Luke said with a hint of sadness in his tone.

"Yeah." Shawn paused and debated with himself whether or not to tell Luke the truth. "I told her I was right-handed," he confessed solemnly.

"That is a shame, Shawn," Luke said with no expression.

"That's all you're going to say?"

"Yes . . . no. There is one other thing." He grinned his closed mouth, completely-satisfied-with-himself grin and waited for Shawn's reaction. "I also want to say thank you."

"Luke, you know that I really hate it when you give me that evil self-satisfied grin."

"I know, Shawn." He grinned with more contentment than before.

"All right, what is it?"

"The recons on Hill 600 got relieved. They're back in Da Nang. Tony and Cassius came to visit. They were there when I talked Elsa into writing a letter for you." Luke snickered.

"Come on."

"I bet Tony ten bucks MPC that you would be stupid enough to tell her that you were right-handed."

"Luke," Shawn began, then stopped. He couldn't think of a defense for what he had done. He felt that same old nagging feeling that maybe he was being the naive jerk that Luke always teased him about being. Shawn wondered. Maybe he was a goody-goody, an oddball of some sort, and just never knew it. Memories of being voted "Most Popular" in junior high and high school flashed through his mind. It felt good. Nobody had thought he was weird then.

"Yes, Shawn, you wanted to explain?" Luke said.

"Where's Tony and Cassius?"

"You were still zonked when they came by. They will return. The First Recons are based nearby."

"Hey, bro," a thin black Marine with a bandage over one ear called from the bed directly across the aisle.

"Yeah," Shawn said.

"Your man there is bleedin'." He pointed at the back of Luke. Luke felt the seat of his pajamas then frowned.

"I better get back, Shawn. See you tomorrow."

"Okay, buddy." Luke hobbled down the aisle and through the swinging doors. The seat of his blue pajamas was quickly soaking up the dark red blood.

Shawn closed his eyes again. He felt as though he were falling back a long distance. A montage of voices and images from home streaked by barely within his peripheral vision, like a strip of film going by a light. Then it slowed and he could see Mom kneeling on both knees with her head pressed against the TV screen and her hands clasped together praying. Flickering black-

and-white images of Marines jumping out of helicopters flashed over Walter Cronkite's shoulder. Tears from his mother's eyes ran down the screen. Eddie knelt beside Opal and put his heavy arm around her shoulders.

"He's fine, Mom. The Lord will take care of Shawn, I know that with all of my heart." Eddie gently pulled Opal to her feet. He turned her pretty face toward him. "God, Mrs. McClellan, I wish I was with him." Eddie's voice quivered. His big blue eyes frosted over.

"PFC McClellan."

Shawn felt something tug at his sleeve. Eddie's face disappeared.

"PFC," a stern voice repeated.

Shawn opened his eyes and focused in on the face of a Marine wearing starched utilities. He held a soft-cover in his hand and had the gold oak leaf of a major on his lapels.

"Yes, sir," Shawn said.

The major turned to a corporal standing at rigid attention beside him. The corporal handed the major a small purple box with gold trim. The major opened the box, took out a medal, and held it by the purple ribbon for Shawn to see. The gold head of George Washington was set in a deep purple-colored stone, and the stone was set into one beautiful golden heart-shaped medal.

"On behalf of the President of the United States and the Commandant of the Marine Corps, I present you with the Purple Heart and the thanks of a grateful nation." He laid the medal on Shawn's chest and nodded to a Red Cross girl standing behind the corporal. She stepped forward with a Polaroid camera.

"Smile." She flashed off a photo, waited a minute, then ripped out the picture and handed it to Shawn. "One dollar, MPC."

"I don't have any money." Shawn felt embarrassed.

"You should get an allotment in a day or so," she said. "I'll catch ya then."

The major cleared his throat as the Red Cross girl walked away. "It is our suggestion that you send this photo and the medal to your next of kin as quickly as possible. It will alleviate some of their concern back home."

"Yes, sir."

"Get well, Marine." He smiled and saluted.

"Sir. I never got a Purple Heart the last time I got hit. Can I get two?"

The major grunted and turned to the corporal. "You have a star handy?"

"Yes, sir." The corporal pulled out a small white box from his pocket and gave it to the major.

The major opened it, pulled out a tiny gold star, and handed it to Shawn. "Put this on the ribbon."

"Thank you, sir," Shawn said. He beamed with pride and he knew it. He couldn't help himself. He knew it was less than cool and not exactly "hard corps," but he had wanted a medal since he was old enough to spell Marine.

Carl turned toward Shawn after the others had gone. "Hey, boot. How old are you?"

"Eighteen."

Carl smiled. "Yeah." He chuckled and leaned back.

The weeks passed. Shawn began to almost get used to sleeping all night on a real bed. Eating real food took some getting used to also. He wasn't sure if his stomach had shrunk that much or if the various parasites that the doctors had discovered within him were unhappy with hot food.

Most of the Marines in the ward were grunts. Grunts did not turn the war off merely by wanting to, that much was plain. Each night someone would wake up screaming in pain or shout a warning of "incoming" from his own mental combat. Some men never spoke. In some ways they appeared worse off than those who screamed. Sometimes a man would break down crying in the middle of the night. It hurt much deeper than the screams.

Luke hobbled through the swinging doors with a spare set of wood crutches under one arm. Shawn watched the big character hop toward him. Luke had learned to move along pretty well on them.

Luke leaned the spare crutches against the side of Shawn's bed. "It has now been three weeks."

"I am ready Luke," Shawn said, mocking Luke's monotone. He sat up and grabbed the crutches. The shrapnel in his shoulder had been removed and the doctors had told him the small pieces in his leg would never be a problem. He wondered. It felt good just to stand, even on crutches. The left leg was weak, but there was no real pain to speak of. Luke led Shawn out of the swinging doors. The sun's heat hit like an open oven as he stepped through.

His eyes teared from the brightness and he perspired immediately.

"It must be a hundred degrees!"

"One hundred and eight, Shawn."

"I'll never gripe about Florida again, even in July, I swear."

"This way." Luke led them down a narrow cement sidewalk. They hobbled past four Quonset-hut wards just like Shawn's, then Luke turned into the swinging doors of the fifth hut. A small white sign hung over the doors. The word BURNS was in bright red letters. He stopped inside the swinging doors and looked back at Shawn. "You won't believe this."

He grinned his evil grin and did his Groucho Marx eyebrow routine. Luke hobbled down the waxed aisle, past bed after bed, until he came to the next to last bed on the left side of the aisle.

A Marine, bandaged from the top of his head to his ankles, lay motionless. His eyes, nose, and mouth had openings. His arms and feet were held up by ropes and pulleys attached to metal bars over his bed. Blue eyes peered from the bandage holes and squinted as if in pain as Luke stopped at the foot of the bandaged man's bed and smiled.

"What do you want?" the bandaged man snapped. His voice was muffled by the bandages.

"I just wanted to make sure you were okay." Luke said pleasantly. He held out a hand as if introducing Shawn. "I have brought you a new visitor. You remember Shawn, don't you?" Luke said with a soft voice and another smile.

"Shawn, this is our old buddy and favorite boot, C. J. Rice, now known affectionately by his close friends as the Mummy." Luke tilted his head and smiled pleasantly at the now-seething blue eyes of C. J. Rice.

"You son of—"

"Now, now, now. We must watch our temper, C. J." Luke turned back to Shawn with his satisfied grin. "What was it you used to tell Rice when he first reached the bush, Shawn?"

Shawn looked at the angry eyes, hating, from under the bandages. "I seem to remember trying to warn some new boot, was that you, C. J. ?" Shawn asked.

"I told you where to stick your advice," C. J. growled.

"Would you like me to come by later, after supper?" Luke asked in his softest tone. "I'll read you that nice story again."

"Get out of here, you jerks, or I'm callin' a nurse."

"Oh, not feeling our best, are we? Well, I'll be around tomorrow to check on you." Luke tickled the bottom of C. J.'s hanging foot, then led Shawn away.

Shawn giggled as quietly as he could until the swinging doors closed behind them. A belly laugh rumbled up from inside. He laughed until his shoulder hurt. A Navy ensign walked by glaring at the two out-of-control Marines. He seemed to be waiting for something from them. He stopped a few feet past them and turned back with a crisp about-face.

"I never saw your salute, Marines!" he barked angrily. Shawn swallowed back his laugh, but his eyes were wet. He couldn't get his face to comply as he lifted his eyes toward the baby-faced officer. Luke somehow managed to stop grinning and stand near attention on his crutches.

"Sorry, Ensign," Luke said.

"You better straighten up, mister!" The baby-faced ensign pointed at Shawn. Shawn stopped smiling and stood straight. The thought of Luke reading to C.J. Rice slipped across Shawn's mind. A giggle forced its way through his lips. Snickering followed. Shawn closed his mouth but the laugh came through his nose in snorting sounds that brought the ensign to a point of near rage. He jumped in front of Shawn. He shoved his baby face into Shawn's, nearly touching noses. Shawn stared cross-eyed at a dab of flesh-colored paste covering a tiny pimple on the bridge of the ensign's pug nose. The familiar scent of Clearasil mixed with Old Spice filled Shawn's nostrils and for one angry moment he would have given his two Purple Hearts for the pleasure of drilling this turd with just one punch.

"Sorry, sir." Shawn saluted.

"We don't salute out in the bush, Ensign," Luke said.

The ensign glared at Luke, then turned and marched away.

"So. What do you read to old C. J." Shawn asked, fighting to control another rush of laughter.

Luke shook his head. "I don't believe you. That jackass butter bar didn't make you mad?"

"Yeah, but I'm not going to let it bug me."

"You have been reading your Bible again." Luke brushed his fingers together like a kid saying "shame on you."

"So, what do you read to C.J.?"

Luke grinned as if extremely proud of himself. He cleared his throat. "I found a copy of *Return of the Mummy* over at the library. I drop by about every day and try to get in a page or so before he yells for a nurse," Luke snickered.

"Luke. I'm in awe. You've done it again."

"Yes, I have."

And so it went. Healing slowly. Gaining back a few lost pounds. Eating with knives and forks and drinking cold milk. Writing letters home, as many as you felt like writing and on dry paper. Wearing skivvies again. Listening to Armed Forces radio—the Beatles had a new song, "Hey Jude." Just lying in bed and hearing the rain on the roof was ecstasy. And each morning, after chow, Luke would hobble through the swinging doors with his mischievous grin and the two would take their morning stroll over to the tiny library.

One day Elsa pushed through the gray swinging doors with a bundle of mail in her hand. For some reason, probably because he hadn't received any mail in the five weeks he had spent in Da Nang, Shawn knew the mail was his. He wasn't sure which excited him most, Elsa's hips swaying toward him or the letters from home. She smiled and laid the stack of mail on Shawn's stomach.

"You must be a popular guy."

He sat up quickly. His mind raced through a dozen "cool" things to say until his tongue felt like a pretzel. He breathed out. "Hi, Elsa."

"Well, I was going to ask if I could write you when you go back to your unit but"—she looked at the stack of mail—"I don't think you would have time for me." She smiled.

"Will you?" Shawn asked. "I'd really like that."

She winked and smiled and walked away.

Carl gave a low whistle. "That's nice stuff," he said. The eyes of every Marine in the ward followed her through the doors.

"There it is, bro," Shawn said. He fixed his pillow against the head of the bed and sat with his back against it. He brought the stack of envelopes to his nose. The sweet scent of lilac was strong. He pulled a pink envelope from the stack and sniffed. Nancy. He put the others down and opened the pink envelope. A newspaper clipping dropped out as he pulled out the letter. He unfolded the clipping.

"Wow, check this out, Carl. I made the *St. Pete Times*."

Shawn held up the clipping. It was a black-and-white photo of him holding the M60 on Truoi Bridge. His shirt was off and his tight muscular build looked even more pronounced in the photo.

" 'St. Petersburg Football Star Wounded in Action,' " Carl read aloud.

Shawn grinned and looked at the photo again. He couldn't believe how much weight he'd lost in four months of beating the bush. "Pretty neat," he said. He put the clipping down and unfolded the letter.

Dear Shawn,

Mom and Dad sent me this clipping from home. I am so terribly worried about you. I called your mother and she said that you had told her that you were fine. I just can't stand to think of what it must be like over there. My professors here at State are all very much against the war. They say that it is morally wrong for you to fight in that war. I went to a big rally here and many of the boys burned their draft cards along with the American flag. I think that they are very courageous for doing it. My friends here at school think that it is wrong for me to write you, they say I am only helping the establishment by doing so. I will continue to write you, Shawn, not because I support what you are doing but because I care for you. If it is okay with you and causes no problem, it would make things easier on me here if you could write to my parents so that they could forward the letters on. That way my sorority sisters won't see the envelopes with the Vietnam stuff and they won't give me lectures on how you are killing women and children. I hope you will understand and not be offended by any of this. Get well soon.

Love, Nancy

Shawn dropped slowly back onto his pillow and stared up at the curved ceiling with a blank expression.

"Bad news?" Carl asked.

"What?" Shawn mumbled. He felt like someone had just kicked his guts out.

"You okay?"

Shawn glanced back at the letter in disbelief. "Yeah," he heard himself answer. It had to be a joke, he thought. Nancy couldn't. She wouldn't. No one, no American would send a wounded Marine this kind of garbage. He leaned back and stared at the ceiling until all of the confusion turned into a silent undercurrent of rage. He sat up straight, grabbed his writing gear from beside the bed, and scribbled out a short letter.

To the Corps, and the cowards they die for.

Semper Fidelis

Shawn folded the letter and shoved it in an envelope then paused and looked over at Carl. "Carl, you got any more of those envelopes with the Marine Corps insignia on it?"

Carl grabbed a box from the table by his bed and pulled out a pale blue envelope with a raised eagle, globe, and anchor insignia in gold on the seal overflap. He tossed it to Shawn.

"Is everything okay?" Carl asked.

Shawn didn't answer. He shoved the letter in the pale blue envelope, addressed it to Nancy at Florida State, and wrote "Free Mail Vietnam" where the stamp would have gone in the States. He sealed it up and slapped it down hard on the metal table by his bed

He closed his eyes and fell into a restless, groaning kind of sleep.

CHAPTER TEN

Just an Ambush

"Stand by!" the copilot shouted over the prop wash.

"Stand by! Might be a hot LZ!" the door gunner yelled. The door gunner's green flight suit was spotted with dried blood from the knees to the ankles. "You a boot?" He shouted with a quick glance at Shawn.

Shawn straightened up against the wall of the chopper. "No!"

"You look awful clean," the door gunner explained.

Shawn looked down at his own boots. Brand new. The clown should have noticed my helmet, Shawn murmured to himself. "I'm comin' back from the NAS at Da Nang. It's my second Heart!" Shawn tried his best to look casual as the door gunner's tone changed.

"Sorry, bro. Wanted to make sure you knew what a hot LZ was."

Shawn signaled with a thumbs-up. Wish old Luke was here, he thought. Luke's injuries were healing more slowly than Shawn's had. He was still back at NAS.

The helicopter began to circle. Shawn caught a glimpse of yellow smoke swirling around the tops of tall green trees as the chopper banked sharply between two steep, forested mountains. He looked at the door gunner's bloodstained trousers.

"Did you get hit?" He pointed at the stains.

The gunner glanced away from the mountains below. "No," he shouted, holding tight to the M60. "We picked up some KIAs. A real mess. That's why we were in Da Nang when you hitched a ride."

Shawn felt like pinching himself. It didn't seem possible that he was going back into the bush. He was scared. He stared down at his new boots and hated them. He had worked hard to earn the look of a salt. Now he was going back just like a boot. Back. Back to the bush. This time without Nancy.

He felt empty inside. No one to fantasize about. No one to

worry about him. No girl. A chill came over Shawn that made him shake. A terrifying fear of going back into the bush, back into the war, overwhelmed him. He looked around the inside of the chopper for a way out, like a man with claustrophobia, and he knew that he was near panic. His stomach sank as the chopper dropped quickly between two mountains. It bumped and rocked as it sped in at treetop level.

"Stand by to jump!" the copilot shouted from the cockpit.

"Jump?" Shawn's stomach churned.

"We got flashes!" the door gunner screamed, and opened fire at a target that Shawn could not see.

Shawn tried to remember the Twenty-third Psalm. He forced himself to breathe. He rose to one knee and scooted close to the side hatch of the old H34-D helicopter. He wondered if any of the guys were dead. The door gunner ceased fire.

"Yea, tho I walk through the valley of the shadow of death, I will fear no evil," Shawn mumbled aloud as he moved closer to the hatch.

"For we are Marines!" the door gunner shouted. "And the meanest mothers in the valley!"

Shawn almost snapped out at the man before he could catch himself, but a voice shouted "Jump!" from the cockpit. Shawn stood, crouching under the weight of his pack, and jumped past the gunner. It was only a few feet to the ground, but the weight of the pack, flak jacket, canteens, and web gear made the landing hard. He hit, rolled forward onto his left shoulder, and landed flat on his pack. The edge of a sharp rock dug into his coccyx. He lay stiff and moaned through clenched teeth. His feet felt cold. Wet. He rolled onto his side and looked down at his boots. They were submerged in a small rocky stream. It was quiet. No gunfire. Only the clapping of the rotors as the chopper lifted away. Yellow smoke shifted around him with the swirling breeze.

"McClellan, man!" The familiar Jamaican accent lifted Shawn's spirits.

"Look out! Old Mackie's back in town." Kayto made his voice as low as he could. Shawn turned his head to see the two coming toward him wearing nothing but their filthy jungle trousers and boots. Each carried a can of C-rations with the white plastic spoon sticking out. Their huge grins settled Shawn's anxious stomach. They stopped a few feet away. Kayto looked up at the taller, square-jawed Cager and began humming a bass rhythm to Bobby Darin's "Mac the Knife." Cager leaned over and set his can of C-rations on the ground, then stood and put an arm around his friend's shoulder. He snapped out a rhythm with his fingers while Kayto drummed his C-ration can with the spoon. They sang. "Old Mac heath, babe . . ."

Shawn shook his head and began to laugh. The fear was gone—for now. He stood up by the edge of the stream. Another familiar voice called from the brush behind Cager and Kayto.

"Mac!" Chip the radioman ran past the duet, who were now totally engrossed in their harmonizing. "Man, it's good to see ya. Where's Luke? How was Da Nang? Get any women?" Chip ripped off his questions in his usual no-pause style. His short fast sentences fit his chipmunklike face.

They clasped hands and Shawn slapped the bare back of the little round radioman. "Slow down, Chipper. I'm glad you're okay, buddy."

Shawn looked Chip in the eyes. Chip glanced down at the ground then back at Shawn. He pushed his glasses back up his sweaty pug nose. His face turned serious and Shawn feared that something had happened to one of the guys.

"Man, we really need a gunner, Mac."

"Did we ever get any new gunners?"

Chip blew a bubble then popped it. "Yeah. We got one from Bravo Company and he got hit by a bamboo viper the first day out. He got medevacked out. Ain't seen him since."

Cager and Kayto stopped singing.

"You honkies got no soul for tunes," Cager said, grinning.

Shawn slapped hands with Cager, then Kayto. "Boy, I'm glad you guys are okay," he said.

"We missed our Bible thumper, man," Cager said. A gust of the hot sticky air wafted an odor into Shawn's nose that made him wince.

"Wooh, get back." Shawn turned his head then looked back with a scrunched-up face as if he had just bitten into something sour. "I don't wanna hurt your feelings but, man alive, you grunts smell worse than dung burning at Phu Bai."

Cager looked surprised. "Bad, huh, man?"

"Bad, man." Shawn imitated Cager's Jamaican accent.

"It ain't rained in a week," Kayto explained.

"I remember how bad everybody smelled when I came back from R&R," Chip said with an accusing sniff toward Kayto.

"Keep your nose to yourself, bubblegum brain," Kayto growled.

"Funny, how you almost get used to it," Cager mused.

"When I get back to the world, bros," Kayto said, looking skyward, "I will never let dirt touch my flesh again."

"I won't even go campin', man," Chip added. "Or walkin'. And no picnics unless it's on shag carpet. Come on, Mac." Chip tugged at Shawn's sleeve. " 'Tenant's waitin'. We're about to saddle up."

"How's old Slo-mo, man?" Cager asked.

"Yeah, man! How's Luke?" Kayto asked.

"He's skatin', but he'll be back in a week or two."

Shawn followed Chip through a few yards of thick brush, then into a small clearing. The lieutenant sat in the center of the clearing talking on the PRC-25 radio and studying a map in his lap.

"Alpha Two . . . over." He put the field phone down and continued to study the map.

"Lieutenant," Chip said as they squatted down beside the radio.

Lieutenant Townsend looked up. "Mac!" He smiled and held out his hand. Shawn hesitated then quickly shook hands. "Welcome back, Marine."

Shawn was surprised. He never expected the lieutenant to be so personable to a mere PFC. He liked it. "Thanks, Lieutenant, but I'd be a liar if I said it was good to be here."

"You sure would, Marine."

"McClellan!" Doc Abernathy slapped Shawn on the pack.

Shawn turned on one knee. "Good to see ya, Doc."

"Like, outstanding. Mac is back and the gun is fun." Doc's head wobbled with his words.

Shawn laughed.

"McClellan." Lieutenant Townsend sounded official. "I want you back on the gun. Go relieve Jake and Sleepy and tell 'em they're your gun team for now. Pick one of 'em for your A-gunner."

"Shakey Jake's been the gunner? That's a pretty nervous finger on the sixty."

The lieutenant shrugged. "Well, he had some time in machine-gun company back at Geiger, so we tried it."

"How'd he do?"

"Thank God we didn't make much contact." He grinned.

"I was hoping old Jake would have gotten his hardship discharge by now."

"Yeah, so was I."

"Where's the Chief?" Shawn asked, looking around.

"Gone."

Shawn's heart felt like it had stopped. "KIA?" His voice cracked.

"No."

"Thank God."

"His old man died. He got a hardship leave to go back for the burial."

Lieutenant Townsend stood up. "Pass the word. Let's saddle up."

Shawn turned away, then stopped. "Where's the gun team?"

"Chip, take Mac over to guns."

"Affirmative." Chip grabbed up his shirt and headed east. Shawn followed.

"Mac," Lieutenant Townsend called. "Will Luke be back soon?"

"Yes, sir."

"Good. That big goofball's good for morale." He grinned.

"Yes, sir."

"You okay, Mac? You seem a little down."

"I sort of got a Dear John—or close to it—while I was in the hospital."

"That right?"

"Yeah." Shawn felt silly. He wished he had kept his mouth shut.

"You squared away, Marine? Your mind better be on business."

"Yes, sir."

"You and Luke are near the top of the list for R&R. Keep your mind on Charlie. I'll see about the R&R."

"Aye, aye, sir." Shawn turned to follow Chip and ran into Doc Abernathy.

Doc sniffed the air and looked accusingly at Shawn. "You smell like soap or something clean. You better dump on some bug juice, man, or you gonna get eaten alive."

"Okay, Doc."

"You get new socks?" the Doc asked.

"Yeah."

"Like, that's almost worth getting hit for."

"Almost. Sorry I didn't get a chance to bring a bunch back."

"Wearin' skivvies?"

"Yeah, I forgot."

"In a month, man, they rot and you got infection where the sun don't shine. And keep an eye on your feet. Those new boots can be bad news. That reminds me, I better check on old Murph's jungle rot." The corpsman's eyes took on their mad-scientist expression.

"Gun team's over here." Chip motioned for Shawn to follow.

Shawn plodded after him. As Shawn and Chip approached, Shakey Jake grinned and started shaking and pointing like someone had plugged him in. Then he squatted down beside Sleepy, who was flat on his back with his helmet over his face, and pounded out a nervous beat on Sleepy's helmet.

"Look here, Sleepy! He's back!"

Sleepy pushed his helmet back and opened one eye. "Mac." He mumbled and pulled the helmet back over his face.

Shakey's glee over Shawn's return faded with the news that he would still be with the M60.

The hump started a few minutes later. The platoon headed in column up the stream, climbing slowly into the mountains. By the first click of distance on the grid map, Shawn's body began to rebel. The protective saddle of callus that had developed painfully between his neck and right shoulder from months of humping with the heavy machine gun was gone. Soft, rear-echelon skin remained. Soon it would blister, then bleed, then get infected—to the corpsman's delight—and finally become hard enough to support the gun again. The thought of going through the painful process all over again was a less than happy one.

By noon Shawn's legs felt weak. Images of Nancy cheering on draft card–burning hippies flashed through his mind. He shook his head to shake away the angry thought. He could smell the lilac on her letters and still see the dark tan on her muscular legs. Shawn reached up with his free hand and slapped himself hard. Water splashed from his hand. It was pouring rain, monsoonlike rain. Enormous black-and-gray clouds rolled sheets of rain across the mountain peaks. It lashed against the tiny column so powerfully that for an instant the men stopped to shield themselves.

A moment ago I didn't even realize it was raining, he thought as he climbed up a muddy mountain trail with his eyes fixed on Sleepy's pack. I'm gonna get killed like this—thinking about Nancy all the time. The rain changed from lukewarm to ice cold.

He slapped himself again and shook his head the way he used

to do when he took a good hit on the football field. Sleepy suddenly knelt down on one knee with his rifle ready. Shawn stopped. He stared up the column of kneeling Marines. Sleepy glanced over his shoulder.

"Down!" He whispered and waved Shawn down.

Shawn dropped to one knee. He bit his lip until he tasted blood.

Pray. Pray, you jerk, he told himself. Father, please clear my mind.

Helmets up ahead began turning.

"Guns up!"

"Guns up!"

"Guns up!"

The whispered call echoed down the column. Sleepy stood to a crouch as Shawn rushed past him. The steep mountain trail turned into a muddy stream as the rainwater rushed downhill. Shawn's feet slipped from under him. He crashed face-first and slid back into Sleepy's boots. Sleepy grabbed Shawn's pack and helped him to his feet. They struggled up the trail for twenty meters with each kneeling Marine lending a hand and a pull. At the crest of the mountain Lieutenant Townsend waved them down. Goody was flattened out just above the lieutenant and Chip.

"Where do you want us?" Shawn asked. Chip shot Shawn a nervous glance. Lieutenant Townsend pressed his ear to the field phone.

"That is affirmative Alpha One . . . over." He handed the phone to Chip and crawled up to Goody.

The rain fell hard against Shawn's helmet. His ears and head ached for relief. He took off his helmet. Someone pushed him from behind.

"Mac! Mac!" Shawn looked back into Sleepy's face, the eyes dark and urgent. "Can't you hear? Pass the word! Gooks comin' up behind us!"

Shawn glanced down the trail. The men were looking back down the forested mountain. He turned to Lieutenant Townsend. "We got gooks comin' up the rear!"

"What?" Lieutenant Townsend turned to look back at Shawn. His face was pale. A touch of panic appeared in the lieutenant's eyes. Shawn had never seen that before, and it scared him. The lieutenant blinked, turned to look ahead, then glanced back down the trail. Goody rolled onto his side.

229

"Looks like better'n a company, sir. We better move. They're comin straight at us. Their point man's close. He's just starting up this hill."

The splash of Sleepy's knees dropping to the mud turned Shawn around.

"Lieutenant! We got a bunch of 'em movin' down that mountain right back there and they're startin' up this one!"

"Who's Tailend Charlie?" the lieutenant asked.

"Dook," Sleepy said.

The lieutenant gave a nervous look back down the trail. "Dook. Good. He won't panic. Okay, Goody." His words came in hurried bursts. He slid back toward Shawn as he tugged Goody to follow. "Come on. You gotta find a trail goin' north or south."

"I didn't see no trail."

"Make one, Marine."

"Where they all comin' from, Lieutenant?" Shawn asked.

"I think we stepped into a battalion staging area," he said as he pushed Goody past him.

Goody half slid, half jogged fifteen meters back down the trail, then turned right off the trail and fought his way through heavy ten-foot-tall brush. The front of the column peeled back around and followed after Goody, Lieutenant Townsend, Chip the radioman, and the gun team. Goody broke a trail around the slope of the mountain as fast as he could fight through the jungle growth and skin-ripping thorn vines.

Shawn thought of Dook, walking Tailend Charlie, and knew that he must be terrified. Up ahead Chip dropped to one knee, turned back to Shawn, and waved him forward. Shawn hustled past Chip, through a briar thicket that ripped into his wet skin, and finally pushed through to an open area overlooking a deep gap between the mountain they were on and another mountain. The two facing slopes were connected by a natural bridge of red mud and rocks that had formed over the years by the rainwater runoff.

Lieutenant Townsend grabbed Shawn's arm and pointed with his rifle across the twenty-foot-wide bridge of mud and rocks. "I want the gun over there where Goody is. Cover the platoon as they cross. Move it, Marine!"

Goody was just on the other side of the bridge, standing atop a huge, moss-covered boulder that abutted the mountainside.

Shawn started across with the M60 at chest level. The thick red mud sucked his boots deeper with each stride. The fifteen-meter run felt like a mile under the weight of his waterlogged gear. Shawn crawled on his knees and one hand, holding the M60 across the back of his neck with the other for the last five feet to the solid footing of the mountainside. He turned to look back as Sleepy struggled behind him like a man running underwater. Jake stopped short of the mud bridge, watching as Sleepy struggled, then moved slightly to the right of the mucky trail the three Marines before him had made. He trotted forward with his rifle at port arms. Halfway across, he froze and looked up at the sky with his eyes closed. That instant the red mud under his boots shot into the air like a small volcano. A muffled explosion sent Jake's limp body straight up. He did a full slow-motion flip in the air.

"Jake!" Sleepy screamed and twisted in the knee-deep mud and clawed back toward the other Marine. Jake landed flat on his back beside his rifle. Shawn laid the M60 down and waded through the mud as fast as he could. Sleepy reached Jake first. He fell crying onto his friend's stomach, then pushed up onto all fours.

"Jake! God! Jake! God!" Sleepy took off his helmet and slammed it into the mud beside his motionless friend.

Shawn reached the two and fell to his knees beside Sleepy. Jake was covered with mud. His face was a solid pack of it, showing no human characteristics other than a bump of mud where a nose should have been. Slowly Jake's hand moved to his face. He wiped the mud away from his nose and eyelids. His eyes popped open. They began to blink. He spit out a mouthful of mud and started quivering all over, like a human vibrator.

"Jake!" Sleepy grabbed Jake by the belts of machine-gun ammo that crisscrossed his flak jacket and shook him once hard. "You're alive!"

"Praise God," Shawn mumbled in disbelief.

Sleepy put his face nose to nose with Jake and shouted, "You step right on a booby trap and you're alive?"

"Are you hurt?" Shawn asked.

"Is he bad?" the lieutenant called.

"I'm okay. I'm okay." Jake's voice vibrated.

"Quit shakin' you jackass!" Sleepy barked.

"He's okay!" Shawn yelled back to Lieutenant Townsend.

"You'd shake too if you got blown up," Jake said as if he'd been insulted. Sleepy laughed and hugged Jake around the head.

"Move out!" Lieutenant Townsend shouted. "Every gook in Nam heard us by now!" He waved Chip forward.

"Is he alive?" Goody called from the giant boulder.

Shawn signaled with a thumbs-up. Sleepy pulled Shakey Jake to his feet while Shawn retrieved his helmet.

"Move it!" Lieutenant Townsend growled. He pointed at Goody. "Get us out of here, Goody!"

Goody spit once, nodded, and turned away.

The gun team hustled to the top of the mossy boulder. It was slippery but relatively flat on top. Shawn set the gun up and waited nervously as the column moved across the bridge.

Shawn, staring through the gray rain at the green mountain, felt his stomach jump each time an American helmet broke through the brush until finally Dook appeared. Dook ran to the muddy span and started across, looking back with each step as if they were close behind.

Sleepy nudged Shawn. "You hear that?"

"What?"

Jake stuck his finger in one ear and shook his head. "I can't hear nothin', man."

Halfway across Dook paused and looked back, then aimed his M14 at something that Shawn couldn't see. Every muscle in Shawn's body tensed as his eyes strained to see movement. Nothing. Dook lowered his rifle and continued across.

"You don't hear that?" Sleepy asked.

"Yeah, I do hear something," Shawn said.

"Something clacking," Sleepy said.

Dook made it across, climbed up to the boulder, and waved the gun team to move on. Shawn cocked an ear toward the clacking that seemed to be coming toward them. "Let's 'de-de-mow'! We're already on the end of the column!"

Sleepy turned and headed after the column. Dook stood on the steep slope where the platoon had beaten down a path leading up the mountain. Shawn and Jake hurried after Sleepy. Fear of being chased and shot in the back pushed Shawn's boots through the thick brush with renewed speed.

Dook gave each man a light shove as they passed him. "Hurry up, I'll take the tail."

They angled uphill for thirty or forty meters until Sleepy caught up with Kayto at the end of the column. The column began heading back down the mountain at a forty-five-degree angle. Shawn glanced over his shoulder. Jake was five meters back and Dook another ten behind Jake. Dook walked sideways, with quick glances back every few steps. Shawn shivered. He felt like he was being chased by death. Nancy's letter flashed through his mind. What were they doing this deep in the bush with eighteen men? He wondered where they were. Near Laos? As if it mattered, he thought. Really, the Nam was all the same when it came right down to it. Rain and leeches and malaria and rice paddies and mountains and the stench of the rotting dead or your own infected body mixing with the stink of oil and fish and human waste; and what for? Back home, cowardice is called bravery and right and wrong are decided by what's the easiest. For an instant he wished desperately he were back in Da Nang. He had an impulse to pray, but he didn't.

The rain lightened as evening approached, and Shawn hurt. His feet were blistered raw in the wet new boots. His neck and shoulder bled from the wear of the M60 rubbing for mile after mile. The shoulder straps of his pack had sunk deep. The drag of four canteens, a K-bar, a .45-caliber pistol, frags, two smoke grenades, and ammo belts had all doubled with the six-hour rain. Fear turned to anger and fatigue, and in spite of all of this crap he still thought of Nancy and he still ached for her.

Suddenly the column turned left along a narrow, overgrown path that led straight downhill. They walked, slid, and stumbled until the path descended to an abrupt end with a sheer fifteen-foot drop into a thirty-foot-wide box canyon. Each man helped the man behind him make a half slide, half jump down to the canyon floor. The boxed end was to the right, and for some insane reason that was the direction the column took.

"Hey, Sleepy, that's a dead end, the way we're going."

Sleepy shrugged. "I think the other way is back where we came from," he whispered. "I guess we're setting up for the night."

The fading light would help, Shawn thought as he stumbled over small, round, white rocks that crushed under the weight of his boots. Near the end of the box canyon the overhanging canopy of trees and vines formed a natural roof that made Shawn feel as though he were entering a cave. At the point where the cave roof began, the platoon bunched up. Murph's squad of six men flattened out in a line across the canyon floor. They aimed straight back down the canyon. The rest of the platoon filed past them and on into the cover. Neader held up a human skull on the muzzle of his rifle and shoved it in front of Shawn's face. Shawn slapped it aside as he walked into the cave.

"Guns," Lieutenant Townsend whispered.

Shawn felt a hand grab him by the shoulder. "Yes, sir."

"Mac, I want the gun set up at the entrance facing back the way we came."

"What about Murph's squad?"

"Tell 'em to scoot over, we got no place to go from here until daybreak."

"Sleepy. Jake," Shawn whispered into the dark.

"Yeah, we're here," Sleepy mumbled close by.

"Come with me. We're settin' the gun up at the entrance." Shawn turned back toward the dim light.

"That you, Mac?" Dook whispered.

"Yeah, Dook."

Dook pulled Mac closer and whispered into his ear. "I guar-rone-tee this much: here's the spookiest place I ever been."

"What's up? Why?"

"I ain't never, I guar-rone-tee never, slept on dead people 'fore." Dook moved on past with an unsettling moan.

Shawn stood still and looked down. He suddenly realized what the crunching white objects were beneath his boots: bones. He knew that six months ago he would have thrown up at the thought of sleeping with a canyon full of dead people. Now he was too exhausted to care.

"Scoot over." Shawn kicked at Neader's boot. "I'm puttin' the gun here."

Neader rolled until he reached Cornhusker. "Move over, Horning." Tony rolled left and into a human rib cage that cracked under the stocky Marine's weight.

"Quiet, fool!" Murph growled from the far left.

Shawn laid the gun down gently as he pulled the second bipod leg down and aimed the M60 into the canyon of bones. Sleepy flattened out on Shawn's left, Jake on the right. Jake linked up two hundred-round belts of ammo and nudged Shawn with his elbow.

"I just"—he shivered—"just can't believe, believe we're spending the night here."

"It's probably the safest place around," Shawn said, but he didn't believe it.

"What do ya suppose it is?" Jake stuttered.

"Psst." Sleepy nudged Shawn's left arm. Shawn turned toward him. "This is where the gooks have been throwing their dead. Probably all from the same unit."

Shawn nodded. It made sense. The enemy went to extremes to keep the Americans from getting an accurate body count.

The night drifted slowly by and Shawn was positive that this would go down as one of the most miserable nights of his life. He took the first watch, but it didn't seem like anyone in the gun team was going to sleep this particular night. Sleepy took the second watch a couple of hours later. Shawn slid out of his pack and used it for a pillow. The vision of falling asleep with his face resting against a decaying skull made his stomach queasy.

The rain stopped. A whiff of something foul floated by on a light breeze. Shawn closed his eyes and tried to keep from wondering how fresh some of these bodies were. Soon he was thinking of Nancy and Elsa the nurse and Passagrille Beach and a big welcome-home parade down Central Avenue and him in the passenger seat of a shiny red Corvette convertible, waving, but always maintaining the look of a humble hero.

Branches cracking underfoot to his left on the mountainside above Murph snapped open Shawn's eyes at the same moment Jake's bony elbow dug into his shoulder.

"Gooks," Jake whispered.

The sound of Vietnamese chattering from above drifted through the damp night air. The cracking of twigs and rustling of leaves grew louder. Shawn stiffened. The movement above seemed to cease, then a Vietnamese voice spoke. Shawn wished that he could understand the language. Men grunted as if straining physically. Something broke through the branches above. Shawn jumped and prepared to fire. Something heavy landed with a crunch just to his left and in front of Sleepy. No one fired. Jake shook so hard that he made noise. Shawn hit him hard with an elbow, and he stopped.

A moment later the men above grunted again, and again something heavy broke through the branches above. The weight of another heavy object hit the bone-covered canyon floor with a crunch. Shawn jumped again. He pulled his hand away from the trigger of the M60 to keep from yanking off a round in fear. As the voices above grunted again and again, something crashed to the canyon floor just in front of Shawn. Then the rustling of men pushing through the jungle brush faded slowly away until all was silent. Shawn stared into the black night ahead. Sweat dripped off his eyebrows. The salt on his lips tasted bitter as his tongue ran nervously back and forth over them. Silent visions of sappers inching forward had Shawn's eyes darting left and right.

Minutes passed. Still no sound. No one moved; no one could be heard breathing for over an hour. Finally a Marine behind them crunched a bone. It was the last sound Shawn could remember hearing for the rest of the night.

A cool drizzle began to hit the back of Shawn's neck as the first shafts of gray-blue light filtered through the tall trees above the canyon floor. He rested his cheek against the wet stock of the M60. The dark outline of a body fifteen yards straight ahead wasn't a total surprise to him.

A few minutes later the bloody, half-naked bodies of the three Vietnamese that lay spread across the canyon were clearly visible. The arms of one were bent back under the torso, broken from the fall. Another had landed facedown, his chin smashing on to the hard skulls of two former comrades. His neck had broken straight back so that his face was looking skyward. The last body had only one leg.

Shawn walked out to see the dead men close up. He did not understand his own curiosity. He hated the thought of people gawking at the dead and yet he did it, like some goofy tourist in a flowered shirt.

"Claymore," a quiet voice behind him said.

Shawn turned.

"What, Jake?"

Shakey Jake pointed at the stomach of one body. It was peppered with hundreds of tiny holes. Jake walked up and shoved the dead man over with his boot. The back was riddled with slightly larger holes and the man's insides oozed through them the way hamburger squeezes through the round holes of a meat grinder.

"Claymore."

"Bad mother."

"Yeah," Jake said. "Payback's a medevac, Charlie."

"Hear any more about your hardship discharge?"

Jake squinted; his eyes looked battle-aged. He shook his head no.

Someone passed the word to chow down but no one acted very hungry. A few minutes later the platoon columned up the mountainside where the bodies had been thrown from the night before. Nothing was found.

The Second and Third platoons linked by midmorning, and together humped back to the trail where the NVA had first been spotted. Two platoons from Bravo Company swept into the area from the east with Alpha's two platoons setting up a blocking action. The enemy was gone. Later in the day Alpha's two platoons joined up with Bravo Company's two platoons and columned east. It felt different with such a large group of Marines. Not safe exactly, but maybe just a little bit less tense.

As the hump went on, the nights turned into platoon-sized ambushes and the days were long, hot marches through impossible terrain. Shawn tried to make a habit of reading his Bible whenever the column fell to the side of a jungle trail. Thoughts of Nancy wrecked his concentration even when he read. Each morning, as the night ambush rustled through packs for breakfast, he started a new letter to Nancy. Each day he burned it in his C-ration stove during chow break. Jake witnessed the ritual for a week. Sleepy usually napped.

"Why do you bo-bo-bother writing?" Jake stuttered as Shawn ripped an already crumpled letter into small pieces and fed them one at a time into his C-ration stove.

"I don't know."

"Ya know, old Dook never talks much but he's never got one letter from his wife or anybody, far as I know."

"Yeah, I know. God, that must be tough."

"Wha-what'd ya get? Dear John?"

"Sort of. Not really. I don't know." Shawn shook his head in disgust. "We were just good friends, not goin' steady or anything, but she's the only girl I've thought of since I got here." He felt a lump slowly rising in his throat.

"Sooo . . . so what did she say?"

The angry crease between Shawn's green eyes grew deeper at the memory of Nancy's letter. "Jake, can you imagine writing a letter to a wounded American Marine and telling him that you have decided that the real heroes are the chicken draft dodgers that burn their draft cards or the faggots that torch American flags on campus?"

Shawn kicked over his stove, stood up, and blew out a long angry breath, then stomped the stove into the dirt.

Jake gave a quiet whistle. "That bad, huh."

Shawn stared off at the purple and scarlet sky. The sun was beginning its descent. "It's more than just losing a girl I liked.

237

Or loved. It's almost like, like getting a Dear John from the whole friggin' country. Know what I mean?''

"Yeah. I know." His thin, nervous face looked almost calm. There was a hint of sadness in his eyes.

"Heard any more about your hardship discharge?" Shawn asked.

"No. Las-last letter from Mom said our congressman had okayed it but the red tape—" He paused and shrugged. "Who knows?"

"Saddle up!"

"Saddle up!"

The inevitable call echoed around the perimeter. Just the words made Shawn's feet ache with expectation. It was hard to decide which was worse, the boring day-after-day humps and ambushes that turned out to be nothing more than mosquito bait, or actually finding the enemy. He would never say it to the men, but after a week or two of boring humps he honestly wanted some action.

The platoons split up, each heading for its own ambush site. The normal procedure was to have an ambush set up soon after the sun disappeared. The sun was gone and the column kept moving. Shawn felt that anxious flutter in his stomach. Somehow the point man stumbled onto a trail. The platoon followed it up a large rocky hill, down the other side, and halfway up another hill overgrown with scrubby bushes. At that point the trail leveled off and skirted around the side of the hill. They followed it around for fifty meters and stopped.

"Set up a perimeter." The whispered voice didn't make any sense, but Shawn was too tired to care. No one had had enough sleep. Shawn felt exhausted. If they were stupid enough to set up a perimeter on the side of a hill, it was fine with him.

Lieutenant Townsend appeared beside Shawn. He tapped the M60 and whispered, "We're ambushing this trail. The flank is all yours." He pointed to a large bush on the downhill side of the trail. "Put the gun down there."

Shawn led Sleepy and Jake down to the big bush. They set the gun up facing downhill just to the right of the bush. Shawn pulled his poncho out of his pack and unfolded it quietly. He leaned back against the hill. "Sleepy," he whispered, "you got the first watch tonight." He pulled the poncho over his head to block out the whining mosquitoes.

"There it is," Sleepy mumbled.

Sleepy's words sounded far away. A heavy dreamless sleep fell over Shawn like a warm blanket. He felt as though he were sinking into the hillside. Falling for miles. The sound of music filled his thoughts as if he were waking from some hypnotic trance. Music. The Beatles. No. The Young Rascals. "Mustang Sally,"? "Midnight Hour"? Music! Music? Music!

Shawn opened his eyes. He rolled left. It was pitch black. The poncho! It's over me. He sighed. Music! God! That *is* music! He sat up straight.

A burst of rifle fire popped in Shawn's ears from above. Bullets tore through a piece of his poncho with a frightening smack. He fought to get the poncho off him. It was wrapped around his head and shoulders. More gunfire shot down at him from above. He ripped the poncho away from him at the same moment as he was jarred from behind by the dead weight of a man rolling into his back. Shawn threw a left elbow straight back as he clutched for his K-bar with the other hand. He heard himself screaming as he ripped the knife from its sheath and stabbed wildly at the man behind him. The dark form of the enemy soldier didn't move as Shawn stabbed the K-bar into his throat. He pulled the knife back to stab again. The man didn't move. Shawn leaned closer with the knife ready to plunge.

"He's dead!" Sleepy whispered and pointed at the man's head. Shawn moved aside, letting the moonlight fall over the man's head. He'd been shot through one temple. The bullet had blown the other side of his head away. Shawn had been stabbing a dead man.

"In the Midnight Hour . . ." The Young Rascals' music blared from the trail.

"Gooks!" a frightened cry echoed from above.

Frightened feet stomped through the brush on the side of the hill thirty meters to Shawn's right. Shawn grabbed the M60 and aimed right. Someone above turned off the radio. Silence engulfed the hillside. A few minutes passed and still no sounds. Shawn leaned close to Sleepy.

"Let's push the body down the hill."

"We better do something; we'll be covered with ants and flies by mornin'."

Shawn spent the rest of the night wondering if his sleep would ever be normal after the war. He knew that no one back home would believe these crazy things had really happened to him.

Even he couldn't believe this. How could anyone go humping through the bush with a radio on. Maybe it was a hippie VC?

Morning found Shawn in no danger of sleeping. Nor Jake. Sleepy snored rhythmically between them, his helmet covering his face and his feet crossed comfortably on top of his M16.

"Jake," Shawn growled. "Did he wake you for watch last night?"

Jake shrugged and shook his head no. Shawn leaned over and punched Sleepy in the arm as hard as he could.

Sleepy groaned from the punch, grabbed at his hurting biceps, and sat up angry. "What the . . ."

"You almost got us killed, Marine! Don't let it happen again!"

Sleepy opened his mouth to speak then seemed to reconsider. He looked surprised at Shawn's anger, but then nodded. "You're right, Mac." He shook his head in disgust. "I just couldn't stay awake. It was stupid."

Shawn had not expected such sincerity from Sleepy. He wished now that he could take back the punch.

"I'm sorry too. It's not like me to lose my temper like that. I probably couldn't have stayed awake either."

"Well, at least one of us bet-bet-better start staying awake!" Jake said.

"He's right," Shawn agreed. "Look at this."

He picked up his green poncho and put two fingers through the new holes.

"I had this sucker on last night when I got the new ventilation."

A whistle signaled someone's approach. Shawn turned around. Goody and Birdman stood behind him. Goody rearranged the tobacco from one side of his mouth to the other.

"Boy. Yer tryin' harder than a heifer in heat to get that third Heart."

"That ain't nothin'," Birdman scoffed. "I had closer calls than that.'Member that time in Phu Loc . . ."

"Now yer fulla bull, Marine."

"Who's confirmed?" Jake asked.

"Mac killed him once," Sleepy said with a chuckle.

"That right, Shawn?" Goody asked.

"You should have seen our man, here," Sleepy said. "I woke up and he's workin' old Charles over with a K-bar like he's carvin' a turkey."

"Get back," Birdman scoffed.

"There it is, bro." Sleepy held up his hands. "Ask Jake."

"It's true," Jake said.

"But he was already dead," Shawn explained.

"But you didn't know that," Sleepy said.

"That's for sure. I was so scared I wet my pants, man."

Jake scrunched up his nose. "I knew I smelled somethin'."

Somebody turned on a radio. A soft voice sang, "Kind of a drag . . . when your baby says good-bye . . ."

"That was the Buckinghams, and this is Hanoi Hannah, your sister American bringing you the sounds from home. Remember home . . ." The radio clicked off.

Dook sneered as he walked down from the trail. "Hannah baby. You got one gook that said good-bye; I guar-rone-tee that much."

"Dook," Sleepy called. "You get that gook last night?"

"Just barely, I guar-rone-tee ya that." He held the cigar-box-size, silver radio out for Goody to see.

"What does just barely mean?" Sleepy asked.

"I gotta tell ya, I was out to the world. Ever'body in our position was out."

"The whole bloody ambush was asleep!" Goody exclaimed.

"He's right," Birdman said. "Townsend is ticked off, bros."

"Why's that?" Shawn asked.

Birdman whistled. "Cuz he woke up when a gook stumbled over him, runnin' right through the ambush. He woke up face-to-face with Charlie."

"Didn't you hear him scream 'gooks' last night?" Goody asked.

"Was that—th-th-that the Lieutenant?" Jake stuttered.

"The gook went stiff and dropped about ten pounds of rice all over the lieutenant, then took off like mad."

Dook cleared his throat. "So, as I was sayin', I woke up when I hear this music."

"Young Rascals, 'In the Midnight Hour,' " Shawn added. A memory of Nancy's love for the Rascals flashed by. He shoved the thought aside.

"Hey," Birdman said. "I just thought of a way to get old Fonda baby a new job."

"How's that?" Shawn asked.

"We get the fifty-two's to put in an arc-light raid on Hanoi Hannah. Then Fonda can take over her job as a gook disc jockey and we get rid of the commie-lovin' . . ."

Dook cleared his throat again. "So, I hear this music and I sit up. Right down in front of me is this column of gooks diddy-boppin' along the trail."

"How many?" Sleepy asked.

"Ten, maybe. So I look for my rifle and I'm sleepin' on it, don't ask me how. By the time I get hold of it, I got the last guy in their column comin' through, and he's tryin' like mad to get the radio turned off."

"Then what?" Goody asked.

"I guar-rone-tee he won't be listenin' to Hannah or nobody else no more." Dook pointed at the body then walked down to it. He bent over it, pulled off a watch, then pulled a small bundle wrapped in thin green plastic out of the dead man's pocket. He unwrapped the plastic. It was a worn, flat brown wallet. He opened it and stared for moment.

"What's in it, Dook?" Birdman moved downhill to get a closer look.

"His family," Dook mumbled. "Wife. Two kids."

Shawn saw Dook's face grow sad. He wondered if the quiet Cajun was thinking of his own wife and kid.

Shawn stood up and walked down to Dook. "Dook. You okay?"

Dook looked up at Shawn. His eyes were teary. He nodded, threw the wallet down and walked back up the hill to his position.

The next day a chopper brought Lukevec back. The next week passed by with no contact, except for a few incoming sniper rounds. One morning the lieutenant walked across a rain-swept perimeter with the hint of a smile on his lean face.

"McClellan. Lukevec."

"Yes, sir."

"Your date's up." Townsend smiled. Shawn and Luke exchanged puzzled stares.

"It's June twenty-first," Townsend said.

Luke shrugged.

The lieutenant laughed. "R&R!"

CHAPTER ELEVEN

The Insincere Baby

Luke stood up from the long, gray bench, stretched, and yawned. "We have to try to look up old Tony Balman and Cassius when we come back through Da Nang."

"Sure," Shawn said, "if we got time." He looked around the crowded Da Nang air terminal and tried to remember how he had felt when they first landed. "It was only about five months ago."

"What was five months ago?" Luke asked.

"That we came in-country."

"It is unbelievable. I honestly feel like I have been here forever."

"I know." Shawn straightened his gold tie clip with the eagle, globe, and anchor. "It's scary, like I stepped into the twilight zone. Sometimes I feel like an old man, like time is different in the bush." He turned to Luke. "You know what I mean?"

"I tried to tell Rachel that in my last letter home. It's no use, though." Luke sounded sad. "Only another grunt could ever understand."

Shawn stood up and stretched. He glanced down the bench filled with Marines and soldiers in dress uniforms waiting for R&R planes. The soldiers had crummy uniforms, Shawn thought, or at least crummy compared to Marines. He knew he had earned the title of Marine, and wondered what the cost would finally be.

"Think we'll be weird when we get home?" Shawn mused aloud.

"You will, but I have an attitude that resists change."

"In your case, Lukevec, no one would ever know."

"The women would know, Shawn."

"I see Joe!"

Shawn turned as Joe ran at him. Joe dropped his sea bag and crushed Shawn's ribs with a bear hug that lifted him off the ground. He set Shawn down and did the same thing to Luke. He put Luke down and stepped back smiling. His dark eyes were frosty with tears. Shawn felt a lump form in his throat. Joe was still "Hank Handsome," but he was different. Hard and thin. He had that haunted face of a grunt Marine that made nineteen-year-olds look aged. Joe sniffed back a tear and stepped back.

"I didn't think I'd ever see . . ." Tears poured from his eyes. He couldn't finish his sentence. Shawn stepped forward and hugged Joe. They slapped each other's back. Luke's big arms hugged them both. The three Marines huddled with their heads together and arms over each other's shoulders the way they used to do when they plotted some prank.

"I'm sorry, Joe," Shawn said. "God, I wish you guys hadn't . . . if it weren't for me you wouldn't be here."

Joe banged heads with Shawn. "Don't ever say that again! Semper fi, do or die, bros." He stared hard into Shawn's eyes.

"There it is, Joe. Always faithful."

"There it is. Hard corps," Luke said with a grin.

Luke nodded toward the men sitting on the long gray bench. "I think we are making a scene, men." He cleared his throat and did his Groucho Marx routine.

Joe smiled at Luke, shook his head, then slapped him on the shoulder. "God, it's good to see that silly mug of yours. It's like I haven't seen you guys for years."

"We know, buddy," Shawn said.

"How was Khe Sanh?" Luke asked quietly.

Joe looked at the floor then back at Luke. "They overran one side of our perimeter in the night. Ran out of ammo. Killed one with my E-tool, split his head like a watermelon." He stared at the floor again.

"We heard Lang Vei got overrun by Russian tanks," Shawn said.

Joe's dark eyes darted nervously from the floor to Shawn. "They kept calling for help but there was no way to get to 'em in the dark, not without bringing choppers in on top of the tanks. They got murdered and we couldn't help."

"We heard the scuttlebutt."

"Yeah." Joe sounded defiant. "Charlie could have taken roll call in a phone booth by the time it was over." He forced a chuckle. "Listen to me—tellin' war stories to you guys like you don't know. And *you* got four Hearts between you."

"Look." Shawn paused. "Maybe we should make a rule before we get on that plane."

"What rule?" Luke asked suspiciously.

"Let's agree to keep Nam talk to a minimum—unless it's something that has to come out."

Joe looked at Luke. They nodded and each held out a hand. Shawn joined them in a three-way clasp that filled Shawn with memories of home. They used to do the same thing in the huddle when the play was crucial. But that had been eons ago, when they were kids.

The sun was bright as the red Braniff touched down in Sydney. The sky was cloudless and blue. Shawn couldn't remember any of the flight. His eyes and every other man's on the plane rarely looked at anything other than the three lovely stewardesses. They wore mini-skirts and continually strolled up and down the aisle with little carts of drinks or food. Shawn suspected that they were working above and beyond the call of duty. They even pretended to like the whistles and groans. The plane exploded with wild cheers when it touched down in Sydney. Shawn took deep breaths of air as the men walked from the plane to the Sydney airport terminal.

"Can you smell that?" he asked.

Joe sniffed. "What?"

"No urine. No human fertilizer. No . . ."

"No fish," Joe added with another sniff.

Shawn sniffed and laughed. "No grunts."

Luke inhaled and blew out with a sigh. "I had forgotten what the rest of the planet smelled like."

They followed an Army captain across the tarmac and into a clean terminal hallway. Shawn touched his hip. No pistol. No canteens. He felt naked and a little nervous. He pretended to whistle. Calm down, he thought. The air-conditioned breeze of the terminal felt wonderful.

"Flight 767 now boarding . . ." an Australian woman's voice echoed through the terminal.

"The sound of civilized life." Luke sighed behind Shawn.

The Army captain led the column of men to the Braniff luggage area. Three smiling young girls walked by. They wore mini-skirts. One hundred and five men whistled or howled at nearly the same instant.

The girls giggled.

"Listen up, men!" the Army captain shouted. "Have a seat in these blue chairs right over here."

The men moved slowly with the air of combat veterans who were in no mood to be rushed.

"Your gear will be searched by these MPs. Any weapons or drugs will be taken, and if drugs are found, the owner will be placed under arrest."

"These men are mostly grunts, Captain." A salty-looking old staff sergeant said from the back of the room.

"Remember us," a black Marine bellowed. "We're the suckers fightin' the friggin' war! *We* ain't comin' from some party in Saigon!"

The room reverberated with angry grumbling. The black Marine was right. Most of the Army guys wore the blue CIB, Combat Infantry Badge, and most of the Marines seemed to be grunts. The captain cleared his throat.

"Sydney is the hub of the South Pacific, capital of New South Wales, and the birthplace of Australia." He pulled a small pad from his coat pocket and opened it. "Now," he read, "all personnel are required to wear civilian clothing while on R&R. The hospitality committee of the Australian Women's Association will be holding their R&R mixer at the Falls Hotel this evening at nineteen-hundred hours . . ."

By the time all of the warnings on Australian law, current VD rate, currency exchange rate, and acceptable military behavior were finished, the men were squirming to get away. When it was over, the room emptied like a fire drill. Luke hailed a cab outside the main entrance and they were off. The driver squealed his tires away from the curb and looked over his shoulder.

"Welcome home, mates." He winked a gray-blue eye and faced the road. "Where to?" He pushed his long, thick gray hair back as he studied the surprised young faces in his rearview mirror.

"Thank you," Shawn said.

"Yeah, thanks," Joe said. "We don't know where to go."

"Some hotel, I guess." Shawn shrugged.

"Round-eyed women," Luke enunciated slowly.

"Professionals?" the driver asked.

"What?" Shawn asked.

"Prostitutes?" Luke asked.

"No." The driver laughed. "You. You're the professionals, right?"

"We're U.S. Marines," Joe answered.

"Yes. The professionals." He smiled into the mirror.

"What's that mean, ah—" Shawn paused to read the driver's name stamped below his photo on the visor. "Mr. Halley?"

"Call me Roger, mate. Yes. We call the American Marines 'the professionals.' "

"Why?" Luke asked.

"I believe it comes from the old days. You know, World War II. They're the best in the world, the professionals. Held in very high esteem here in Australia, I'll tell you."

Shawn turned to Luke. "Wow, that's neat."

"And remember, mates, the Japanese were a kangaroo's hop from bein' right in our homes when the American Marines showed up."

"I guess that's true," Joe said.

"Where would you suggest we stay, Roger?" Luke asked.

"Leave it to me, mates." He pulled a business card out of the visor and handed it to Shawn. "For a fair rate I'll be your cabby for the week. Call that number, mates, I'll be over in a jif."

He winked in the mirror and made a sharp right turn onto a busy street. The sounds of horns blowing and brakes squeaking were music to Shawn's ears. Just riding in a car felt new and strange, as if it were the first time he'd ever done it. The three Marines stared at the shoppers along the busy streets, like men visiting from another time. It was all a dream. A rush of fear swept over Shawn, fear that he would wake up in a minute, back in the bush. He began to sweat.

"Here's the place, mates," Roger said as he turned left down a broad street lined with modern buildings. He pulled up to the curb in front of a six-story, white building with large double-glass doors. A doorman in a red-and-black uniform stood on the brown marble steps of the hotel.

"Bay Hotel," the cabbie announced. "Now, right down this street"—he pointed out of the rear window—"see that blue neon sign?"

"La Rue Sans Issue?" Luke said in perfect French.

"That will be the place you are looking for. Lovely young ladies and American music."

Shawn leaned forward and held out his hand. "Gosh, this is really nice of you, Roger. Thank you for being so hospitable to total strangers."

Roger smiled and shook Shawn's hand with a firm grip. "My pleasure, mate."

"Can you drop by that place tonight, Roger?" Joe asked. "I'd like to buy you a drink or two."

"Quite kind of you, mate. I'll have to see what the Mrs. says. Maybe I'll see you tonight, but if not, God be with ya."

The guys tried to tip Roger but he wouldn't hear of it. The Bay Hotel was plush but affordable. They got three adjoining rooms on the fourth floor with Shawn in the middle one.

"Wow!" Joe's shout came through the white adjoining door like it was made of paper.

"Get back, GI!" The white door burst open.

"Shawn! Come here! Quick!"

Shawn jumped off the bed. He paused a moment to let his feet sink into the gold shag carpet.

"Guns up!" Joe pointed back at his room.

"What is it?" Shawn ran after Joe.

"Look!" Joe pointed at a color TV. Combat films of Marines loading into troop choppers flashed on the screen. "It's the news. That's the Ninth Marines leaving Khe Sanh!"

"What's up?" Luke called from the door on the other side of Shawn's room.

"Films of the Ninth Marines on TV," Shawn answered.

"Turn it off!" Luke waved in disgust. "I am departing for La Rue Sans Issue in five minutes. Time check!" He closed the door.

"He's right, Joe. Come on." Shawn turned the TV off.

"Think they're seeing that back home?"

"Probably."

"Hope they're seeing it at JC." Joe kicked the side of the TV.

"JC? St. Pete Junior College?"

Joe sat on the end of his bed and stared silently at the TV.

"What's up, Joe?"

"Nothin'."

"You're holding something in."

"Holding what in?" He kept staring at the blank screen.

"Cut the crap, man. I know you. Something is wrong." Shawn sat beside Joe and gave him a nudge. "Might as well tell me while you're sober. I'll get it out of you when we get bombed, anyway." He smiled and poked Joe with an elbow.

Joe's brooding stare remained on the blank screen. "Sandy had my baby," he said.

Shawn felt his mouth fall open, but nothing came out. He closed his mouth and opened it again. "Wow," he said quietly.

"Yeah. Wow," Joe mumbled.

"Well, that's great!" He slapped Joe on the back. "You always loved Sandy anyway. Boy or girl? We gotta celebrate!"

"She met this hippie named Keith out at JC. He's the leader of the SDS on campus. She's moved in with him. With my kid."

Joe's eyes remained fixed. The veins in his neck swelled. The grinding of his teeth got louder.

"I'm sorry, Joe." Shawn knew that wasn't enough.

"Yeah. Chuck wrote me. Says the guy's got a ponytail down to his rear end."

"That doesn't sound like Sandy."

"Chuck says he's the main pusher at JC. Sandy's on uppers."

"Uppers?"

"Pills."

Shawn closed his eyes, bowed his head, and made a silent prayer for God to give guidance to Joe.

"Shawn." Joe pulled his glare off of the blank screen and faced Shawn. He grabbed Shawn's shoulders.

Joe didn't speak. He looked to be in deep thought. "Promise me." He looked hard into Shawn's eyes.

"What?"

"If I don't make it back, promise me you'll see my boy."

"Of course I will, man."

"And if this long-haired fag isn't the best father a kid can have, I want you to put your boot up his rear end until he is. I mean it, Shawn!" Joe's tone was vehement, his dark eyes fierce.

"Joe."

"Promise!"

"I promise, Joe, but no more talk like that. We're going home together, brother."

Shawn pulled out his wallet, opened it, and showed Joe a stack of bills clipped together with a broken Marine Corps tie clip. "Now, I got seven hundred bucks, so let's go drink to a new baby Elbon."

"Aye, aye, Marine. The drinking lamp is lit."

Civilian clothes felt strange. The Marines stood out like big green military thumbs with their jarhead haircuts as they entered

249

La Rue Sans Issue. Shawn's green-and-orange-flowered Hawaiian shirt was still crumpled from months in a sea bag. Luke's blue-and-white surfer shirt still smelled like old canvas.

"Joe," Luke mumbled as every head in the crowded nightclub turned to look at the Americans, "think surfer shirts are out?"

Joe glanced down at his brown surfer shirt and shrugged.

The club was large and plush. Thick, red, wall-to-wall carpet surrounded a beautiful wood dance floor that was vacant of dancers. The twenty to thirty dark wood tables with four chairs each were all filled with staring faces. A blue-gray fog spiraled up from overflowing ashtrays, hovering over each table of half-empty bottles and glasses like a cloud layer. To the right, in front of the dance floor, was a small, round stage. Four guys dressed in black, with Beatle haircuts, banged out a loud version of the Rolling Stones' "Satisfaction." Shawn stopped and stared at flashing blue, yellow, and red lights above the stage. Joe nudged Shawn from behind.

"They ain't flares, bro."

Shawn laughed politely, but deep inside it didn't seem funny.

Luke headed for a long mahogany bar along the left wall. Shawn and Joe followed him to two empty brass-and-leather stools.

"Sit, Joe." Shawn nodded at the two chairs. "I'll stand."

"Here, mate." A young man in a tan suit stood up from a stool. "You can have this one, I'm leaving."

"Thanks," Shawn said as he sat on the stool.

"What'll it be?" A burly, round bartender made a quick wipe with a towel on the bar.

"Three shots of Kentucky bourbon," Luke answered quickly.

"Right-o."

"Why isn't anybody dancing?" Shawn asked with a look over his shoulder at the empty floor.

"Can't say. You boys Americans?"

"Yes, sir," Shawn said.

"Marines," Joe added.

The bartender looked back at the Americans as he reached for three glasses. He set them down and poured the bourbon.

"It's on the house, gents." He turned and walked toward the far end of the bar.

"These people are great," Shawn said.

"I'm so very happy that you like us, love." Shawn turned to

see the face that belonged to the soft sexy voice. Her face didn't quite match her voice, but she had round eyes and that was enough. She brushed her long blond hair aside and smiled. She looked better with a smile.

"I'm Kathleen McKinney."

"My name is Shawn. Shawn McClellan."

"Like to buy us a drink, gents?" she asked. Beside the blonde stood two young brunettes. They weren't knockouts either, but they wore high heels and short, tight mini-skirts that pulled the eyes of the young Marines down like magnets.

An hour later the three couples were mixing drinks in Luke's hotel room. Somehow the conversation got around to comparing tales of past parties and topping each other's story of, "Once I got so drunk that . . ." The laughter felt like home. Even the girls had a couple of good stories as the group sat laughing and drinking in a circle on the gold shag carpet. Their accents were great.

"Your turn, Joe," Luke said, rubbing an ice-cube back and forth across his forehead.

"What are you doing, Luke?" Joe asked.

"Ice, Joe. I want to remember it."

No one spoke. Joe and Shawn exchanged glances. Smiles faded. Nam.

Then, suddenly, Joe jerked his head back as if shaking the thought away. He smiled. "Girls, you know who this guy is?" he said, and took a gulp of his drink. "You're lookin' at the soberest Marine to ever join the corps!" Joe slapped Shawn's back.

Shawn felt embarrassed. Luke pointed at him.

"I want to see you get plastered, Shawn McClellan."

Joe handed Shawn a glass of bourbon.

"Drink."

"Drink!" the girls yelled in unison.

"Chug it, Shawn!" Luke shouted.

Shawn drank. And drank.

A painful bright light stung his eyes open. The sun? He shut them again. Something flashed. He forced open one eye and groaned. A blurry, four-headed Lukevec stood at the foot of the bed smiling out of dual mouths. A white flash stung his eyes closed.

"What the . . ." Shawn grimaced and tried to cover his eyes with his right hand. The hand wouldn't budge. He wiggled his

251

fingers. Flesh. Somebody was lying on it. He tried to move his left hand. Somebody was lying on it too. He opened both eyes. A two-headed Joe Elbon stood beside the blurry shape of Luke. He aimed a camera at Shawn.

The flash closed Shawn's eyes. He rolled his head to his right and the spinning started again. He belched up the bitter taste of bourbon-flavored bile. He opened his eyes again and blinked them clear. The fuzzy face of the blonde lay on a pillow facing him. She smiled. He blinked again. Joe and Luke were laughing like thunder. Shawn's head hurt. The camera flashed again. Joe and Luke laughed louder. They sounded as if they were in a drum. Shawn forced his head to roll the other way.

One of the brunettes smiled and kissed him. He pulled his arms from under the girls and sat up. He tried to focus, but the room was still spinning. He looked right then left. All three girls lay beside him, two on the right and one on the left. He couldn't be sure, but they didn't seem to be fully dressed. Shawn forced a smile then swallowed back a belch. He looked at Luke and Joe. They stomped their feet and laughed.

"Payback's a medevac, you clowns," Shawn threatened. He closed his eyes to stop the spinning. "And I want that film."

"So sorry, GI." Joe laughed.

"These photos go directly to Virginia Tech," Luke said.

Shawn tried to open one eye.

"Yes, Eddie will have to see this for himself." Joe gave his camera a pat. "Maybe we should send copies to the school newspaper at St. Petersburg Senior High School."

"Come, ladies," Luke said, "let Shawn barf alone."

"I'll stay here with Shawn," Kathleen said softly. "And make sure he's all right."

Luke howled like a wolf. The room began to spin faster. The black unconsciousness that followed was a relief.

Painful chimes from what had to be the biggest, loudest church bell on planet Earth told Shawn that it was noon. By one P.M., 1300 hours Marine Corps time, he was able to sit up in bed. By 1400 hours he had barfed for the final time, and by 1430 he could stand and think.

It was during these first moments that he realized he was alone. He looked around the room. His wallet, open and thinner than before, was on the carpet. Too thin to contain his seven hundred dollars of R&R leave money. His headache got worse. He picked up the wallet and Roger the cabby's business card fell out along with one ten-dollar bill. He stared at the phone number. R&R was over without the money and he still had a full week ahead of him. Kathleen McKinney. He felt like a fool. She'd probably given him a phony name, he thought.

Shawn got dressed and caught the lift down to the lobby. He got change for the ten and called Roger the cabby.

Five minutes later the familiar blue Holden Fairmont pulled up in front of the hotel. Shawn jumped into the front passenger seat.

"Hi, Roger."

"How are you on this lovely morn, Yank."

"Not good. Look, I think I have enough money to pay you for coming by, but that's all. I hate bothering you with my problems, but you're the only person I know here . . ."

"What is it, mate?"

"I guess I got rolled this morning."

"What?" His eyes opened wide. "Here?" He pointed at the hotel.

"It's not the hotel's fault. I met this girl last night at the nightclub you told us to try and she said her name was Kathleen McKinney."

Roger instantly started the car and made a U-turn. He pulled up in front of the club, turned off the ignition, and looked at Shawn. "You say her name was Kathleen McKinney?"

"She probably gave me a phony name."

"I know Pinky. He owns this place, and he's the barman. He'll not put up with this sort of thing."

Shawn followed Roger into the club. Pinky was the same barman that had bought the guys drinks. He remembered Kathleen. He was sure that one of the waitresses knew her. It was her day off, so he called her at home. Pinky hung up the phone and faced Roger.

"Lilly says she lives over at Terry Road, she was a 'grouse-lookin' Sheila' that Kathleen, but she ain't from Pitt Street and I'd say she ain't from Kings Cross either."

"What?" Shawn asked.

Roger smiled. "He says she's a good-looking broad and she ain't from the fancy part of town, but she ain't from the red-light district either."

"Oh." Shawn scratched his head.

Roger turned to Pinky. "Terry Road, you say?"

"Beyond the tracks, fourth little white shack with a corrugated-iron roof."

"Is her name really Kathleen McKinney?" Shawn asked.

"That's right, mate."

The drive was not too far. Five miles, Shawn guessed. The city ended abruptly and turned into open fields. There were houses that sat far apart along a dusty road that ran parallel to some railroad tracks. Roger parked the cab in front of a small wood frame house that was badly in need of a fresh coat of white paint. It had a front porch with a broken rocker and a large front yard with no grass. The backyard was big, too, and ended at the tracks. The tin roof reminded Shawn of old farmhouses back home. The roof was old and rusty in spots. It was a quiet area, and the air smelled clean. A storm was coming in from the west.

"This is it, mate."

"I'll go up alone, Roger."

"I'll be right here."

"Thanks."

Shawn walked up to the house. He was filled with apprehension. He wasn't sure what to say. He tried to put his thoughts in order. Should he demand the money back, maybe threaten to call the police? But he knew he had no proof. Keep it simple, he thought. He climbed the steps to the porch. The front door was open and a tattered screen door was doing a poor job of keeping out the flies.

"Oh, wonderful!" The screen door pushed open behind the shout of an old lady wearing a dirty flowered apron. She rushed onto the porch. Her face was tan and wrinkled and she was in a huff about something.

"I've a man coming in from the city. Oh my, he's probably there already!" She put her palms over her ears and rocked her head back and forth.

"Be a doll, won't you matey? It won't be a mo'."

"Ma'am?" Shawn said.

"Just keep an eye on the 'bub' and I'll be back in a jif, I'll be needin' the cab."

"But, ma'am . . ."

She was gone, rushing out to the cab. Roger looked questioningly at Shawn as the old lady jumped in the backseat and motioned him to take off. Shawn shrugged. Roger shrugged, started the cab, and drove off with the old lady burning his ear with chatter.

Shawn stood on the porch for a few moments wondering what had just happened. "Just keep an eye on the bub," she had said. What's a bub? Somewhere inside the house a baby started crying. Shawn opened the screen door and called out loud, "Hello, anyone home?"

The baby cried louder. A bub?

The realization that he was now on "baby duty" came swiftly and with much trepidation. He stepped through the door like he expected a trip wire. The living room had clean wooden floors, but it looked barren of furniture, except for two plain wooden chairs and a well-worn leather couch. A big ceiling fan rotated slowly above. There was a kitchen straight back and two doors to Shawn's right that he supposed went to bedrooms.

One door was slightly open. The baby's crying was coming from there and it sounded louder. Shawn moved slowly toward the half-open door. He pushed it all the way open and found himself facing the solid end of a crib. Suddenly the head of a black-haired baby, less than a year old, Shawn guessed, popped up. Shawn jumped slightly. The baby stopped screaming. Two little hands with short fat fingers gripped the end of the crib and the baby chinned up over the edge until he could see Shawn through wide-open blue eyes. He smiled a happy, baby smile and dropped back down. Shawn relaxed.

Suddenly incoming fire from the crib smashed with bruising force against the top of the doorway just above Shawn's head. Shrapnel from the shattering plastic object hit Shawn in the back of his neck. He stiffened, then moved back and forth like a boxer trying to anticipate a left jab. A bright yellow object shot up out of the crib like a mortar round. The baby's fire was uncommonly accurate and only a quick parry with both hands saved Shawn from being struck in the face. Then with no warning there was a lull in the incoming fire. The fat little fingers grabbed the end of the crib and the baby chinned his way over the edge to recon Shawn.

Shawn took one cautious step forward. Stay calm, he thought. Let's try a quiet, mellow greeting.

"Hi Baby. I'm Shawn. Cease fire, now, friendlies approaching."

The baby disappeared down behind the solid end of the crib and began giggling. Shawn smiled and approached like a point man going uphill. He prayed that the baby wouldn't cry. The baby giggled again. Shawn paused and sighed. He peeked into the crib just as the baby unleashed a small toy car like a Sandy Koufax fastball. Shawn dodged left and retreated temporarily, but quickly moved forward again. He wrinkled up his nose as the odor of something foul attacked the fresh air like a hot breeze off a rice paddy. He looked to his right. There was a basket filled with white cloth diapers. Shawn moved closer, with his guard up.

"Hi little—guy, I guess?"

The baby giggled.

The odor was worse.

Shawn stepped forward boldly, right up to the kid's bunker. Close up, the baby looked about a year and a half old. His throwing arm must have developed early, Shawn surmised. He was fat and disgustingly cute, but his aroma could have knocked a buzzard off a crap wagon at fifty meters. It was too much. Shawn gagged and retreated to the living room. The baby cried.

Shawn paced in circles under the living-room fan. He tried to think of something that grated his nerves as badly as a baby crying. The baby screamed. He thought harder. In the distance here was the thump of incoming mortar rounds; now that was awful. The baby screamed. Fingernails on a chalkboard. He grimaced. Now *that's* awful. The baby screamed. Shawn clutched his ears. Dumb baby will probably be an opera singer before he starts his pitching career with the Dodgers. The baby screamed.

Shawn retreated nervously to the front porch and searched for reinforcements. The dirt road was empty in both directions. He was desperately alone. The baby cried; he sounded really hurt now. A command decision had to be made. Shawn reconned the road for signs of help that might be coming. None. The baby cried. Shawn paced the porch nervously as dark rain clouds blackened the horizon, mocking his mood.

Time passed. The crying came in waves that tied Shawn's stomach in knots.

"Crap!" he screamed. "She can have the seven hundred bucks!"

The baby screamed.

"Seize command, McClellan!" he shouted to himself as he did a sharp about-face and marched back into the house. He did not stop until he reached the crib. The baby spotted him, stopped crying, and giggled with mysterious merriment. The smell was terrible.

"You need an oil change, baby."

The baby giggled.

Shawn stepped back and reconned the area. He grabbed up a white cloth diaper and laid it on the wood floor. It looked too small. Probably takes a couple, Shawn thought. This baby could stand to lose some weight. Shawn looked accusingly at the fat baby. The baby cried out loud then suddenly stopped and smiled. This baby is insincere, Shawn thought. He scares me. Shawn turned back to the basket of diapers. He got two more out and tied them by the corners to the one already on the floor. He stood up, stepped back, and tried to picture how this project would work. They looked almost like a small toga.

"That's it!"

Shawn picked the baby up, keeping him at arm's length. The baby did not object. Shawn laid him on the floor beside the toga and stood up to study just how it might fit. The baby seemed willing to go along with the operation. Shawn knelt down and began work. He unpinned the foul diaper and carefully removed it and its contents, again holding the cause of discontent out away from him at arm's length.

He stood up. "Now what?"

He looked around the room. It was empty except for the rocking chair. A side window was open. He pitched the diaper through. The baby's giggle again seemed insincere somehow. Shawn knelt back down and rolled the baby onto the toga, wrapped one end between his legs, and tied it all together over one of his shoulders.

Shawn stood up to survey the job. The insincere baby giggled and made baby noises that Shawn assumed were normal. There still seemed to be a problem. Danger of a potential leak. A second toga tied over the other shoulder and through the legs, crisscrossing his chest, would shore that up.

Shawn set about the task. By the time he had finished, a storm had rolled in with the force of a monsoon. He put the baby back in his crib and closed the window. Thunder shook the house. Lightning streaked across the dark sky, sending white flashes through the window. The baby cried. Heavy rain pelted the tin roof. Drops of water splashed off of the edge of the crib. Shawn moved the crib and searched for a bucket in the kitchen. He found two metal ones, but they were already catching water from other leaks.

The thunder grew louder and the baby cried, so Shawn was forced to pick him up. It wasn't so bad, now that he didn't stink.

257

Shawn rocked him until he fell asleep. He looked more sincere when he was asleep, Shawn decided. He gently laid the baby back in his crib and went back into the living room.

He decided to investigate the closed door. He opened it. It was another bedroom with a big old feather bed and a dresser with a mirror that tilted. On the dresser was a stack of money held together by a broken Marine Corps tie clip. For some reason, confirmation of the theft saddened him. Shawn picked up his money and shoved it into his trouser pocket.

"Hey, Yank! You still here, mate?" Roger called from the living room.

"Yeah, Roger, right here." Shawn walked back into the living room.

"She come back yet?"

"No."

"My Lordy, Lordy, Lordy, Yank!" The old lady in the flowered apron came out of the baby's room. "Is that the way you Yanks put nappies on a bub?"

"What?"

"Nappies, Yank," Roger explained. "You know, diapers I think you Americans call 'em. On the bub."

"Bub? Baby?"

"That's right."

"Oh, well . . ." Shawn stuttered.

"Strange land, America," the old lady mumbled, and went back into the baby's room.

Shawn turned to Roger. "What would it cost to put a roof on this place?"

"Corrugated iron, not sure, probably a couple hundred quid, I imagine."

"If I gave you the money, think you could round up all the material we'd need to do the job?"

Roger smiled. "Don't be a drongo, mate."

"What?"

"A fool. A sucker, as you Yanks say."

Shawn laughed. "You've been talking to Lukevec."

"You sure this is what you want?"

"Yeah. It shouldn't be raining on a baby, even if he is insincere."

"What? What kind of baby, mate?"

"Little. Little baby."

They turned together and walked outside to the porch.

"This is her place, Kathleen's, I mean?" Shawn asked.

"That's what the old broad says. Says she got knocked by a Yank, and he wouldn't marry her. The old broad says she ain't no pro."

"Pro?"

"Prostitute."

Shawn nodded. He was glad. Kathleen and the insincere baby were sitting on the porch when Shawn and Roger arrived early the next morning. Kathleen stood up with the baby but did not speak. The insincere baby cried and held out his arms for Shawn. Kathleen seemed shocked at the baby's reaction. A friend of Roger's brought all the needed supplies in an old, red Chevy truck: corrugated iron roofing, rivets, drills, hammers, and ladders. At the end of the first day, Kathleen managed to walk up to Shawn and, teary-eyed, she spoke. "I'm sorry," she said. "Thank you." She was sobbing so hard that she got Shawn wet with her tears when she kissed him on the cheek. Then she ran back into the house.

Luke and Joe had staunchly refused to work that first day— after all, they were on R&R. But on the second, they came out in Roger's cab, each bearing three cases of Foster's beer and swearing he wouldn't work hard or sober. For a while, Kathleen tossed bottles up to Joe, the designated receiver. Then he began climbing down for them and often stayed with Kathleen until Luke complained. Joe seemed happy.

It took four days to complete the roof, and even then Shawn wasn't satisfied. He bought paint and brushes and immediately set to painting the outside walls of the house. Luke used Shawn's name in vain and swore he was finished doing anything that did not wear a mini-skirt, but when Joe pitched right in, it didn't take long for Luke to follow. By the end of R&R, the house looked practically brand new.

The cab ride to the airport was crowded and quiet. Kathleen and Joe stared into each other's eyes the whole way. Luke and Shawn tried to finish up the remaining Foster's before they reached the terminal, and they let the insincere baby throw the empties out the back window until Roger called for a cease fire. The good-byes at the airport were short. Kathleen kissed everybody and cried. Then she kissed Joe again, this time longer and harder, the kind of kiss that makes a guy sweat—then it was over, and so was R&R. To Shawn, the kiss looked almost serious. He wondered.

Touching down in Da Nang was a real stomach growler. It was worse than the first time, maybe because Shawn knew what was coming. He looked at Joe and Luke across the aisle. He loved them like brothers. Could all of us go home, he wondered? Three gunners? It would take a miracle. He fought the temptation to panic the same way he always had. He pulled out his Bible. His hand shook too much to turn pages, so he read the first pages he came to.

Joshua 1:5: "As I was with Moses, so I will be with thee: I will not fail thee, nor forsake thee."

Shawn read the verse again and again. The fear faded by the time the plane taxied to a stop. The men were quiet as they left the plane and filed toward the briefing area. Sweat poured through his skin until his uniform clung to him. He pulled his shirt away from his body.

"Look at this." Shawn looked back at Joe. "I've walked fifty feet and I'm soaked. I hate this country."

"Oh, really?" Joe said sarcastically. "I was thinking of building a summer home up by the Rock Pile."

"No way, GI!" Luke said from behind Joe. "You should check out the real estate prices over in Elephant Valley." Luke signaled a thumbs-up. "Very reasonable."

They were led to a big tent for a briefing and a roll call. The briefing was short. The men were given times for travel back to their units then issued any gear they had left before going on R&R. Changing back into jungle utilities didn't feel all that bad to Shawn. He liked the salty look of his helmet, with A ⅕ GUNS UP! printed across the camouflage cover. Part of him got so charged with the adventure of being a grunt Marine at war that he had to calm himself to keep from looking like a kid. Another part of him was scared stiff and wanted to wake up from this nightmare.

Shawn threw his sea bag over his shoulder and grabbed his rifle. The M16 was too light, but at least it was a weapon. He had felt naked without one for the last week.

Joe gave his orders a long solemn stare.

"What's the word, Joe?" Luke asked.

"Got a convoy headin' north at—" Joe paused to look at his

watch. "—zero-nine-hundred." He looked at Shawn, then Luke. "De-de-mow, Marine. How 'bout you guys?"

"We got one night in Da Nang, chopper out tomorrow," Shawn said.

Luke held out his hand.

"See ya in seven months, Hank Handsome."

Joe grinned and held out his hand. They shook hands. He turned to Shawn and held out his hand.

"Don't give me that garbage." Shawn pushed Joe's hand away and hugged him and slapped the back of his flak jacket. "Love ya, buddy." Tears filled Shawn's eyes. He hated being so emotional. He pulled back, embarrassed. Joe's dark eyes frosted over. He cleared his throat and wiped at a tear with his sleeve.

"Yeah," Luke growled as if he were angry. He stepped up and gave Joe a bear hug.

"Joe." Shawn pulled a little pocket Bible out of his sea bag. "I hope—" He hesitated, looking for the words, then handed it to Joe. "Here."

Joe held it, staring at the gold printing on the cover. "Wow, you put my name on it," he said quietly. "Thanks, Shawn. I mean it."

"You better saddle up, Marine!" a young second lieutenant with a bandage over one ear shouted. "That convoy's ready!"

"Aye, aye, sir," Joe said as he tightened his grip on his sea bag. He looked back at Shawn and Luke. "No John Waynes now! We go home together, right?"

"There it is, Marine." Shawn held out his palm and Joe slapped it.

Luke put his palm out. "Keep the bursts short, Joe."

Joe slapped Luke's hand. He looked at the ground like he was embarrassed.

"I love you guys," Joe mumbled.

He looked back at Shawn. "Keep your promise, Shawn."

"I won't have to."

Joe turned away and followed the lieutenant. He stopped and looked back over his shoulder. "Hey, Shawn."

"Yeah, Joe?"

"Pray for me, will ya?"

"There it is, Joe." Goose bumps rushed down Shawn's back. He had never in all the years of their friendship heard Joe make such a request.

Luke was extra quiet after Joe left. They found the tent where they were supposed to stay until their ride came. After an hour in the tent with no conversation, Shawn finally figured that Luke was too quiet.

"You okay?" he asked as he stared at the top of the tent from his cot. "Luke?"

Shawn rolled his head toward Luke's cot. Luke rested on his back with his hands behind his head. His eyes were open. A long pause got longer. Shawn sat up. "Luke!"

Luke crossed his arms across his chest and cleared his throat. "We have been through some things that very few friends have ever experienced together." He stared at the tent ceiling.

"Yes, we have."

"How long have we been friends, Shawn?" His eyes remained fixed on the ceiling of the tent.

Shawn scratched drips of sweat from his scalp. "Well, ever since I moved to Florida."

"Since the seventh grade at Mirror Lake Junior High, to be precise."

"Right. Old Paul Wells, math class."

"Who would you say are your closest friends in the world—after Eddie, I mean?"

"You and Joe," Shawn said quickly. "And Chuck's a good friend, and Jay too."

"Your closest."

"You and Joe. Why?" Shawn asked impatiently.

Luke didn't move. "Do you consider me as a good friend, as good as Joe?"

"Of course."

"You never gave me a gift," Luke said indignantly, still staring at the ceiling. "I have fought and bled beside you through this war. You are my best friend. I would not give Joe a gift and not give you one also."

Shawn's mouth fell open. "A Bible?"

"That is not the point. I do not care what the object is, but after nearly dying together on numerous occasions . . . I practically bottle-fed you your first beer. Who gave you a mirror for your bike in the eighth grade?"

"You stole that mirror from Ted Kotcheff."

"I didn't ask how the mirror was obtained; besides, Ted was rich. What is the highest sign of friendship in the bush, McClellan?"

Shawn fought back a laugh. "Sharing peaches and pound cake, Luke."

"Correct!" Luke put his hands behind his head.

"And dry socks."

"Correct!"

"And drawing fire off your buddy by exposing yourself."

"Aw, baloney. Any Marine will do that. But peaches and pound cake . . ." Luke stopped talking. He looked mad.

Shawn pulled his sea bag from under his cot and opened it. He felt around for a few seconds then pulled out a small black pocket Bible with "Eric Lukevec" printed in gold letters at the bottom right-hand corner. He laid it on Luke's stomach, crossed his arms proudly, and grinned the most satisfied grin he could muster.

Luke's eyes glanced down at the Bible on his stomach. He peered at Shawn from the corner of one eye then back to the Bible without moving his head. He cleared his throat, then removed one hand from under his head and slowly reached for the Bible. He held it up and stared for a long time at his name on the cover before he sat up.

Luke turned slowly to face Shawn. Shawn flashed his eyebrows up and down. Luke's brown right eye closed and he glared at Shawn with his left black eye. Shawn blinked and grinned.

"You did that on purpose, McClellan." Luke looked down at the Bible and shrugged. "Thanks."

Da Nang was no small place. Finding your way around was like trying to navigate an extra-scummy version of Tampa, Shawn thought. After a few hours of asking directions and trying to hump it on foot, Luke asked a young recon corporal who was jumping into a Jeep outside an officers' club. He looked drunk, but he tried to point and give directions to Camp Reasoner.

"Left. No, I mean, right. Then, past Graves and Registration, take a left before you hit China Beach." He dropped his pointing finger and turned his long, sad face toward Luke. His eyes were blood red. He shook his head. "Grunts?" he asked.

"0331s." Shawn said.

"Oh, crap! Just jump in, I'll take ya there."

He did. Camp Reasoner was made up of small houses with plywood-and-screen walls and tin roofs surrounded by enough concertina wire to stop a tank. Some of the houses had regular bunks and some even had refrigerators filled with cold beer and

Cokes. Tony and Cassius had both. It seemed an unbelievable luxury to Shawn and Luke. Tony and Cassius shoved cold beer at the two grunts as fast as they could drink.

"Wait a minute." Tony held up a finger and leaned over to pull something from under his bunk. "You ain't seen nothin', grunts." He pulled out a big Pioneer stereo receiver as Cassius produced a Dual turntable. They hooked the two together and dragged out two large Pioneer speakers from behind the refrigerator.

"Pioneer eighty-eights, bros," Cassius said. "The best. You dudes just stay here tonight. We'll get you back tomorrow."

Shawn stared at the huge wood speakers in disbelief. "How can you guys get this stuff?"

Tony laughed. "PX. Where else?" He laid a Young Rascals album on the turntable and tossed Shawn the album cover.

"Wow." Shawn opened it up. "It's Japanese. Look, Luke, it has the words to the songs in Japanese."

"Yes. I am sure that they like music, Shawn." He grinned and flashed his brows.

Ten or fifteen repeats of "Groovin' " later, a major portion of the beer was gone. Shawn was woozy. Tony opened the small white door of the refrigerator. He leaned on the door and stared into the empty box. He slammed it shut with a big smile. He held up a finger.

"I know where we can get some more beer."

"It's almost dark, bro. We ain't goin' nowhere," Cassius warned.

"The vill," Tony said with a twinkle in his eyes.

"Oh, no," Cassius groaned, and rolled his eyes.

It didn't seem all that dangerous to Shawn as the four left the compound. Compared with the bush, it was like walking through Williams Park back home. The vill was just across a couple of dried-up rice paddies, two hundred meters away, Shawn guessed as he glanced at the big yellow ball sinking behind the mountains. The villagers were closing down for the night as the four Marines crossed the second paddy, climbed in and out of a six-foot ditch, and stumbled onto the main dirt street. A wrinkled, leather-skinned old mama-san squatted in the doorway of the first hootch. She cast a suspicious stare at Shawn as the Marines passed. Suddenly Shawn began to wonder just how safe this was.

Tony led them to the fourth hootch on the right. It was made of plywood with a thatched roof and a dirty blue curtain for a door.

"Apple-san!" Tony called through the curtain. "Apple-san, baby." Luke and Shawn exchanged questioning glances then looked around nervously.

"Tony-san!" a sensuous voice called from inside. The curtain pulled open and a smiling Vietnamese girl peeked out. "Come in, please." She pulled the curtain back and bowed as the Marines entered.

"I go get girls," she said as she giggled and darted out.

The inside of the hootch was too dark to make out the furnishings. The stink of fish was strong. Tony struck a match and found a candle on a mirrorless dresser in one corner of the hootch's only room. The floor was packed-down dirt. A white card table sat in the center of the room with a bowl of rice and a bottle of Tiger Beer on it. A green Army blanket lying on a straw mat in one corner was the only bed Shawn could see.

"We here, Tony-san," Apple-san said. Her voice was squeaky. She giggled as she pushed through the curtain door. She was followed by three other giggling young Vietnamese girls.

"Guns up! Take your pick." Tony put an arm around Apple-san, leaned down, and gave her a kiss. "This one's mine."

Shawn looked at the girls. They were thin and ugly and two of them were missing a front tooth. He fought the urge to groan and wondered why he hadn't been smart enough to figure this would happen.

"De-de-mow! Soldier come!" The frightened shout belonged to a young, panic-stricken girl standing in the doorway and pointing down the street.

"VC?" Luke snapped as he brought his rifle to the ready.

"ARVN!" she shouted, and ran away.

Tony released Apple-san and hit Luke in the shoulder.

"Come on!" Tony grabbed up his rifle and ran through the door with Cassius right behind.

Luke looked at Shawn and shrugged. "She said ARVN."

"Yeah," Shawn said.

Tony's girl shoved Luke toward the door, then pulled Shawn forward. "ARVN! Husband-san! You go! Husband-sans! They shoot!"

"Oh, my God!" Shawn groaned and pushed Luke through the curtain door and into the dirt street. Shawn glanced right.

The silhouettes of helmeted ARVN soldiers walked toward them in two columns down the center of the dirt street.

"Here they come, Luke!"

Luke froze and looked right. "Come on!" He broke into a run toward the rice paddy.

Shawn took off after him. Someone shouted an angry command in Vietnamese from behind them. Shawn ran faster. He could see Tony and Cassius scrambling out of the ditch and starting across the paddy ahead. He jumped into the ditch behind Luke. They clawed up the other side and started across the first paddy. An automatic burst of M16 fire shot from the village.

"God! They're shootin' at us!" Shawn shouted ahead. He pushed his body to run faster. Another burst of fire came from behind. Luke started across the wide dike separating the two paddies. Shawn glanced back. The muzzle flash of an M16 shot out of the dark paddy behind him. It was closer.

"Luke! They're chasin' us!" More rifles opened up behind him. The dim silhouette of the Camp Reasoner gun towers looked close against the dark gray skyline. A sparkling flare hissed into the sky from the camp. It popped open above the paddy like a small red sun and swung lazily beneath its tiny parachute. Suddenly an M60 machine gun opened up from one of the towers. Orange tracers streaked close overhead as Shawn dove for the ground. An instant later heavy small-arms fire thudded into the paddy around Shawn and Luke from the Camp Reasoner perimeter. Shawn lifted his face from the dirt and looked back. He pushed up from the ground and ran. The ARVNs opened up full automatic. Shawn dove to the ground beside Luke. Their fire was high. The Marine fire was more accurate. Dirt spit out of the dusty ground two feet from Shawn. He flinched, gritted his teeth, and shoved his face so close to Luke's that they banged helmets. Dirt stuck to the sweat on Luke's frightened face.

"Luke!"

"What?"

"We're going to be killed by the husbands of those girls!"

"I didn't think they would be so testy about it!"

"You knew?"

Tracer rounds from the Marine machine gun ripped across the paddy to Luke's right.

"Friendlies! Marines!" Tony's screams were muffled by the chaotic cross fire.

"Please don't let me die like this, God!" Shawn shouted.

"We're Marines, you jackass!" Cassius screamed through a lull in the shooting.

A moment later the perimeter ceased fire.

"Recons! We're recons!" Tony screamed at the top of his lungs. Another blast of fire from the ARVN rifles shot overhead. The perimeter opened fire at the ARVNs. The ARVNs ceased fire. The perimeter stopped firing.

"Come on in!" someone shouted from the wire.

Shawn dropped his face into the dirt and sighed and thanked God for saving them, then pushed into a sprint for the wire. Why no one demanded an explanation was a mystery to him, but he was thankful for not getting busted to private. He put it down as one more story no one back home would ever believe— except Eddie, he thought. He'd tell Eddie everything, just like he'd been doing since he was four years old. And Joe. Joe would believe it. He'd write to Joe.

CHAPTER TWELVE

The Letter

The ride back to the bush turned out to be a flight on a big, fat troop-transport plane, packed with fresh-faced boot replacements right out of staging battalion at Camp Pendleton. They still wore starched, stateside utilities and soft-cover hats. Shawn and Luke stuck out like cavemen in their tattered jungle utilities, jungle boots that looked like Indian moccasins, and helmets and flak jackets with "GUNS UP!" printed in black across the camouflage canvas cover.

Shawn wore Dusty's NVA pack too, but it was more than clothing that made the veterans stand out. Shawn could see another difference and it left him feeling uneasy. He looked at Luke's face, then glanced at the row of young healthy Marines facing him along the opposite wall of the troop plane. The faces stared back with a curious awe in their eyes. Shawn felt older than the boots, yet he knew he wasn't. At least not in years.

The plane landed in Phu Bai around noon. The heat was blistering. They dropped off their sea bags at a big tent filled with Alpha Company's sea bags. An hour later Shawn and Luke got their first ride on a Huey gunship. It was an Army chopper; of course, the Marines were still using the old Korean-era H34-Ds for the most part. As bad as landing in Da Nang felt, it was nothing compared with the sickening wave of anxiety that swept over Shawn when the chopper began to circle down toward a rocky knoll in a barren and bomb-cratered valley in central Thua Thien Province. Yellow smoke swirled on the ground at his feet as he jumped from the hatch behind Luke. The chopper lifted away.

"Mac! Luke!" Doc shouted. He ran toward the guys with a can of C-rations in one hand and his white plastic spoon in the other. His blond crop of hair stuck straight up in the back like always.

"Dennis the Menace!" Shawn shouted.

"How was it? Catch the clap?" Doc stuck his spoon in his mouth and held out his hand, palm up. Shawn slapped it, then Luke did.

"Luke! McClellan! Outstanding!" a deep, familiar voice called.

"Sergeant Ghosthorse?" Luke said, surprised.

"Chief!" Shawn yelled.

"How was R&R?" Doc repeated.

Shawn moaned with satisfaction. "Outstanding, Doc."

"It is very difficult to come back," Luke added as the Chief slapped him on the shoulder.

Shawn shook his head and laughed and held out his hand. "Why didn't you stay in the world, Chief? You didn't have to come back."

Sergeant Ghosthorse shook hands and grinned. "The Marine Corps is here; I'm a Marine," the Chief said matter-of-factly, as if there had been no choice. He pushed his thick glasses back on his long straight nose. "How was Australia?"

Shawn smiled. "It was great."

The big Indian looked at Luke. "You get him laid?"

"Hey, come on, you guys," Shawn complained.

Luke cleared his throat as if he were announcing something important. "I did manage to get young Mr. Bible Thumper, in the words of our local Cajun, Dook, 'Drunker'n a red-eyed skunk.' " Luke laughed. The others were silent. Doc looked at the ground and kicked lightly at a small rock. Luke stopped laughing. His big face turned serious. "What's wrong? Doc?"

"Old Dook found a trip wire a couple of days ago," Chief said.

"Dead?" Luke asked.

"No, but he's gonna be walkin' on pine."

Doc looked at Luke. "You know how he never got mail."

"Yes," Luke said.

"Yeah," Shawn mumbled. Visions of Dook and his big walrus mustache flashed by, and he wondered what kind of life old Dook would have without legs.

"Well, you knew he was married and had a kid. She finally wrote. Asked for a divorce."

"He never told anybody," Chief griped.

"Yeah, he'd never talk about that. Not old Dook," Shawn said.

"Got careless," Chief said.

"He was trying to catch a bag to the world, man," Doc added with an angry glance at the Chief.

"He demanded to walk point every day," Chief continued. "We didn't know."

"Cager, like, found the letter in his helmet after he hit the booby trap," Doc said. He kicked at the stone again.

"Anybody else?" Shawn asked.

"No." Chief shook his head. "Haven't even made contact since you left. Least not since I got back."

"Mac! Luke!" Chip the radioman bounced up with a big friendly grin. "Welcome home, dudes!" He blew a bubble and popped it and chewed and grinned at the same time.

"Chipper, my man!" Shawn gave the shorter radioman a pat on the top of his head.

"What is the latest scuttlebutt, Chip?" Luke asked.

"You're not gonna like it," he blurted with a tilt of his head.

"I *already* fail to like it, Chip," Luke said, frowning.

"Go relieve Sleepy and Shakey Jake on the gun and—"

"Saddle up," Shawn moaned sarcastically.

"There it is, bro." Chip turned and walked away. Shawn and Luke headed for the M60.

"Shawn?" Luke said.

"Yeah?"

"I hope they never throw pieces of me into the South China Sea."

It was strange how a day or two back in the bush wiped out any good that a rest might have done. By the third day of humping through the sweltering jungle heat, even the memory of Australia was blurred and faded with fatigue. Shawn's stomach adjusted slowly to the C-rations. It rejected the Halazone water. By the sixth day back, he had dysentery. But the daily hump didn't stop because someone had the runs. Doc gave Shawn some pink horse pills that didn't help. Shawn ripped the seam of his trousers open with his K-bar so he could drain while he walked. No head calls on the hump. That left his skin exposed to the bloodsucking leeches and teeming jungle insects. The misery of your own excretion running down your legs as you marched fifteen miles each day through the hottest jungle in the world brought Shawn to the limit of his endurance. Luke refused to walk behind him. The gap in the column behind Shawn seemed to grow each day. He couldn't stand himself. Biting flies covered him. The night ambushes became worse than the daily humps. Ants ate him alive as he fought to remain motionless.

After a week of the suffering, it began to rain. Shawn cleaned himself as the column marched. They broke through a line of bamboo trees and into a narrow valley of razor-sharp elephant grass that towered fifteen-feet high. The rain began to fall harder as the point of the column intersected a well-trodden footpath running east to west through the valley. The column turned left onto the path, which was like a tunnel with a ten-to-fifteen-foot wall of elephant grass on either side. Shawn was growing weaker from the dysentery. He stared in a light-headed trance as helmets ahead dropped like dominoes.

Luke motioned Shawn down. Shawn dropped and waved the man behind him down. Heads began to turn with a whispered word, then moved off the trail to the right.

Luke turned and whispered, "Gooks, move right." He slid into the thick grass and quietly flattened out.

Shawn turned to pass the word.

"Gooks . . ."

A burst of AK-47 fire cracked from the front of the column. M16s answered. The firing stopped.

"Guns up!" someone shouted from ahead.

Shawn jumped to his feet. Dysentery twisted his stomach into knots as he ran forward. The path snaked left. Ahead Lieutenant Townsend and the Chief stood over a Vietnamese body lying spread-eagled with a Russian AK beside it.

"Shawn"—Lieutenant Townsend pointed ahead—"set the gun up there." Shawn stopped by the body and looked down at it. "He's just a kid," Shawn mumbled.

No one spoke. The black-haired little boy looked to be no more than fourteen years old. Dark red blood gushed from his throat. His boyish face reminded Shawn of Phan the Coke boy.

Doc shoved Shawn aside and knelt down by the boy. He checked his pulse and looked up. "Lieutenant, he's still alive."

"He is?"

The lieutenant looked surprised. He pushed his helmet back with the barrel of his M16. He studied the boy. "Okay. Let's carry him back to that last hill." He turned to the Chief. "We can get a chopper in there, can't we, Chief?"

"Yes, sir."

"Put a poncho and two rifles together for a stretcher and let's move."

They moved, but by the time the column reached the barren hilltop, the boy was dead. They laid the body in the center of the perimeter, near the CP. One at a time most of the men found a reason to walk by the child. Including Shawn.

"Don't get scared, now."

Neader's nasal tone sent a surge of anger through Shawn as he stared down at the dead boy's face. Neader laughed and spit on the body. He pulled an ace of spades card out of the band around his helmet cover and knelt beside the body.

"What are you doing, Neader?" Shawn barked, louder than he intended.

Shawn's stomach cramped hard with dysentery and for a moment he thought he'd have to vomit.

"Keep it down over there," Chief ordered from the CP twenty meters away.

Neader looked up. He seemed surprised at Shawn's tone. He pushed his helmet back and turned back to the body. He pulled a thumbtack out of a small canvas pouch on his cartridge belt then pulled his K-bar from its sheath. He laid the ace of spades card on the boy's forehead and tacked it into the skull with the handle of his knife. Shawn's stomach cramped. He grabbed his knees and began vomiting.

"What are you doing in the Marine Corps, McClellan?" Neader sounded angry.

Shawn closed his eyes and tried to keep from throwing up again. He felt light-headed and broke into a cold sweat.

"Dead gooks ain't supposed to make you sick, little girl. It's the live ones that make me sick." Neader laughed his grating laugh.

"Shawn, you look bad," Luke said.

Shawn opened his eyes and looked up at Luke. "I'm really sick."

"Hey, Doc!" Luke called.

Neader laughed. "He lost his cookies when he looked at this dead gook."

"Shut up, Neader." Luke growled.

"Bible thumpers like this guy belong in the Boy Scouts, not the corps."

An hour later Shawn was still vomiting.

Lieutenant Townsend grudgingly ordered a medevac chopper when Shawn's temperature went to a hundred and four.

* * *

272

The medevac chopper dropped Shawn off at Truoi Bridge instead of Phu Bai. The CAP unit had an aid station set up in a hootch across the road from the ARVN compound. The two corpsmen that ran the aid station were good. They treated Shawn like a king once they had burned his clothes and made him jump in the river with a bar of some yellow soap that smelled like medicine. Two days of pills and shots and sleep got him on his feet. On the third day a welcome face peeked through the bamboo-and-straw door.

"Feel like a visitor?" Chaplain Elliott asked.

"Hey, Chaplain! How ya been? Come on in."

The chaplain walked in and closed the door. "Well, I heard you were here, and I can only stay a minute, but I wanted to say hello, make sure you're okay."

"Heck, I'm fine now. I caught dysentery and thought I was gonna die." Shawn pointed at three cases of C-rations stacked against the wall. "Have a seat."

The tall, lean chaplain walked like he was on stilts. He sat down with a sigh, stretched out his legs, lifted his soft-cover, and wiped beads of sweat from his forehead with his sleeve. He grinned and closed one eye. "Every once in a long while, I get real tempted to ask the Lord if Vietnam was his work or just where he washed his hands when he finished making the real world."

"There it is, Chaplain." Shawn chuckled. "Chaplain, there is something I've been wanting to talk to you about."

"Fire away, Shawn." He put his hat back on and leaned forward, resting his elbows on his bony knees. His long, friendly face looked eager.

"Sometimes I feel like some weirdo," Shawn said. "I mean, like I'm not one of the guys, you know what I mean?"

"Sure, I understand that feeling, Shawn." The chaplain's lack of hesitation surprised Shawn. "And so does God. Remember, the world rejected Jesus himself. Just make sure people aren't persecuting you for being a jerk."

He smiled.

Shawn chuckled. "Okay."

"I hope I was of some help with your question, Shawn." Chaplain Elliott stood up and held out his hand. "I really have to get going. You take care, now. I'll be praying for you."

Shawn shook his hand. "Thank you, sir. Oh, yeah, one more thing, Chaplain. Have you seen Phan?"

"Oh, yes." He beamed. "I got him a Vietnamese Bible and he is full of questions."

"How 'bout the plywood?"

"No, sorry, Shawn. Not yet. The Sea Bees have some policy going right now because of shortages, but we won't give up."

"Well, thanks for trying."

"Right." He turned and walked through the bamboo door, then peeked back in. "I'll see if I can pick up your mail while I'm in Phu Bai." He closed the door.

Shawn lay back down. He thought over the chaplain's words. Soon, he drifted off to the warm world of sleep.

"Hey, jarhead! You gonna sleep the war away?"

Shawn's eyes popped open and he groped for the M60 that wasn't there.

"Don't shoot, grunt." The voice chuckled. "I'm your doctor, remember?"

Shawn sat up and looked toward the door. The black Navy corpsman smiled.

Shawn yawned. "What time is it?"

"Time for you to go for a walk. Doctor's orders."

"Sounds good to me, Doc." Shawn reached for his boots and socks by the end of the bunk. "Where to?"

"Why don't you go on down to the Dinkie-Dow Bar and Grille, get yourself a bottle of Tiger piss and see if the old stomach can take it."

"Okay by me." Shawn gave the mattress a pat. "I still can't believe you guys managed to get a real mattress."

"Semper fi, Mac. We're in the Navy. We ain't no Spartans and don't wanna be." He laughed and closed the door.

A feeling of Marine Corps pride went through Shawn. Esprit de corps, he thought with a grin as he laced up his worn-out boots. He wouldn't trade uniforms for all of the "pogey bait" in Da Nang.

The walk felt good. The sun was bright in the pale blue sky. A rumbling convoy of trucks turned him beige with dust by the time he reached the Dinkie-Dow Bar and Grille on the south side of the bridge. The Dinkie-Dow was sort of a restaurant and outdoor cafe, Vietnamese style, a few round wooden tables under a thatched roof with bamboo shades for walls. There was a little room in the back where the old couple that owned the place cooked and slept. Like everyplace else in Nam, it smelled like a combination of urine and fish and burnt oil.

In spite of the smell, sitting at a table with your boots resting on another chair, drinking hot beer and watching convoys go by was just about heaven to a grunt. Three beers later it didn't even smell all that bad. Shawn looked around the cafe. Two ARVN soldiers seemed to be arguing at a table in the back. Other than himself, that was the extent of business, it appeared.

"Got your mail, Shawn."

Shawn turned back to the road. "Chaplain. Man, that was fast."

"Here." He flipped a small stack of mail wrapped with rubber bands onto the fly-covered table. "Having flies for dinner?"

"Have a seat. I'll buy you a beer."

"Talked me into it, Marine."

Shawn pulled his boots off the second chair and dropped them to the packed-dirt floor. He turned back toward the room in the rear. "Papa-san, beer!" he shouted. The gray-haired old man stepped through the brown curtain door of the rear room, bowed twice, and went back in.

"Office pogues," the chaplain mumbled angrily. He sat down shaking his head. "You know"—he frowned—"half of those typewriter pushers in Phu Bai are wearing full camouflage utilities."

Shawn chuckled. "You sound like a grunt, Chap." He glanced at the bundle of dirty white envelopes. No pink ones. No lilac scent. No Nancy. "You married, Chaplain?"

"Sure am. Got a boy and a girl too. Go on and read your mail. Don't mind me."

"Okay." Shawn took a swig of beer and snatched up the bundle. He recognized his mother's handwriting on the top letter. He pulled the rubber bands off and spread the letters on the table like a deck of cards.

The papa-san set a brown bottle of beer with a Tiger label on the dusty tabletop.

"Thank you, Papa-san. Papa-san, is that Armed Forces radio I hear playing back there?"

"Is number one," Papa-san said.

He bobbed his head with short quick bows and grinned. His teeth were black. "American music number one."

"Would you turn it up, please, so that we might listen too?"

The old man grinned and bowed as he left. A moment later the soulful sound of "Dock of the Bay" blared from the back room. Shawn thumbed through the envelopes.

PFC Shawn McClellan
A. Co. 1st Bat. 5th Marine Regt.
APO San Fran. Calif.

"Got a letter returned to me," Shawn mumbled quizzically. He pulled the envelope out of the fan-shaped pile.

"Wrong address?" the chaplain asked.

Shawn stared at the envelope. "It's a letter I sent to Joe. He's my buddy in the Ninth Marines." Shawn looked at the chaplain. "We joined together with Luke, my A-gunner."

He looked back at the envelope.

"But I sent this to him back before we went on R&R. Look at it. It's been all over the place."

He handed it to the chaplain and pointed at two red-stamped fingers pointing to forwarding addresses. The chaplain held it up closer to his face to study it. Shawn's heart stopped beating as his eyes focused in on the letters WIA printed in pencil across the back of the envelope. Wounded in action.

"It's been to First Med at Phu Bai, Shawn. He might be wounded but—" Chaplain Elliott laid the envelope down and looked at Shawn's frozen stare. "Shawn. What's wrong? You look pale."

Shawn picked up the first letter from his mom and ripped it open.

Dear Son,

We don't know if you have heard the news about Joey or not, so I decided I better write and tell you just in case.

Joey is in Japan. He is in critical condition. He stepped on a land mine. He lost one leg and the other leg may have to be removed. He is supposed to be flown back home as soon as he's strong enough.

I pray for you and Luke every hour of every day . . .

Shawn dropped the letter. He leaned his elbows on the table and covered his face with both hands. Chaplain Elliott laid a hand on his shoulder. No one spoke for a few seconds.

"Shawn. May I—" He paused, "—read the letter?"

Shawn couldn't speak. He felt sick and empty. He heard the rustle of the letter being shoved back into the envelope.

"Shawn, I'm so sorry. Is there anything I can do?"

"Go away," Shawn whispered from behind his hands.

"Can we pray together, Shawn?"

Shawn stared at the tabletop. "Semper fi. Do or die. That's what Joe always said." He spoke with his stare fixed on the table.

"Let's pray, Shawn."

"Semper fi," Shawn mumbled down at the table.

"Semper fidelis means always faithful, doesn't it? Have faith in God, Shawn."

Shawn covered his face again. "I wanna be alone, Chaplain."

"Okay, Shawn." He stood up. "Let me know when you feel like talking." He turned and walked to the edge of the road then looked back. "I heard your platoon is coming back to the bridge for a couple of days. They should get here about dusk. Would you like me to tell your friend Luke?"

Shawn shook his head no. The chaplain walked back toward the ARVN compound on the north side of the bridge. Shawn turned and shouted, "Beer!"

He looked back at the dusty road. His expression was hard with anger. He drank through a montage of memories. Joe's diving touchdown catch in the corner of the end zone against Dixie Hollins High School was so clear. He wanted to reach out and touch Joe's white jersey with the green 84. He wanted to cry, but he couldn't. He wanted to pray, but couldn't. He stared at the table covered with empty bottles and remembered his last promise to Hank Handsome.

"Talk about the life of Riley." Luke's tired complaint lifted Shawn's reddened eyes from the bottles. Luke stood by the table in full combat gear.

He set the M60 on the floor and pulled two belts of ammo off. He stared down at Shawn with a questioning frown. "Man, you look terrible. Did you drink all these?" Luke dropped his pack and sat down as Murph and Cornhusker came in and began dropping their gear at a nearby table.

Birdman shrieked out a whistle like a parrot. "Talk about a skatin' girene!"

Shawn glanced up. Birdman grinned and pointed at Shawn. Goody and Sergeant Ghosthorse shoved Birdman aside and sat down at the first table they came to. Shawn looked back down at the tabletop.

"Look at this garbage." Neader's nasal tone pierced Shawn like an angry arrow. "What'd you do, McClellan, take a few extra salt tabs? That's a good way to get out of the bush. You learn that one in church?"

Shawn stood up fast and slapped his chair back out of his way. He glared hard at Neader. Neader slid his pack straps off his shoulders and let the pack drop to the floor. He leaned his rifle against a chair and laid his helmet on a table beside him, then grinned at Shawn.

"Calm down, Shawn," Luke said. "What's wrong?"

With no warning Shawn sprang toward Neader. He hit him with a running right cross that lifted Neader off the ground and put him flat on his back. Neader got to his feet only to be bloodied by a furious series of accurate punches. He staggered backward away from Shawn then charged forward, but another flurry of straight left jabs battered Neader's face as his knees buckled.

A follow-up straight right and left hook put Neader on his back again. He sat up. His face was red with smeared blood.

"I learned *that* in church, Neader. My pastor was golden gloves," Shawn said calmly. He turned and walked back over to Luke. Everyone except the Chief was standing in silent awe, gawking at the unexpected outcome.

Luke stared at Shawn in disbelief.

Somebody snickered.

"Friggin' Neader will be getting baptized in the next slop-shute!"

"Hey, Neader," Birdman called. "I think you got some new teeth for your necklace."

Luke looked stunned. "You never told me that your preacher was golden gloves. I've never seen you fight . . ."

"Luke. Joe tripped a booby trap."

"What?"

"He's bad."

"How bad?"

Shawn picked his mom's letter up and handed it to Luke. Luke sat down and read it.

"Hey, McClellan!" Birdman yelled.

"I wanna be left alone," Shawn said clearly as he sat down.

"You heard him," Chief growled. No one spoke.

Huge tears rolled down Luke's cheeks. He looked past Shawn with a blank stare. They didn't speak from that moment on, except to call for more beer. Darkness came and the bar closed. They walked back across the bridge as an ARVN soldier pulled the big rolls of concertina across the road for the night. Shawn threw up and passed out on the floor of the aid station. He wasn't sure what had happened to Luke when he woke up the next morning. His head throbbed like a thumb that just got smashed by a hammer. By noon things stopped spinning. He tried to keep his mind off Joe but nothing worked. He wanted to pray but he felt too angry. His head throbbed. Someone was hammering. Sea Bees. He thought of Phan. The plywood. Shawn grabbed his M16 from the foot of the bed and stormed out of the hootch. He looked left. Three shirtless Sea Bees were nailing a plywood shed together over in the CAP unit compound. One Sea Bee dropped his hammer and put on his shirt.

"Chow time!" he yelled.

A few minutes later the Sea Bees strolled past Shawn on their way to the Dinkie-Dow Bar. Shawn stood by the edge of the road, staring at the ground. He thought of Joe. Then he thought about Phan and the plywood. He remembered Eddie yelling at old Mr. McCovey and trying in vain to sniff back tears.

"Shawn doesn't steal! It was me!" Eddie pleaded.

"He was just trying to save me," Eddie said. "Shawn would never steal in his whole life. He wasn't even in your old Ten-cent store! He knew my dad would kill me more than his would kill him, that's why he said he did it! Shawn would never steal!"

Shawn felt a tap on his shoulder.

"You okay?" Luke asked.

Shawn lifted his eyes to Luke and nodded, then looked back at the ground. The sun glistened off a piece of silver foil from a gum wrapper. Shawn leaned over and picked it up.

"Luke, will you help me carry some sheets of plywood to Phan's hootch?"

"Sure. Where you plan on getting it?"

"Just go along with me, okay?"

"Sure."

"Here." Shawn handed Luke his rifle and squatted down on one knee. He folded the foil into a small silver rectangle.

"What are you doing?" Luke sounded suspicious.

"Just go along with me." Shawn took off his soft-cover and looked around to see if anyone was watching. "Hey, Chip!" He waved across the road at Chip the radioman walking out of the ARVN compound.

"Yeah?" Chip said.

"Give me a piece of bubble gum, will ya?"

"No way. This stuff is priceless."

"How about used?"

Chip took a piece of gum out of his mouth, bit it in half, and tossed it across the road. It landed at Luke's feet.

"Thanks."

Chip gave Shawn a thumbs-up as he headed toward the bridge. Shawn grabbed the gum.

Luke frowned. "Shawn, what are you doing?"

Shawn brushed the dirt off of the gum and pressed it to the back of the foil rectangle, then he stuck the foil against the black eagle, globe, and anchor stenciled on the front of his soft-cover cap. He put his hat on, stood up, and looked at Luke.

"Let's see a salute, Marine," he barked.

"Are you losing your mind? That is impersonating an officer, Shawn. People go to prison for long periods of time for that."

"Come on." Shawn grabbed his rifle, turned, and headed for the CAP compound.

"I don't believe this, McClellan," Luke murmured as he followed a few paces back.

"Hey, Marine," Shawn called to a shirtless young redheaded Marine sitting against a tree under the shade of a huge camouflaged parachute.

"Yes, sir." The Marine stood up.

"This was a good idea." Shawn pointed at the parachute tied to four trees.

"Yes, sir."

"Look, I'm here to pick up some of these sheets of plywood." He motioned toward the half-completed shed. "Lend a hand."

"Oh, yes, sir."

"And police up a couple of hammers and some nails and bring it along."

"Yes, sir."

Luke started coughing from behind Shawn. He continued coughing all the way across Truoi Bridge. He didn't stop coughing until the redheaded Marine set his end of the four sheets of plywood down in front of Phan's wall-less hootch. Old papa-san and mama-san looked puzzled. They squatted by their bunker, nodding and grinning and chewing on betel nuts. The three Marines spent the better part of the afternoon nailing the little house together. Phan rushed about, retrieving dropped nails or running to the river to fill wood bowls of drinking water for the Marines. He was like a kid on Christmas morning.

When the work was done and the Marines started back for the bridge, Phan cried and clung to Shawn's leg. Shawn picked him up and hugged him tight and fought back tears of his own by taking deep breaths. He kissed the little boy's cheek and set him down. The love in Phan's tear-filled eyes seemed to ease Shawn's pain for a while. No one ever questioned the missing plywood. A few days later the Fifth Marine Regiment was convoyed south, down Highway One, through Da Nang and all the way to a place called An Hoa Valley.

CHAPTER THIRTEEN

An Hoa Valley
August 1968

An Hoa Valley made a natural supply route for the NVA coming off the Ho Chi Minh Trail and across the Laotian border. The Laos-Vietnam border region consisted of mountains and jungle as rugged as any in the world. The thick jungle canopy blacked out the sky in some areas. The valley floor was all knee-deep mud and was full of leech-infested rice paddies, fields of waist-level elephant grass, and small rolling hills. All of it was a maze of booby traps.

The enemy's main target in I Corps Tactical Zone was Da Nang. An Hoa Valley was the most accessible attack route. The NVA had taken a serious beating-up north around the DMZ, and they were shifting their main effort to the central provinces, with Da Nang as the ultimate target.

An Hoa Combat Base was twenty-five miles southwest of Da Nang. It wasn't much to look at, but then again, what was there to look at in Vietnam besides the hostile terrain? The base consisted of one portable airstrip made of pierced-steel planking and one artillery unit, made up mostly of .105-millimeter pop guns that were just slightly more deadly than spitballs when used here, in the thickest jungle on earth. It had one chow hall, one bar for officers, one bar for office pogues, and rows of large, dust-covered tents. The tents were for those rare occasions, every sixty to ninety days, when the grunts marched into An Hoa looking like murderous, heavily armed savages out of some pre-historic era. They would get one hot meal and resupplies and head back out within twenty-four hours. It was not much to look forward to, but after two months in the bush, everyone did. Shawn laid his chin on the feed cover of the M60 and tried to visualize a giant red-and-white can of ice-cold Budweiser rising out of An Hoa like a volcano.

Luke struck a match.

Shawn flinched.

"Hold still," Luke demanded.

He touched the lit match to the burrowed head of the six-inch-long slimy black leech attached to the back of Shawn's left ear. It dropped to the mud, Shawn groaned, and looked at the squirming leech. It was fat with his blood. He pulled his K-bar out of the sheath.

"You son of a . . ." he growled, and hacked the leech in half.

"That is the closest thing to a curse I have ever heard you say."

Shawn threw an irritated glance at Luke. Luke's brows pinched together.

"Don't give me that 'biology project' look of yours, all right, Lukevec?" Shawn gazed across the vast span of flat rice paddy fields. A green oasis of trees on a square island of firm ground four hundred meters straight ahead was the next nearest cover.

Luke gave the bolt of his rifle a casual swipe with his toothbrush. "Haven't seen you read your little Bible in a while, Shawn."

"Haven't seen you reading much, either."

Luke threw his toothbrush in the mud. "Look, jerk-face, I would just feel better if you would at least do your prayer thing for Joe."

Luke picked up his toothbrush and tried to find a clean piece of clothing to wipe it on. Shawn ran through a half-dozen angry responses to Luke's shocking request but ended up scratching his head and saying nothing.

"Hey, guns," a voice from behind the gun position ended the silence. Shawn looked behind him. Kayto dropped to one knee as he wiped dirt from the back collar of his flak jacket and rubbed it on his trousers. "You guys hear the scuttlebutt?"

"What's up, Kayto?" Luke asked slowly.

"Chip says it looks like Shakey Jake is getting his hardship."

"That's out-Marine-Corps-standing!" Shawn slapped his thigh.

"When?" Luke asked

"Soon as we get to An Hoa, I guess."

"That's great," Shawn murmured, and tried to ignore the scary feeling of envy that began to gnaw at him.

"You guys hear any word on your buddy yet?"

"No," Luke said with a glance at Shawn.

Kayto pointed left. "Check out this face."

Shakey Jake diddy-bopped toward the gun position with an ear-to-ear grin. He had a happy bounce to his step, rarely seen among the tired grunts.

"Sucker walks like Fred Astaire."

"You guys hear?" Jake blurted out. His head bobbed with nervous excitement.

"You lucky sucker!" Shawn stood and slapped Jake's extended palm. "There it is, bro!"

"You wouldn't need anyone to help carry luggage home by any chance?" Luke's envious smile seemed to mirror everyone's feelings. Happiness for Jake, mixed with fear that it might never happen for them. It was a feeling everyone understood.

Jake blinked and shook like a frail old man. "Shawn . . ." He laid a hand on Shawn's shoulder. "Because of you I started praying for the first time since I can remember."

"Sure, Jake," Shawn said as if he expected a wisecrack to follow.

"No, man. I . . . I . . . I mean it. Somethin' feels different, in here," Jake touched his closed fist to the chest of his flak jacket. "It all started to make some sense. Well, not all of it, but, you know what I mean?"

Shawn looked into Jake's twitching eyes. They were calmer than usual. Jake wasn't joking. "Yeah, Jake, I know what you mean." Shawn ached. He thought of Joe and knew that something was wrong inside. He could feel Luke's stare but he refused to look at him.

"Boy, I bet old Sleepy's sure gonna miss you, Jake," Kayto said.

"Yeah, you guys take care of him. I'm 'fraid he'll fall asleep in the middle of a firefight someday." Jake laughed, but his eyes looked serious. "Really. Take care of him, okay?"

"No sweat, GI," Kayto said with a grin. "Jake, you said you were the only surviving son to carry the family name?"

"Yeah. That can get ya home, but my mom has terminal cancer too."

"I'm the only son to carry our family name."

"That right, Kayto?" Luke asked.

"Yeah."

"Even in Japan?" Shawn asked.

"Yeah."

"What are you doing here, man. You could sky out to the world," Jake said.

Kayto grinned a grin that said his decision had been made a long time ago. He was like most Marines, Shawn thought. He would gripe about this stinking green machine known as the U.S. Marine Corps until he ran out of breath. He'd call it every name under the sun and mean every word of it. And then he'd deck the first non-Marine who dared insult the corps.

"Saddle up!" the Chief shouted around the muddy perimeter. The smiles evaporated. Jake shook his head.

"Bros, I sure ain't gonna miss hearing those two words."

"You said that about 'guns up,'" Luke kidded.

"Yeah. Maybe I'll just learn a new language when I get my bird out of the Nam," Jake stuttered.

Kayto slapped Jake on the shoulder. "Semper fidelis, Jake." He headed for his gear with a big grin across his Oriental face.

Jake threw up his hands. "Well," he said, "that rules out Latin."

The column sloshed across the paddies, past the island of solid ground, and into a big field of elephant grass. Beyond that the terrain became rocky and flat. Soon the platoon fanned out into a sweep across the flatlands of the "Arizona Territory" two miles west of An Hoa. The brush grew in scattered patches, usually surrounding clumps of wide-leafed banana trees. From the corner of his left eye, Shawn caught a sudden waving of the Chief's arm from atop a small rise in the landscape. A patch of tangled brush surrounded four banana trees with yellowed leaves. Ghosthorse waved the sweeping Marines to his left and right to a halt. The men dropped to one knee. The big Indian ran back off of the small knoll and huddled quickly with Lieutenant Townsend. They both waved to Shawn.

"Guns up."

"Guns up."

"Guns up."

The whispered call came from each Marine's lips as they turned toward the gun team. Shawn and Luke stood up and moved to the lieutenant in a hunched-over run. They dropped to one knee beside the Chief and the lieutenant.

"See the color of those banana leaves?" Lieutenant Townsend pointed at the clump of trees on the other side of the knoll.

"Yeah," Shawn said.

"Chief noticed that they're the only ones around that seem to be dying."

285

Shawn looked at the brown-and-yellow leaves drooping from the tops of the trees, then made a quick eye sweep of the area. It was true. All the other banana trees were green-leafed. Tunnel. Suddenly a burst of fire shot from behind the knoll. The platoon returned fire with withering force. The enemy fire ceased.

"Corpsman up!"

"Jake's hit!"

"We hit that gook, Lieutenant!" Sleepy shouted from the far left. He pointed at the clump of yellow-leafed banana trees.

"Cease fire! We're goin' over the top to check it out! Murph!" Lieutenant Townsend shouted, and waved Murph forward on the far left. "Flank 'em with your squad!"

The big black Marine signaled a thumbs-up. His squad of six men moved forward on the far left, forming the line of Marines into an L shape with the enemy position in the center.

"How 'bout if we put the gun on top of the knoll, sir?" Chief asked.

"Right," the lieutenant said. "Get up there and cover us."

Shawn and Luke ran up the knoll, staying as low as they could. A moment later the Chief and the lieutenant moved cautiously around the right. The lieutenant stopped and pointed at a blood trail leading into a small triangular crevice between two large boulders.

"We need a tunnel rat with a forty-five!" Lieutenant Townsend shouted.

"Right here!" Shawn shouted.

"I'll do it, sir." Sergeant Ghosthorse handed the lieutenant his rifle.

"No, Chief." He pointed at the crevice with his rifle. "You're too big to get in there."

"Here, Luke." Shawn took Luke's M16. "You got the gun."

"Shawn—" Luke stopped as if he weren't sure what to say.

"Right, buddy." Shawn gave Luke a pat on the helmet and ran down to the lieutenant.

"Drop your pack and gear."

"We throwing in a frag first?" Shawn nodded toward the dark opening between the huge boulders as he dropped his pack.

"No." He pointed twenty meters beyond the opening. "See that fresh dirt over there?"

Shawn could see the dark red earth spread over the whiter, sunbaked surface ground. He gave a nod.

"We think we stumbled onto a tunnel complex, Mac," the Chief said.

"We throw a frag and we close up our way in. You sure you want this job?"

Shawn didn't answer. He checked his .45 clip to make sure it was full, then chambered a round. He looked at the dark entrance. Terror suddenly seized him and he wasn't sure he could do it. He dropped to his hands and knees, took off his helmet, and set it down. He had to flatten onto his stomach and roll onto one side in order to squeeze his shoulders through. He put the pistol through first.

"Shawn. Let your eyes adjust to the light before you go any farther," Sergeant Ghosthorse whispered as Shawn's head entered the black tunnel.

Shawn felt the Chief's calming pat on his calf as he wiggled his body forward. The blackness turned to brown, then to gray as his eyes adjusted. He could feel the pistol shaking with fear. The faint outline of the tunnel grew clear. He paused as he pulled his boots into the narrow cavern. A soft moan came from the darkness ahead. Shawn froze. He aimed at the sound as he lay motionless on his stomach. His sight increased. He could make out a bend in the tunnel five to ten feet ahead. The size of the tunnel increased quickly. He could get to his hands and knees before he reached the bend. The air was stale and damp.

He heard the soft moan again. Closer. A surge of claustrophobia swept over him. The .45 nearly trembled out of his sweating hand. He froze stiff. Warm urine ran down his thighs. He tightened his stomach. He couldn't go on. God! Pray, Shawn, pray. His head began to tremble. He tried to force his mind to work. Psalms. Psalms. "The Lord is my light and my salvation; whom shall I fear? The Lord is the defense of my life; whom shall I dread?"

The gurgling moan of a man in pain sounded close. Shawn tried to swallow, but his saliva was gone. He stopped trembling and inched forward. The tunnel widened as he reached the bend. He crawled forward on his left hand and aimed ahead with the right. He stopped as his fingers touched a puddle of something wet and sticky. He knew it was blood. A whiff of rotting fish stung his nostrils as he leaned slowly around the bend in the dark tunnel. His eyes burned from salty sweat and from the strain to see.

Around the bend was a small room. It looked big enough so

287

that he could stand to a hunch. But as Shawn leaned around the dirt corner, something moved. Shawn flinched. A man's feet. He wore black Ho Chi Minh sandals made of American tire treads. Shawn inched forward. Then he froze, aiming his pistol at a dark figure sitting against the wall of the tunnel. The enemy soldier moaned and clutched at his stomach with both hands. His AK-47 assault rifle lay five feet away on the floor of the small dirt room.

Shawn leaned closer. He could see something dark oozing between the clasped fingers of the moaning VC. Shawn stood to his knees and grabbed one ankle of the wounded man with his left hand while he aimed the .45 at the VC's chest with his right. He pulled him forward. The man didn't resist; he was nearly dead.

Shawn glanced left, more from nerves than reason. Another VC sat in a dark corner eight feet away with his rifle across his lap. The VC straightened up as he spotted Shawn at the same instant. He jerked his AK-47 off his lap as Shawn pointed and fired until the pistol stopped recoiling. Shawn turned back to the wounded man. The VC didn't move. Shawn's ears pounded from the noise of his own shots as he began to back out. He grabbed the ankles of the wounded man again and pulled him back toward the entrance. The ringing in his ears seemed to be getting worse. Someone grabbed Shawn's ankles and began to pull.

"Mac! You okay?" Lieutenant Townsend's voice had never sounded better.

The black-pajama-clad Viet Cong died a few minutes after Shawn dragged him out. Shawn took a sip out of his canteen and crawled back into the tunnel. He dragged out the two AK-47 rifles and a wood box with an old Singer sewing machine and two stacks of communist propaganda leaflets that no one could read.

"Is that it?" Lieutenant Townsend asked.

"Yes, sir, except for the stiff inside."

"Just leave him there. Good a place as any to get buried."

"Hey, check out Mrs. Charles over here!" Neader stood over the dead VC laughing. He knelt down and yanked a fake ponytail off the back of the dead man's head. Neader laughed, "Bet he's wearin' falsies."

It wasn't uncommon for the enemy to dress like women. They knew Americans. They knew an American Marine or soldier would hesitate if there was a chance of killing women or children, and hesitation was the difference between living or dying.

Shawn turned back to the lieutenant. "How's Jake?"

The lieutenant smiled. "He's fine. Shaking like mad, and he's goin' back to the world without an earlobe, but he's hyped up."

"Why?"

"He thinks it's great that he got a Heart on his last day in-country."

The platoon set up a perimeter around the tunnel for a quick meal. Luke, Shawn, Kayto, and Cager slopped their C-rats together in Cager's steel pot for some "Nam stew." Cager tossed in some Cajun hot sauce just to kill the taste. The chow still tasted like dog food, but the empty feeling got filled. Corporal Murph and Cornhusker ambled over to the body of the dead VC. They knelt down to look inside the entrance of the tunnel then walked over to Shawn.

"Shawnie Mac. That took some brass balls, bro." Murph gave a sleepy nod of approval and a thumbs-up.

"Ditto, McClellan." The stocky Cornhusker signaled a thumbs-up and the two walked back to their position.

Cager poured some water into his helmet from a canteen. "Lookin' hard corps. You will never find me crawlin' in some dark hole, man." He shook his head and gave the inside of his steel pot one last wash.

"Yeah, man." Kayto squinted. "Ain't no way in this green mother you get me down that hole. How'd you do it?"

"One too many 'guns up.' " Cager made small circles with his finger around his ear. "He's gone 'dinkie-dow.' "

Goody and Birdman walked up and squatted down near Shawn. "Took some Texas-size guts, Gunner," Goody said.

"Thanks, Goody."

"That was almost as bad as that hole I went in, 'member Goody, up at Hai Van Pass." Birdman whistled and brushed a fly off his bony face.

"You ain't ever reconned no hole that weren't big 'nough fer a dad-blamed battalion of Marines to sweep in, on line!" Goody shot a squirt of tobacco juice out of one corner of his mouth.

"Hey, Birdman," Luke prodded. "Did you ever acquire that elusive address?"

"I ain't hearin' it!" Goody threw up his hands. "Ain't no dang Marine ever writin' my Bonnie Kay."

"Now that ain't no way for a Marine to be, Goody!" Birdman stomped his boot.

"You stop houndin' me, boy." Goody covered his ears.

"Now, Goody . . ."

"Tell it to the chaplain, Girene!" Goody walked away with his hands over his ears and Birdman dogging his steps.

Shawn felt someone standing beside him. He looked up.

The stone-faced Indian put out his hand. "Give me your helmet."

"How come, Chief?" Shawn handed him the helmet. The Indian pulled a blue-and-white Bic pen out of his breast pocket and drew an X under the PFC chevron that Shawn had drawn under the big black letters spelling "Guns Up!"

He tossed the helmet back. "Here, Lance Corporal."

"Oh, no!" Luke shouted. "You can't promote him and not me!" Shawn looked at the X under the PFC chevron that represented the crossed rifles.

"Lance Corporal. I like the sound of it."

"So you get fourteen cents per hour, now, instead of eleven, Shawn," Luke said ironically.

A few minutes later somebody shouted "Saddle up!" The platoon began a roundabout hump that would eventually end back in An Hoa. Second Platoon was a bunch of weary Marines, bent forward with exhaustion, fatigued minds working hard just to get one foot in front of the other. The hump always felt a little easier just knowing that a hot meal was at the end of the trail. Shawn watched Jake, up ahead in the column, and tried to imagine how he must feel, knowing this was it. The last hump. He wanted to be happy for Jake but it wasn't there. Memories of Joe constantly saddened every other thought. Luke was right. He needed to pray. Shawn looked at the ground as he forced his legs to keep moving. "Dear Jesus, forgive me, Lord. I just don't understand. Please take care of Joe, Lord, let him not be too hurt. Don't let him die, Lord. Let him be happy again, with his little boy."

Kayto looked back over his shoulder as the tired column of Marines moved through the small village and entered the maze of concertina wire around the base. The stink of the "piss tubes" brought a frown to his Oriental face.

"Think we'll have mail?"

"Man, I hope so. I just want to lay down for one entire night." Shawn glanced at two twin-bladed troop choppers settling onto the landing pad in a cloud of dust at the far end of the base. He shifted the M60 to his left shoulder and tried to work a kink out of his neck. He also shifted the heavy cartridge belt higher on his hip, but nothing could make all of that weight feel good. Sometimes the belt felt heavier than his pack.

The column stopped just inside the wire. Shawn could see the lieutenant on the field phone up ahead. He had out a map.

"I don't like what I see, Shawn," Luke mumbled from behind.

Lieutenant Townsend handed the phone to Chipper and quickly folded the map into a canvas pouch on his cartridge belt. He motioned at the big Indian, then turned to look down the column of menacing faces.

"Jake! Make your bird over to HQ!" He pointed toward the tin-roofed hootches of the regimental headquarters. "Good luck, Marine!"

"Double time! Let's move it out, Marines!" Chief's commanding shout brought a chorus of curses. A moment later the dusty platoon was jogging toward the landing pad. Jake stood and watched as the men jogged by. He signaled a thumbs-up. He looked almost sad, like a little nervous boy who had just been kicked off of the team.

"Hey, Jake!" someone shouted. "Flatten the first hippie for me, man!"

"Jake! Send me a bottle of Jack Daniel's, bro!" another Marine yelled.

Jake signaled a thumbs-up.

"Semper fi, bros!"

Two new boot replacements were standing like scared orphans beside the landing pad when the platoon jogged up. They had that fat-faced look of health that every Marine coming out of boot camp had. The bigger of the two new men had "Mad Mike" freshly printed across the front of his brand-new camouflaged helmet cover. He carried an M16. The smaller one had blue eyes and freckles and Shawn would have bet money on red hair under his helmet. He carried an M60 by the carrying handle, something that no salt would ever do.

Lieutenant Townsend yelled something to the two new men, but the rotors of the helicopters drowned out his voice. He ran up to them, and they snapped to attention. Motioning them to follow, he turned and jogged back down the column of Marines.

He stopped in front of Shawn with the harrassed expression of a man under too much pressure.

"You and Luke have to split up. Luke, you take this gun." He grabbed the M60 from the freckle-faced boot and handed it to Luke. "Give the boot your sixteen. He's your A-gunner." The lieutenant pointed a thumb at Mad Mike. "Mike's your A-gunner, Shawn." He turned and pointed at the rear ramp of a twin-bladed CH-46. "Sergeant Ghosthorse! Move 'em out!"

"Luke," Shawn said.

"Yes."

"You were right. I mean, I tried praying for Joe."

Luke flashed his bushy brows in his Groucho routine. He didn't say anything and Shawn was glad.

Twenty minutes later the two choppers swooped down to some narrow flats thickly overgrown with elephant grass and thorn-covered brush. To the south ran the wide Vu Gia River and to the north the Thu Bon River. The Green Beret camp at Thuong Duc was on a mountain five-miles to the west. The platoon linked up with the Third Platoon led by Lieutenant Sayers. Chip the radioman mumbled something about "Operation Mameluke Thrust," but like most of the operations, what they decided to call it mattered very little to the grunts doing it.

Night was about an hour away when the column cut through the bush to a well-used enemy base camp. They counted over seventy fighting holes spread in a large triangle. Quickly and silently, the two platoons circled into a perimeter. A few minutes later the word came to move out.

Kayto looked back over his shoulder. "Psst, Mac."

"Yo," Shawn whispered.

"Point man found over seventy gook foxholes in a big triangle."

"Seventy!" Shawn looked back at his new boot A-gunner. What a time to lose Luke, he thought.

The column headed west along the edge of the Vu Gia River for another mile, then broke south along a wide jungle trail that had recently been cut. Helmets began to turn. Marines pointed silently at a sandy patch of ground as they passed. Kayto glanced over his shoulder, his lips giving a silent whistle and his head shaking no as he pointed down at two deep tire treads about three feet apart. Shawn pulled the M60 off his shoulder and waved Mad Mike forward as the column continued along the trail.

"Tear off a belt and link it up as we walk," Shawn whispered. Mike's eyes and mouth popped open. "Now!" Shawn growled quietly.

The boot Marine fumbled with one of the four belts of ammo crisscrossing his flak jacket while his eyes searched the bush on both sides of the trail. He pulled it off and linked it to the strip belt of fifty rounds already in the gun. Shawn threw the long belt of ammo over his shoulder and carried the machine gun on his hip. He missed Luke.

The column followed the trail into a small hamlet of three hootches. Darkness was twenty minutes away at best. Two of the hootches had had recent fires. Smooth river rocks surrounded coals that were still warm. The point man for the Third Platoon found an SKS sniper rifle in the third hootch. Contact was close; the signs were clear and Shawn knew it. He faced his new A-gunner as the column moved out again.

"If you hear 'Guns up,' you be on my tail, got it?"

Mike nodded yes but he looked worried. The column cut left off of the trail, hacked through thick brush with the point men using machetes for fifty meters, then down into a narrow gully of moss-covered rocks, up the other side, and finally up a slight incline to a rocky knoll. The knoll was barren of any large trees, but the surrounding terrain was wooded.

"Hurry up and dig in!" Lieutenant Townsend ordered as the end of the column filed up the incline to the top of the rounded knoll. "Second Platoon, this half of the perimeter."

He pointed out a half circle facing in the direction they had just come. "Murph."

"Yes, sir."

"Round up the canteens, one from each man in both platoons, and take your squad down to the river on a water run. Move it! We're runnin' out of light. McClellan, you ride shotgun."

Murph nodded yes but his big sleepy eyes said he didn't like it. He led his squad around the perimeter, collecting canteens. Shawn dropped his gear on the southeast corner. His field of fire down the forty-five-degree incline was adequate but not great. A few fallen trees and some large rocks littered the twenty-five meters to his front all the way to the narrow gully.

"How 'bout here, Chief?" Shawn pointed at his position. The stone-faced Indian gave a quick nod then turned back to digging his fighting hole in the CP area in the center of the perimeter.

Shawn turned to Mike. "This is home. Hurry up and scratch out a hole; we got water detail." Shawn unstrapped his E-tool from the back of his pack and started digging. A steady drizzle made the digging a little easier.

"How long you been here, McClellan?" Mike wiped sweat from his eyes and stuck his little shovel into the rock-hard earth.

Shawn glanced up. "Since February. About a million years ago."

"The lieutenant called you a salt."

"Yeah," Shawn mused. He tried to keep the boot from seeing how pleased he was to hear that. "Guess I am," he mumbled as he lifted a large rock out of the hole.

"Why'd you join the corps?"

"I was a dumb kid."

"No, really, why?" Mike prodded.

"You writin' a book?" Shawn snapped.

"I might," Mike said matter-of-factly.

Shawn looked up at the big sweaty blonde and debated the pros and cons of answering. He didn't like being unfriendly. His attitude was in the crapper and he knew it.

"I always wanted to be a Marine. I like being the best."

"What do you think about being here?"

"It stinks like nothing you ever dreamed, but I've seen communism for what it really is. It sucks just like a lot of good people have been saying for a long time. You think that's corny?" Shawn looked at the boot with an intensity that said he was ready to fight.

"Corny! Hey, I'm from Iowa, man. Put her there, Marine." Mike smiled and extended his hand. Shawn was surprised. For some reason he had expected some wisecrack. He shook Mike's hand and started digging again.

Mike cleared his throat, blew out, and winced. "Hope you don't take this personal, McClellan, but the smell of you guys could knock a fly off a crap wagon at twenty meters."

Shawn chuckled. "Yeah, you got a lot to look forward to, boot, and smellin' like a Tijuana commode is the easy part."

Mike's dog tags clinked together as he stuck his E-tool into the ground.

"First thing you do is put those tags in the laces of your boots. And blacken 'em. Chip the radioman has a black marker."

"Okay. How come?"

"You trip a 155 artillery round that the gooks have booby-trapped and there ain't enough of you left to send home. The boots usually stay together, so they can identify you."

"Wonderful," Mike mumbled.

"How many rounds you got in that magazine?" Shawn nodded toward Mike's M16 leaning against his pack.

"Twenty."

"No way, boot. Take two rounds out, now."

"Why? It holds twenty."

"Twenty rounds weakens the spring in the magazine. Only a matter of time before she jams."

Mike dropped his shovel, picked up his rifle, removed the magazine and slid out two rounds. "Keep talkin'." He grinned.

"First chance you get, borrow some tape off Doc. Tape two magazines together end to end. That way you can reload fast and you won't get killed looking for that second magazine."

"Guns up," Murph said. Shawn looked up. Murph stood over him with a dozen canteens strung together by a canvas NVA belt and thrown over one shoulder.

Tony the Cornhusker wiped a handful of sweat from his tree-trunk neck and motioned at Mike. "Where's the boot from?"

"Iowa," Mike said. Birdman whistled. "I had a woman from Iowa once." He stared at the sky with a foolish grin that pushed his high cheekbones even higher.

Shawn picked up the M60 and pointed a thumb at Mike. "This is Mike House. This is Corporal Murph, Cornhusker, Birdman and Sleepy and Goody."

"Let's make our 'bird,' man, I ain't fetchin' no water after dark." Murph headed down the hill as a sudden cloudburst drenched the perimeter. He led the water detail through the narrow gully and back down the path that the column had just hacked out. They reached the wide jungle trail that led through the hamlet and down to the river just as the rain lightened up.

Suddenly Murph stopped and knelt down. The trail bent to the left. He pointed at a fresh tire-tread sandal imprint in a muddy patch of ground on the side of the trail. Water still trickled into the sandal imprint.

"God, we're right on top of 'em!" Cornhusker whispered as he leaned over Murph's shoulder.

"Gooks!" Mike shouted.

Shawn jerked around. Mike stood straight up, aiming back down the trail. A Vietnamese woman holding a chicken in her arms stood frozen in panic fifteen meters away. Beyond her, two helmeted North Vietnamese soldiers lifted AKs as they saw Mike.

"Fire!" Murph shouted.

"Get down!" Mike shouted at the woman. An instant later AK fire blew the woman to the ground on her face. Mike slumped to his knees. Goody and Birdman opened fire on the two fleeing NVA. The NVA vanished into the thick brush to the right of the trail. Shawn grabbed Mike's shoulder with his free hand. The boot Marine fell onto his side, dead, with two holes through the heart of his flak jacket.

"Take the gun!" Shawn handed the M60 to Murph and knelt down beside Mike.

"Ya shoulda shot through her!" Cornhusker shouted down at the ashen face of the dead Marine.

"He ain't hearin' ya, bro," Murph said.

Shawn lifted the big dead Marine over his shoulder and neck with Cornhusker's help. They moved as quickly as possible back toward the perimeter. Shawn could feel Mike's blood running down his shoulder and back until his shirt was sticky and wet.

"That ain't the wind, bro!" Birdman pointed at the tall elephant grass twenty-five meters to their right. It was bending and shaking from the movement of enemy troops. The squad started running. They reached the gully. Shawn stumbled to his knees under the weight of his dead A-gunner. Cornhusker lifted the body off Shawn and pushed it up the steep edge of the gully. They scrambled up and out of the rocky ditch as fast as they could pull and pushed each other forward. Shawn hoisted the dead Marine over his shoulder and started running. The run up the twenty-five meters of incline felt endless. Ten meters from the perimeter, Shawn felt the weight of the dead Marine lifted from his shoulders.

"Let go, I got him!" Luke shouted. Luke threw the dead man over one shoulder and gave Shawn a shove up the hill as the first cracks of AK fire shot from the rocky gully. Bullets thudded into the ground nearby. The water detail dove into the safety of the perimeter. Luke carried Mike's body on into the center of the perimeter and laid it down. The firing stopped after the first few shots. Shawn did a low crawl to the gun position, pulled Mike's poncho out of his pack and ran it over to the CP to cover the body. Luke and Doc were kneeling over the big blond Marine as Shawn slid in beside them.

"No chance," Doc said.

Luke looked at Shawn as he helped spread the poncho over the body. "What happened, Shawn?"

"He couldn't shoot first. A mama-san was in the way."

Doc tucked the poncho under the dead man's head. "That didn't stop Charlie, I bet."

"There it is, bro," Shawn said quietly. "The mama-san's facedown in the mud."

"Dumb boot." Doc sounded as sad as he looked.

"Quit the jaw-jackin', Doc." Shawn sneered. "You'da done the same thing. I'da done the same thing." He sent an angry finger at Luke. "He'da done the same thing! We don't murder women and kids!"

"Sure we do, bro," Murph growled from behind Shawn. "Ain't you learned to read, man? That jive's in the white man's paper, brother. Makes it true."

"Yeah. Right, Murph." Shawn stood up and looked down at the new jungle boots sticking out of the poncho. "Dumb boot Marine probably never read the newspapers."

Luke stood up and looked Shawn in the eye. "Shawn. Take care, little quarterback. This might get nasty."

"You too, buddy. Twenty-round burst."

"Semper fi." Luke gave Shawn a thumbs-up.

Shawn held out a thumbs-up, "Semper fi."

The sun dropped away as Shawn reached his shallow fighting hole. A few minutes later Sleepy jumped into Mike's fighting hole two feet to Shawn's right. He spit back toward the command post.

"Shoulda just been a friggin' gunner," Sleepy griped.

"Better lay out some frags, man."

"Straighten the pins?"

"Yeah."

"Man, I hate being by this frigging gun!"

"Sleepy," Shawn whispered. "You see somethin' move?"

"Where?"

"Twenty yards down. The brush between that boulder and the fallen tree."

"I can't hardly see the tree." Sleepy leaned forward out of his hole and shook his head. "Nothin'."

Shawn squinted to see more. "Man, I wish the moon would pop through those clouds." He stared at the dark outline of the bush until his eyes watered from the strain.

"Pssst! Hey, Mac!" A whispered call from the next position ten yards to Sleepy's right sent a chill through Shawn.

"Who's that, Sleepy?" Shawn whispered.

"Kayto, I think." Sleepy looked right and cupped his left hand to shield his voice from their front. "Yeah?" he whispered.

"I hear somethin', man!" Kayto's voice rang with urgency.

"Hey, get down, man!" Sleepy snapped.

Shawn looked right. A shadowy figure stood straight up five yards to Sleepy's right front. "Get down, man! You crazy?" he growled at the shadowy figure.

"What?" Kayto's voice sounded from farther to the right as the shadowy figure walked straight at Sleepy.

A faint sliver of moonlight glistened off the long point of a Russian bayonet on the end of an SKS rifle as the shadowy figure lunged forward. Sleepy's agonizing scream drowned out Shawn's warning as the NVA soldier rammed the bayonet clean through Sleepy's right shoulder, pinning him to the earth wall of his fighting hole. Sleepy grabbed at the rifle with his left hand as the enemy soldier stumbled forward into the fighting hole, landing on top of the screaming Marine. Shawn jumped out of his fighting hole and grabbed the enemy soldier from behind in a choke hold. He yanked the NVA's head back as he grappled for his K-bar. He pulled it out at the same moment that Sleepy stabbed the man with his own K-bar. Shawn stuck the knife into the man's side as he held tight around his throat with his forearm. Shawn's knife hit a rib. He stabbed again. Sleepy sank his knife into the man's chest a second time. The NVA soldier went limp with a sickening gurgling sound. A burst of M16 fire flashed from Kayto's position. Suddenly a red star cluster shot out of the darkness below. Whistles blew. Vietnamese voices shouted. The slower *rat-a-tat-tat* of two old .30-caliber machine guns shot two streams of green tracers, crisscrossing the perimeter from the Second Platoon's front.

"He's dead!" Shawn yelled at Sleepy as he dragged the NVA out of Sleepy's fighting hole. Shawn pushed the body down the hill with his hands and then his feet, until it rolled a few feet away.

"Corpsman up!" Sleepy screamed as he slumped back into his hole.

Shawn searched for the M60 like a blind man, feeling the ground around him. Another cluster shot into the dark sky. This one was white and came from the CP. Another flare burst open from the far side of the perimeter as the Third Platoon opened fire then ceased.

"Gooks!" Kayto shouted. Six quick semi-automatic shots came from Shawn and Sleepy's right.

Grenade explosions erupted around the Second Platoon sector of the perimeter. Kayto and Cager opened up full automatic. Two sharp white blasts to Shawn's right silenced Kayto and Cager's firing. Shawn ducked down, then peeked up again as two more blasts erupted from the same spot.

"Corpsman!" Sleepy shouted again. He pulled at the SKS. The bayonet slid out of his shoulder. He screamed.

Shadows to Shawn's front dove and dodged for cover fifteen meters away. Another flare spread an eerie red light over the black jungle. Shawn searched the ground around him. He grabbed an M26 grenade off the floor of his fighting hole, pulled the pin, and tossed it at the last point where he saw a man duck down. He slapped at his cartridge belt until he felt another frag. He straightened the pin and pulled it. The first grenade exploded. A scream from below told him he hit his target.

He peeked up and over the edge of his hole. Shawn stared in disbelief, frozen for an instant. Four NVA were moving straight toward him, hunched over but still not firing, with bayonets fixed. They weren't even spread out. They were almost shoulder to shoulder and not running but walking up the incline ten meters away. Shawn let the spoon on the grenade fly, counted one-thousand-one, and tossed the grenade at the oncoming skirmishers. He ducked down as the grenade exploded. Screams rose from below Shawn's position. He lifted up again and aimed the M60 at two shadowy figures jumping over the fallen tree straight ahead. A series of explosions rocked the Second Platoon perimeter.

"Corpsman up!" a Marine shouted from Shawn's left. A strange horn sounded from the gully below. Suddenly AK rifles and .30-caliber machine guns opened fire against the perimeter.

"I'm hit! I'm hit! Corpsman!" another Marine shouted.

Shawn squeezed the trigger. The four NVA walking forward were gone. He sent a stream of orange tracers toward an enemy machine gun firing to his left, twenty-five meters downhill. The full weight of a man crashed into Shawn's back, shoving him into the butt end of the M60. His mouth split open against the side of the feed cover. He straightened up and threw an angry elbow into someone's helmet.

"It's me!" Doc shouted. "Who's hit?"

"Sleepy!" Shawn pointed at Sleepy's helmet in the next hole. Doc scrambled toward Sleepy with his canvas aid bag as a hail of bullets pounded into the earth around them. Shawn pulled a grenade off his cartridge belt. He squinted to see the grenade more clearly in the flickering red light of dying flares. He couldn't tell if it was a hand-lum or an M26 grenade; they looked the same.

"Who cares?" he shouted as he pulled the pin and tossed the grenade toward the fallen log. Sizzling white light torched the area below. Shawn couldn't believe his eyes. The NVA that Shawn had stabbed and shoved down the hill was up and staggering forward again. A burst of M16 fire from a position to the right of Cager and Kayto hit the NVA on his left side and blew him to the ground. Shawn snapped his eyes back to the fallen log and the boulder. He saw movement behind the brush between the two. He opened fire and laid on the trigger until the gun went silent.

"Corpsman! We got wounded Marines over here!" Shawn recognized Birdman's angry shout from a position to his left as he ripped a belt of ammo off his shoulder and over his head. He tried to lift the feed cover and lay in the belt of bullets. His fingers felt too stiff to function. Doc crawled out of Sleepy's fighting hole and low-crawled toward Birdman's position.

"How's Sleepy?" Shawn shouted as he snapped the feed cover down and took aim at muzzle flashes spitting from below.

"Dead!" Doc crawled away.

Luke's M60 opened fire from Shawn's right as he stole a glance at Sleepy, slumped over the SKS and his M16. A bullet whined off a rock to Shawn's front. He jerked his eyes straight ahead. An enemy .30-caliber machine gun thirty meters away and to Shawn's right shot a murderous stream of green tracers at Luke's M60. Shawn cringed as the shrill whistle of an artillery round whisked by low overhead. A mushroom cloud of white smoke shot out of the gully to his front. It was a spotter round and it was right on target. AK fire flashed out of the darkness like angry lightning bugs. Shawn winced as bullets hit the hard earth around him. He pulled the trigger and guided his orange tracers at flashing muzzles below. Twenty-round burst. Twenty-round burst. Twenty-round burst. Enemy flashes blinked out like lights being turned off. It felt good. The cocking lever slammed forward; the gun fell silent. His jaw ached from grinding his teeth.

Shawn turned toward the CP and screamed at the top of his lungs. "Ammo! Get me an A-gunner up here!"

He jumped out of his hole and rolled to his right. He pulled Sleepy's slumped-over body to a sitting-up position and broke off a belt of machine-gun ammunition. An artillery round whistled overhead. Chipper's voice shouted from the darkness behind Shawn.

"Fire for effect! Fire for effect! All you got!"

"Outgoing!" Sergeant Ghosthorse's warning echoed through the chaotic firing.

A ripping explosion sent white-and-yellow fire out of the gully below. Another flare popped open above. Then another and another. The faint drone of the old C-47 cargo plane signaled the presence of "Puff." Another flare popped open, then another until the jungle below was lit by twenty tiny suns, swinging down slowly under small parachutes. The glare of sudden light stole Shawn's night vision. He searched below but saw only spots. He blinked and rubbed at his eyes until he saw what did not seem possible. The same NVA soldier that had bayonetted Sleepy, that he had stabbed and shoved out of the perimeter and was cut down by rifle fire, was on his knees again. He threw something.

Shawn ducked down, instinctively pulling Sleepy's dead body down too. The explosion covered him with dirt. He peeked back at the M60. It was gone. Shawn ducked down and came face-to-face with Sleepy. Sleepy's white face was streaked with blood from two holes in his forehead. Shawn grabbed up Sleepy's E-tool, which had been lying on the back edge of the fighting hole. He peeked down the slope. The NVA was flat on his stomach. Shawn jumped out of the hole, darted down the incline toward the prone figure. The enemy soldier didn't move. Shawn's heart pounded with fear and adrenaline until he felt close to fainting. He heard himself screaming. He hacked at the back of the man's head with the shovel end of his E-tool until the man's skull split open like a watermelon. Shawn turned and ran back to the gun position. He dove into the hole, headfirst, his nose smashed against the edge of his helmet. He licked blood off his mustache as it streamed out of a gash across the bridge of his nose. The cringing whistles of artillery rounds ripped overhead. The earth shook as they rattled off like giant firecrackers. Men screamed below.

"Mac! Friendly comin' in!" a voice shouted from the interior of the perimeter.

"Come on!"

Chip lifted his short pudgy form to a hunched-over all-out sprint toward Shawn. Shawn waved him in. Chip dove the last five yards. He hit hard on his stomach and rifle just at the edge of Shawn's fighting hole, then rolled in on top of Shawn with a painful groan.

"Ain't no way to make a livin'," he quipped as he rolled off Shawn. "Why don't you guys build bigger holes?"

"What are you doin' here?" Shawn shouted into Chip's glasses.

"When arty stops, I got Puff ready to work over the tree line and that ditch down there or wherever the heaviest fire's comin' from, so spot 'em with the gun. Luke's doin' the same thing from the other side. Third Platoon didn't get touched, so the gooks are only on our side of the perimeter!" Chip seemed to blurt it all out with one breath. He rose to run back toward the CP. A shrill faraway whistle grew loud as it ripped in at bewildering speed. The chilling whistle went silent overhead.

"Short round!" the screaming warning came from across the perimeter. Chip flattened out. The earth beneath Shawn shuddered. Fire, rocks, dirt, and shrapnel shot into the air from the right side of the perimeter. Chip pulled his face out of the dirt.

"Chip, wait!" Shawn grabbed the back of his flak jacket. "My gun's gone, man! Blown away! I can't point for Puff!"

"God! We got medevacs on the way! Okay, I'll go tell Luke. His A-gunner got hit, lost an eye. I'll tell him to beat-feet over here."

"You better get arty on the phone, Chip, many more short rounds and it ain't gonna matter!"

"There it is, bro!"

Chip scrambled forward and darted across the perimeter toward Luke. Shawn pulled out his .45 and faced downhill. The artillery ceased. The night fell strangely silent as if the war had paused to catch its breath.

Suddenly a staccato of explosions to Shawn's right erupted one after the other. The right side of the perimeter exploded with small-arms fire. Shawn lifted up, half expecting to see the enemy charging forward. Nothing. The terrain to his front and

302

left was clear of NVA or even muzzle flashes. The right side of the pear-shaped perimeter was taking the brunt of the attack. Bullets whizzed across from his right. Another grenade exploded to the right, then came two more quick explosions, followed by the chattering of a .30-caliber machine gun. The *bloop* of an M79 was followed by another *bloop* before the first round exploded. Two M16s zipped through clips with automatic fire. A bad sign. Shawn knew the Marines wouldn't fire automatic unless they had to. He still couldn't hear the speedy power of the M60. A sudden fear for Luke gripped him. He scanned the slope around him.

Two minutes passed before the fierce fighting on the right side of the perimeter slowed to scattered exchanges. The sound of boots running yanked Shawn's head around just as a young black Marine with an M60 hit the ground ten meters back.

"Where's McClellan?" he shouted. "Guns!"

"Over here!" Shawn waved and turned his attention back down the slope.

"Look out!" The black Marine hit the ground behind the fighting hole and slid in beside Shawn. He laid the gun over the edge. "Where are they? We got a medevac comin' in!"

"Give it to me! Who are you?" Shawn pulled the gun into his shoulder and shot a stream of tracers along the edge of the gully below. He ceased fire.

"Walker! Third Platoon!"

The clapping sound of a medevac chopper whisked by overhead, then hovered just above the CP. Two hand-lums popped near the CP. It was like turning on floodlights. Lieutenant Townsend and Doc stood waving the chopper down toward a hasty LZ.

"Where's Luke? The other gunner?" Shawn screamed as he shot another stream of tracers across the jungle below. Suddenly the roaring *BAAAAAAAAAAAAAAAAAUP* of Puff's mini-guns streaked out of the sky like a giant golden rod.

"They pulled me off the other side!" Walker shouted into Shawn's ear. "They said both of Second Platoon's guns were gone! They said the gunners were dead!"

Shawn's fingers went limp on the trigger. He pushed the gun back to Walker and shoved his face into the black Marine's until their helmets banged. "What?"

"Yeah. Short round got one!"

"Where?"

"Over there, I think." Walker pointed across the perimeter, just left of the H34-D bouncing to the ground near the CP. Shawn could see the lieutenant and Doc carrying a poncho-covered body toward the chopper hatch. He jumped out of the hole as Walker opened fire with the M60.

"Where you goin', man!"

"Keep pointing for Puff!" Shawn screamed as he ran toward the CP.

Cracks from Russian AKs opened up on the chopper from the gully and were immediately silenced as Puff made another roaring pass. Shawn ran as fast as he could move, but he felt slower than he had ever felt before, like he was running but not moving forward. Doc and Lieutenant Townsend lifted the body into the chopper. The door gunner dragged it toward the back of the old bird. Sergeant Ghosthorse struggled toward the chopper with another wounded Marine over his shoulder.

"Chief!" Shawn shouted as the big Indian sat the wounded Marine at the door gunner's feet. It was the boot, Spellman, Luke's A-gunner. He held a bloody bandage over his right eye and the right knee of his trousers was soaked with blood.

Lieutenant Townsend helped the corpsman with PFC Blaine. He was naked from the waist down and the entire right cheek of his rear end was completely gone. Townsend noticed Shawn and looked surprised. "Mac! Why ain't you workin' that gun?"

Shawn ignored the lieutenant and grabbed the Indian by the front of his flak jacket. "Chief! Where's Luke? Chief!"

"I don't know, Shawn!" He shoved Shawn's hand away and headed toward the perimeter.

Shawn turned to the boot gunner, Spellman, as the copilot pulled him back into the chopper. Shawn grabbed the wounded Marine by the boot. "Spellman! Were you Luke's A-gunner?" The groggy Marine nodded. "Where is he?" Shawn screamed.

"He got blown out of the perimeter. I never saw him again."

Shawn pointed at the copilot. "Hold this chopper till I get back!"

"No more room, Marine!" The copilot waved Shawn away.

"Be right back! God! Please wait!" Shawn tore off in a panicked sprint toward the right side of the perimeter. The smack of AK rounds hitting the chopper rang clear as he ran away.

"Get down, you idiot!" A hand motioned for Shawn to hit the dirt ten meters ahead.

Muzzle flashes spit from a thin bamboo tree line twenty meters beyond the waving hand. Shawn zigzagged as he ran. Flares popped open, one after another across the black sky, like white Christmas lights strung together. The bush beyond the perimeter was lit up, every rock, every thicket, and every body became visible. Shawn dove headfirst beside the foxhole with the waving hand.

"McClellan!" Tony Horning, the Cornhusker, rose up. "You tryin' to get killed?"

"Where's Luke?"

"Think he bought it, Mac." Tony's eyes winced with Shawn's pain.

"Where was the gun team? Quick!"

"Right over there." Tony pointed to his right along the perimeter. "See that bush 'bout ten yards over there? Murph is on this side of it and the gun team was just beyond that. That's where that short round hit."

Shawn was up with his .45-caliber pistol and running before Cornhusker finished. The frightening bellow of Puff's mini-guns shot out of the sky.

"Murph!" Shawn shouted as he ran toward the bush.

Murph's helmet poked up out of a hole. He opened fire on the bamboo tree line. Shawn belly flopped to the ground near Murph.

"Murph! Where was the gun team?"

Murph fired twice then nodded to his right. "Next door, but they're gone, bro."

"You see Luke?"

Murph faced Shawn. His black skin glistened with sweat and the whites of his big sad eyes showed clear. He shook his head no.

Shawn dropped his face into the damp earth. "Dear Christ, Jesus, please save Luke."

He started to cry, then remembered the Indian's words when Billy the Kid got killed: "Never cry, grunt; it blurs your vision and you miss targets."

"Come on, Mac, let's look-see." Murph rolled over the edge of his fighting hole and crawled past the bush on his elbows and knees. Shawn followed. Ten feet past the bush Murph stopped in front of a crater filled with white sulfurous smoke. The surrounding brush was scorched and smoldering. The damp air was thick with the acrid smell of gunpowder. Murph looked back at Shawn and tossed a floppy NVA pack over his shoulder.

"That's Luke's, Murph! The boot A-gunner said he got blown out of the perimeter!"

Shawn jumped to a crouch and scanned the knee-level brush just beyond the perimeter. A burst of machine-gun fire shot out of the bamboo tree line. The slapping sound of bullets ripping through the tin shell of the old helicopter turned Shawn's head back to the CP. Green tracers seemed to go right through the old chopper. Sparks shot out of the main rotor, then flame. The noisy engine choked, then stopped as the rotor blades whirled silently on momentum alone.

"Get those men out!" a voice shouted as another stream of green tracers shattered the cockpit windows of the crippled helicopter. Marines scrambled out of the hatch of the chopper while others carried dead and wounded away from the old bird. Tony the Cornhusker opened fire at the enemy gun an instant before the entire right side of the perimeter sent a hail of gunfire into the bamboo tree line. The enemy gun went silent. Shawn darted out of the loose circle of Marine positions. He jumped down a five-foot drop just beyond the perimeter and into the knee-high brush that ran twenty meters to the bamboo tree line.

"Luke! Luke!" he shouted as he swung the .45 back and forth with each scan of his eyes. Suddenly a hand-lum exploded with light to Shawn's left. Shawn hit the dirt. The warm wet feel of his own urine ran down his legs.

"See him?" Cornhusker shouted.

Shawn tried to blink out the spots in his eyes from the sudden burst of light. He lifted himself up out of the brush and searched all around him. The dark shadow of a man lying in the brush ten feet to Shawn's right sent a chill through him. Shawn rose up to get a better look. The rounded silhouette of an American helmet lying beside the dark figure brought Shawn to an all-out sprint. He hit the dirt beside the body and looked around, ready to fire at a charging NVA, but none came. The body was face-down. The weeds and grass were wet with blood. Shawn looked closer. He lifted the man's face out of the dirt. His heart sank. It was Luke; his eyes were closed.

"Luke. Luke. It's me! Shawn!"

His eyes opened; they looked distant, unseeing, like a blind man's. "Shawn," Luke whispered.

"Luke! It's me, I got ya."

"My legs are cold, Shawn."

"I got ya, buddy, you're okay." Shawn cradled Luke's head to keep his face off the ground.

"Shawn. I feel cold. My legs are cold."

Shawn moved to his knees and laid Luke's face gently on the ground. The flare light was dim. Luke's eyelids were swollen and heavy looking. Shawn felt for wounds. His back seemed okay. Shawn touched his legs. They were gone. Blood had oozed into warm puddles around the lower half of Luke.

"Am I okay, Shawn?" He sounded weak like a man falling asleep.

A belch of vomit swelled up out of Shawn's stomach and he turned away to puke.

"Shawn." Luke's weak moan snapped Shawn's head around.

"Luke!" Shawn slid his arms under Luke's stomach. "Hold on, buddy, I got ya, it's okay, we're okay now." Shawn gently cradled the heavy upper torso of Luke in both arms with Luke's face pointing at the ground. He stood up slowly.

"He found him!" Murph shouted.

"Medevac comin' in!" someone from the CP yelled.

"Cover fire!" another Marine screamed at the top of his lungs.

The perimeter opened fire. The prop wash of the hovering medevac chopper blew dirt in Shawn's eyes as he neared the perimeter. The helicopter dropped down over the CP, then landed just beyond the crippled helicopter. It was another old H34-D. Shawn could see the tail end of it sticking out beyond the crippled chopper as he lumbered up the hill. He passed the perimeter line, past Murph's blazing M16 and on up to the CP. Doc and Chipper shoved a poncho-covered body into the hatch of the rumbling medevac as Shawn rushed past the chopper. Sergeant Ghosthorse and Lieutenant Townsend lifted a wounded Marine up and into the hatch. The door gunner dragged the man back into the chopper, turned, and signaled a thumbs-up as Shawn ran forward screaming.

"Hold that chopper! Hold it!"

Lieutenant Townsend turned toward Shawn. His eyes opened wide. He turned back to the door gunner, waving and screaming something Shawn couldn't hear over the loud engine. The old chopper's two front tires lifted off the ground, then set back down. Shawn ran under the rotor as Lieutenant Townsend ran forward to help.

"Is he alive?" The lieutenant put his arms under Luke's

bloody stumps. Shawn shifted his arms under Luke's head and shoulders.

"Yes!"

They lifted Luke gently up and laid him on the floor of the crowded helicopter. The door gunner pulled Luke in. Shawn and Lieutenant Townsend backed away, cowering under the whipping overhead rotor as the old bird strained to get off the ground. Suddenly a stream of green tracers shot high over the CP.

"Open fire!" the lieutenant screamed toward the right side of the perimeter.

"Cover fire!" Sergeant Ghosthorse grabbed up his rifle and ran in that direction.

The helicopter's front tires lifted off of the ground. The engine strained to gain altitude, but the tail end wouldn't lift off. The chopper dropped back to the ground with a bounce. A bullet smacked through the tin hull with a loud crack. Shawn grabbed Lieutenant Townsend's shoulder and pushed his face up into the taller lieutenant's face.

"Too much weight to get off the ground!" he screamed. His eyes filled with tears. He turned toward the chopper as it tried in vain to lift off again. Shawn ran up to the helicopter and looked in the hatch. The pilot, door gunner, and copilot of the first medevac chopper huddled together just behind the pilot seat. Shawn looked left. At least five bodies were piled under ponchos in the tail end of the chopper. Luke lay on his back on the deck, a few feet from the hatch. Three wounded Marines sat, bandaged and bloody, leaning against the hull of the helicopter. Shawn looked back at Luke. His eyes opened and closed. Luke's hand made a fist. Shawn turned to the cockpit and screamed through a flood tears.

"Get off the ground!" He pulled himself up and into the chopper hatch.

"What are you doing?" The door gunner stepped away from his M60 and grabbed Shawn by the front of his flak jacket.

Shawn hit him hard in the chest with both palms. The door gunner fell backward over the legs of the crew of the disabled helicopter and landed on his back. Shawn pulled his .45-caliber pistol out of the holster and pointed it at the four men on the deck. The copilot of the medevac chopper pivoted around in his cockpit seat.

"What are you doing, Marine?" he shouted at Shawn, and

looked at the four men on the deck. Shawn raised the pistol and pointed it at the copilot.

"I kill the first man that tries to stop me!" Shawn moved to the rear of the chopper. He stepped over the outstretched legs of the wounded Marines, bent over Luke, slid Luke to one side, and grabbed up a fistful of green plastic body bag. He dragged it to the open door hatch and pushed it out.

"What the . . ." the copilot's shout from the cockpit stopped short as Shawn aimed the .45 at his head.

"Shut up or you're dead!" He grabbed another body bag and dragged it with one hand to the hatch as he aimed the .45 with the other. He shoved the dead Marine out of the hatch. It landed at Lieutenant Townsend's boots as he ran up to the chopper and looked in.

"Mac! Are you crazy! Get off that chopper, Marine! That's an order!"

Shawn grabbed the muddy boots of another dead Marine and dragged the body from under a blood-splattered poncho liner. The light of a bursting flare glistened off the lifeless Oriental face of Kayto. Shawn froze for an instant, gaping at the dead stare on the face of his friend, then bit through his bottom lip and pushed the body out of the hatch. Lieutenant Townsend jumped back. Kayto's body landed on top of the other two body bags and rolled onto Townsend's boots.

"Lift off!" Shawn screamed at the stunned faces of the two helicopter crews, then jumped out of the door hatch. The pilot gave the old bird full throttle. The helicopter lumbered into the air.

"Those stiffs ain't even from this unit!" the door gunner shouted, and opened fire at muzzle flashes beyond the perimeter as the chopper gained altitude over the hill.

"They're with Marines, Jack!" Chipper shouted back. "They don't care!" Chip's round face looked angry. He gave Shawn a thumbs-up.

"There it is, McClellan!"

"Shut up and get a poncho over this Marine!" Lieutenant Townsend pointed down at Kayto, then spun around to face Shawn. "Get back on line, Marine! Who's manning the gun?"

"The gun got blown up," Shawn mumbled, and stared down at Kayto as if he had no interest in anything around him.

Lieutenant Townsend slapped Shawn's helmet with a quick,

angry swing. Shawn's neck twisted from the blow and his vision blurred.

"Get the M60 out of that chopper! Move it, Marine!"

Shawn glared at Lieutenant Townsend and fought an instinctive urge to swing back. He holstered his .45 and walked like a zombie toward the crippled helicopter. He climbed in. The M60 was strapped to the roof of the chopper by old parachute cords so that the door gunner could let it rest in firing position when he was strapped in at the hatch. Shawn cut the cords with his K-bar. He grabbed the gun and two metal boxes of ammo then jumped out and ran for Luke's old gun position.

"Comin' in, Murph!" Shawn called.

Puff was still dropping flares. Visibility was good. The shooting seemed to slack off when Shawn reached the artillery crater to Murph's right. White gunpowder smoke still hovered at the bottom of the crater as Shawn jumped in. His right ankle twisted over something under the smoke. He grabbed at his canvas boot top. The wet feel of cold flesh touched the back of his hand and he jerked away with a violent shiver. He kicked at the object under the knee-deep sulfurous cloud. The heel end of a jungle boot stuck up out of the smoke, then fell back down. Shawn laid the M60 on the edge of the crater and looked at the jungle beyond the perimeter. It was as bright as day from the flares being dropped by Puff. He couldn't see any movement.

"Murph!" Shawn called to his left.

"Yeah," Murph's voice answered from the other side of the bush.

"I'm comin' over."

"Stay put. You'll leave a gap in the line."

Shawn looked down at the smoke around his feet. He kicked at the boot under the smoke until he felt the weight of it on his own foot. It was heavy. He lifted it up with his toe. Blackened dog tags were laced into the tongue of the boot. Shawn knew it was Luke's. He had to get the tags. He reached down, knowing in his heart that he could never do it. He lifted the boot up. It was heavy. A foot was still inside, then the remainder of Luke's leg emerged from the smoke. Shawn dropped it and puked until his ribs hurt.

"Shawn. You sick?"

"Murph. I'm comin' over."

* * *

The rest of the night was quiet. There weren't the usual groans of the dying or wounded. It was as though the war had gone to sleep and left the Marines to keep watch.

"All right! Marines! Let's get a body count!"

Shawn stared at the greens, yellows, and browns of the line of bamboo trees at the foot of the small hill and knew that he had been staring at it for hours.

"Murph!" Lieutenant Townsend shouted from beside the crippled helicopter.

"Yo!"

"Get your squad down there for a count! McClellan! You got cover!"

Shawn heard the lieutenant but kept his stare on the tree line.

"You okay?" Murph nudged Shawn with his canteen, then chugged half of it down.

"Yeah. I'm great," Shawn mumbled, his weary eyes still fixed on the trees. Shawn rubbed a grimy palm across his stiffened neck. His skin was sticky, not with sweat but with the slimy stuff that oozes through a man's pores when he's killing and crying and suffering. Shawn pulled his stare away from the tree line and settled on the dead body of a khaki-clad NVA soldier lying spread-eagled on his back, fifteen yards downhill from the artillery crater. He wore a pistol and some sort of yellow embroidery on his collar. An officer.

"Horning!" Murph shouted.

"Yo."

"Is Neader over there?"

"Yeah, I'm here," Neader yelled from the position ten meters to Tony's left.

"Let's go get a count."

Shawn straightened his spine. It cracked and felt good. He looked at the bush to his right. Tears began to stream down his dirty face. He climbed out of the fighting hole and stood up with the M60 on his hip.

Murph's squad gathered at the edge of the perimeter. Shawn looked at the crater on the other side of the bush. As he walked toward it, everything seemed strange and dreamlike. He stared down into it. The leg lay in the bottom, severed clean four inches above the knee. Even the trouser leg had been cut cleanly, as if by a giant razor.

Shawn set the M60 down and jumped into the crater. His vision was blurred with tears, but he made no sound. He paused

311

and tried to swallow but there was no saliva. He fell to his knees and unlaced the boot, fumbling with the two blackened dog tags as his hands started shaking. He pulled the tags out of the boot lace and wiped his blurry eyes with his dirty sleeve, stiff with dried salt from the sweat of sixty-five days in the bush. He held the tags close to his face until the letters came into focus. PFC Lukevec, Eric. Shawn's chin dropped to his chest so hard that his helmet fell to the ground against the bloody stump end of the leg. He sobbed quietly and squeezed the dog tags with both hands until they cut deep into his palms. Someone above him cleared his throat and Shawn looked up out of the crater. The dirty, sullen faces of Murph's eight-man squad stood around the edge of the crater staring down at Shawn. Cornhusker sniffed, wiped angrily at tears in his eyes, and turned away.

"You all right, bro?" Murph asked softly.

Shawn nodded, swallowed back a huge lump in his throat, grabbed his helmet, and stood up. Neader leaned forward and held out a hand. Shawn glanced at the hand, then into Neader's dark eyes. He grabbed the outstretched hand and Neader pulled him up out of the crater.

"Thanks," Shawn mumbled as he picked up the M60.

"KIA?" Neader asked.

"Don't know." Shawn wiped more tears from his eyes and stared at the ace of spades sticking in the band of Neader's helmet. Shawn nodded at it. "Can I have your card?"

Neader's eyes opened wide with surprise. He looked into Shawn's eyes for a moment, then shrugged and tilted his head so that the card was in Shawn's face. Shawn pulled it out of the band, turned, and walked down to the dead NVA officer. He stared down at the dead, yellow face, the mouth open as if in some silent anguished scream of death. The body was riddled with holes from knees to neck, holes too large for M16 rounds. They were from the M60. The officer's lower stomach was gone.

Luke got him, Shawn thought, kneeling beside the body. He laid the ace of spades in the open mouth, stood up, and kicked the jaw closed. Bones broke with a loud crack. Half of the card stuck out from the dead man's brown teeth. Shawn turned to face the sober stares of the platoon. No one spoke. They went on with the body count.

An hour later a medevac picked up the KIAs and one grunt from the Third Platoon that had blown half his hand off with his own grenade when it exploded too soon. One of the huge helicopters known as Jolly Green Giants lifted the crippled H34-D out later.

The two platoons saddled up after the Jolly Green made it away safely. The hump was long but Shawn felt no fatigue. He felt only light-headed. Numb. Two days passed like some wide-awake, walking dream. The two platoons headed back to An Hoa on the third day. No one spoke to Shawn, and he wanted it that way.

The battle had no name, like most battles in Nam. The final word from above said that two platoons from Alpha One-Five had made contact with a suspected enemy battalion of the 308th NVA Regiment. The enemy had attempted to overrun the Marine position and was beaten back, suffering what appeared to be heavy casualties. The Marines were aided by tactical air support from Da Nang and the 11th Marines' artillery. The enemy then retreated northwest across the Thu Bon River where Delta Company First Battalion Fifth Marine Regiment and two companies from the Seventh Marines had set up a blocking action. The enemy again suffered heavy casualties. Alpha Company: four dead, five wounded. Enemy confirmed: twelve dead.

CHAPTER FOURTEEN

"The Two-Thousand-Pound Bomb"

The walk through the wire at An Hoa Combat Base seemed to lift the spirits of the angry Marines. Scuttlebutt murmured up and down the column even before they reached the tents. Goody leaned close to Shawn as the men stood in formation in front of their tent.

"Chipper says we got seven friggin' boots."

"We'd better get some replacements or there won't be a Second Platoon," Shawn replied.

"It's stomp-down good to hear you talk again, gunner." Goody spit tobacco juice into the hot, dusty ground. "Heard tell Martin Luther King got killed."

Shawn turned to look the crusty Marine in the eye. Goody shrugged, "Ain't sure. Chipper's usually on target."

" 'Tennntion!'" Sergeant Ghosthorse shouted with the authority that only he commanded. The tired Marines straightened. It was as close to attention as combat grunts would get.

"At ease," Lieutenant Townsend said. "We got twenty-four hours. Every Marine will shave, shower, or bathe in some manner, dress in new utilities, and wear a soft-cover or helmet at all times. We have replacements. I will place each boot replacement with a salt. You will square these Marines away."

He unfolded a piece of yellow paper.

"I have word—" The Lieutenant's lean, tan face seemed to relax as he looked down at the yellow paper. A pang of fright shot through Shawn's stomach. He sensed some sort of resignation in Lieutenant Townsend's manner. The lieutenant lifted his deep-set eyes and ran them down the column of dirty, unshaved faces until he came to Shawn. "Spellman, PFC, the boot A-gunner, didn't lose his eye." Townsend looked away from Shawn.

"Out-Marine-Corps-standing!" a deep voice bellowed from the other end of the formation.

"All right," another Marine mumbled his approval.

"Keep it quiet, ladies!" the Chief barked.

Lieutenant Townsend's long jaw tightened. He looked straight at Shawn. Shawn felt his heart drop. He mumbled a silent prayer. Dear Jesus, save Luke, God, please save that big dummy. Please, God . . . Life without Luke . . .

"Sorry, Mac. Luke didn't make it." Lieutenant Townsend folded the yellow paper and put it back in his breast pocket. Shawn stared at the ground. He felt hot and numb.

"Sergeant. Dismiss the platoon. Formation at oh-five-hundred."

"Aye, aye, sir." Sergeant Ghosthorse raised a salute and held it until Lieutenant Townsend returned it. The Chief faced the platoon. "Attention!"

The men straightened. Shawn did not.

"One more word. You will not be too drunk to hump out of An Hoa at zero-five-hundred! You will not batter or maim any office pogues! You will write at least one letter to your next of kin! You will leave your frags, hand-lums, or smoke grenades in your tent! Pins bent! You will not carry weapons into the enlisted pogues' bar! Diss-missed!"

Shawn stood still.

"Sorry, Mac," Birdman mumbled as he walked by.

"We'll be taking names, Mac," another voice growled.

Goody slapped Shawn's shoulder. "Payback's a medevac, Shawn." He spit at the ground and walked into the tent.

"Lance Corporal McClellan!" Ghosthorse shouted as the somber platoon moved into the long dust-covered tent. Shawn looked at the Chief. He waved Shawn over. Shawn lifted the M60 to his shoulder and trudged over to the big Indian but did not speak.

"Murph and Cornhusker told me about you carrying Luke to the 'evac under fire. I've asked the lieutenant to put you up for the Bronze Star with Combat V. He said he'd try. You know how the corps is about giving out medals. Seems there's a couple of fly-boys that wanted you nailed with a Section 8. I think he told 'em you were a KIA so they dropped it."

"Okay, Chief," Shawn said in low monotone.

"He died a Marine. There ain't no better way to die," Sergeant Ghosthorse said.

"Yeah. There it is, Chief."

"Chaplain wants to see you."

"I don't want to see anybody," Shawn growled.

315

"I'm right here, Chief, " Chaplain Elliott said from behind the big Indian. He stepped around the sergeant. "Could you excuse us, Chief?" The sympathy in the chaplain's dark eyes made Shawn look at the ground.

"Yes, sir." Ghosthorse walked away.

The chaplain stood straight with his hands clasped and a look on his face that said this was hard for him. "Shawn, is there anything I can do?"

"No. Just don't tell me that the Lord has a plan." Shawn looked at the ground and couldn't believe the words that had come out of his mouth, but he was too angry to apologize.

"He *does* have a plan, Lance Corporal." The chaplain paused. "I know things don't make much sense right now," he continued. "A lot of innocent people get killed in war, good people. I know it sounds hollow, Shawn, but sometimes you've got to just hang on to your faith by an act of will. In the end we've got to trust God to even things out. He's promised that war and misery, injustice and pain are all temporary."

"Not in the Nam, Chaplain. It's never-ending here."

" 'God will wipe every tear from their eyes,' " the chaplain recited quietly. " 'There will be no more death or mourning or crying or pain, for the old order of things has passed away. He who was seated on the throne said, 'I am making everything new.' "

"Look, Chaplain," Shawn said angrily, then stopped. "I just don't wanna hear it right now."

"Let me know when you feel more like talking, Shawn. I'll be praying."

Shawn shrugged and watched the chaplain walk away. A sick feeling that something deep inside was horribly wrong made him feel suddenly weak and overwhelmed with sadness. He had never felt more alone in his life. He thought of Eddie. Thank God he stayed home. Shawn's shoulders sank with a deep sigh.

"Hey. Are you McClellan?"

Shawn turned back to the Second Platoon tent. The clean healthy face of what had to be one of the new replacements pushed through the tent flap.

"I'm your new A-gunner. Boy, I got a pile and a half of questions for you." He smiled a smile that was too happy for the way Shawn felt. The boot came forward with his hand out. He looked awkward. Shawn gave his hand a quick shake and pushed past him.

"Wait! McClellan, I need to talk to you."

"Not now, boot." Shawn pushed through the tent flap and headed toward an empty cot at the far end of the tent.

Tony the Cornhusker sat up in his cot as Shawn passed. "You okay, Mackie?" Shawn didn't answer. "Mac, me and Murph and the guys thought we'd follow you on down to chapel today. We know it's important to you."

Shawn paused but did not answer. He continued toward the back of the tent.

"Yeah," Neader said, "count me in too, McClellan."

Shawn looked at Neader. Neader turned away as if he were embarrassed.

The new boot nudged Shawn from behind as Shawn walked toward an empty cot. "Name's Smith. Larry Smith. I hear you make Baby Face Nelson look like a beginner with a machine gun. They were sayin' that you're about the best 0331 in the Fifth Marines."

The boot Marine stepped on the heel of Shawn's jungle boot. Shawn stumbled forward, then fell on his stomach. The barrel of the M60 rammed into the dirt before he could protect it. Two of the new fresh-face replacements started laughing.

"You better stow those giggles away, boots," Neader snapped.

The hardened stares of the old salts came down on the two new men with all of the friendliness of a drunken mob looking for a reason to fight. The boot replacements exchanged puzzled glances. They weren't part of the Fifth Marines yet; they hadn't earned the title of Marine grunt. They were outsiders, and judging by their expressions, they understood.

Shawn rolled onto his side and looked back at the pale, embarrassed face of PFC Larry Smith.

"Gosh, I'm really sorry, McClellan! I think my boots are too big. Here"—Smith extended a hand—"let me help you up."

Shawn sat up with the M60 and looked at the dirt rammed into the flash suppressor. He shoved the gun barrel into Smith's hand. "Clean it. Oil it. And clean the gas cylinder." Shawn stood up, straining under the weight of his pack.

"The gas cylinder?"

"Right." Shawn dropped his pack by an empty cot.

"Where's the cleaning gear?"

"The oil's in my pack, side pouch. Use your toothbrush to rub it on." Shawn pulled off his flak jacket and dropped it in the dirt.

"My toothbrush?"

"Right, 'less you got somethin' else."

Shawn sat down hard on the cot and looked at the long-faced A-gunner. His clothes didn't fit him. Everything looked a size too big or a size too small. He had that gangly look that young boys get when they outgrow their coordination.

Shawn motioned at a cot beside him. "Move your gear over to this cot and start cleaning the gun. I don't feel like talking now. I'll tell ya what you need to know later."

"Okay by me. Boy, I got some questions. Did you really lose two A-gunners in one night?" His mouth was open in disbelief.

Shawn stared at his open mouth; the vision of the dead NVA officer's open mouth flashed through his mind. He bowed his head and searched for the proper attitude to bring before the Lord in prayer but found only frustration.

"I guess you can tell me later," Smith said. He sat on the cot next to Shawn and started looking for the gun oil in Shawn's pack.

"Mail call!" Chip shouted from the front of the tent. He pulled the top letter off a stack of mail in his hand. "Doc Abernathy!"

"He's with the CP," someone said.

"Cager!" The chattering tent went silent. Chip looked down. His round face turned sad. He shoved the letter to the back of the stack.

"McClellan!"

"Yo."

Chip sailed it toward the back of the tent. It landed at the foot of Shawn's cot. The raised gold letters VIRGINIA POLYTECHNICAL INSTITUTE felt like a warm blanket on a cold night. Shawn scooped up the letter and tore it open. Just seeing Eddie's messy handwriting seemed to soothe the pain.

Dear Shawn,

I feel awful about Joe. I sent his folks a card, via your mom.

Sorry I haven't had time to write much lately. Have met the perfect chick!!!!!!! School is more fun now, some wild parties, buddy. Tell Luke he would have some competition for most insane human around this place.

Take care,
Eddie

Shawn couldn't help smiling. He tried to picture his big friend at some fraternity party. He loved it. He pulled out his writing gear and removed the plastic. The letter to Eddie was hard to write, but just knowing Eddie was still there to lean on made the struggle of writing about Luke bearable. By the time Shawn finished spilling his guts to Eddie, the only person he could or would tell, he fell back exhausted.

"Get out of the rack, Marines! It is zero-five-hundred!"

Shawn opened his eyes and knew immediately that he had been sleeping since he finished writing. The angry grumbles of the grunts awakening filled the tent. Shawn sat up.

"McClellan. I got ya some new utilities, on the end of the cot."

"Thanks, boot," Shawn said.

Smith smiled, then his face turned serious. "Put 'em on, will ya? You stink, man. You gotta explain what I'm supposed to do, McClellan. I'm really nervous, man. Don't get me wrong," he went on, shaking his head, "I joined the corps. I'm gung ho, man. I just don't want to screw up."

"No sweat, GI. Me make numba-one Marine."

By noon the Second Platoon was deep into the Arizona Territory and heading for a spot called Dodge City on the grid maps. The column stopped on the edge of a rice paddy. Across the paddy was a small village of thatched-roof hootches amid scattered banana trees. The platoon split in half and approached the vill from the east and north.

Luke's gun had not been replaced yet, so the platoon was down to one gun again. The gun team came in from the north with the CP and Murph's squad. The Chief led the other two squads in. For some reason crossing the open paddy didn't bother Shawn as it usually did. He felt eager for contact. He wanted some personal payback.

"Guns up!" Lieutenant Townsend waved from the front of the column.

"Come on, boot!" Shawn shouted, and ran forward, through the ankle-deep muck of the rice paddy. Something splashed behind him. He glanced over his shoulder as he ran. Smith was flat on his face in the mud. Shawn stopped beside the pointing lieutenant.

"Recon that vill with fire. Ain't no friendlies there," the lieutenant said.

"There it is." Shawn pulled the gun off his shoulder as his mud-caked A-gunner sloshed up beside him.

"What's up? What's up? Gooks?" Smith gasped as he spit mud out of his mouth.

Shawn leveled the M60 to his hip and opened fire. He raked a stream of tracers through the village, then back again, trying to draw enemy fire. No return fire.

"Cease fire!" Townsend shouted. "Move out!"

Halfway through the village a muffled explosion dropped each man to a firing position. A few seconds later two more grenade-sized blasts came from the east part of the vill.

"What ya got, Chief!" the lieutenant shouted toward the blast.

"Goody reconned a bunker! Got hit in the knee with a Chi Com and ran out. We tossed in two frags! Goin' back in!"

"Lieutenant! There's a big bunker over here!" a black Marine called from atop a large mound of dirt beside a hootch with no walls. He was one of the new boot replacements and his voice quavered with excitement.

"Recon with some frags!" Townsend shouted, then turned to Shawn. "Go make sure he doesn't blow himself up. Everybody stay put! We made contact!"

Shawn started for the bunker. A grenade exploded on the other side of the mound. Two more quick blasts shot a cloud of dust and smoke into the air.

"Cease fire! Boot!" Shawn shouted as a fourth grenade vibrated the ground. "Hold your fire, boot!"

Shawn ran to the top of the ten-foot-high mound with Smith stumbling close behind. The black Marine crouched by a large opening that led inside the mound. He stood up with his rifle and fired five shots into the bunker, then walked in.

"Wait!" Shawn's shout went unheeded. "You stupid boot," Shawn turned back to the lieutenant.

"Lieutenant, you better talk to these jerk-off boots about following orders!"

Lieutenant Townsend pulled the field phone away from his mouth. "What's wrong?" He looked mad.

"I told this jerk to wait for me before he went in this bunker and he ignored me. He threw four frags in!"

"Send him over here!"

Shawn looked down at the larger than normal entrance of the bunker, then back at Lieutenant Townsend. "He hasn't come out!"

"Give him a minute."

A minute passed. Then four minutes passed. The lieutenant walked to the left side of the entrance. Shawn sat down on top of the mound while Smith crouched and bit his fingernails.

"Williams! Get out of there! Now!" Townsend yelled into the dark cave. Williams didn't answer. "Mac." He looked up at Shawn and shook his head. "Go get him."

Shawn frowned. He laid the M60 down, slid his pack off, and pulled out his .45-caliber pistol. He checked the chamber and flipped the safety off, then slid down the mound.

"Eleven cents an hour," he mumbled at the lieutenant.

"Fourteen," the lieutenant grumbled. "You got a raise."

Shawn crouched with his pistol at the ready, then walked into the black bunker. He moved to the damp earth wall on his left and waited for his eyes to adjust. Something metal glimmered on the floor of the bunker. The air was bitter with sulfur fumes from the four grenades. Now he could see. Williams lay motionless beside the large metal object on the floor. Shawn searched every inch of the bunker with his eyes before he moved. It was empty. The fumes burned in his lungs. He scanned the bunker one more time, then moved over to Williams, grabbed him by his boots, and dragged him out into the harsh light.

"Move." Doc shoved Shawn aside and searched for a pulse. "He's alive," Doc mumbled as he opened his aid bag.

"I think he passed out. The jerk threw four frags in there and went right in."

"See anything?" Lieutenant Townsend asked.

"There's something real big in there, Lieutenant. It's half buried and it's metal, maybe eight feet long."

"Is that right?" The lieutenant pulled out his penlight and his pistol. He walked into the bunker. A few moments later he rushed out.

"That's a bomb! I mean bomb! It's huge! Get away from this bunker! Move it, Marines! Chip!"

"Yo." Chip ran forward, tugging at the antenna of the PRC-25 on his back.

"Get Alpha One. See if we can get some engineers in here."

An hour later a squad of engineers jumped out of a Chinook troop helicopter with enough wire, blasting caps, and explosives to build a canal to Hanoi. What they found was a shocker, even to the salts in the platoon. It was a two-thousand-pound American bomb. How it got there was anybody's guess. Even the giant B-52 Bombers only dropped one-thousand-pounders. The Chief said that he had heard scuttlebutt about dropping the monster bombs out of the back of C-47 cargo planes. When the engineers blew it, the platoon was a good two hundred meters away. The ground shook as if an earthquake had struck and a huge brown mushroom-shaped cloud blew into the hot blue sky.

Birdman whistled long and slow, like an old train. He squatted beside Shawn and watched the mushroom cloud. "You been prayin', Mac?"

"What are you running your mouth about, Birdman?"

"Just seems weird that four frags on top of that sucker didn't put us up in that cloud."

"Saddle up!" someone shouted.

"You hear what Neader did?" Birdman whistled again.

"No," Shawn said.

"He took that gook stiff that Goody and the Chief fragged and put him in the big bunker with the bomb."

"He did?" Shawn looked back at the brown cloud. "Tell me that sucker ain't kissin' Buddha right now."

Birdman stopped and turned to face Shawn. He tilted his head, gave a curious grin, then whistled. "The Nam's sure done a number on you, bro."

"What's that supposed to mean?"

"Not much." Birdman stood up. "The Nam changes everybody," he mumbled. "Even Bible thumpers."

"Keep your mouth to yourself."

"Semper fi, bro, semper fi."

"Mail call."

Shawn turned around. Goody pulled out his red bandanna and wiped sweat from his droopy mustache before he thumbed through a handful of mail.

"Where did that come from?" Birdman asked.

"Engineers brought it out."

"Anything from Bonnie Kay?"

"Here, Mac." Goody flipped Shawn a letter. It was from Opal McClellan. Shawn found a soft piece of dirt and sat down. He felt nervous. He knew that it was news about Joe. Somebody had to have heard something by now. He tore it open.

Dear Shawnie,
    How's my baby? I pray for you every day and every

322

night. Joe is due home from Japan this week. His dad told me that they had to remove his other leg. . . .

Shawn read on, but the rest of the letter became a blur. He sat with his head between his knees for a long time. He tried to pray, but it seemed so meaningless now. He pulled his writing gear out of his pack, unwrapped the plastic protection, and wrote a letter to Joe. He mailed it to his mother and told her to give it to him. A stupid letter, he thought as he watched the engineer chopper fly away. He had tried to sound upbeat in it, but he knew that he came off as phony as he felt.

"Saddle up!"

"What's cookin', bro?" Murph asked.

"What?" Shawn said.

"Your body is here but your head is elsewhere."

"Yeah."

"You look like you lost your best friend, Mac. What you got on your mind?"

"Payback."

"Stay cool now, Mac. Short burst. We're going into Dodge City, I hear. That ain't no place for short-timers, man."

CHAPTER FIFTEEN

Dodge City

"Hey, Chipper," Shawn shouted, and struck a match to a small white lump of C-4 plastic explosive.

"Shawn!" PFC Larry Smith pointed at the C-4, his mouth hanging open and his eyes wide. He dropped his can of meatballs and beans and rolled from under the green poncho lean-to into the mud. He crawled away on his hands and knees like a man on fire. Shawn watched the frightened boot with a melancholy expression.

Chip dropped down to his knees and crawled in out of the driving rain. He pointed at Smith and laughed. "The C-4?" he asked.

Shawn nodded.

"What you thinkin' of, Mac? You look all depressed." He peeked into the olive-green can sitting on top of the C-ration can stove. "What's cookin'?"

"Boiling water for some hot chocolate."

"Hey, boot!" Chip called as Smith stopped crawling and looked back over his shoulder. "You can light C-4! It don't blow unless you wire it with an electrical charge."

Smith sat in the mud with a dumb, openmouthed expression. "What?"

Chip laughed again. "The C-4 needs a charge!"

"I didn't see any C-4." Smith shrugged as water cascaded off his helmet. "It's that hot sauce!" He opened his mouth and looked up to let the rain cool his tongue.

Chip turned to Shawn. "Cager's sauce?"

"Yeah."

"How'd you get it?"

"Doc gave it to me. He took it out of Cager's pack when they threw him on the last ride."

"I thought you hated that stuff?"

"Yeah, I did. Things change in Nam."

Chip blew a bubble and popped it. "There it is, bro."

PFC Smith looked silly sitting in the rain with his mouth open.

"I can't even remember being a boot," Shawn said.

"Makes ya feel old, don't it?"

"I feel like I've been here for my whole life, like the world ain't really there anymore." Shawn looked at Chip's round gum-chewing face. "Know what I mean?"

"Yeah. The only thing that keeps me sane is my girl; one letter from Evelyn and I . . ." Chip paused. He looked apologetically at Shawn and shrugged. "Sorry. You ever hear from that broad again?"

"No. She's bangin' some hippie fag that's probably prettier than her."

"Man, you really have changed." Chip grinned. "I didn't think I'd ever hear you crack off somethin' like that."

"Everybody changes in Nam," Shawn said, and checked his tin can of boiling water.

"You hear from any other women?"

"Yeah, some, but she was the one that mattered. I do have a buddy that sort of keeps me sane. Eddie. We've been best buddies since we were four years old. Sometimes I think I'd be a Section Eight case without old Ed."

"You hear the scuttlebutt?"

"What?" Shawn tore open his pack of hot cocoa mix.

"Delta Company knocked out two T34 Russian tanks."

"In Dodge City?"

"There it is. They say they're the first tanks ever knocked out with LAAWs." Chip watched Smith slosh slowly back to the lean-to.

"Tanks!" Smith's mouth was open. He squatted down in the rain, facing Shawn and Chip. "Did you say Russian tanks?"

"Yeah. Dyin' Delta knocked out a couple of T34s in Dodge City."

"Really! Wow! Where's Dodge City? Why do you call 'em Dying Delta?"

"Come on, Smith, don't start with the five-million questions again," Shawn griped.

"This is Dodge City, boot," Chip explained, "You know that wooded area we went through yesterday?"

"Affirmative."

"That is part of Dodge City."

"You're in Dodge City." Shawn pointed at the ground, then poured his cocoa mix into the C-ration can of boiling water.

"Shawn showed me the number markings on the trails," Smith said.

"There it is, boot. When Charlie starts numbering trails and movin' tanks across the Laotian border"—Chip pushed his glasses back up his pug nose—"things are gonna get hot."

Shawn glanced at the long, gaping face of his young A-gunner. "There it is, man. Don't fret, Larry. We're going to kick some butt and take names, bro. Payback's a medevac for Charlie."

"Gungho, sucker," Chip said.

Shawn looked at Chip. Chip stared back quizzically. Shawn turned away.

"What's 'kick butt and take names' mean?" Smith asked.

"Confirmed." Shawn sipped his hot cocoa, then stirred it with the tip of his K-bar.

"It means killing so many gooks out of one unit that the unit ain't no more," Chip added. "We take their name off the roll."

"Chipper, you in there?" a strong voice called from behind the poncho lean-to.

"Yeah, Chief." Chip moved out from under the shelter.

"Saddle up."

Sergeant Ghosthorse moved around to the front of the lean-to as Chip headed for the CP. He squatted down beside Smith, facing Shawn. "Get over to the CP, we're saddlin' up. The gun team's staying here with Murph's squad when the platoon moves out."

"What's up?" Shawn asked.

"Charlie's been comin' into our position after we move out."

"Scrounging for food?"

"Whatever some dumb grunt leaves. Been tailed for the last three days."

"How do you know that, Sergeant?" Smith's droopy brown eyes widened.

Ghosthorse ignored him. "We have to make it look good. Won't be close enough for support."

Shawn looked down at the M60. "Okay by me. I got some payback to issue."

"Mac—" The stone-faced Indian stopped, then turned and spoke to Smith. "You go recon the perimeter."

"Huh?" Smith leaned closer to the Chief.

"De-de-mow, boot. I wanna talk to Mac."

"Oh!" Smith jumped to his feet, grabbed his rifle, and headed

326

toward the next position. The Chief removed his glasses and looked for a dry spot on his shirt to clean the water off his thick lenses.

"Come on in out of the rain, Chief."

The Chief scooted in under the lean-to, took off his helmet, and pulled a dry, green piece of an old T-shirt out of the helmet liner. He cleaned his glasses and put them back on.

"You miss Luke?" The big red-skinned face never changed expression. He stared at the Vu Gia River forty meters to their front.

"I don't think about it," Shawn lied.

"How 'bout the other buddy? The one with One-Nine?"

"Lost both legs."

"You have good spirit. Don't lose it."

"Charlie has to pay."

"Twenty-round burst, Mac."

Sergeant Ghosthorse slid out of the tiny shelter, stood up, and walked back to the CP without another word. Shawn felt honored. Since his first hour in the bush, he had wanted that Marine's respect more than anyone else's. He stared through the driving rain at the jungle river and tried to remember St. Pete High. He blinked and tried to remember Australia. Luke's big oval face with his two-tone eyes. Joe, so deep, so serious. He thought of Sandy and the baby and the promise.

A voice rang across the rain-swept perimeter.

"Saddle up!"

"What are you thinking about?" Smith asked as he picked up his pack.

"Just thinking of a girl I used to like."

Shawn glared at the muddy ground and Joe's words screamed from his memory. *"Promise me, Shawn. Swear it. . . . Promise me, Shawn. Swear it."* An angry vision of pounding his fist into Sandy's faceless hippie boyfriend sent a surge of hot rage through Shawn. He stood up and kicked the bamboo stick that held up one end of the poncho.

"Looks more like you're thinking of her new boyfriend." Smith chuckled.

Shawn turned an icy stare toward the smiling A-gunner.

Smith's smile washed away with the rain. "Hey, McClellan, I'm sorry, I was just jokin', I—" He paused and shrugged. "Your girl?"

Shawn began wrapping up the wet poncho. "No. My buddy's.

You know anything about this SDS crap that's on the college campuses?''

"Never heard of it. Why?''

Shawn unsnapped half of the makeshift tent and handed it to Smith. "Here. Pack your poncho. Put your writing gear inside it; helps keep it dry.''

"Yeah, but then I'll have to repack it when I need the poncho.''

"You won't need it. Rain on a poncho makes a noise that Charlie knows. You ain't wearin' no poncho in Dodge City, boot.''

"Oh. Thanks. So why does this SDS bring out that kind of anger?''

"A promise I made.'' Shawn pulled on his pack and looked down at the M60 sitting on its bipod legs in the rain.

"Sounds like somebody won't get no slack.''

"Did you put plenty of oil on the gun? It ain't beading up like it should.''

"Yeah, I did.''

"She jams and you me and some other Marines go home in a bag.''

"I put plenty on, Mac. Cleaned Old Betsy like a pretty girl.'' He smiled. "So what was the promise?''

"Nothing. Drop it.''

"How old are you, Mac?'' Smith draped a belt of ammo across his chest.

"I'll be nineteen in October.''

"What? Really? God, I thought you were a lot older than that! I'm nineteen too! I thought, I mean I would have guessed you to be at least twenty-five.''

"Yeah. I feel like forty. What do you think would happen if a guy came home from the Nam and blew somebody away back in the world?''

"Hey, Mac, don't talk like that, man.''

"Mac,'' another voice called.

Shawn turned to his right to see Murph give a wave. "Over here.'' He bent over, grabbed a handful of mud, and smeared it on his face and forehead. "Come on, Smith. Blacken your face with some mud.''

Shawn headed toward Murph. He knew Smith was right. It was stupid to think of going home and blowing that little queer away. I'll just beat him to death, he decided.

The platoon filed off toward the south. Murph's squad and the gun team stayed behind and silently melted into the brush facing north toward the river. Fifteen minutes later a squad of ten pith-helmeted NVA soldiers wearing Ho Chi Minh tire sandals, empty packs, and rifles strolled toward the abandoned Marine position like they were on a Sunday walk along the edge of the river.

Smith lifted the long belt of ammo out of the mud with both hands. "God, Shawn," he whispered, "I'm scared."

"Me too. Be cool. Don't panic."

Shawn took aim through a break in the knee-high brush. The third man in the column smiled and said something to the man in front of him. They were thirty to forty yards away and closing.

Shawn focused the lead man's stomach on the tip of his site. Smith started to shake. Suddenly an M16 opened fire from Shawn's left. Shawn fired. The lead man exploded backward, his lifeless grip on his rifle released. Shawn raked his tracers up the line of NVA.

The enemy disappeared like roaches caught in the light, scrambling, running, rolling, and gone.

"Cease fire!" Murph shouted from the left.

Shawn laid on the trigger through twenty, forty, eighty, and a hundred rounds.

"Cease fire!" Shawn released the trigger. Smith shivered like he was cold.

Murph stood up out of the brush and gazed cautiously ahead. "Let's get a body count!"

The Marines stood up slowly and swept on line, one careful step at a time, toward the dead NVA. Shawn and Smith walked up to the lead man that Shawn had killed. They stood over him. Smith looked pale. His eyes were glued on the dead man's face.

"Wow, man, check this out," Cornhusker said. He stood ten yards from Shawn in knee-level brush. He was looking down. Shawn could hear a strange, uneasy noise, like something gurgling. He left Smith standing over the dead man and walked over to Cornhusker.

"These people are sick, Mac." Tony stared down and shook his head in disgust.

Shawn stopped beside Tony and looked down. An NVA soldier lay dead on his side, the back of his head gone. His face looked older than most, wrinkled and weather-beaten. His dead right hand gripped a huge hook, the kind that men lift blocks of ice with. The hook was rammed under the chin and out of the mouth of a young NVA soldier like a human fish. The young NVA was still breathing. Blood bubbled out of his mouth, making a grotesque gurgling noise with each gasp for air.

"My God, why would they do that to their own men?" Smith exclaimed at Shawn's side.

Shawn turned to face the openmouthed A-gunner. "That's the way they drag the dead away so we can't get a body count."

Tony the Cornhusker spit at the ground. "Yeah, but when they start draggin' away the living, you get to know what Charlie's really about."

Tony walked away. A few minutes later the count was over.

"That's it, Murph!" Tony shouted. "Three confirmed!"

"Search the bodies!" Murph barked. He turned to his left, walked straight for PFC Williams, and didn't stop until his own face was shoved into the boot's.

"Get out of my face, man," Williams growled.

"I told you, boy! Don't open up till the gun opens up!"

"No honky calls me boy, and I ain't havin' that jive off no brother!"

"You follow orders in the bush or you die, boot!"

"Get outa my face, man!"

Murph stuck the business end of his M16 under Williams's chin. "We ain't honkies or niggers here, Marine, and you ain't back on the block, Jack. You will follow orders or somebody's gonna kill you. Now tell me that you will follow orders." Murph lifted the boot's chin with his barrel.

"I will! I will, Corporal."

Murph lowered his rifle. "Now get back to your position."

Tony nudged Shawn from behind. He grinned and winked.

"I agree," Shawn said. He nodded toward the NVA that had stopped gurgling. "Can Doc help?"

"No. He croaked."

From May 18 to October 23 the Seventh Marine Regiment and the Fifth Marine Regiment participated in Operation Mameluke Thrust. Enemy killed: 2,728. Marine losses: 267 killed, 1,730 wounded. On October 6, Alpha Company First Battalion, Fifth Marine Regiment, joined up with the Second Battalion, Fifth Marines for Operation Maui Peak along with the Seventh Marines and the 51st ARVN Regiment in the Relief of Thuong Duc.

CHAPTER SIXTEEN

Relief of Thuong Duc

It seemed like the rain would never stop, but it did and the temperature quickly rose to one hundred fifteen degrees, according to the thermometer in Doc's helmet band. Scuttlebutt was flying up and down the column as Alpha Company waded across a shallow spot on the Thu Bon River. The thunder of heavy air strikes reverberated through the mountains as the long column of Marines climbed out of the river and filed down a dirt road called Highway Four. A mile down the road Birdman held up his hand and whistled back at Shawn.

"Move off the road."

"Move off the road."

"Move off the road."

The call echoed down the column as the tired Marines slumped in utter fatigue to the right side of the road. The all-night hump had sapped every ounce of Shawn's energy, and every part of his body ached. He fell back on his pack and let his head hang back over it to rest his neck.

"If it's true, I wanna know."

Shawn opened one eye to peek up at the source of the voice. "What do you want, Birdman?" He closed his eye again.

"You got it, don't ya?"

"Got what?"

"Goody gave it to you, didn't he?"

"Gave me what?" Shawn opened his eyes and sat up.

"He gave you Bonnie Kay's address, that scumbag!"

Goody shuffled up beside Birdman. "Now—" Goody spit a shot of tobacco juice on Birdman's boot. "—ain't no need to go name callin'." He twirled at one end of his droopy mustache.

"What's this all about, Goody?" Shawn asked with a grin.

"It's about you movin' in on my woman!" Birdman snapped, then scowled at Goody.

"What?" Shawn asked.

"He gave you Bonnie Kay's picture too, didn't he?" Birdman turned his scowl down at Shawn.

Shawn smiled and crossed his heart. "Not me, Birdman."

Birdman's bony face flushed red as he turned back to the salty Texan. "I heard him say it. He told Cager, back at Hai Van Pass, that you'd be the only Marine that he'd even think about lettin' write his sister. I heard ya. Go on, deny it."

Goody rolled a wad of tobacco around his tongue, turned his head, and spit. "Ain't denyin' nothin', cuz I said it."

"There it is!" Birdman gave a sharp whistle. "That tears it, Goody! We ain't friends no more!" Birdman huffed past Goody and on past the next two Marines sitting on the side of the road. He stopped, gave one more angry look back at Goody, and sat down with his rifle across his lap.

Shawn looked up at Goody. "Who pulled his pin?"

Goody rocked his head back and forth like a bashful cowboy. "I can't leave my pack anywheres near him. He keeps tryin' to steal a peek at Bonnie Kay's picture 'n her address so's he can write her."

"Yeah."

"Well I told him I already gave it to somebody else. Wellll, he goes on like a crazy man 'bout how I stabbed my best friend in the back."

"Why did you say you gave it to me?"

"Didn't," Goody said.

"What's he talking about, then?" Shawn pulled out his canteen and offered it to Goody.

"No thanks. Well, I guess he's thinkin' you're the one I gave it to cuz I told old Cager one time how you'd be the one, if I gave it to any dang Marine."

"Thanks, Goody." Shawn nodded at the Texan and took a drink. "How come?" he asked suspiciously.

"I figured you for a God-fearin' man. Texans respect that."

Shawn didn't speak. Goody walked back up the column and sat down. A Phantom F-4 whisked overhead at treetop level. The bombing was louder up ahead. The cracking of small-arms fire could be heard more clearly.

"Hey, Shawn," Smith called. Shawn turned to look back. Smith pointed at three big American tanks rumbling up the road toward the company.

"There must be boo-coo gooks up this road."

"Boo-coo?" Smith asked.

"A bunch, boot. Throw some oil on the gun."

A minute later the column started out again as the giant steel monsters churned past. Two more Phantoms streaked over. Black clouds of smoke rose into the blue sky up ahead. Napalm. A surge of fear and excitement swept over Shawn. This was big. Rarely had he seen tanks. They were mostly useless in the jungle war, but it made them no less impressive.

The column rounded a bend in the narrow road that followed the meandering Thu Bon River. They marched past another company of tired Marines sitting on the side of the road, then stopped behind the three tanks with their big diesel engines rumbling out puffs of black smoke as they idled in the shade of three massive oak trees. Beyond them was a large open area. No cover at all. The wide river was to the left, and three steep hills forming a triangle were on the right of the dirt road.

"Second Platoon! Move up!" an anxious voice screeched from the front of the column.

Second Platoon ran past the rest of Alpha Company. Shawn felt adrenaline pound through his system at jackhammer speed. A Huey gunship dove like an old World War II fighter at a battered and smoking hilltop across the open field beside the dirt road. Two fiery orange rockets spiraled into the hilltop. The Huey pulled up and banked away. Green tracers chased after it from the barren hill. The tracers stopped as the rockets exploded on target. Rocks and smoke blew into the air just as another Huey dove at the hill.

"Form up over here!" Lieutenant Townsend shouted. More rockets exploded into the hill. "Chief! Get 'em into squads!"

"Murph's squad! Right here! Over here! Third squad! Right here!"

"Where you want the gun team, Chief?" Shawn shouted.

"You cross with the first squad that goes! We got another gun team from Third Platoon. They're crossing with second squad!"

"Listen up!" Lieutenant Townsend shouted. "We will cross this field! Two hundred meters away you will reach a small stream! The bridge across that stream has been blown! Wade across! Establish a beachhead at the foot of that hill." He indicated a hill that was taking heavy rocket hits. "That is Hill 65. It lies approximately twenty meters from the other side of the stream! You will receive incoming fire from Hill 65 and the two other hills to its right forming a triangle with it."

"We're movin' across, Lieutenant!" a Spanish-looking Marine shouted down from the turret of the lead tank. He signaled thumbs-up and then said something into a hand-held radio. The three tanks started down the dirt road, one at a time, with thirty yards between them.

"We shouldn't get any fire from across the river! The ARVNs are sweeping that side!" Townsend shouted, but the way he said the word "ARVNs" told Shawn not to count on it.

"Right," Goody snarled. "And there ain't no drunken Marines in the slop-shute."

"Listen up!" Sergeant Ghosthorse shouted, and pointed at Doc Abernathy. "The corpsman will bring up the rear! Do not—repeat!—do not stop for the wounded! Is that clear?"

A few helmets gave tired nods but no one spoke. The men were somber. A sleek Phantom fighter bomber roared overhead, swooped low over Hill 65, then banked sharply up. It circled, swung low over the approaching tanks, and released two long canisters that tumbled toward the hill as if in slow motion. Black smoke shot into the blue sky. A wave of fire engulfed the top of the hill.

"Fix bayonets!" Sergeant Ghosthorse yelled as he attached a bayonet to the end of his rifle.

Smith's mouth dropped open. "God. Is he serious?"

"You kiddin', boot?" Shawn coughed and tried to hide his nervousness. "The Chief was born serious."

Shawn stared down the dusty road as the lead tank's turret rotated its big ninety-millimeter cannon toward the hill.

"Serious?" Cornhusker stepped from behind the stunned A-gunner. "The Chief did a low crawl out of the womb, boot."

"Then he came to parade rest till somebody named him," Murph added. He pulled a rusty bayonet out of its scabbard and showed his big white teeth to the nervous A-gunner.

"This looks big-time," Shawn said.

"You see all of those guys bandaged up?" Murph asked.

Shawn looked back down the road at a group of bloodied Marines being attended to by three corpsmen on the river side of the road. "Yeah."

"Echo Company. They already tried to go up this sucker."

The first two tanks rocked back as their big guns opened fire. Rocks and dirt exploded out of the side of the hill.

"Guns up!" Lieutenant Townsend waved at Shawn.

"Come on, Smith!" Shawn ran over to the lieutenant.

"Did you tell him what to do, McClellan?" Lieutenant Townsend asked. Townsend's eyes looked over the understrength platoon then burned in on the boot A-gunner before Shawn answered.

"Smith! If Mac gets hit, you do not stop! You grab that gun and set up a base of cover fire on the other side of the tributary! Is that clear, Marine?"

"Yes, sir!"

"Ten-meter intervals!" the lieutenant shouted at the platoon.

"Stand by!" Sergeant Ghosthorse bellowed.

"Murph! Move out! Go!" Lieutenant Townsend barked, and shoved Shawn after Murph's squad.

"Guns up!"

"Yeeeehiii!" Shawn screamed, and ran into the open field. The heavy weight of the M60 evaporated as he ran past Murph's jogging squad. He sprinted until he caught up with the last tank in the column of three. A sudden hail of AK fire shot out of the triangle of hills on the right. Green tracers blurred between the two tanks up ahead. The fire was coming from across the river on Shawn's left. Hatred for the useless South Vietnamese Army flashed through his mind. He gained on the second tank.

"Corpsman up!"

"Corpsman!" someone behind Shawn yelled.

Three quick mortar blasts exploded behind Shawn. Shrapnel and rocks whipped across the open field in every direction. Someone screamed in agony. Shawn could see the stream thirty meters ahead as he reached the second tank. Four successive bullets rang off of the steel hull, then two more. Shawn flinched. Suddenly his right leg blew out from under him as if some huge sledgehammer had batted it away. He fell forward beside the churning tread of the tank. He hit the hard dirt road on his helmet and right shoulder, tumbled forward, then flattened out on his back with his left leg lying across the M60. A burning pain screamed out of his right thigh.

"Shawn!" Smith's terrified face leaned over Shawn and looked down out of the hot blue sky.

"Grab the gun!" Shawn yelled through clenched teeth. "I'm hit! Corpsman!"

Smith dropped his M16 beside Shawn, lifted Shawn's leg off the M60 machine gun, grabbed it up, and ran. Shawn lifted his head to see the wound. There was a dark hole in the right thigh of his blood-soaked trouser leg. He dropped his head back to the ground.

"Corpsman!" A vision of going home without his leg pushed him to a sitting-up position. He put both hands on his thigh and squeezed, but the blood gushed out. He looked back. A mortar blast hit close to the Chief, twenty meters back. Ghosthorse flew into the air and landed in a cloud of dust facedown. He didn't move. Murph and two other Marines ran past Shawn, gasping for breath.

"You okay?" Murph's strained words went unanswered. A surge of unbearable pain rushed out of the gaping hole in Shawn's thigh. A mortar round clanged off the turret of the lead tank like a giant church bell.

Lieutenant Townsend ran past with Chip the radioman on his heels. They ran up to the lead tank as it rumbled to a stop and fired its big gun into the top of the hill.

"Pull back!" Lieutenant Townsend shouted at three Marines on the other side of the tributary.

Boots ran to a stop beside Shawn.

"Mac! How bad?" Doc Abernathy knelt down. A burst of automatic fire kicked up dirt on Shawn's left. Doc pushed Shawn's hands away from the wound, ripped at the hole in his trousers, then felt the back of Shawn's thigh. "Got a bullet clean through. Like, calm down! Don't go into shock! You'll be okay, man!"

"How is he?" Murph slid in beside the corpsman.

"Give me a hand, Murph!" Doc grabbed Shawn by the boots.

"No! Help me get him over my shoulders, Doc!" Murph pulled Shawn up onto one leg.

The two lifted Shawn to Murph's shoulders for a fireman's carry. Murph started running back toward the cover of the big oak trees. Shawn closed his eyes. He felt sick and feared that he was about to pass out. The rumble of a big diesel sounded close. The tanks were pulling back.

"Lay him over here, Murph!" somebody yelled, and Shawn opened his eyes. Murph stopped. Shawn could feel the shade of the big oaks on the back of his neck as Murph leaned over to set him down.

"I got him, Murph," a familiar voice said. Cornhusker grabbed Shawn under the arms and laid him beside the trunk of a large tree. "How is it, Shawn? You want to sit up or lay down?"

"Sit up," Shawn moaned.

Cornhusker pulled Shawn to a sitting position and leaned him against the tree trunk. A young corpsman with hairy forearms knelt down beside Shawn. He slit the bloody trousers open with a K-bar, then pulled a roll of gauze and a morphine needle out of his medical kit.

Shawn looked at the corpsman and smiled. The corpsman glanced up at Shawn, shook his head, and stuck the morphine needle into Shawn's thigh, just above the bullet hole.

"I know you jarheads are gung-ho idiots, but you'll never make me believe this feels good." He pulled the bandage tighter with each wrap.

Shawn read the words on the corpsman's helmet again and chuckled weakly. " 'Join the Navy and see the Marine Corps.' That's great."

The corpsman was too busy to answer.

"Over here, Goody!" Cornhusker shouted.

Shawn looked left. Goody lumbered forward with Birdman in his arms. Birdman's eyes were closed and his body looked limp. Huge tears streamed down the Texan's dirty face.

"Corpsman!" Goody screamed, and laid Birdman beside Shawn.

"Get him, Doc! I'm okay!" Shawn pointed at the pale thin face of Birdman. Goody fell to his knees beside his friend and slapped Birdman hard across the face. Birdman groaned and one eye popped open.

Goody grabbed him by the front of his flak jacket and shook him. "Birdman! Say something!"

"I'm hit, Goody." He sounded weak. "I'm sorry."

"Hold on, you useless bull slinger or I'll slap ya into heaven, now!"

"Goody." Birdman lifted a bloody hand to Goody's shoulder and pulled him closer.

"I'm here, Birdman. Right here, bro."

"I love ya, Goody. Bonnie Kay—" Birdman groaned, and didn't finish.

Goody pulled away and wiped tears out of his eyes. He yanked off his helmet, pulled out the helmet liner, and removed his wallet. He tore off the rubber band and plastic that was wrapped around it. He pulled out a photo that Shawn couldn't get a good look at and shoved it into Birdman's breast pocket.

"Here, pardner. The address is on the back." Goody sniffed back another wave of tears. Shawn did too.

Goody gave Birdman a light pat on the shoulder, then leaned over and hugged him around the helmet.

"Move, Marine." The corpsman shoved Goody aside and opened Birdman's flak jacket. "Do you know where you're hit, Marine?"

"All over. Shrapnel." Birdman closed his eyes.

"Lieutenant!" Cornhusker shouted as he jumped out of the path of the last tank pulling back out of the open field. He pointed back at the hill. "We still got three Marines on the hill!"

"What?" Lieutenant Townsend's eyes bulged with fear and rage. He looked back at the hill. "Chief!" He snapped around, searching for the big Indian.

"Chief got hit, Lieutenant." Doc Abernathy looked up from bandaging the bleeding eye of one of the new boots. He pointed at two corpsmen working on a motionless Marine a little farther down the dirt road. Lieutenant Townsend's lips tightened with the strength of a leader, but the pain in his eyes was too strong to hide. He jerked his stare away from the wounded sergeant and searched the faces around him.

"Chip! Radio up!" He looked around again. "Chipper! Who's on that hill?"

"Lieutenant." Doc Abernathy pulled a needle out of the arm of the boot marine. He looked at the lieutenant and pointed at a poncho-covered body a few feet to Shawn's right. Shawn hadn't noticed it. The PRC-25 radio lay beside the body. A round pink ball of used bubble gum was stuck to the top of the antenna. Shawn's heart sank.

A stocky corporal from Third Platoon ran up to the lieutenant. Lieutenant Townsend stared at Chipper's body.

"That's a gun team from Third Platoon up on the hill, Lieutenant! Clark and Chan and Doyle! They're pullin' back, Lieutenant. Here they come!"

Lieutenant Townsend turned around to face the hill again. "Give 'em cover fire! Guns up!" He looked around until his eyes met Shawn's. He grimaced and mouthed a curse.

"I'm here, sir!" Smith ran up to the lieutenant with his mouth open.

The lieutenant looked at Smith like he had just received bad news, then pointed at the hill. "Fire!"

The three Marines waded across the tributary with their weapons above their heads. Withering automatic fire shot out of the triangle of hills. Green tracers from enemy machine guns raked the field from across the river as the three Marines climbed out of the water and started the long run back across the open area. Two mortar blasts peppered the running Marines with dirt but they kept coming. Men fired and cheered as the three charged through what seemed a rainstorm of bullets without getting hit. The two-hundred-meter run looked like it would never end. Shawn watched and prayed for God to let them make it. They dove into the cover of the big trees to the cheers of the Marines. Shawn leaned back against the tree and sighed. He was out of breath from just watching.

"Lieutenant!" A pale white captain named Karas waved from beside the third tank in line of the road. Lieutenant Townsend jogged over to him. Captain Karas pointed toward the hill. They exchanged what appeared to be sharp words. Lieutenant Townsend saluted and ran back to the edge of the clearing.

"Form up! Marines! Guns up! Saddle up! We're taking that hill!" His angry command seemed to silence everything around.

"That's stupid!" the baby-faced gunner from Third Platoon snapped.

"Shut up, Marine!" Townsend barked. He turned to Goody. "You got Birdman's squad!"

Goody gave a nod, turned his head, and spit. "Don't move out till I give the word!" He caught the attention of the Marine on the turret of the lead tank and waved him forward.

Birdman whistled and sat up beside Shawn. "Hey, Goody!" he yelled.

Shawn laid a hand on Birdman's shoulder. "Hey, Doc! Should he be sitting up?"

"Yeah, he's all right."

"Corpsmen!" Captain Karas shouted from twenty yards back down the road as he pulled the pin on a smoke grenade. "We got medevacs! Let's get those wounded over here!" He dropped the smoke grenade in the center of the road. Red smoke filled the air and swirled into the sky.

"Goody!" Birdman shouted again. He whistled again, this time louder and stronger.

A medevac helicopter hovered above the road, then settled down beside the smoke grenade. Two corpsmen grabbed Birdman under both arms and legs as his shrill whistle pierced the surrounding chaos.

"Goody!"

Goody cocked an ear, then turned around. Birdman whistled

again as the corpsmen picked him up and headed through the cloud of dust being kicked up by the chopper's rotors.

"Birdman!" Goody shouted, and grinned and signaled a thumbs-up.

Birdman whistled again and held up the photo of Bonnie Kay. "Goody! Thanks, my man!" He laughed and whistled out a catcall.

Goody's smile disappeared. His face flushed red. His eyes widened with rage. "You ain't dyin'!" he screamed, and ran toward the grinning Birdman. "I'll cut yer lyin' heart out! You bull-slingin' father to sheep dip!"

The corpsmen lifted Birdman into the helicopter. He waved and smiled at Goody. Goody stopped ten feet from the chopper and shook his fist at him. Two more corpsmen lifted the limp body of Sergeant Ghosthorse into the open hatch while a weary grunt held a bottle of clear liquid over the Chief. It was connected by a tube and needle taped to his wrist.

"I'll get you for this, Birdman! Yer gonna need a medevac if you write my sister, you, you—Marine!"

Shawn looked away from the screaming Texan. Smith stood over him, his mouth open and his eyes pleading for help.

"God, Mac! I'm scared!"

"You're gonna be okay, gunner," Shawn said, staring into the frightened Marine's face. His mind raced for the right words.

"But I don't even know what to do!" Smith's voice cracked.

"Snap out of it, Marine! Now listen up! Twenty-round bursts! Clean her every day! Lots of oil, clean the ammo with your toothbrush, and don't forget the cylinder! Fifty-round strip belt when you're humping, no more than that! The weight of the belt can jam the gun."

"Can you walk, Marine?" a corpsman yelled as he ran toward Shawn.

"No."

"Guns up!" Lieutenant Townsend yelled at Smith. Smith turned and ran toward the platoon, then stopped and looked back at Shawn. He closed his mouth as if he were biting his lower lip. He gave Shawn a thumbs-up and turned away.

"Wait!" Shawn shouted as two corpsmen lifted him up onto his good leg. Smith turned back to face Shawn. "Here!" Shawn unhooked his cartridge belt and threw it toward Smith.

Smith picked up the cartridge belt. He looked at the holstered pistol for a moment then looked back at Shawn. He stopped

340

biting his lower lip. His face suddenly looked almost calm. He signaled a thumbs-up.

"Guns up, Shawn."

"Semper fidelis, gunner."

Smith turned and ran as each of the corpsmen put a shoulder under Shawn's arms. The tanks opened fire. The corpsmen cradled Shawn past the dusty poncho that covered Chipper's body. The sounds of battle grew louder as they lifted Shawn into the chopper. He felt light-headed, but the burning had lessened. The morphine was working.

The door gunner dragged Shawn away from the open hatch and leaned him against the hull of the chopper beside Birdman. He looked around Birdman to see the Chief. The Indian's eyes were closed beneath his thick-lensed glasses. A white bandage covering his left jugular was turning red. His shirt was off. His lean, muscular body was peppered with small bleeding shrapnel holes that the corpsmen didn't have time to bandage. The boot Marine with the bandaged eye lay beside the Chief with both hands over his face. The chopper began to lift off the road. The door gunner stood up with the M60 ready to fire.

Shawn slumped back. "How bad's the Chief?" he asked.

Birdman waved his hand and looked away. "Shoot, I seen him worse than this back at Hai Van Pass. These little scumbags couldn't kill that Marine if he walked unarmed all the way to Hanoi."

Birdman smiled, then chuckled. "You see old Goody scream?" He slapped his thigh, then winced from the pain.

The helicopter lifted above the trees and swung out over the Thu Bon River. The door gunner opened fire at muzzle flashes on the other side of the river. Shawn flinched as a bullet slapped through the hull of the helicopter. He looked around for the bullet hole but couldn't find it. The helicopter began to gain altitude. The door gunner ceased firing. He turned toward Shawn.

"Anybody get hit?"

Shawn stared up at a dark visor covering the door gunner's eyes. He felt dizzy and warm. He blinked again and the dark of the visor was all there was. He blinked again and felt as though he were falling. He reached out to hold on to something, anything. God, he asked inwardly, am I dying?

CHAPTER SEVENTEEN

Kin Village, Okinawa
April 1969

"Your wound has healed."

The calm voice of Master Shimabuku could put anyone at ease, Shawn thought. He studied the old Okinawan's tanned face. They sat cross-legged, facing each other, on Master Shimabuku's rooftop Dojo.

"Yes, sensai," Shawn replied, using the term of respect reserved for the master. "I've gained back nearly forty pounds." He gave his thigh a pat where the bullet had entered. "The leg is stronger than ever."

"No pain?"

"Some, but not bad."

"You have trained harder than all of my other students. I will miss you, McClellan-san."

A wave of pride swept over Shawn. He looked down at the cement deck of the outdoor Dojo he had grown to love, then he gazed toward Camp Hanson and wished that he could find the proper words to thank the wonderful old man. He looked around the Dojo where he had spent every free minute of the last many months since his release from Yokosuka Naval Hospital in Japan. In the far corner was his hemp-wrapped makiwara post, where he had stood for hours on end practicing karate punches, thousands of times, over and over. Shawn remembered with a smile the first time he had questioned the master after being cracked across the back with the long bamboo stick, the sheenai, for relaxing from his stance.

"Master, I have been here for forty days and all I ever get to do is punch the makiwara board. When can I learn to kick?" Shawn had asked eagerly.

"But, McClellan-san," Master Shimabuku had replied softly, "you cannot yet punch perfectly. Why would you want also to know so little about kicking?"

Shawn grinned at the memory of the old man's wisdom. He

had learned so much; he loved this little man. He pulled his gaze from the hemp-wrapped post and into the clear searching eyes of the gentle Okinawan.

"But the wound in your spirit has not healed, and Shorin-Ryu will not heal such a wound, Shawn."

"I—" Shawn hesitated, not knowing what to say. He wondered what the old man thought was wrong. How did he know?

"You train for more war, but your war is over."

"I know that you are right, master." Shawn looked down at the ugly lumps of callus on his knuckles.

"Who would you blame for the deaths of friends? Your God?"

"Maybe. I don't know. There are some traitors and cowards back home that I want to blame."

"Sometimes the good cannot be heard over the noise of the loud." The old man uncrossed his legs and stood with the agility of a young man. Shawn stood at attention and bowed. Master Shimabuku bowed.

"This is true, sensai," Shawn said.

"Find a good school, Shawn, when you return to your home. Learn. Then teach Shorin-Ryu. Maybe I come to America. Visit school."

He smiled and walked to the stairs leading down to his home. Shawn watched him leave, then took one more look around the rooftop Dojo that had helped him keep his sanity as well as heal his wounds. He bowed one last time and left.

The ten-minute walk through Kin Vill felt sad. He knew that he would never return. And even though he was anxious to get home, part of him wanted to stay. A chunky Mexican MP waved a white glove at Shawn as he approached the main gate of Camp Hanson.

"McClellan! Hey! I hear you got orders for the world, bro."

"There it is, Quintana!" Shawn stepped up to the cement island that the guardhouse rested on.

"That's outstanding, man. I can't wait to get off this rock."

"I was starting to think I'd never go home."

"How long have you been an MP here?" Quintana asked.

"Since I got out of the hospital in Yokosuka."

"You were in Japan?"

"Yeah. Yokosuka wasn't bad, but then I get here and that gung-ho gunny sergeant tells me that anybody with two or more Hearts gets to be an MP."

"Yeah." Quintana frowned. "But if you weren't an MP, you couldn't get liberty all the time."

"They can keep their liberty pass," Shawn griped. "I'll take goin' home for Christmas."

"Well, the poop I heard says they were trying to keep guys here until they gained back their weight or stopped limpin' so's they would look good when they go home."

"I wouldn't doubt it. My mom woulda fainted away if she saw me forty pounds lighter and on crutches."

"Yeah. Mine too."

Shawn held out his hand. "Good luck, Quintana."

They shook hands.

"Back to the world. Hey, eat a cheeseburger for me, bro."

"There it is."

Shawn checked his watch. "Wow! I gotta make my bird!" He slapped Quintana on the shoulder and ran for the MP barracks. It didn't seem possible. Going home.

CHAPTER EIGHTEEN

El Toro, California, the World

"Outstanding!" a voice from the front of the plane screamed at the top of his lungs.

"It's the world!" another Marine shouted.

"I see it!" A freckle-faced Marine pressed his nose against the porthole. He turned to face Shawn in the seat beside him. "I see it!"

Shawn grinned and tried to keep his eyes from going below the man's neck. The freckle-faced Marine didn't have any legs. Shawn looked across the aisle. A hard-faced staff sergeant with an empty sleeve where his right arm should have been stared back. He didn't smile. Shawn looked away. His palms were clammy. A Marine in the front of the plane stood up in the aisle to get a better look at the coast of California below. He looked a little like Joe. Same size. Same hair.

Shawn had never dreamed of coming home alone. He thought of Sandy Hendry and Joe's baby boy and the SDS character. He punched the back of the seat in front of him before he could stop himself.

"Cool it with that crap, Marine!" a deep voice growled from over the top of the seat.

"Sorry," Shawn mumbled.

"You okay, Corporal?" The freckle-faced Marine looked concerned.

"Yes. I think so." Shawn felt embarrassed. He looked away in an effort to avoid conversation.

"Anybody meeting you?" the legless Marine asked.

"Not here, but when I get home." Shawn turned back to the freckle face. "I'm glad you asked me that; my lifelong best buddy and my mom will meet me in Tampa. Stupid time to be mad or sad, isn't it?"

"There it is, bro." He stuck out his hand. "Kiefer, Jon Kiefer."

"Shawn McClellan." Shawn shook his hand.

"That's funny. My best buddy's meeting me too!"

"Really?" Shawn asked.

"Yeah. In Denver. We been friends since junior high. If it weren't for old Bobber, I never would have found out what girls were for." He laughed a good, happy laugh that put Shawn at ease.

"That's weird. My buddy Eddie told me how girls worked right after we saw the *Sands of Iwo Jima* with John Wayne."

"This is your pilot, Captain Paul Wells. We will be landing at El Toro in five minutes. The sky is clear and blue. It is nine-thirty A.M. Temperature, sixty-eight degrees. Leave your seat belts fastened until we stop. Remain seated until those Marines requiring assistance have been helped off of the plane. Thank you."

"Where you from?" Jon asked.

"Charleston, West Virginia, till seventh grade, then I moved to Florida."

"*Sands of Iwo Jima*, huh?"

"There it is." Shawn grinned.

"Me too," Jon said. "I love the Duke."

"I sort of discovered the Marine Corps and sex on the same day," Shawn said.

Jon pointed at Shawn's hands. "What's wrong with your knuckles?"

Shawn looked at his ugly hands. The fore knuckle and middle knuckle were joined by one large round callus a half inch higher than the other knuckles.

"I studied martial arts on the Rock."

"I always wanted to do that," Jon said quietly. He glanced down at his pinned-up trouser legs.

Shawn tried to think of something cheerful to say, but the words would not come. The squeal of the 727's wheels touching down at El Toro Air Base was a rescue from the silence. The big plane taxied to a stop as the pilot's intercom cracked with static.

"Welcome home, Marines. Job well done."

Shawn swallowed back the lump that swelled up in his throat. He could hear some of the other Marines sniffing and clearing their throats. Others cheered.

"Corporal," a soft, feminine voice said from beside Shawn.

346

Shawn turned and looked up at the face of a pretty black stewardess. "Yes, ma'am?"

"Would you give us a hand with your friend?" She patted the handle of a wheelchair.

"Yes, ma'am." Shawn unbuckled his seat belt, stood up quickly, and banged the top of his head into the overhead luggage compartment.

"Good move, Shawn," Jon said, then laughed.

"They shouldn't have put you in the window seat." The black stewardess sounded apologetic. A flash of annoyance shot from Jon's blue eyes. He pressed himself up out of the seat, both hands on the armrest, and pushed his legless body up and over one armrest. He landed in Shawn's vacated seat and looked up defiantly at the stewardess. Shawn helped him into the wheelchair, then pushed him to the exit door and out onto an elevator-type lift.

"I can't believe it's over, man." Jon made a quick swipe at a tear.

The air was crisp. The sky looked like a painting, a few white puffy clouds on a turquoise canvas. Another Marine in a wheelchair was pushed onto the gray metal platform. He didn't speak. He just stared down at a long red carpet that led from the plane to a small one-story, yellow-brick terminal.

"Got room for one more?" a cheerful voice said from the open door of the plane. Shawn looked back at a smiling corporal sitting in a wheelchair, arranging his barracks cover. He had a stocky build that reminded Shawn of Cornhusker. Both legs were gone from the hip down. An Oriental lance corporal pushed him onto the platform.

"Hey! Will somebody help me out of this chair when we get down?" the stocky corporal asked.

"Yeah, sure," Shawn said.

"Thanks, bro."

The corporal's joy was catching. The big elevator platform started down. A rush of excitement covered Shawn with goose bumps.

A Marine Corps band in dress blues stood at attention in three rows just to the left of the red carpet and in front of the terminal. Their brass-and-silver instruments glimmered in the sun. Facing the band, on the right side of the red carpet, a group of ladies rushed about behind two long chow-hall tables, carrying glass pitchers of what looked like lemonade and plates of cookies.

"What's goin' on over there, Shawn?" Jon asked as the platform hit the ground. Shawn pushed the wheelchair off the elevator platform and onto the plush red carpet. Jon pointed at a noisy group of people standing on the outside of a ten-foot-tall chain-link fence that started at the right side of the terminal building and surrounded the airstrip. Some of the people were shouting and waving signs. Others seemed to be singing or chanting something that Shawn couldn't hear.

He pushed Jon away from the elevator platform. Two Marines in starched utilities rolled the platform away from the plane while two others pushed a portable stairway into its place. Shawn looked back at the stocky corporal in the wheelchair.

"You want down here?"

"Yeah, Marine. I sure do." His eyes sparkled with a joy that Shawn did not fully understand.

Shawn and the Oriental lance corporal lifted the stocky corporal out of his wheelchair and set him on the red carpet. He just sat there, staring down at the cement. The clamor of shoes hustling down the metal stairs turned Shawn's head back to the plane. The first Marine down the steps stopped and stared as he touched the ground and noticed the legless corporal. Then each of the Marines hurrying down the stairs behind the first stopped cold and stared. The corporal leaned forward slowly and kissed the ground. He stayed there for a moment, his forehead pressed against the cement, as large tears darkened the concrete under his eyes. He sat up, wiped away the tears, looked up at Shawn, and gave a nod. They lifted him back into his chair as the band struck up "The Marine Hymn." Shawn felt his chest expand as he pushed Jon's wheelchair up the red carpet.

"Man"—Shawn blinked back a tear—"I know it's corny but I still get goose bumps every time I hear the hymn."

Jon looked back over his shoulder and gave Shawn a thumbs-up. The shouts of the people on the other side of the fence grew louder as Shawn neared the terminal.

"You see that?" an angry Marine shouted behind Shawn. Shawn looked back. A tall Marine wearing a Purple Heart ribbon with two gold stars walked past the pointing Marine to get a better view of the crowd behind the fence. He bent over and pulled up his trouser leg. A black-handled K-bar and sheath were strapped to his calf. He pulled the knife out of its sheath. Two Marines grabbed him from behind while a third twisted his wrist until he dropped the knife.

"Hide that K-bar! We got MPs coming!" a faceless voice warned.

"Baby killers!" a young girl screamed from behind the fence.

Shawn looked at the crowd. Most of them were young, but not all of them. It was hard to tell if they were girls or boys. They all had long stringy hair and wore blue jeans. A young shirtless boy with long blond hair that went past his shoulders climbed halfway up the chain-link fence. An older man with a bald head and a dark beard handed the boy a big white cardboard sign. The blond boy held the sign high for the returning Marines to see. YOU MURDERED INNOCENT WOMEN AND CHILDREN!

Jon pressed himself up, out of his chair. "You cowardly little queer!" he screamed at the top of his lungs.

The blond teenager jumped from the fence, pulled down his jeans, bent over, and pressed his naked rear end against the fence.

Shawn released his grip on the wheelchair handles. He headed for the fence along with every Marine that could walk. A loud whistle sounded from the terminal. A detachment of fifteen to twenty MPs with nightsticks ran between the approaching Marines and the fence. The MPs gently herded the Marines back toward the terminal as the protestors taunted them with insults. The Marines were strangely quiet afterward. The mood had changed. The unspoken foaming rage was as sharp as a knife. Everyone understood. No one spoke.

The men in wheelchairs or those still disabled from wounds were bused to a nearby naval hospital. Shawn watched the busload of disabled Marines pull away and knew that he would never see Jon Kiefer again. He wondered what his life would be like, then he thought about Luke and wondered how he would have done with no legs. He thought of Joe and wondered what the baby looked like. He threw his sea bag over his shoulder and climbed into the olive-green bus for a ride to a nearby barracks. Casual Company.

Processing was a monumental pain in the posterior. There would be no liberty until it was done. Military money exchange. Medical check. Debriefing. Civilian opportunity classes. VA benefits counseling. And on. And on. By the time the Los Angeles Police Department made their pitch, most of the men were ready to go AWOL. Shawn looked on in shock as four Marines actually signed up to be cops after their discharge was final. A dark-skinned PFC in the chair beside Shawn leaned close, with one hand shielding his voice so that no one else would hear.

"Ten to one they're office pogues," he whispered. "Who were you with?" he asked.

"Alpha One-Five."

"I was in One-Seven. You going into L.A. when we get liberty?"

"Yeah, guess so."

"Let's split the fare on a taxi. If you wait for a bus, it takes forever. I know. I live here. Name's Beaton."

"Sound's good to me. My name's McClellan."

By 1800 hours Shawn and the dark-skinned PFC from California were standing outside an L.A. bar with a pink neon sign flashing SAMMY'S just above a green wood door with a brass knob. Taped to the door was a small hand-printed sign: NO DOGS OR MARINES ALLOWED IN.

"Don't let it bug ya, McClellan." Beaton walked past the door and gave Shawn a tug.

Shawn followed reluctantly. "I don't believe this!" he yelled, and stopped and looked back at the green door.

"Hey. Who cares, man? Screw 'em."

"How can Americans do this?" Shawn shouted at the green door.

Beaton pulled Shawn forward by his coat sleeve. "Hey, come on, man. Don't make a scene. We'll be in jail before we can get a beer."

Shawn took a deep breath and blew out hard. He turned away from the door and started down the litter-strewn sidewalk beside Beaton. "I really need to call home." He looked at the sidewalk as he spoke.

"There's a phone booth in the bus terminal, right around the corner. Make your call and let's find some women and cold beer."

"There it is," Shawn agreed. He lifted his eyes off the dirty sidewalk and tried to clear the frustration from his mind. "I'll snap out of this crap when I hear good ol' Ed again."

"Is that your brother?"

"No, he's closer than a brother."

"Good. Let's make that call and get into some serious drinking. Bus station's over here."

The bus terminal was huge. It echoed with engines, cash registers, babies crying, and a thousand other sounds that Shawn had almost forgotten. Each sound seemed to sing the same word: America. Even the disgusting Greyhound Bus exhaust fumes smelled good.

"Wow! Recon that, Marine." Shawn stopped in front of a row of phone booths and gaped across the cavernous room. Two college-age girls stood by a ticket counter. They wore matching paisley mini-skirts and they both had long blond hair.

"Hurry up and call."

"Look at those mini-skirts."

"I don't want to look, grunt! I want to chase them. Make your call."

"Gee, they look so good it almost hurts." Shawn forced himself to turn away. He dug into his pockets and laid a handful of quarters on a small shelf under the phone. He pulled his tattered brown leather wallet out of his hip pocket and found Eddie's high school graduation photo. The number was on the back. He put a dime in the slot.

"Yes, operator. Would you dial this number for me in Virginia. . . ."

"Please deposit one dollar and seventy-five cents." The phone rang. Shawn shifted his weight from one foot to the other in nervous anticipation.

"Hello."

"Ed?"

"No, man, this is Bill."

"Sorry, I must have the wrong number."

"You looking for Ed Price?"

"Yeah."

"He got an apartment off campus with his chick."

"Oh. Have you got his number?"

"No, man, they don't have a phone yet, but I got his address here. You got a pen?"

"Yeah go."

"It's 3507 Washburn Ave. Northeast."

"Got it. Is there an airport very close by?"

"Yeah, sure. Roanoke."

"Thanks."

Shawn hung up, then he called the L.A. airport. He made reservations on a flight to Roanoke with next-day reservations from Roanoke to St. Pete.

He hung up the phone and then picked it up again. He dropped in a dime. "Operator, I'd like to make a collect call to . . ."

351

Shawn waited nervously until he heard his mom squeal with joy and begin to cry. "Mom."

"Shawnie! My baby! Thank God!"

"I love you, Mom. I don't want to talk over the phone. I'll probably be there Friday."

He could hear his mother crying. "Mom. Don't cry now. I'm home." Opal's crying came through more clearly. Shawn pressed his ear against the receiver and covered his other ear with his palm.

"Mom. Are you all right? Answer me. Mom!"

"Yes, honey." Her voice sounded weak.

"Mom. You're crying too hard. I'm home. I'm fine, Mom!"

"My baby," Opal sobbed.

"It's okay, Mom."

"Oh, baby . . ." Opal cried hard.

"Mom, come on, I'm back, it's okay. Me and ol' Ed will be chasing mini-skirts around before you know it. I tried to call Ed. I got his address. I'm going to stop over for a night in Virginia."

"I haven't heard from Eddie since you left. I saw Joey yesterday."

"You did!"

"Oh, Shawnie."

"Is something wrong?"

"No, honey."

"Joe!"

"Yes. He's out at Bay Pines now. We'll go see him as soon as you get home."

The promise flashed through his mind and his stomach tightened with anger. "Sure, Mom."

"I love you, son."

Shawn hung the phone up and stood still for a moment. He thought of Joe and felt sad. He had to keep the promise. He pushed Joe out of his mind and thought about Eddie. Good ol' Ed. He smiled and sighed.

The rest of the night was a blur of bars and loud music and cigarette smoke. No one seemed very interested in two Marines just home from the war. The grogginess of too many beers began to clear up the next day with two fantastic words: Officially Discharged. By that afternoon Shawn was on a flight for Roanoke, Virginia.

The flight to Roanoke was fast. He slept most of the way. It was four P.M. when the plane taxied to a stop. Shawn got an airport limo van for the twenty-mile trip to the VPI campus. Eddie's two-story town house was in an upper-middle-class neighborhood just off campus. The air was crisp for April. It smelled as good as it felt.

Shawn walked up to the door with his sea bag over his shoulder. A wave of pride swept over him. All of his life it seemed that he had dreamed of coming home from a war with medals on his chest and a sea bag over his shoulder just like John Wayne. He laughed to himself for being so foolish. His stomach growled nervously as he neared the front door of the town house and he remembered the hundred times his stomach had done the same thing before opening up on an ambush or walking across a clearing or stepping onto a well-trodden trail. He shivered and felt embarrassed. Eddie. Best friend in the whole world.

Shawn took a deep breath to control his excitement. He rang the doorbell. A moment later the door opened.

"You're early!" A short, cute, dark-haired girl exclaimed. Her perky smile faded into a frown as she realized that Shawn was obviously not whom she expected to see.

"Hello. I'm Shawn McClellan. Does Eddie Price live here?"

"Yes."

"Is he here?"

"Yes," she said with the slightest hint of displeasure. "Wait a minute and I'll get him."

"Thanks."

She closed the door. A few moments later the door opened again. Eddie stood in the doorway with his mouth open and no words coming forth.

Shawn laughed. "Well. Can I come in?"

Eddie moved forward and bear-hugged Shawn and the sea bag off the ground. He set Shawn down and pulled him inside. "Judy! It's Shawn! Shawn McClellan! I've told you about Shawn!"

"Yes. Of course. It's nice to meet you, Shawn." Judy held out her hand. Shawn shook it as he dropped his sea bag onto the thick white shag carpet.

"You can put that over by the door. Shawn, be careful not to scratch the wall, we just had it painted."

Shawn leaned the sea bag against the wall by the front door and faced Eddie.

"Shawn, Judy and I are engaged!"

"What! Really?"

"Yeah!"

"Congratulations, Eddie!" Shawn slapped Eddie on the shoulder.

"Hard to believe, isn't it?"

"When did this happen?"

"We've been engaged for four months now," Judy said without a smile.

"That's great! That explains why you never wrote!"

"I know. I'm sorry about that, Shawn. You wouldn't believe how busy and hectic our lives are around here. Trying to keep a grade average and fraternity work . . ."

"Eddie is president of Sigma Chi Sigma," Judy said proudly.

"That's super, but I'm not surprised. This guy can do anything he sets his mind to."

"I disagree," Judy quipped with a pretend glare at Eddie. "He has to be pushed in order to excel."

Shawn winked. "She sounds tough, Ed."

"She keeps me in line."

"Hey, how about football?"

"I hate football," Judy said.

"I kind of quit playing," Eddie said. "It interfered with my class work."

"Eddie didn't really like football."

"Hey, enough about me; look at the ribbons on this guy!"

"Yes, indeed," Judy said. "You'll have to tell us what they're for sometime, Shawn. How long are you in for?"

"Well . . ."

"Where will you be staying?"

"He's staying right here," Eddie said.

Judy laughed and smiled politely at Shawn. "Shawn, would you excuse us just for a moment?" she asked, turning and tugging Eddie to follow before Shawn could answer.

"Sure," Shawn said as they closed the swinging kitchen door behind them.

He looked around the immaculately clean apartment. He felt like an intruder. He moved closer to the kitchen door where Judy's voice could be heard clearly.

"And we have Professor Mosely and his wife coming over tonight for dinner."

"So we set an extra place, honey."

"No way! This is special and he just won't fit in, you know that."

"Well, what do you expect me to do? I can't just tell him to go away, Judy. He just came back from a war."

"I know, but that's another reason. No one wants to get all bummed out talking about Vietnam war stories. Not tonight and certainly not during dinner."

"Maybe you're right. Especially, Professor Mosely, Mr. Pacifist himself."

"And I don't want to spend our first free weekend in a month entertaining the troops."

Shawn's heart sank into his stomach. He picked up his sea bag and quietly left. A city bus was stopping to let someone off on the street in front of Eddie's apartment. Shawn ran for it. He boarded the bus, dropped his sea bag, and dug for change.

"I need to get to the airport."

"This is the wrong bus, Marine."

"Don't matter."

CHAPTER NINETEEN

Semper Fidelis

"I suppose that you are very proud of all of those little ribbons," the woman next to Shawn on the airplane said.

Shawn tensed but said nothing. He stared out of the small square window at the white puffy clouds below.

"I've often said it to my son, William, that if they would stop giving out medals to soldiers for killing innocent men, women, and children, we would have far fewer soldiers. My William would have had to go over there, but thank God we had a good family doctor."

"I can't believe my ears. How can any American be that insensitive?" an angry but pretty voice said.

Shawn turned away from the window to see who had spoken. A young, brown-haired stewardess stood in the aisle beside a small drink cart.

"If I hear you so much as open your mouth one more time to this—" The stewardess glared down at the middle-aged woman with her salt-and-pepper hair sprayed stiff, in a pile on top of her head. "This—" She fumbled angrily for the right words. "—American hero, I'll have you removed from the plane in Atlanta!"

"How dare you speak to me in that tone?" the older lady huffed, lifting her long, straight nose and brushing a wrinkle off her expensive silk dress.

"Would you like to sit somewhere else, Marine?" The stewardess sounded apologetic.

"Yes." Shawn pulled his diddy bag from under his feet, stood up, and scooted past the middle-aged lady, who then looked around at the other passengers as if she were embarrassed. Shawn moved to an empty seat near the front of the plane.

It was dark by the time the big airliner touched down in Tampa. Shawn watched the blue-and-white runway lights flash past. It didn't feel real. He was scared. It didn't seem possible that it was all over. He wondered who would be there to meet him. He thought of Luke and swallowed back a lump in his throat. Maybe Nancy would be there to meet him, he thought. But he knew she wouldn't. He didn't understand why, but he hoped that Joe would not be there at the terminal.

He filed down the enclosed gangway that led into the receiving area. The laughter of various reunions echoed from ahead. Shawn felt nervous. He stepped into the terminal and quickly scanned a crowd of faces.

"Shawn!" a familiar voice shouted from his right. He turned as someone else shouted.

"Shawn!"

"Uncle Bob!" Shawn dropped his diddy bag. Bob ran forward with his arms outstretched. Bob still looked like a Marine—short hair, stout as ever, and with a drill instructor's granite jaw. He hugged Shawn hard and quickly, then stepped back so that Opal could take her turn.

"Shawnie!"

"Mom!" Shawn picked his charging mother up off of the floor and hugged her for a long time. Her face smelled fresh and clean and safe, the way it had smelled when he was a little boy and ran, in need of love, into her arms. He set her down and looked into her teary eyes. Opal smeared mascara across her face with a brush of her quivering hand. She tried to keep from crying with a bite at her lower lip, then fell against Shawn's chest and sobbed. She clung to him, crying as hard as he had ever heard the strong old country girl cry. Shawn squeezed her. He cried slowly at first, his face not changing, then he cried hard, with his eyes closed, and buried his face in the top of Opal's shoulder. He burrowed into her neck, hiding his tears behind her shoulder-length brown-and-gray hair, just the way he had done at Dad's funeral. They stayed that way for a time. No one spoke.

When Shawn finally looked up, the arrival area was mostly empty. Mrs. Elbon stood beside Uncle Bob. Her silver-white hair was uncombed, her clothes wrinkled. He couldn't remember ever seeing Joe's mom so unkempt looking. She rushed forward, removing her glasses as she came. She put her chunky arms around Shawn, hugged him once, stepped back and tried to speak, then broke down crying against his chest.

"Welcome home, Shawnie." She pulled away and the curly

head of Chuck Caldwell blurred into Shawn's midsection with a fake football tackle.

"He's thrown for a loss!" Chuck shouted, then straightened up laughing. He looked exactly the same way he had looked on graduation day a million years ago. It wasn't fair, Shawn thought, noticing the absence of age or strain in Chuck's bright blue eyes.

"Chuck."

"Thank God you're home." Chuck spoke slowly. His eyes darted back and forth, brow pinched forward with a suddenly serious stare as if he were searching Shawn's face for something hidden or something missing. Chuck's stare bothered him.

"Been a long time."

"Are you okay, Shawn?" He slapped Shawn's shoulder and smiled. "Boy, you been workin' out!"

"Thanks for coming to meet me, Chuck."

"Are you kidding? You think I wouldn't be here?"

Shawn looked around the emptying room and smiled. "Where's the rest of the guys?"

Chuck looked around, then back at Shawn. He shrugged. "Well, Jay had to work and . . ."

Shawn held up his hand. "No. Don't. It's okay. I didn't expect anything."

"Come on, son." Opal squeezed Shawn's callused hand. "Let's get you home. Are you hungry?"

"Yeah, Shawnie-boy, Opal's been cookin' up stuff all day long," Bob bellowed. "You'd think the whole Fifth Marines were comin' over for dinner." He laughed and grabbed up Shawn's diddy bag.

The ride across the Howard Franklin Bridge was quiet in Mrs. Elbon's big new 1969 Buick. Shawn stared out at the moon glistening on the bay like a man seeing water for the first time. Something loud popped from behind him. Shawn's forehead banged into the hard dash as he dove forward. Opal screamed. He sat back up, then hunkered down at the sight of overhead lights flashing by like tracer rounds.

"Shawn!" Chuck called from the backseat. He sounded scared.

"It's champagne, Shawn," Bob said calmly, also from the backseat. "It's just a bottle of wine popping open."

Shawn could feel his mother's nervous hand rubbing his back. He sat up slowly and looked back out of the window. "Yeah," he mumbled. "No sweat, GI."

The next morning Shawn sat up straight in bed and tried to shake away the ringing in his ear. Telephone. He looked at the white phone on the nightstand to his right.

"Hello." Shawn looked away and yawned.

"Shawn, it's me, Chuck. You up?"

"Nope."

"Get dressed. I'm comin' by to pick you up for breakfast with Jay and Rachel."

"No thanks, Chuck. Maybe later. I need to look up Sandy Hendry first."

"She got married."

"Is she still with him?"

"Yeah." Chuck sounded hesitant.

"They still go to JC?"

"I don't know. I haven't seen Sandy in ages."

Shawn's voice lowered. "What's his name?"

"Keith Adams."

"Come on by and pick me up."

"Now, Shawn, wait a minute."

"Come on by and get me. I'll be ready in twenty minutes."

"What?" Opal said from the bedroom doorway. Shawn hung up the phone and climbed out of bed wearing nothing but his white boxer shorts. He grabbed his trousers and pulled them on.

"I won't be too long, Mom."

"Well"—she shook her head dejectedly—"go say good-bye to Uncle Bobby. He's leaving this morning. He flew in from Virginia just to see you get off of that plane. He's got to be back at work today."

"Sure, Mom. It was really good to see him. Is he up?"

Shawn sat down on the edge of the bed and pulled on his black Marine Corps socks.

"Yes. He slept out in the Florida room after he carried you to bed."

"Carried me to bed?" Shawn searched his mother's face for the joke. "The champagne wasn't that good." He smiled.

Opal laughed. "I'll let Uncle Bobby answer that one. He says you'll never hear the end of this. I think he's got a present for you."

She walked over to her handsome, muscular son and kissed the top of his head. "Thank you, Lord," she whispered.

"No!" Shawn snapped. "Thanks for nothing. Thanks for . . ." He stopped and yanked hard on a shoelace.

"Shawn McClellan!" Opal gasped.

"Drop it, Mom. I don't want to talk about it."

"I've never heard such a thing come out of your mouth."

"Mom." Shawn stood up and looked down hard at his mother. His face relaxed. "Sorry, Mom."

Opal looked anxious. She forced a worried smile, turned, and left the room. A moment later someone knocked at the bedroom door.

"Shawn."

Bob pushed the door open.

"Come on in, Bob." Shawn picked up his long-sleeved khaki dress shirt.

"I got a little something here." Bob tossed a cigar box–size package onto the bed. It was wrapped in blue paper with a red ribbon.

"Just you being here was enough, Uncle Bob."

Bob sat on the edge of the bed and clapped his strong hands together. "It's from me 'n Carolyn."

"Thank her for me, Bob."

"Shawnie, your dad would have been so proud of you, son. Well"—he stood up, put his hands on Shawn's shoulders, then hugged him—"I'm so proud of you right now, I could bust." Bob stepped back. "Put on your jacket, Marine. I want to look at you."

Bob's face beamed with pride as Shawn buttoned his dress green jacket and straightened the brass buckle on his fair weather belt.

"Ready for inspection, sir," Shawn said.

"Your military alignment is off center, Marine."

"Aye, aye, sir." Shawn saluted and turned to look in the mirror. He straightened his brass buckle so that it was on line with his tie and jacket buttons.

"Those anchors will face outboard, Marine." Bob sounded like a DI as he checked Shawn's eagle, globe, and anchor collar pins.

"Aye, aye, sir."

Bob pulled a loose thread off Shawn's jacket collar. "And what are those Irish pennants doing on a Marine uniform, Corporal?"

"I'll try to square away, sir." Shawn saluted and smiled.

"Shawn," Opal called from the living room, "Chuck is out front."

"Thanks, Mom!"

"Well, look, I don't want to hold you up from seein' all of your friends." Bob backed toward the door. "Open your present real fast." He pointed at the box.

"Oh, yeah." Shawn grabbed up the box and ripped the ribbon and paper off. He pulled the cardboard top away. The bright gold letters HOLY BIBLE jumped off a red leather binding and held Shawn's eyes to them.

"I can't imagine what you've been through, Shawnie. I know it's been bad. When we heard the word about your two friends, well, it just took the air right out of me. Carolyn and me tried to think of some way to help and we knew we couldn't. It's up to the Lord Jesus."

Bob stepped closer. He opened the cover. "I just didn't know what to write in there, but this is from me to you."

He pointed at an inscription in black ink.

"Semper fidelis, Uncle Bob, April 2, 1969."

Bob shut the cover and stepped back. He looked uncomfortable at showing so much emotion.

"Thanks, Bob." Shawn laid the Bible back down on the bed and grabbed his barracks cover.

"You all right Shawn?" Bob looked concerned.

"Yeah. I better be gettin', Bob."

"Oh, heck, yeah! Here I am talking your ear off and you got things to do."

The drive in Chuck's old yellow Packard brought back memories. More memories than Shawn wanted to deal with. Chuck chattered all the way to the junior college, but Shawn could only hear Joe's voice. "Promise me, Shawn. Promise me."

Chuck pulled up to the curb in front of the old administration building. It was a pretty little college with Spanish architecture dominating most of the buildings.

"Are you going to tell me why you have to see Sandy so bad?" Chuck asked.

"I just do."

Chuck turned off the engine and checked his watch. "It's almost eight-thirty." He looked up. "They probably got class."

"Who watches the baby?"

"What baby?" Chuck's blue eyes opened wide.

361

"Don't they have a baby?"

"I don't know. I haven't seen Sandy since Joe went into the Marines. I don't like the way your old 'McClellan crease' keeps getting deeper. What's up?"

"Just keeping a promise." Shawn opened the door and got out. He headed for the administration building.

"Wait for me!" Chuck jumped out of the car and trotted after Shawn.

"Where do you think they'd be?" Shawn asked as Chuck jogged up beside him. "Or do you think I can get the info in the administration building?"

"Probably not. Let's just go to the quad and wait for the bell. They'll probably walk by, everybody does, and wait'll you see the chicks."

"Lead the way."

Shawn followed Chuck through the administration building and out the side entrance. They followed a long narrow sidewalk lined with crisp-smelling pine trees.

Chuck pointed at a red-brick building on the right as they passed.

"That's the new Theresa Goss Library. Here's the quad." He pointed ahead to a large grassy area about the size of a football field. The grassy area was surrounded by the campus buildings. Four long-haired boys in faded blue jeans were sailing a bright orange Frisbee back and forth in the center of the field. A small group of students sat under a big pine tree to Shawn's left listening to a young guitarist strumming and singing Simon and Garfunkel's "Scarborough Fair."

"What's that?" Shawn pointed at a large white banner, taped to two long poles. Beneath it was a card table where three long-haired men wearing camouflaged jungle jackets were sitting. Two male students stood with books in hand looking down at a stack of pamphlets on the table.

"You mean over there in front of the bookstore?"

"Yeah." Shawn's eyes squinted as he tried to make out the big red letters on the banner.

"Some protest, probably. Come on over here to this bench. If Sandy still goes here, she'll come through the quad."

"Does that banner over that table say SDS?" Shawn's voice turned low and cold.

"It might. Why?" Chuck sounded worried.

Shawn started walking toward the banner until he could see

362

the big red letters clearly. SDS. He stopped and looked back as Chuck approached.

"Stay here, Chuck."

"What? Shawn!" Chuck grabbed Shawn's shoulder. "Don't do something stupid, man. I don't want to get in trouble, man. No fighting."

"Stay where it's safe, Chuck. Just like the rest of the little girls who are against anything they might have to fight for."

Chuck's mouth fell open. He stared at Shawn in disbelief. Shawn pushed Chuck's hand away, turned, and walked to the SDS table.

The three camouflaged jungle jackets turned to stare at Shawn as he neared the table. A bearded one, seated in the middle, stood up and walked around the table. He was big. His long, brown, curly hair surrounded his pale face and made him look like a lion. He folded his arms and cocked his big hairy head to one side as Shawn stopped three feet in front of him. Shawn stared at the canvas cartridge belts that crisscrossed his chest. Joe's face flashed through Shawn's mind.

"*Promise me, Shawn.*"

"You here to join up, dude?" His taunting smile matched his gruff, alcoholic voice. One of his friends laughed, pushed his chair slightly away from the table, and put a toothpick between his teeth.

"Would you be the man to see if I did?" Shawn asked with his eyes fixed on the big man's solar plexus.

"That'd be me, soldier boy." He glanced back at his friends and winked so that Shawn could see the wink. His two comrades chuckled again.

The one with the toothpick shoved a pamphlet across the table. "Here, I think soldier boy needs some literature."

"Marines can't read," the other one said.

Shawn's eyes didn't move from the leader's midsection.

"You got a problem, dude?" the leader asked. Shawn could hear the mumbling of the crowd growing around him but his eyes didn't move.

"Are you the leader of the SDS on this campus?" Shawn's voice was calm but his insides churned like a volcano of fear and anxiety.

"That's me."

Shawn closed the distance between himself and the big bearded man with one well-learned shuffle of his feet. Before the big man could unfold his arms, Shawn had delivered a devastating front kick to the man's groin. The bearded SDS leader folded forward with a loud gasp, only to be straightened back up with Shawn's follow-up knee to his face. Two rapid-fire elbow strikes snapped his head from right to left then back again. Shawn grabbed his long hair with both hands and he pulled the big man forward and delivered a crunching head butt to the bridge of his nose. The SDS leader crumpled to the ground and didn't move. Shawn faced off toward the other two men, now standing behind the table, staring down at the puddle of blood forming around three white pieces of broken teeth on the sidewalk in front of their leader's unconscious face.

"Hey, look, man"—Toothpick held up his hands—"I just hand out pamphlets."

"Me too, man!" the other one blurted.

"I don't know what you got against Big Mic but I don't want no part of it, man." Toothpick stepped back.

"Mic?" Shawn looked down at the bloody face. He looked at the cartridge belts. "What's this guy's name?" Shawn demanded.

"Mickey Sumpter," a girl shouted from behind Shawn. He turned around. A crowd of fifty to seventy-five faces gawked at him like he was from another planet.

"Yeah." A pretty red-haired girl in a blue mini-skirt pointed at the unconscious man. "I got him in Mr. Gamage's English class. His name's Mickey Sumpter."

Shawn turned back to face Toothpick. "Where's Keith? The guy who was going with Sandy Hendry?" His fist clenched as he stepped over the bleeding SDS leader.

"He's gone, man!" Toothpick held up his hands and backed up another step along with the other SDS man.

"What do you mean, gone?" Shawn stopped. He glared at Toothpick.

"He got married and moved away. He ain't in school no more! Honest!"

Shawn turned and looked down at the unconscious man. His bleeding face turned yellow. His bleeding mouth was open. His shattered teeth clenched a black-and-white ace of spades card. Shawn stiffened at the vivid memory.

"Shawn. Come on." Chuck's familiar voice blew the vision of death away. Shawn shuddered, then looked up. Chuck's worried face stared back at him.

"Chuck."

"Come on, Shawn. Let's get out of here." Chuck leaned closer. "Before the cops show up," he whispered, and looked nervously around the crowd of faces. He gave Shawn a tug and started through the crowd, heading for the car. Shawn followed.

"Let's go get a newspaper. I wanna get a room somewhere."

"Your mom will hate that, so soon."

"I have to be alone."

"Warmonger!" a voice shouted at his back.

"American losses for the week stand at twelve killed and forty-eight wounded. While the Pentagon insists that bombing will bring Hanoi to the peace table and has cut American losses by more than half by cutting off enemy supplies. Ramsey Clark, among others, is calling for an end to the bombing. Jane Fonda led . . ."

Shawn leaned forward and turned off the small black-and-white TV, then fell back against the armrest of the old blue couch and rubbed a hand across the two-day stubble on his face. He looked around the shabby, dark, one-room apartment, cluttered with empty beer cans and an empty bottle of Johnny Walker Red. He grabbed a half-filled shot glass of Scotch and downed it. He kicked a dozen empty beer cans off a battered rectangular coffee table, leaned forward, slapped the shot glass down, and picked up a silver-plated .32-caliber pistol. He held it up against the sunlight filtering through the drawn shades. His mind was drowsy with booze. Death would be a relief. He put the barrel of the pistol in his mouth. The cold steel of the barrel tasted metallic. He fingered the trigger lightly but knew that he wouldn't pull the trigger.

"Hey! Shawn!" a voice called from outside. Shawn put the pistol down and leaned back on the couch. The sound of someone coming up the stairs of the old garage apartment made him angry.

"Come on, Shawn!" Chuck pounded on the door. "Enough's enough, man! Your mom is real worried, Shawn!"

Shawn sat quietly. Chuck would finally give up and go away.

Chuck pounded on the door again. "Can you hear me? I got some news! I found Sandy Hendry! She's Sandy Adams now. Her husband's name is Keith!"

Shawn sat up straight. He tried to blink away the blur of a

thousand drinks, but it didn't work. Keith Adams, Keith Adams, he repeated the name in his mind.

"Did you hear me?" Chuck shouted again.

Shawn struggled to his feet and staggered toward the door.

"Okay, Shawn. I'm leaving!"

"Chuck!" Shawn yelled as he reached for the dead-bolt lock on the door. "Wait." His drunken hands trembled as he fumbled with the lock. The bolt slid back. Chuck pushed the door open. Shawn stumbled backward, then gained his balance.

Chuck stood still in the doorway. He frowned. "Shawn, you look bad, man."

"Where do they live?" Shawn demanded.

"Your eyes look like a road map."

"Where do they live?"

Chuck closed the door and looked around the filthy room. "What do you pay for this hole?"

"Eighty bucks a month. Where is he, Chuck?"

Chuck kicked an empty beer can across the dirty kitchen floor. Two huge cockroaches scurried out of the can. "Do they cost extra?"

"Where does this Keith live?"

"Take a shower, get some coffee in ya, and I'll take you to him."

Shawn looked hard at Chuck for a moment, then nodded.

"Got any coffee? I'll make up a batch while you take a shower."

"Yeah, think so. Look over the sink."

A shower, four cups of black coffee, and an hour later Shawn climbed into the old yellow Packard. The bright morning sun stung his eyes the way it used to sting when he came out of an enemy tunnel. Chuck turned left off of Central Avenue and headed south on Sixty-second Street.

"The streets seem empty," Shawn said.

"It's Sunday."

"Is it?" Shawn's tone said that he didn't care. "This is a dead-end street, isn't it?"

"Yep."

"Did you see Joe's kid?" Shawn asked.

"Yeah, he's a real neat little guy. Looks like Joe."

"What are all of the cars about?" Shawn asked. The street was lined with parked cars on both sides. A big empty lot on the right was filled with cars too.

366

"It's Grace Bible Church."

Chuck turned right, up a small dirt driveway that led into the lot. He parked between an old pickup truck and a beat-up red Volkswagon.

"What are you doing, Chuck?" Shawn sounded serious.

Chuck turned off the engine and opened his door. "You wanna see Keith Adams or not?" Chuck got out of the car and walked toward the front of the little white concrete block church. Shawn got out slowly and followed. Chuck walked past the main entrance of the chapel. A long one-story building shaped like an L was attached to the back of the main chapel. The L-shaped building had bright red doors, each one numbered. Chuck pointed at a red door straight ahead, on the short end of the L. "He's in room seven."

"Don't pull any crap on me, Chuck," Shawn threatened. His fist clenched tighter with each step.

Chuck stopped a few feet from the red door with the black numeral 7 on the front. He pointed at a big square window beside the door. "That's him. The dark-haired guy teaching the class."

Shawn walked up to Chuck. He couldn't see through the window very clearly. White curtains on each side of the window hindered his view. He walked up to the window and looked in. A pleasant-looking, dark-haired man of about twenty-five pointed at a green chalkboard as a group of captivated children seemed to hang on his every word.

"Come on in." Chuck opened the red door and motioned to Shawn. Shawn hesitated, then shook his head no. Chuck closed the door and stood staring at Shawn, his hand still on the doorknob. "Wanna see Sandy and little Joe?"

"Yeah," Shawn said quietly.

Chuck pointed at a red door on the opposite end of the building. "She's right over here. The door with the number one. She's got nursery duty today." Chuck cut across the green lawn. Shawn shoved his hands into his pockets and followed. He felt angry.

"Is that his name?" Shawn asked.

"What?" Chuck looked over his shoulder.

"Joe. Did they name the baby Joe?"

"Good name, don't ya think?"

Shawn didn't answer. He felt confused and frustrated. He wondered if the booze had clouded his mind too badly to think or reason. Chuck reached the door, opened it, and peeked in.

An instant later Sandy pushed past Chuck and ran straight at Shawn with arms out. Big tears streaked tiny trails through her makeup.

"Shawn!" she shouted as she collided with him before he could pull his hands out of his pockets. She hugged him tight, pinning his arms and sobbing against the ribbons on his chest. They stood that way for a long minute, Sandy sobbing, Shawn staring blankly at the white cinder-block wall of the building, his mind racing with thoughts of suicide and murder and loss and pain and Joe and Luke and Eddie and an ungrateful country that he was beginning to hate.

Chuck cleared his throat. "I got somebody for you to meet."

Chuck's voice sifted through the confusion and pain in Shawn's mind. Shawn pulled his eyes off the wall and focused on Chuck's smiling face now standing in front of him. A chubby, dark-haired little baby boy clung to Chuck's neck with two fat little arms.

"Mr. McClellan, I'd like you to meet Mr. Joe Clark Adams."

Sandy gave Shawn one last squeeze, then released him and stepped back. "You've never seen him!" Chuck handed the baby to Shawn.

Shawn pulled his hands out of his pockets and held the little boy out away from him. He studied his round little face. "He's got Joe's dark eyes," he said.

"Check out the boy's duds." Chuck laughed.

The hint of a grin cracked across Shawn's unshaven face for the first time in a long time as he looked at the way the baby boy was dressed. Little Joe wore a button-down short-sleeve white shirt with a red bow tie, red pants, and red suspenders. Shawn held the baby to him and kissed his soft cheek. He smelled like baby powder.

"The guy decks out like Hank Handsome. Here, Sandy." He gently handed the baby to Sandy, but his eyes stayed on the little Joe's face.

"It's so good to see you, Shawn." Sandy wiped away a tear. Her bottom lip began to quiver.

Shawn pulled his eyes away from the baby's face and looked at Sandy. He nodded toward Room Seven. "Is this guy good to the baby?" His face turned stone hard again.

"He's the best father in the whole world, Shawn, and"—Sandy sniffed and looked at the grass—"Joe even likes him."

Shawn frowned at Sandy as she looked up to meet his eyes. "What do you mean?" he grumbled.

"We visit Joe almost every day. Keith insists upon it, and Joe gets to see little Joe as much as he wants."

"Joe *likes* him?"

"Yes. Joe's changed, Shawn. He has a new girlfriend and she had a baby just three months older than little Joe."

Sandy paused and wiped away another tear. "Haven't you seen Joe yet?" She looked surprised.

Shawn's stomach suddenly swelled up to his tonsils. He looked away. "I better be going."

"Shawn?"

Shawn turned and walked away. Tears streamed down his face. He began to walk faster. He had to get away.

"Shawn!" Sandy's shout stopped him. He didn't look back. "Try to get out to Bay Pines real soon. Joe has a surprise for you."

Shawn stopped, stared ahead, and cried silently. "Yeah, Sandy. I will."

Shawn walked back to the yellow Packard, got in, and waited. A minute later Chuck walked up, got in, and started the engine without speaking a word. They drove back to Central Avenue and Chuck turned left.

"Where you going?" Shawn asked.

"Bay Pines."

Shawn started to speak but didn't. It was a ten-minute drive to Bay Pines Veterans' Hospital. They didn't speak all the way there. It was a beautiful old hospital, large Spanish-style buildings right on the bay with acres of tall Florida pines and a well-kept military graveyard and memorial park. If a young man had to lie around with no legs, it seemed like as pleasant a place as any.

Chuck parked in front of what looked like the main admitting building. He turned to Shawn as he opened the car door. "The amputee ward is on the fourth floor. He's due to get out next week. They're fitting him for new legs."

Shawn got out and followed Chuck into the building. An old lady wearing a Red Cross cap handed them visitors' passes and they walked to an elevator. Shawn was nervous and it angered him. Why should he be nervous? Joe was as close as any brother could be. The elevator doors opened with the ring of a bell and Shawn stepped into a long hallway. They walked down the hall and turned right into a modern-looking waiting room. In the far corner, sitting in a comfortable-looking chair, was Mr. Elbon. Joe's dad was as fat and funny looking as ever. He was bouncing a little baby boy on his lap. Shawn walked across the room toward him. The little boy looked strangely familiar. He had a green rubber hammer in his hand. He turned in Mr. Elbon's lap as Shawn approached and smiled and giggled at Shawn. Suddenly the baby's arm cocked and with no warning he drilled Shawn square in the forehead with the green rubber hammer. Shawn groaned and rubbed the instant goose egg on his forehead.

"The insincere baby!" Shawn said aloud, pointing at the fat little face still smiling happily. No. It couldn't be, he thought. It had to be, he thought. There couldn't possibly be two babies with an arm like that. Not two babies who would smile before they drilled you.

"Shawn!" Mr. Elbon stood up with the baby and stepped forward. He handed the baby to Chuck and hugged Shawn so hard that Shawn's back cracked.

"It's good to see you, Mr. Elbon."

Mr. Elbon stepped back and smiled. He had bushy eyebrows and gray hair growing out of his ears.

"God, I'm glad you're home, son! Hurry up and go see Joey. He's been asking about you every day."

"Who's this baby?" Shawn pointed at the insincere baby.

Mr. Elbon's eyes lit up. "He's a champ, Shawn. He hit a pigeon with that little hammer on the first throw!"

"Shawn! You're here!"

Shawn turned around. Kathleen McKinney rushed toward him with her arms out.

"Kathleen! What are you . . . ." Shawn was cut short by her hug and a kiss full on the lips.

Kathleen stepped back and laughed. "You look like you've just been kissed by a ghost, mate."

"You look great!" he managed to stammer.

"You're an eyeful yourself, Shawn."

Of course, she *did* look sensational in her short blue dress, but there was something else, something more elusive that made her come alive in a way he'd never seen before. Her smile seemed electric with some newly found happiness, not at all the expression of the desperate young woman Shawn remembered. He wondered at the change in her.

"Kathleen, how? I mean, what are you doing here?"

"Joe and I have been writing every day since he left Australia. We've fallen in love, Shawn, and we've decided to get married. We want you to be the best man." She tugged him toward a room numbered 407 and gave him a little nudge through the open door as she whispered, "We'll have plenty of time to talk later. Joe's anxious to see you. I'll wait out here."

Joe was sitting in a crank-up bed. He wore the blue pajamas everyone in Bay Pines wore. A white sheet covered him from the waist down. His dark eyes opened wide at the sight of Shawn, and a radiant smile burst across his face as he held out his arms.

Shawn heard a little sigh escape his own chest, then suddenly felt faint. He stepped forward slowly. There were a million words he wanted to say, and just as many emotions he wanted to hide. He bit at the inside of his mouth until he tasted blood, then leaned over to hug his old friend. Like a dam breaking, Shawn collapsed against Joe in a flood of uncontrollable tears. Joe patted Shawn's back and hugged his head against his own chest like a mother comforting a hurt child. They stayed that way for a little while, not speaking. Shawn finally stood up straight, wiped away his tears with the sleeve of his dress green jacket, and looked around the room. There was another young guy in a bed a few feet away, next to a window. Shawn felt embarrassed as their eyes met.

"It's okay, bro," the young guy said. "We have to welcome each other home. Nobody else cares."

"That's not true, bro," Joe said. "There's one person who is 'always faithful.' " Joe looked at Shawn and winked. "Right, Shawn?"

Shawn hesitated in answering. Joe looked so happy and content. It didn't make any sense. He'd lost half his body. Shawn lowered his dull stare to the gray tile floor and mumbled, "I don't know anymore, Joe." His own words filled him with shame.

"Yeah," Joe said quietly, "that's what I heard through the grapevine. You know, McClellan, there was a time when me and Luke felt like that—like maybe the choppers had dropped us into the wrong LZ without a map."

Shawn sighed and forced a grin. "Yeah, somewhere north of the DMZ."

"Then this buddy gave us a map," Joe said as he reached back under his pillow and pulled out a small, tattered black

371

Bible. "It's been through the bush, but it's the same map you gave me in Da Nang." Joe held out the Bible. "Here, get squared away, Marine."

Shawn stared at it but didn't move. A river of painful memories rushed through his mind, and with each memory, the words "semper fidelis" shouted at him like the bark of a Parris Island drill instructor. Finally, Shawn stepped forward and took the Bible. The way it felt surprised him—warm and peaceful and safe. He hadn't felt that way in a very long time.

"Yeah, Joe . . ." He paused. "Maybe it's time I checked my coordinates."

Glossary of Military Terms

AK-47 - A Russian assault rifle

ARVN - Abbreviation for Army of the Republic of Vietnam

AWOL - Absent without leave

B-40 Rocket - A communist antitank rocket

betel nut - A nut, widely chewed by the Vietnamese, that stains the teeth and gums a pomegranate red

body bags - Plastic zipper-bags for corpses

boot - Slang for a new recruit undergoing basic training

bush - The outer field areas and jungle where infantry units operate

Charlie - Slang for "the enemy"

Chi-Com - Chinese communists

choppers - Helicopters

claymores - Mines packed with plastique and rigged to spray hundreds of steel pellets

Cobras - Helicopter gunships heavily armed with rocket launchers and machine guns

concertina wire - Barbed wire that is rolled out along the ground to hinder the progress of enemy troops

C-rats - C-rations or prepackaged military meals eaten in the field

C-S - A caustic riot-gas used in Vietnam

C-4 - Plastique explosive

C-130 - A cargo plane used to transport men and supplies

C-141 Starlifter - A large jet transport

deuce-and-a-half - A heavy transport truck used for carrying men and supplies

dinks - Slang for an Oriental person, especially in reference to the enemy

EM club - Enlisted men's club

E.R. - Emergency room

flak jacket - A vest worn to protect the chest area from shrapnel or bullets

I Corp Tactical Zone - The northern five provinces of South Vietnam, called "Marineland" by some. I Corp stretched 225 miles from the Demilitarized Zone to the boundary with Binh Dinh province and II Corp Tactical Zone.

frags - Slang for fragmentation grenades

Freedom Bird - Slang for the flight that took a soldier home after his tour

friendlies - Friendly Vietnamese

gooks - Slang for an Oriental person, especially in reference to the enemy

grunt - Slang for any combat soldier fighting in Vietnam

Hueys - Helicopters used extensively in Vietnam

Ho Chi Minh Trail - The main supply route running south from North Vietnam through Laos and Cambodia

hooches - Slang for any form of a dwelling place

humping - Slang for marching with a heavy load through the bush

K-bar - A Marine Corp survival knife

KIA - Killed in action

klick - One kilometer

LAAW - Light antiarmor weapon

LZ - Landing zone

MACV - Military Assistance Command Vietnam

medevac - A term for medically evacuating the wounded by chopper or plane

M14 - An automatic weapon used in Vietnam by American ground forces

M16 - Standard automatic weapon used by American ground forces

M60 - A machine gun used by American units

M79 - A 40 mm grenade launcher

nouc-mam - A strong smelling Vietnamese fish sauce

NVA - North Vietnamese Army

pogue - A derogatory term for rear-area personnel

punji sticks - Sharpened stakes used to impale men

RPG - Rocket propelled grenade

R & R - Rest and Relaxation

sappers - Viet Cong infiltrators whose job it was to detonate explosive charges within American positions

satchel charges - Explosive packs carried by V.C. Sappers

SDS - Students for a Democratic Society

search and destroy - American ground sweeps to locate and destroy the enemy and his supplies

short-timer - Someone whose tour in Vietnam is almost completed

smoke grenade - A grenade that releases colored smoke used for signaling

Tet - The Chinese New Year

III Corp - The military region around Saigon

Tiger beer/33 beer - Vietnamese beers

tracer - A bullet with a phosphorous coating designed to burn and provide a visual indication of a bullet's trajectory

VC - Viet Cong

Viet Cong - The local communist militias fighting in South Vietnam

Web-gear - Canvas suspenders and belt used to carry the in-fantryman's gear

WIA - Wounded in action

Willie-Peter - White phosphorous round

ABOUT THE AUTHOR

Johnnie M. Clark, a thirty-eight-year-old disabled veteran of the United States Marine Corps, lives with his wife and two children in St. Petersburg, Florida. At age 17, he joined the Marines upon graduation from high school and served with the 5th Marine Regiment as a machine gunner during the 1968 Tet Offensive, where he was wounded three times. His first book, *Guns Up!*, is about those experiences. While recuperating in Okinawa from wounds suffered in Vietnam, Mr. Clark studied karate as part of his rehabilitation program, and after his discharge taught martial arts at the University of South Florida. A 1971 graduate of St. Petersburg Junior College, Mr. Clark has also worked for the United States Postal Service and is now a freelance writer.

MOVING, ACTION-FILLED WAR STORIES OF UNMISTAKABLE AUTHENTICITY